Experiments With People

Revelations From Social Psychology

Experiments With People

Revelations From Social Psychology

Robert P. Abelson
Kurt P. Frey
Aiden P. Gregg

2004

LAWRENCE ERLBAUM ASSOCIATES, PUBLISHERS
Mahwah, New Jersey   London

Lawrence Erlbaum Associates, Inc., Publishers
10 Industrial Avenue
Mahwah, NJ 07430

Cover design by Sean Sciarrone

Library of Congress Cataloging-in-Publication Data

Abelson, Robert P.
Experiments with people : revelations from social psychology /
    Robert P. Abelson, Kurt P. Frey, Aiden P. Gregg.
        p.   cm.
Includes bibliographical references and index.
ISBN 0-8058-2896-6 (cloth : alk. paper)
ISBN 0-8058-2897-4 (pbk. : alk. paper)
1. Social psychology—Experiments. I. Frey, Kurt P. II. Gregg,
    Aiden P. III. Title.
HM1011.A24   2003
302—dc21   2003040768
                                                          CIP

Books published by Lawrence Erlbaum Associates are printed on acid-
free paper, and their bindings are chosen for strength and durability.

Printed in the United States of America
10 9 8 7 6 5

Contents

Introduction

Welcome! This book provides an opportunity to explore the fascinating, underpublicized, and sometimes misunderstood subject of social psychology. In it, twenty-eight intriguing studies that throw light on human social thinking and behavior are reviewed. These studies, mostly laboratory experiments, address topics such as people's unawareness of why they do what they do, the tenacity with which they maintain beliefs despite contrary evidence, and the surprising extent to which they are influenced by the social groups to which they belong. The results of these studies help the reader understand many social phenomena that would otherwise remain deeply puzzling, such as the operation of unconscious prejudices, belief in mental telepathy, intense loyalty to questionable groups, the occasional cruelty and indifference of ordinary people, and the nature of love relationships. We chose to include each study because, in addition to being ingeniously designed and carefully executed, it raised a question of theoretical significance or addressed a problem of practical importance.

This volume is not a reader—we do not reproduce (lawyers take note!) any of the original journal articles. Rather, each chapter offers a detailed exposition of, and commentary on, a single study (though often citing closely related research). We first introduce the problem that the researchers sought to solve ("Background"). We then describe how the study was conducted ("What They Did") and what its findings were ("What They Found"). Next comes a "So What?" section, the purpose of which is to persuade anyone inclined to view the study as trivial that his or her misgivings are unfounded. We continue with an "Afterthoughts" section, in which we discuss some of the broader issues that the study raises, of a conceptual, practical, or ethical nature. Finally, each chapter concludes with an explicit statement of the unique "Revelation" that each study affords, often a profound and counterintuitive truth.

One of our goals in writing this volume was to make a convincing case for the use of *experiments* in social psychological research. Colloquially, the word *experiment* refers to the trying out of some new idea or technique. Our usage is more technical: It refers to the random assignment of many subjects—here human participants—to different groups (conditions) where these groups are treated identically except in one or a few crucial respects (the independent variable[s]). The impact of these independent variables on how participants think or act (the dependent variables) is then assessed—did the manipulation have an effect? Experiments have a unique advantage in that they allow causal inferences (i.e., X causes Y) to be made with confidence. They also permit alternative explanations for a phenomenon to be efficiently ruled out. Although we do not claim that experimentation provides absolute knowledge, we do claim that it enables researchers to better distinguish between viable and untenable theories about the mind and behavior. Indeed, when the findings of social psychological studies come in, the pitfalls of commonsense are often shockingly exposed.

Two issues seem to cling to any discussion of psychological experimentation: *ethics* and *artificiality*. First, ethics. Social psychologists are often depicted as monsters in lab coats who do not scruple to take advantage of unsuspecting participants. (Indeed, perhaps the very title of this volume, "Experiments With People," sends a shiver down some spines!) This depiction is a perversion of the truth. Social psychologists are, in fact, acutely sensitive to the impact of their procedures on participants. It is common practice, for example, to tell participants in advance what will happen in a study, and to obtain their informed consent. Moreover, before any study can be carried out, an independent ethics committee must first approve it. Such precautions are all to the good, but it should be noted that the majority of social psychological studies, even those that involve deception, rarely raise ethical concerns. Most participants regard them as interesting and informative ways to spend half an hour, and are often found afterwards chatting amiably with the experimenter. This gives the experimenter the chance to debrief participants thoroughly (let them in on the purpose of the study), as well as to obtain feedback from them. Human participants are the lifeblood of social psychology, so researchers are understandably keen to make participation as appealing as possible.

Second, artificiality. Criticism of the experimental method has centered on the claim that, because laboratory settings do not, for the most part, resemble the real world, they do not tell us anything about it. This criticism is specious for several reasons (see Mook, 1980). Primary among them is that artificiality is necessary if ever one is to clear up what causes what, because the only way to get rid of confounds (extraneous factors that might complicate interpretation) is to strip phenomena down to their bare essentials. For example, suppose you wish to test whether the metallic element potassium burns brightly (as it does). Unfortunately, because of potassium's chemical reactivity, it is always found in nature as a salt. Consequently, to test the hypothesis that potassium per se burns brightly, you must first artificially purify potassium salts by electrolysis, in case the other elements with which potassium is combined obscure its incandescence, or turn out to be misleadingly incandescent themselves. In a similar manner, to test any hypothesis about social thinking or behavior, you must first purify the phenomenon of interest in an experimental laboratory, in case the ebb and flow of everyday life obscure its true nature, or misleadingly create the impression that its true nature is other than it actually is.

Artificiality is only a drawback if researchers are seeking to generalize their findings immediately to a specific setting or group of people (as is done in applied research). However, researchers spend much of their time testing general theories or demonstrating classes of effects. This is a worthwhile enterprise because our knowledge of what generally causes what enriches our understanding of specific problems and suggests more effective solutions to them. In any case, social psychological experiments are not always artificial, nor is everyday life always real. The studies featured in this volume, for example, have participants doing a variety of interesting things: they lie to others, submerge their hands in ice water, recall their menstrual symptoms, try to send telepathic messages, contemplate the personalities of the fictional inhabitants of a faraway planet, offer assistance to epileptics, and prepare to deliver a sermon. We daresay that such artificial activities are no less real than many everyday activities, such as flipping hamburgers, driving cars, or watching television (Aronson, Wilson, & Brewer, 1998).

What would happen if social psychologists were to study only everyday experiences in people's lives? Years ago, Barker (1965) pioneered what he called the ecological approach to human behavior. He and his colleagues had the goal of recording the activities of people in a small Kansas town using large numbers of observers stationed in various strategic locations. Much data was collected in grocery stores, on park benches, near soda fountains, and so on. Although the observations collected added up to a number of curious factoids about what really went on in this small town, almost none of these contributed significantly to our general knowledge of human nature. The laboratory is the place to create conditions that put theoretical positions to the test.

On a more personal note, the writing of this book has been, by turns, challenging and gratifying, frustrating and exhilarating. It began when fate, and a common passion for chess, brought the three of us together at Yale University; it has ended, years later, with us living and working continents apart. The process has had its fair share of ups and downs. We sometimes clashed over which studies to include, which issues to address, and which conclusions to draw—hardly unexpected, given the differences in our ages, areas of expertise, and perspectives on life. Yet, through mutual openness, a willingness to compromise, and a principled commitment to democratic decision making, we ultimately succeeded in turning into a reality a wild idea that struck one of us while out for a jog. (Little did that jogger, *KPF*, realize what he was letting himself or the rest of us in for!) Moreover, we believe that this book distills our common wisdom and insight, for, as we collaborated, we could not help enriching each others' knowledge and understanding and curtailing each others' biases and oversights. We are consequently confident that the following pages present an enlightened and evenhanded account of experimental social psychology, past and present. Although our book may well have featured different or additional studies—we preemptively apologize to any researchers who feel unjustly sidelined—we nonetheless flatter ourselves that the studies we do showcase make a prize package. Enjoy!

Please visit our website at: http://www.experimentswithpeople.com

REFERENCES

Aronson, E., Wilson, T. D., & Brewer, M. B. (1998). Experimentation in social psychology. In D. Gilbert, S. Fiske, & G. Lindzey (Eds.), *The handbook of social psychology* (4th ed., Vol. 1, pp. 99–142). New York: Random House.

Barker, R. G. (1965). Explorations in ecological psychology. *American Psychologist, 20*, 1–14.

Mook, D. G. (1980). In defense of external invalidity. *American Psychologist, 38*, 379–388.

ACKNOWLEDGMENTS

We wish to thank Mark Lepper of Stanford University for his detailed and useful comments on an earlier version of this book. Thanks also go to the folks at Lawrence Erlbaum Associates, especially to Larry Erlbaum, Debra Riegert, Marianna Vertullo, and Jason Planer for their support and patient help.

To Kurt Lewin, Stanley Schacter, Leon Festinger, and Harold Kelley, champions of experimental social psychology at MIT in the mid-1940s, and especially to Alex Bavelas who gave me my first research job.

—RPA

To Tae Woo, Alice Eagly, and Eliot Smith, who turned me on to Social Psychology.

—KPF

To my family, for their constant support and love (and hoping this clarifies my occupation!).

—APG

1 Strangers to Ourselves: The Shortcomings of Introspection

"Consciousness is the mere surface of our mind, and of this, as of the globe, we do not know the interior, but only the crust."
—Arthur Schopenhauer (1788–1860), German philosopher

BACKGROUND

Have you ever looked at a friend through a goldfish bowl? If not, try it out when you get the chance: you will find that your friend appears upside down. In itself, that is not too surprising. What is surprising, however, is that your own eyes bend light rather like a goldfish bowl does. That is to say, although the image of an object lands upright on your cornea, it does a vertical flip within your eye, and reaches your retina upside down. Nonetheless, you do not normally perceive your friends to be hanging by their feet from the ground above. There is consequently a contradiction between how things are in the world and how they are presented to your visual system. This contradiction is brought out even more clearly by the following remarkable fact: if people wear special goggles that invert their field of vision, they start to see the world the right way up again after a few days (Stratton, 1897). Somehow, regardless of how the world actually is, the visual system is bent on making vertical sense of it.

Findings like these carry a profound implication: our visual system does not simply reflect external reality but rather actively constructs it. Although this view seems bizarre at first sight, there is plenty of evidence to support it. Consider, for example, what happens when different parts of the occipital cortex (the outer layer of the brain towards the back of the head) are damaged. Several types of specific visual deficit then occur, many of an exceed-

eyes make sense of the world.

1

ingly odd character. Thus, some brain-damaged patients cannot name objects that they can draw; others cannot draw objects that they can name; and still others cannot see the movement of objects that they can both name and draw (Blakemore, 1988). Normal perception, then, would appear to depend on distinct brain circuits making specialized interpretations of the world around us and weaving them together into a coherent fabric.

News of this constructive process comes as a surprise to anyone unacquainted with the science of vision. The reason is straightforward: We are not naturally aware of all the preparatory work that the brain does to produce a perception. We are only aware of the final result itself. The extent to which our unified experience is put together behind the scenes is glimpsed only under rare or artificial circumstances, such as when the visual system breaks down. Under such circumstances, the limitations of our everyday intuitions are exposed, and we find ourselves grappling with the possibility that we see the world not as it is, but as we are.

The thesis of this chapter is that what is true of the visual system is true of our mental life generally. Echoing the philosopher Immanuel Kant, we argue that our understanding of the world and everything in it—objects, people, groups—is a psychological construction determined by the structure of our minds. It is not a literal reflection of things as they are in themselves. Nevertheless, we mostly go about our lives assuming that it is, blithely endorsing what is called naive realism. The inevitable consequence is bias—a reduced sensitivity to the possibility that reality may be very different from how it appears to us (see chap. 4). For example, we tend to assume that others are more likely to share our outlook than they actually are, the so-called false consensus effect (Ross, Greene, & House, 1977).

The point that we wish to emphasize in this chapter is that, if conscious understanding is indeed a psychological construction, then we cannot be directly aware that it is taking place. We can only infer that it is taking place by relying on indirect kinds of evidence, of the sort yielded by scientific investigation. A concise way of expressing the situation is that we are aware of the products of our mind (beliefs, feelings, desires, and judgments) but not of the processes that give rise to them. A major goal of social psychology is to characterize these processes by finding links between what goes on in the world and what goes on inside our heads.

Now consider a commonplace activity that requires conscious understanding: the act of providing explanations for your own thoughts and deeds. You might conclude, for example, that you nagged your boyfriend because you had a stressful day at work; that you liked a humorous movie because you needed cheering up; that you believed in God because you experienced His love; or that you chose a career in accounting because of your punctilious personality. Such explanations, as varied as they are, nonetheless share one common denominator: They all make reference to factors that you are aware of and able to understand. This being so, a deep question arises: If so much of mental life is invisibly constructed behind the scenes, how sure can we be that the explanations we provide are true or complete? Might not the limited range of our awareness prevent us from apprehending factors that are equally if not more important determinants of our thoughts and deeds?

Suppose you wished to *prove* that this was the case. How would you proceed? Well, you would need to satisfy two criteria. First, you would need to show, beyond reasonable doubt, that some factor did (or did not) influence people's thoughts or deeds. Second, you would need to show that, when explicitly questioned about this factor, people did not (or did) believe they had been influenced by it.

Imagine a psychology experiment in which participants are shown the photograph of a woman. Their task is simply to form an impression of her. There are two conditions. In one, the woman's hair is dyed black; in the other, it is dyed brown. Suppose it turns out that participants judge the woman with black hair to be dumber. This proves that hair color influenced participants' impressions. Suppose further that all participants, when later asked if hair color influenced their impressions, reply that it did not. This proves that participants lacked conscious access to the mental processes underlying the formation of their impressions.

You would probably be surprised if black-haired women really were judged dumber than brunettes. However, if, in a variant of this experiment, blondes were judged dumber than brunettes, you would probably be less surprised. This is because, in Western society at least, everybody is familiar with the "dumb blonde" stereotype and expects it to influence impressions. However, because no corresponding stereotype of dumb blackheads exists, no one expects it to influence impressions. The point we wish to bring out here is that you would probably rely on prevalent stereotypes to predict the outcome of a hypothetical hair-color experiment. As a consequence, the accuracy of your predictions would depend on the accuracy of those stereotypes.

Now consider this: Participants in psychology experiments are also familiar with prevalent stereotypes. Hence, they too are likely to draw on those stereotypes when trying to explain the origin of their own impressions. Indeed, the possibility arises that all people ever do when they explain their own thoughts and deeds is to ransack intuitive theories of what makes people tick that are widely shared within a culture (stereotypes are one kind of intuitive theory). Hence, although it may feel as though our introspective reflections yield infallible insights into our minds, this feeling is misleading. We have merely absorbed popular psychological lore so completely that we do not realize that we are relying on it. It follows from this analysis that, if our intuitive theories are correct, then so too will be our explanations for our thoughts and deeds. However, if our intuitive theories are mistaken, then so too will be our explanations.

A surprising implication follows: Whether or not people actually think a thought or do a deed will have little bearing on the correctness of their explanation for why they did so. Observers, to whom the provoking situation is merely described, will arrive at the same explanation as subjects, who experience the situation for themselves. This is because both observers and subjects share the same intuitive theories, and it is these theories that inform their explanations, not insights based on their personal experience. For example, in the hair-color experiment previously mentioned, subjects who actually formed an impression of the woman, and observers merely told what the experiment involved, would come to very similar conclusions about why the subjects had formed the impression that they did.

Social psychologists Nisbett and Bellows (1977) conducted a more complex experiment based upon the above logic. As you read the following details, keep in mind that the researchers' goals were to show, first, that people's verbal explanations for their mental processes are often mistaken, and second, that these mistaken verbal explanations are derived from widely shared intuitive theories.

WHAT THEY DID

A total of 162 female university students participated. Of these, 128 served as subjects. These subjects were placed in a scenario where they were provided with several items of information about a target person. On the basis of this information, they formed an impression of her. The remaining 34 participants served as observers on the sidelines. These participants had the scenario described to them briefly, and were asked to guess what sorts of impressions they would have formed had they themselves been presented information about the target person.

The 128 subjects were asked to judge whether a young woman named Jill had the personality traits needed to become a staff member at a fictitious crisis center. Each subject was handed an application folder containing three pages of information about Jill. The information was supposedly derived from three sources: an interview, a questionnaire, and a letter of recommendation. The portrait of Jill that emerged was of a well-adjusted and competent person who could nonetheless be a little cool and aloof.

Against the background of all this personal data (which gave the study the appearance of realism) five of Jill's attributes were varied. She was described as having, or as not having, each of the following: an attractive appearance, good academic credentials, a car accident some years earlier, the opportunity to meet participants in the near future, and the misfortune to accidentally spill coffee over an interviewer's desk. Each of these attributes was ascribed to Jill exactly half of the time, though in a rather complex way. Specifically, the presence or absence of any one of Jill's five attributes was made independent of the presence or absence of any other. Why so? Because if the researchers had merely, say, led half the subjects to believe that Jill had all five attributes, and the other half to believe she had none, they would not have been able to rule out the possibility that any results obtained, for each of the five attributes, depended on the presence or absence of some combination of the remaining four. Hence, the researcher employed a *factorial* design, in which every possible combination of Jill possessing and not possessing each of the five attributes was featured (adding up to 32 combinations in all). Again, this prevented the effects of any attribute being confounded (mixed up with) the effects of any other. The upshot was that each participant received one of 32 possible descriptions of Jill.

Once subjects had finished reading the contents of the folder, they gave their opinions about how suitable a crisis center employee Jill would make. In particular, subjects rated how much Jill exhibited the following four relevant traits: sympathy, flexibility, likability, and intelligence. Directly afterward, subjects rated on 7-point scales how much they believed each of Jill's attributes had influenced their ratings of each of her traits. The researchers could now compare the actual impact of Jill's attributes on subjects' impressions to subjects' own judgments of their impact. Actual impact was indexed by subtracting subjects' average ratings of Jill when each attribute was present from their average ratings of her when that attribute was absent. Judged impact was indexed by taking subjects' average ratings of each attribute's impact when it was present.

The 34 observers, in contrast, only had the experimental scenario described to them (much as we have described it to you). They were asked to imagine having had access to information about a young female job candidate, and to estimate how their opinion of her would have shifted if she had possessed each of the five attributes systematically manipulated in the experiment. Observers responded using the same 7-point scales as subjects. This made the ratings given by the two groups directly comparable.

WHAT THEY FOUND

As predicted, participants who served as subjects were largely mistaken about the impact that Jill's five attributes had on their impressions of her. For example, subjects who read that Jill had once been involved in a serious car accident claimed that the event had made them view her as a more sympathetic person. However, according to the ratings they later gave, this event had exerted no impact whatsoever. Conversely, subjects also claimed that the prospect of meeting Jill had exerted little if any impact on their judgments of how sympathetic she was. However, subjects' later ratings revealed that the impact of this factor had been substantial (Fig. 1.1). Much the same results were found for the ratings of Jill's flexibility and likability. Indeed, on 6 of 20 occasions, participants' ratings actually shifted in the *opposite* direction to that in which they believed they had. Thus, participants' perceptions of how their judgments of Jill had been swayed, and how their judgments of her actually had been swayed, bore little relation to one another.

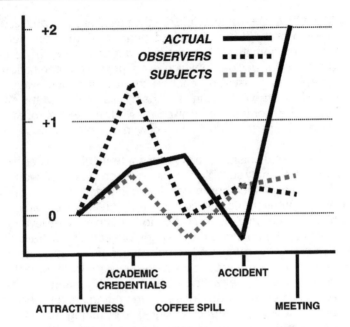

FIG. 1.1. The actual effects of Jill's five attributes on subjects' judgments of her flexibility, and what subjects and observers judged those effects to be.

However, a different picture emerged for ratings of Jill's intelligence. Here, an almost perfect correlation obtained between how subjects' judgments had actually shifted and how much they believed they had shifted. Why so? The researchers argued that there are explicit rules, widely known throughout a culture, for ascribing intelligence to people. Because subjects could readily recognize whether a given factor was relevant to intelligence, they could reliably guess whether they would have taken it into consideration, and therefore whether it would have had an impact on their judgments. In contrast, the rules for ascribing fuzzier traits, like flexibility, are poorly defined or nonexistent. Hence, subjects had no sound basis for guessing whether a given factor had exerted an impact on their judgments in these cases. Introspection could not remedy the deficiency.

If subjects were generally unable to figure out how their judgments had been shaped, how did observers fare? As it turned out, they fared no better or worse than subjects themselves. The determinations of subjects and observers coincided almost exactly. This is quite remarkable given the obvious differences between the concrete judgmental task that subjects engaged in and the abstract scenario that observers read about. It provides powerful support for the hypothesis that people's ideas about how their minds work stem not from private insights but from public knowledge. Unfortunately, however, this public knowledge is often not accurate. It is based on intuitive theories, widely shared throughout society, that are often mistaken.

SO WHAT?

The significance of the present study can be brought out by drawing a distinction between two types of knowledge: familiarity and expertise. Consider a patient who suffers from a disease and the physician who treats him. The patient is familiar with the disease, being personally afflicted by it. In this sense, he might be said to know the disease better than the physician. Nonetheless, the patient's intimate acquaintance with the disease does not provide him with deep knowledge of how the disease developed, how it will progress, or how it should be treated. Yet the physician, who may never have suffered from that disease, is liable to be adept at understanding and treating it. In other words, familiarity does not entail expertise, nor vice versa, where the body is concerned. The same is true, we would argue, of the mind. The bare experience of, say, making a judgment, does not make someone an expert on the factors that shaped it. Moreover, someone who never made that judgment could nonetheless be an expert on the factors that shaped it. In the present study, for example, subjects were unable to determine how Jill's attributes had influenced their ratings, despite being familiar with what it was like to rate her suitability for a job. In contrast, the researchers, despite being unfamiliar with what it was like to rate her suit-

FIG. 1.2. Introspective "reflections" often fail to illuminate the real causes of behavior.

ability for a job, were able to determine (by experimental means) how Jill's attributes had influenced subjects' ratings.

The upshot is that we are more of a mystery to ourselves than we realize. That is why social psychology exists as an objective science. It seeks to illuminate—by theorizing, measuring, and experimenting—how the human mind operates within the social world. Many of its most provocative discoveries would never have been unearthed by introspection alone. Have you, for example, ever suspected that you initially believe every statement that you understand? That changing your mind causes you to forget the opinions you held earlier? That engaging in an activity for a reward makes you enjoy it less? Probably not, even though you are undoubtedly familiar with understanding statements, holding opinions, and receiving rewards. (You can read about these and other "revelations" in the rest of our book!)

The notion that real reasons for our thoughts and deeds defy everyday understanding is, of course, hardly new. Psychoanalysts have long contended that much of what we think and do is unconsciously caused. Social psychologists agree that the real causes of behavior are often unconscious. However, they disagree about where they are to be located. Instead of locating them solely within the person, they also tend to locate them outside the person. So, whereas a psychoanalyst might explain war in terms of an all-embracing death instinct, a social psychologist might do so in terms of social pressures to conform or obey (see chaps. 17 and 21), or people's penchant for identifying with competing social groups (see chap. 25). Of course, social psychologists do not dismiss person-based explanations altogether; on the contrary, they recognize the continual interplay between the individual personality and the social world. However, they are nonetheless apt to point out subtle aspects of situations that exert a surprisingly powerful impact (see chaps. 19 and 23).

The failure of introspection to detect social influence has been documented many times (Nisbett & Wilson, 1977a; Wilson & Stone, 1985). Consider the following study, which investigated people's awareness of the "halo effect"—the tendency for feelings about one thing to contaminate feelings about something else associated with it. Participants watched different videotapes of a college instructor who spoke with a pronounced Belgian accent. On one videotape, seen by half the participants, the instructor came across as warm, engaging, and likeable. On a second videotape, seen by the remaining participants, he came across as cold, aloof, and unsympathetic. All participants then rated how appealing they found three specific features of the instructor: his appearance, mannerisms, and accent. Note that these specific features remained the same regardless of his general demeanor (warm or cold). Nevertheless, participants regarded the instructor's appearance, mannerisms, and accent more favorably when his general demeanor was pleasant than when it was unpleasant. Moreover, participants were completely unaware that the instructor's general demeanor had shaped their opinion of his specific features. In fact, they reported exactly the opposite, that his specific features had shaped their opinion of his general demeanor (Nisbett & Wilson, 1977b).

The tendency to explain psychological states in terms of the wrong antecedent—*misattribution*—takes many forms. Some of these are as amusing are they are informative. In one study, male participants watched an erotic videotape (all for the sake of science, no doubt!). Before watching it, some did nothing, some exercised vigorously, and some exercised vigorously and then waited awhile. It turned out that participants in this last group later reported being most turned on by the videotape. The reason? Exercising had heightened participants' arousal, but because several minutes had passed, they no longer attributed that arousal to the exercise, but rather to the videotape, which happened to be the most salient (noticeable) stimulus in their environment (Cantor, Zillman, & Bryant, 1975). So, if you wish to use misattribution to your personal advantage, here is a suggestion. Bring your date to a scary movie, or on a rollercoaster ride. Then—this is the key point—wait for a few minutes. Finally, make your move. With any luck, your unsuspecting date will misattribute his or her still-elevated arousal to you!

Our lack of introspective insight can also reduce our appreciation of how irrational our judgments can be. Consider, for example, the *above-average bias*. It is well established that most of us rate ourselves more favorably than is warranted on a variety of broadly desirable traits (Dunning, Meyerowitz, & Holzberg, 1989). Yet, most of us also consider ourselves better than our peers at avoiding this above-average bias, thereby ironically confirming its existence (Pronin, Lin, & Ross, 2002). Thus, we believe that our own perceptions of superiority are factually justified whereas those of our peers are the product of vanity.

In closing this section, we would like to briefly address two criticisms that have been leveled at the present study and others like it. The first begins by noting that there are always several valid explanations for what people think or do. As a result, when the explanations of researchers and participants conflict, it is not that the participants are mistaken, but that the researchers have adopted too narrow a view of what constitutes a valid explanation. Admittedly, it is true that any thought or deed can have multiple explanations and that these need not exclude one another. For example, my writing this chapter can be simultaneously explained in terms of personal motivation (I like writing), economic reality (I need the money), or brain science (neuronal firing makes my fingers flex). However, what this criticism overlooks is that participants are not just theorizing at their leisure: they are asked specific questions about factors that have been experimentally proven to affect them. Whatever other valid explanations participants may privately entertain, they are still demonstrably mistaken about the impact of the factors they are questioned about.

The second criticism is that the accuracy of participants' verbal reports is misleadingly compromised by two cognitive defects: An inability to remember what factors affected them and an inability to articulate them. This criticism fails on two counts. First, it is not a sufficient explanation for the inaccuracy of verbal reports. The near-perfect match between the verbal reports of subjects and observers, for example, indicates people's overwhelming reliance on intuitive theories. Second, the criticism seems not so much to argue for the potential accuracy of verbal reports as to describe some additional reasons for why they might be inaccurate.

AFTERTHOUGHTS

Could our introspective insight into ourselves be more limited still? Could we be mistaken about what our true thoughts, feelings, and desires are, not merely what causes them? Freud certainly thought so. Unfortunately, his accounts of our hidden obsessions (e.g., our mothers naked) were more brilliant than believable. Unawareness of our true selves may amount, more modestly, to something like the following. Although we may know for sure what thoughts, feelings, and desires we currently experience, we may still be mistaken about how long they will last or how typical they are of us (Gilbert and others, 1998; see chap. 3). That is, we may think that the contents of our consciousness reflect deep and abiding dispositions, but they turn out to be mere fleeting fancies, entertained one day, but forgotten the next.

Consider how we truly know that we love our romantic partner. Although our immediate feelings may sometimes convince us that we do, there are other occasions on which we recognize the need for a more objective appraisal (Bem, 1967). Have we behaved toward our partner like a lover is supposed to? Are we prepared to live with them for the rest of our lives? What is true love, anyhow? The answers to these questions are not subjectively obvious. If we get the answers wrong, we may also be wrong about whether we truly love our romantic partner (i.e., have a genuine disposition to love them).

Now consider again what happens whenever we ask ourselves why we think, feel, or want something. We come up with reasons that, as we have seen, are typically wide of the mark. However, having come up with them, we may also use them as a source of information about our beliefs, feelings, and desires. Unfortunately, the beliefs, feelings, and desires implied by these reasons may not be the ones we have an underlying disposition to experience. Hence, the very act of explaining ourselves can put us out of touch with who we really are.

One indication that this is so is that engaging in introspection undermines the link between what we say and what we do (Wilson, Dunn, Kraft, & Lisle, 1989). In one study, participants reported how they felt about their romantic partners. The correlation between the feelings they expressed and the ultimate fate of the relationship was then assessed. Normally, a reasonable correlation between the two was observed: Participants who liked their partner stayed with him or her, whereas those who did not, left. However, if participants had first asked themselves why they liked their romantic partners, then no correlation was observed. Introspection evidently disrupted participants' accurate perception of their underlying levels of love for their partner (Wilson & Kraft, 1993).

The pitfalls of introspection do not stop there. Based on the reasons we come up with, we may also make decisions. However, because these decisions fail to take account of our underlying dispositions, we may be setting ourselves up for disappointment. This possibility was nicely illustrated in another study (Wilson et al., 1993). Participants began by viewing posters depicting either fine art or pop art. Afterwards, some participants, but not others, wrote down reasons for why they liked or disliked each poster. All participants then rated how much they liked each poster. Next, participants were given the opportunity to privately choose one surplus poster to take home with them. Finally, 3 weeks later, the researchers telephoned participants to find out how satisfied they were with their chosen poster. Results showed that, normally, participants overwhelmingly preferred the fine art posters. However, if participants had first asked themselves why they liked the posters, they reported liking both types of posters about equally. In addition, those who had engaged in introspection reported being less satisfied with their poster at follow-up. Apparently, introspection had temporarily overridden participants' disposition to prefer fine art. However, this disposition had reasserted itself, leading them to ultimately regret their choice of a pop art poster.

Note that the disruptive effects of introspection are limited to circumstances where people are uncertain of their own attitudes; strongly held attitudes are immune to self-reflective distortion. Nonetheless, the sorts of people who are most likely to engage in introspection are precisely those who are unsure of themselves to begin with, typically individuals with low self-esteem (Campbell, 1990). Thus, those individuals most in need of a certain self-concept may be those most liable to inadvertently spoil their chances of acquiring one.

The general implication is that, given how poor we are at explaining our own behavior, introspection may hinder rather than help us acquire accurate self-knowledge. So, rather than get bogged down in unproductive navel-gazing, we might be better off exposing ourselves to a variety of circumstances and observing how we respond in each. This would enable us to compare our responses and thereby make informed guesses about what causes us to think and act in different ways. (Note that participants in the present study did not have this luxury: they had to determine how their attitudes toward Jill were determined by a unique set of circumstances and attributes.) Perhaps this is why travel broadens the mind: The

introspection → disrupts underlying dispositions.

environment is always changing, making it possible to observe a range of responses. This raises the intriguing possibility that backpacking across a distant continent may tell us more about ourselves than a year on a psychoanalyst's couch.

REVELATION

The fact that we are aware of our own beliefs, feelings, and desires does not automatically make us experts on where they come from. Introspection is therefore an unreliable guide to how the mind works, reflecting cultural truisms rather than providing infallible insights.

— APG —

CHAPTER REFERENCE

Nisbett, R. E., & Bellows, N. (1977). Verbal reports about causal influences on social judgments: Private access versus public theories. *Journal of Personality and Social Psychology, 35,* 613–624.

OTHER REFERENCES

Bem, D. J. (1967). Self-perception: An alternative interpretation of cognitive dissonance phenomena. *Psychological Review, 74,* 183–200.

Blakemore, C. (1988). *The mind machine.* London: BBC Books.

Campbell, J. D. (1990). Self-esteem and clarity of the self-concept. *Journal of Personality and Social Psychology, 59,* 538–549.

Cantor, J. R., Zillman, D., & Bryant, J. (1975). Enhancement of experienced sexual arousal in response to erotic stimuli through misattribution of unrelated residual excitation. *Journal of Personality and Social Psychology, 32,* 69–75.

Dunning, D., Meyerowitz, J. A., & Holzberg, A. D. (1989). Ambiguity and self-evaluation: The role of idiosyncratic trait definitions in self-serving assessments of ability. *Journal of Personality and Social Psychology, 57,* 1082–1090.

Gilbert, D. T., Pinel, E. C., Wilson, T. D., Blumberg, S. J., & Wheatley, T. P. (1998). Immune neglect: A source of durability bias in affective forecasting. *Journal of Personality and Social Psychology, 75,* 617–638.

Nisbett, R. E., & Wilson, T. D. (1977a). Telling more than we can know: Verbal reports on mental processes. *Psychological Review, 84,* 231–259.

Nisbett, R. E., & Wilson, T. D. (1977b). The halo effect: Evidence for the unconscious alteration of judgments. *Journal of Personality and Social Psychology, 35,* 250–256.

Pronin, E., Lin, D. Y., & Ross, L. (2002). The bias blind spot: Perceptions of bias in self versus others. *Personality and Social Psychology Bulletin, 28,* 369–381.

Ross, L., Greene, D., & House, P. (1977). The false consensus phenomenon: An attributional bias in self-perception and social-perception processes. *Journal of Experimental Social Psychology, 13,* 279–301.

Stratton, G. M. (1897). Vision without inversion of the retinal image. *Psychological Review, 4,* 441–481.

Wilson, T. D., Dunn, D. S., Kraft, D., & Lisle, D. J. (1989). Introspection, attitude change, and attitude-behavior consistency: The disruptive effects of explaining why we feel the way we do. *Advances in Experimental Social Psychology, 22,* 287–343.

Wilson, T. D., & Kraft, D. (1993). Why do I love thee?: Effects of repeated introspections about a dating relationship on attitudes toward the relationship. *Personality and Social Psychology Bulletin, 19,* 409–418.

Wilson, T. D., Lisle, D. J., Schooler, J. W., Hodges, S. D., Klaaren, K. J., & LaFleur, S. J. (1993). Introspecting about reasons can reduce post-choice satisfaction. *Personality and Social Psychology Bulletin, 19,* 409–418.

Wilson, T. D., & Stone, J. I. (1985). Limitations of self-knowledge: More on telling more than we can know. In P. Shaver (Ed.), *Review of Personality and Social Psychology* (Vol 6., pp. 167–183). Beverly Hills, CA: Sage.

MORE TO EXPLORE

Ramachandran, V. S. (1998). *Phantoms in the brain.* London: Fourth Estate.

Wilson, T. D., Lindsey, S., & Schooler, T. Y. (2000). A model of dual attitudes. *Psychological Review, 107,* 101–126.

2 Mythical Memories: Reconstructing the Past in the Present

"The most faithful autobiography is less likely to mirror what a man was than what he has become."
—Fawn M. Brodie (1915–1981), American biographer

BACKGROUND

To prepare yourself for this chapter, try the following exercise. Sift through your memory until you locate an episode from your distant past. Next, attempt to recall as clearly as you can the events making up that episode, paying special attention to visual details. Spend a few moments clarifying your memories before proceeding to the next paragraph.

Ready? Now, replay the entire autobiographical episode once again. Looking at it with your inner eye, what precisely do you see? Though the imagery may be faint, and the scenes disjointed, an odd fact may be apparent. Your recollections may not completely or even remotely resemble the visual images that a camera on your head would have recorded. Rather, in accordance with cinematic convention, the remembered events may be depicted from a third-person perspective. You may picture yourself as part of the scene (Nigro & Neisser, 1983).

The existence of such impossible memories proves a surprising but important point: not only are memories capable of being retrieved, they are also capable of being *reconstructed*. In today's hi-tech culture, people could be forgiven for thinking that human memories, once properly stored, can be retrieved from the mind as faithfully as computer files are downloaded from a disk. However, the analogy is mistaken. The memories people retrieve are often biased by the state of mind they are in. A better analogy for how human memory operates (staying within the hi-tech world) might be an eccentric word processor that keeps reinterpreting the contents of documents as it opens them.

Several factors can lead memories to be unreliably reconstructed. Consider, for example, mood. People remember information better when it matches their current mood, or when they learned it in a mood similar to their current one (Clore, Schwartz, & Conway, 1994). In other words, people's minds select some memories, but ignore others, based on their current emotional state. This tendency is especially apparent in people suffering from depression. So-called diurnal depressives—people who feel progressively gloomier as the day wears on—recall fewer happy memories, and more unhappy ones, at sunset than at sunrise (Clark & Teasdale, 1982).

Memories for once-held opinions provide another vivid example of how the past is reinterpreted in terms of the present. In one experiment (Goethals & Reckman, 1973) high school students were first classified, on the basis of their questionnaire responses, as being either for or against the busing of poor Black kids to better-off schools. (At the time, this was a controversial proposal aimed at achieving better racial integration in classrooms.) Several days later, in a different setting, these students were divided into discussion groups based on their pro-busing or anti-busing opinions. In each group, the discussion came to be dominated by an ex-

FIG. 2.1. Far from being digitally hardwired, our memories are distorted by what we currently think and feel.

perimental confederate, posing as a respected senior student. The confederate presented compelling arguments against the position originally endorsed by the other group members. The effect, predictably, was to induce students to radically revise their opinions. The critical part of the experiment, however, came 4 to 14 days later. All students were asked to fill out repeat versions of the original questionnaire. To ensure that students were highly motivated to accurately recall their original opinions, the experimenter claimed that he would be carefully checking the correspondence between responses to the old and new questionnaires. Nevertheless, students' recall of their opinions was highly distorted. They falsely remembered their original opinions as having been consistent with their newly acquired ones. The authors of the study interpreted these results in terms of cognitive dissonance theory (Festinger & Carlsmith, 1957; see chap. 6), the idea being that participants, driven by the motivation to hold consistent opinions, were averse to concluding that their opinions had changed. However, a nonmotivational explanation is also possible. Participants may have reconstructed their past opinions on the basis of false theories about the rate at which their opinions were likely to change, using their current opinions as a benchmark (Ross, 1989). Whatever the explanation, retrospective editing of one's opinions appears to be no fluke. For example, one large study found that, over a 9-year period, people's current political attitudes were much more strongly related to the attitudes they remembered holding than to the attitudes they actually held (Marcus, 1986).

Such findings have an Orwellian feel to them. Yet at least the characters in George Orwell's infamous book *1984* knew that a vast propaganda campaign was being waged against them. In contrast, we seem to be largely unaware that our minds fabricate and revise our personal histories (Greenwald, 1980). Our ignorance of these mental mechanisms should not come as a surprise to readers of chapter 1. There, research was reviewed showing that our intuitive theories about how the mind works, and about the factors that influence its operation, can be woefully wide of the mark. We should hardly expect the experience of remembering to be accompanied by better insight into how remembering occurs, or how faithfully the past is recorded.

The challenge for the experimental social psychologist is to demonstrate that people's intuitive theories can bias recall. To meet this challenge, three things need to be assessed: people's intuitive theories about the mind, the events addressed by those theories, and people's memories for those events. To satisfy these requirements, McFarland, Ross, and DeCourville (1993) seized upon a phenomenon that might at first glance seem a strange candidate: menstruation.

In Western culture, the negative impact of menstruation on well-being is taken as a given (Brooks-Gunn & Ruble, 1986). Premenstrual syndrome is the household name for the array of symptoms, from chocolate cravings to homicidal impulses, that falling levels of the hormone progesterone are supposed to trigger. The syndrome is popularly regarded as a scientific fact, being forever soberly discussed by physicians and clinicians, and the subject of a thriving self-help literature. Many readers will be surprised to learn, therefore, that evidence for the syndrome is very thin on the ground. Numerous studies have failed to substantiate any systematic change across the menstrual cycle in women's psychological symptoms (Klebanov & Ruble, 1994). Indeed, it can be argued that premenstrual syndrome is not so much a bona fide medical disorder as a cultural myth that persists as a way of explaining women's distress in terms of their presumed emotional and biological fragility (Tavris, 1992). (Lest readers think that these claims reflect male bias, we point out that women have done most of the relevant research on the topic.)

For the purposes of demonstrating that memory is shaped by intuitive theories menstruation was an ideal choice. First, it was associated with a prevalent stereotype; second, the reality of menstrual events could be approximately assessed from daily reports; and third, memories for those same menstrual events could be assessed from retrospective reports.

In the study we describe the researchers made two specific predictions. First, they predicted that participants' intuitive theories of menstrual distress, being shaped by negative cultural stereotypes, would be at odds with their actual experience of menstruation. Secondly, they predicted that women's intuitive theories of menstrual distress would lead them to recall their menstrual symptoms as being worse than they actually were, and that the more strongly those theories were held, the more biased their recall of those menstrual symptoms would be.

WHAT THEY DID

Sixty-five Canadian females, mostly college students in their late teens and early twenties, participated in the study. To assess the nature and strength of their intuitive theories of menstrual distress, the researchers had them complete a subset of items from the *Menstrual Distress Questionnaire*, or *MDQ* (Moos, 1968). These items tapped the extent to which participants typically experienced three general types of symptom over the course of their menstrual cycle: pain, water retention, and unpleasant emotion. Participants rated the severity of 18 more specific symptoms, 6 for each general type, on scales that ranged from 1 (symptom absent) to 6 (symptom acute and disabling). The researchers' assumption that the MDQ items would reflect intuitive theories about, rather than actual experience of, menstrual distress, was supported by two previous findings. First, MDQ scores and daily reports of menstrual distress tend to correlate only modestly (Ascher-Svanum, 1982); second, responses to the MDQ before the onset of menstruation resemble responses to it afterwards (Clarke & Ruble, 1978). The MDQ was administered approximately 2 weeks after the rest of the study was over, in order to avoid arousing participants' suspicions.

To assess actual symptoms over the course of the menstrual cycle, the researchers had participants fill out daily questionnaires that asked, among other things, about their experiences of pain, water retention, and unpleasant emotion. The researchers, however, disguised the purpose of these daily questionnaires. Prior research had shown that people report extra symptoms if they believe that they are participating in a study on menstruation (Ruble & Brooks-Gunn, 1979). Hence, the daily questionnaires consisted mostly of bogus items, designed to back up the researchers' claim that they were investigating the links between legal drug use, life events, psychological states, and physiological states. Only one other questionnaire item was genuine. It asked unobtrusively whether participants were currently menstruating.

Participants agreed to complete the daily questionnaires at bedtime for a period of 4 to 6 weeks. They deposited each completed questionnaire the next day in a public mailbox. If participants ever failed to submit a questionnaire, they were immediately contacted and given a reminder. It is a tribute to the management abilities of the researchers, and the conscientiousness of the participants, that over 99% of the questionnaires given out were returned.

Finally, some days after the daily questionnaire phase of the study had concluded, the researchers assessed participants' recall of their menstrual symptoms. Participants were asked to remember, as best they could, the responses that they had given to the daily questionnaire exactly 2 weeks earlier. The administration of the recall measure was scheduled so that half the participants had been in the menstrual phase of their cycles when they had filled out the original questionnaire, and half in their post-menstrual phase. (The menstrual phase was defined as the first 3 days of menstruation, and the post-menstrual phase as the 3-day period beginning 5 days afterward.) The researchers assumed that only participants made aware that they had earlier been menstruating would use their intuitive theories of menstrual distress to inform their recollections. To ensure participants were in fact aware of their prior menstrual status, the experimenter let them see their responses to the first three items on its life-events section of the questionnaire (supposedly to help jog their memory for the remainder of their responses), with the third item indicating whether or not they had been menstruating. Finally, to oblige participants to rely solely on their memories of menstrual symptoms, the researchers ensured that no participants were menstruating at the time they attempted to recall their responses to the daily questionnaire.

WHAT THEY FOUND

Participants' intuitive theories of menstrual distress, indexed by their MDQ scores, bore out cultural stereotypes. Specifically, participants believed that they had experienced more pain, retained more water, and felt worse during the menstrual (and premenstrual) phase of their cycle. On a 6-point scale of severity, they indicated that each type of symptom had been, on average, 1 scale point worse than at other times. However, participants' intuitive theories of menstrual distress did not match their actual experience. Participants' responses to the daily questionnaires indicated that their pain and water retention levels had only been a quarter scale point worse during their menstrual (and premenstrual) phase. Even more strikingly, participants' levels of unpleasant emotion did not show any fluctuation across the whole of their cycle. Thus, the undergraduates in the present study seemed blessedly immune to the premenstrual blues. Statistical analysis confirmed that participants' daily reports across the different phases of their cycle were at odds with their intuitive theories about how they typically felt during those phases. The overall pattern of results suggested that participants not only overestimated the intensity of menstrual (and premenstrual) symptoms, but also underestimated the intensity of symptoms during the remainder of their cycle (Fig. 2.2).

Such results demonstrate that participants' theories of menstrual distress did not correspond with the reality of their symptoms. But could they also *distort* participants' specific recollections of their menstrual distress? One way to test this would have been to check whether, for each type of symptom, the discrepancy between daily reports and subsequent memories was greater for participants scoring high on the MDQ than for participants scoring low, but only when the reports and memories per-

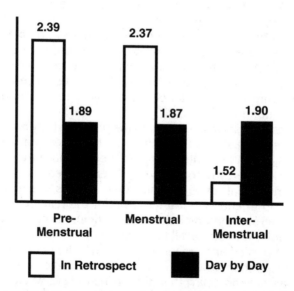

FIG. 2.2. The levels of unpleasant emotion that participants reported across different phases of their menstrual cycle, both in retrospect and day by day.

tained to the menstrual phase of participants' cycle (as they did for half the sample), not when they pertained to the post-menstrual phase (as they did for the remaining half). In fact, the researchers conducted a series of conceptually similar, but statistically more powerful, analyses to address these questions. The predicted findings emerged. The more severe participants expected their period to be (based on their intuitive theories about menstrual symptoms), the more they retrospectively exaggerated the severity of their symptoms. However, this only happened when the period of recollection pertained to the menstrual phase of their cycle; when it pertained to the post-menstrual phase, the severity of the symptoms recalled was not predicted by theories of menstrual distress. The effects obtained were most pronounced for pain and unpleasant emotion.

A supplementary analysis underlined the very specific nature of the memory distortion. The MDQ items, you will recall, surveyed intuitive theories of menstrual distress for the whole of the monthly cycle, not just the menstrual phase. As expected, participants' intuitive theories about the distress they would experience during the nonmenstrual phases of their cycles did not predict their recall of menstrual symptoms.

Taken altogether, these findings neatly show that intuitive theories of menstrual distress (but not of nonmenstrual distress) biased participants' memory for menstrual symptoms (but not for nonmenstrual symptoms). They provide rigorous proof that intuitive theories about the mind—in particular, about how it is affected by bodily events—can distort recollections. In fact, it is conceivable that the results obtained even underestimated the magnitude of the distortion, for convenience. Participants' daily reports of their symptoms had been equated with objective reality. However, these reports, being themselves somewhat retrospective in nature by several hours, were also liable to have been somewhat influenced by participants' intuitive theories of menstrual distress. The fact that positive findings were obtained nonetheless points to the potency of the memory distortion found.

One final issue deserves mention. In the present study participants' intuitive theories were assessed only after they had attempted to recall their symptoms. Might participants' mistaken theories have therefore been a consequence of the symptoms they misremembered rather than the cause of them? A final set of analyses ruled out this alternative explanation. We had not mentioned it until now, but the researchers also conducted a parallel study in which they had participants complete the MDQ immediately following the recall task, rather than 2 weeks later as in the main study. If participants' recollections had influenced their theories, then the correspondence between the measures would have been greater in the comparative (no delay) than the main study (2-week delay). However, no greater correspondence was found. Hence, this alternative memories-cause-theories hypothesis was not supported.

SO WHAT?

Though we may believe ourselves to be remembering events exactly as they occurred, we may be unconsciously constructing them on the basis of erroneous beliefs. An analogy with a familiar perceptual illusion helps to illustrate the point. The moon looks bigger over the horizon than it does directly above us. Nonetheless, the moon subtends a constant angle of half a degree to the eye no matter where it is in the sky. One explanation for this moon illusion is that faraway overhead objects typically do subtend a smaller angle to the eye than nearby overhead objects (e.g., airplanes get smaller as they recede into the distance). Consequently, our visual system cleverly corrects for the reduced angular disparity to impart the useful impression that objects remain the same size, wherever they (or we) go. However, because the angle subtended by the moon remains the same size regardless of its position overhead, our visual system is conned into correcting for nonexisting lunar shrinkage, and the illusion results (Baird, Wagner, & Fuld, 1990). The point is this: We are not aware of the underlying inferences that shape our false perception of the moon, only of the final perception itself. Similarly, we are not aware of the unconscious beliefs that shape our false recollections, only of the recollections themselves. In the first case, it takes a cognitive psychologist to highlight our errors, in the second case, a social psychologist.

Our lack of insight into how our minds work can be explained (see chap. 1). However, what explains the persistence of our intuitive theories when our ongoing experience repeatedly disconfirms them? In particular, why did participants in the present study, veterans of many menstruations, not learn that menstruation was unrelated to psychological distress?

Perhaps the main reason is that memories shaped by intuitive theories feel subjectively compelling, which in turn is taken as evidence that these intuitive theories are true, creating a sort of *self-fulfilling prophecy* (Snyder, Tanke, & Berscheid, 1977; see chap. 14). Apparent memories of menstrual distress, taken at face value, confirm that menstruation causes distress. Another general reason why false intuitive theories may persist is that espousing them enables desirable conclusions to be reached. For example, in one study, students who enlisted in a study skills program known to be ineffective later recalled their prior studying habits as having been poorer compared to a matched control group (Conway & Ross, 1984). Wanting to believe that all the effort they invested had been justified (Aronson & Mills, 1959; see chap. 7), they espoused the theory that the program worked, and then altered their recollections to match. A final reason why false intuitive theories persist is that the evidence bearing on them may be processed in a biased manner (Kunda, 1990; see also chap. 4). A useful distinction can be drawn here between one-sided and two-sided events (Madey & Gilovich, 1993). Two-sided events capture our attention no matter how they turn out, whether they confirm or violate our expectations. For example, a honeymoon in Vegas is likely to prove memorable whether it turns out to be exhilarating or exasperating. In contrast, one-sided events only capture our attention if they turn out a particular way. For example, if I guess correctly who is calling before I pick up the phone, I may marvel at my clairvoyance; but if I guess incorrectly, I may instantly switch my attention to other topics. Consequently, my hits will be recalled, my misses forgotten. Given that estimates of likelihood depend upon the ease with which material can be retrieved from memory (Kahneman & Tversky, 1973) I might then lean towards the false conclusion that I possess psychic ability (see chap. 15, for other antecedents of this impression). Similarly, participants in the present study may have been more impressed by, and hence have better remembered, those occasions on which their psychological distress coincided with menstruation than those on which it did not. Occasions confirming the stereotype would likely have been more dramatic (because of the emotional upset they have entailed) whereas occasions disconfirming the stereotype would likely have been less so (because they entailed no departure from normal well-being).

AFTERTHOUGHTS

It is likely that many participants in the present study felt they were genuinely recalling their menstrual symptoms, not simply inferring them or imagining them. To the extent that this was so, they were exhibiting *false memories*. This brings us neatly to our final topic of discussion. Questions concerning the reliability of memory have in recent years attracted intense public and scientific scrutiny due to the heated controversy surrounding the alleged phenomenon of *recovered memory* (Loftus, 1994). Many clinicians believe, following Freud, that traumatic experiences in childhood, too harrowing to be consciously assimilated, get involuntarily repressed (split off from conscious awareness) and remain so for many years. Although the repression initially allows the trauma to be endured, it later gives rise to an array of psychological symptoms that the patient is at a loss to explain. Diagnosis of these symptoms by a clinician is followed by intensive psychotherapy aimed at enabling patients to recall their traumatic past, the underlying premise being that remembering is a necessary or sufficient condition for healing. Clinicians typically rely heavily on techniques such as guided hypnosis and suggestive prompting to get to the root of their patients' repression. Patients undergoing the therapy often find themselves supported and encouraged by a community of like-minded survivors.

Unfortunately, patients' alleged reminiscences often push the limits of credibility. Impassioned crusaders urge us to accept that the abuse of children by Satanists, or the abduction of humans by aliens, is alarmingly commonplace, a silent epidemic that our society refuses to face (Bass & Davis, 1994; Mack, 1995). The impressionable would therefore do well to heed an argument first formulated by the philosopher David Hume (1990), which he hoped would "serve as an everlasting check on superstition of all kinds." Hume asked which we have better grounds for believing: that a religious miracle occurred and was accurately reported, or that it did not occur and was mistakenly reported? He concluded that, given our background knowledge of how the world works, the latter possibility is always the more likely. Consequently, there can never be adequate grounds for believing in miracles on the strength of testimony alone (not even if such miracles actually occurred). A similar argument could be brought to bear on the more extravagant claims of those who champion the cause of recovered memory.

Nonetheless, some recovered memory claims do fall within the bounds of credibility. In such cases, memory-based testimony cannot simply be dismissed out of hand. It seems improbable, on the face of it, that large numbers of patients would allege traumatic abuse without due foundation, or that memories for such abuse would be so vivid were they mere mental fictions. Yet are things how they seem? The stakes are high. On the one hand, every moral person rightly recoils from the prospect of dismissing a genuine case of abuse as bogus. On the other hand, accepting as genuine a false allegation of abuse risks ruining the lives and reputations of those who stand unjustly accused. In the absence of decisive physical evidence, the evidential value of memory-based testimony must be carefully determined. Scientific psychology has played a key role in this regard. As it turns out, its findings tend to justify skepticism about the validity of recovered memories.

First of all, the available laboratory evidence does not support the view that people repress unpleasant memories (Holmes, 1990). (Note: Repression differs from suppression in that it is involuntary; see chap. 10, for more on the effects of voluntary suppression.) Indeed, one of the hallmarks of real traumatic memories, observed in people who have been through verifiable ordeals like wartime killing, is that such memories cannot be forgotten. They intrusively recur during both waking and sleep (Krystal, Southwick, & Charney, 1995). Admittedly, post-traumatic amnesia does occur, but when it does it is global in character, making no distinction between traumatic and nontraumatic events (Schacter & Kilstrom, 1989). However, even if a trauma were selectively forgotten, repression would not be automatically implicated. Everyday forgetting, due to competition from other material or to the decay of memory traces, would be an equally if not more plausible explanation. True, unpleasant autobiographical memories do tend to fade faster than pleasant ones, but repression does not appear to be involved (Walker, Skowronski, & Thompson, in press). A more general psychological immune system is responsible (Gilbert, Pinel, Wilson, Blumberg, & Wheatley, 1998; see chap. 3). Hence, the prima facie case for recovered memory is not compelling.

Moreover, numerous studies attest to the surprising malleability of memory. Taken as a whole, these lend credence to the view that recovered memories, for all their drama and vividness, can be artificially induced. For example, when people read a list of related words (e.g., bedtime, yawn, pillow) most of them then recall having read, or report having recognized, other thematically related words that did not in fact appear (e.g., sleep; Roediger & McDermott, 1995). Moreover, people's confidence in the accuracy of their memories, and their feeling of remembering rather than guessing, is no higher for words previously presented than for words falsely identified. Hence, subjective judgments about the validity of memories can go astray when highly consistent mental concepts are activated.

Other research shows that post-event questioning can modify memories. In one study, for instance, a series of slides was presented in which a car came to a halt at a *stop* sign. Some participants were then asked, misleadingly, what the car did after coming to a halt at the *yield* sign. These participants were more likely to later remember having actually seen a yield sign than were those who were not asked the misleading question. Such findings have been replicated for attributes like speed and color, and carry obvious implications for the reliability of eyewitness testimony (Loftus, Miller, & Burns, 1987). Clearly, how questions are asked can bias the content of what is recalled.

However, can recollections be fabricated from nothing if others merely insist that fictitious events occurred? Remarkably, yes. In a study of false confessions (Kassin & Kiechel, 1996) participants performed a computer task at either a hurried or a leisurely pace. The experimenter warned participants at the outset not to press the ALT key accidentally, as this would later cause the computer program to crash. All heeded this warning, but later found themselves wrongfully accused of pressing the key. For some participants, the accusations were backed up by a confederate, who whispered audibly to the experimenter that he had witnessed the alleged transgression. Of those participants who performed the computer task hurriedly, and who overheard the confederate ratting on them, one third fabricated detailed false recollections about pressing the ALT key. This study shows that, when memory for an event is vague, and others make a credible case for its having occurred, that memory stands a reasonable chance of becoming integrated into one's mental autobiography. Indeed, a substantial minority of people remember fictitious childhood events when it is only casually suggested to them that they occurred (Ceci, 1995).

Sessions with recovered memory therapists are anything but casual however. First of all, patients are openly pressured to generate memories in order to surmount the retrieval block that repression is presumed to impose. Second, recovered memory therapists often employ hypnosis or guided imagination to facilitate patients' recall of events. Although research shows that such techniques can improve memory for real events, it also shows that they can do the same for fictitious events (Spiegel, 1995). Third, patients are liable to be steeped in the lore of the recovered memory movement, ensuring that they will possess rich intuitive theories concerning the nature of trauma, memory, and therapy. Extrapolating from the present study, we could expect such theories to spawn theory-consistent recollections. Fourth, paradoxical as it may seem, patients may be powerfully motivated to believe that they are victims of trauma. Full assimilation into a sympathetic community of fellow survivors requires that a patient exhibit the authenticating signs, and the emotional stress of the therapy itself is likely to strengthen a patient's commitment to that community (Aronson & Mills, 1959; see chap. 7).

At the end of the day, the fact that recovered memories do assume fantastic forms is the best evidence for their potential unreliability. Devotees of recovered memory therapy, now legally compelled to admit the reality of some false memories and the devastation they can wreak, nonetheless continue to maintain that genuine instances of repressed trauma do exist, and that these can be diagnosed by experienced clinicians with tolerable accuracy. However, it is difficult to see how such clinicians could acquire such expertise in the first place. They have rarely if ever had access to individuals who can be positively identified as abused or nonabused by any criterion independent of their own clinical judgment.

Even if genuine cases of recovered memory do exist, the therapeutic value of dredging up a traumatic past is still debatable. Modern scholarship has documented that Freud, the originator of supposed memory cures, never actually cured any of his patients, despite his extravagant claims to the contrary (Crews, 1995). Certainly, it is good to face unresolved psychological issues. Even confiding one's woes to a diary modestly benefits one's physical health (Pennebaker, 2000). However, becoming preoccupied with the past, and bogged down in one's own victimhood, is an unlikely recipe for triumphing over adversities past. Forging ahead courageously, finding hope in the new rather than fault with the old, is a more reliable road to recovery.

REVELATION

Our intuitive theories about how things are subtly shape our memories for what has been .Thus, we unknowingly reconstruct the past in terms of the present rather than simply remembering the past in its original form..

— APG —

CHAPTER REFERENCE

McFarland, C., Ross, M., & DeCourville, N. (1993). Women's theories of menstruation and biases in recall of menstrual symptoms. *Journal of Personality and Social Psychology, 65,* 1093–1104.

OTHER REFERENCES

Aronson, E., & Mills, J. (1959). The effect of severity of initiation on liking for a group. *Journal of Abnormal and Social Psychology, 59,* 177–181.

Ascher-Svanum, H. (1982). *Alcohol use and psychological distress during the menstrual cycle.* Unpublished doctoral dissertation, University of Minnesota, Twin Cities, MI.

Baird, J. C., Wagner, M. F., & Fuld, K. (1990). A simple but powerful theory of the moon illusion. *Journal of Experimental Psychology: Human Perception & Performance, 16,* 675–677.

Bass, E., & Davis, L. (1994). *The courage to heal: A guide for women survivors of sexual abuse.* New York: Harper Perennial Library.

Brooks-Gunn, J., & Ruble, D. N. (1986). Men's and women's attitudes and beliefs about the menstrual cycle. *Sex Roles, 14,* 287–299.

Ceci, S. J. (1995). False beliefs: Some developmental and clinical considerations. In D. L. Schacter (Ed.), *Memory distortion: How minds, brains, and societies reconstruct the past* (pp. 91–128). Cambridge, MA: Harvard University Press.

Clarke, A., & Ruble, D. N. (1978). Young adolescents' beliefs concerning menstruation. *Child Development, 49,* 201–234.

Clark, D. M., & Teasdale, J. D. (1982). Diurnal variation in clinical depression and accessibility of memories of positive and negative experiences. *Journal of Abnormal Psychology, 91,* 87–95.

Clore, G. L., Schwartz, N., & Conway, M. (1994). Cognitive causes and consequences of emotion. In R. S. Wyer & T. K. Srull (Eds.), *Handbook of social cognition* (2nd ed., Vol. 1, pp. 323–418). Hillsdale, NJ: Lawrence Erlbaum Associates.

Conway, M., & Ross, M. (1984). Getting what you want by revising what you had. *Journal of Personality and Social Psychology, 47,* 738–748.

Crews, F. (1995). *The memory wars: Freud's legacy in dispute.* New York: The New York Review of Books.

Festinger, L., & Carlsmith, J. (1959). Cognitive consequences of forced compliance. *Journal of Abnormal and Social Psychology, 58,* 203–10.

Gilbert, D. T., Pinel, E. C., Wilson, T. D., Blumberg, S. J., & Wheatley, T. P. (1998). Immune neglect: A source of durability bias in affective forecasting. *Journal of Personality and Social Psychology, 75,* 617–638.

Goethals, G. R., & Reckman, R. F. (1973). The perception of consistency in attitudes. *Journal of Experimental Social Psychology, 9,* 491–501.

Greenwald, A. G. (1980). The totalitarian ego: Fabrication and revision of personal history. *American Psychologist, 35,* 603–618.

Holmes, D. S. (1990). The evidence for repression: An examination of sixty years of research. In J. L. Singer (Ed.), *Repression and dissociation: Implications for personality theory, psychopathology, and health* (pp. 85–102). Chicago, IL: University of Chicago Press.

Hume, D. (1990). *Principal writings on religion including dialogues concerning natural religion and the natural history of religion.* New York: Oxford University Press.

Kahneman, D., & Tversky, A. (1973). On the psychology of prediction. *Psychological Review, 80,* 237–251.

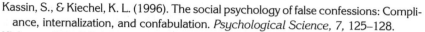

Kassin, S., & Kiechel, K. L. (1996). The social psychology of false confessions: Compliance, internalization, and confabulation. *Psychological Science, 7,* 125–128.

Klebanov, P. K., & Ruble, D. N. (1994). Toward an understanding of women's experience of menstrual cycle symptoms. In V. J. Adesso & D. M. Reddy (Eds.), *Psychological perspectives on women's health* (pp. 183–221). Philadelphia: Taylor & Francis.

Krystal, J. H., Southwick, S. M., & Charney, D. S. (1995). Post-traumatic stress disorder: Psychobiological mechanisms of traumatic remembrance. In D. L. Schacter (Ed.), *Memory distortion: How minds, brains, and societies reconstruct the past* (pp. 150–172). Cambridge, MA: Harvard University Press.

Kunda, Z. (1990). The case for motivated reasoning. *Psychological Bulletin, 108,* 480–498.

Loftus, E. F. (1994). *The myth of repressed memory.* New York: St. Martins Press.

Loftus, E. F., Miller, D. G., & Burns, H. J. (1987). Semantic integration of verbal information into a visual memory. In L. S. Wrightsman & C. E. Willis (Eds.), *On the witness stand: Controversies in the courtroom* (pp. 157–177). Newbury Park, CA: Sage Publications.

Mack, J. E. (1995). *Abduction: Human encounters with aliens.* New York: Ballantine.

Madey, S. F., & Gilovich, T. (1993). Effect of temporal focus on the recall of expectancy-consistent and expectancy-inconsistent information. *Journal of Personality and Social Psychology, 65,* 458–468.

Marcus, G. B. (1986). Stability and change in political attitudes: Observe, recall, and "explain." *Political Behavior, 8,* 21–44.

Moos, R. H. (1968). The development of a menstrual distress questionnaire. *Psychosomatic Medicine, 30,* 853–867.

Nigro, G., & Neisser, U. (1983). Point of view in personal memories. *Cognitive Psychology, 15,* 467–482.

Pennebaker, J. W. (2000). The effect of traumatic disclosure on physical and mental health: The values of writing and talking about upsetting events. In J. M. Violanti & D. Paton (Eds.), *Posttraumatic stress intervention: Challenges, issues, and perspectives* (pp. 97–114). Springfield, IL: Charles C. Thomas.

Roediger, H. L., & McDermott, K. B. (1995). Creating false memories: Remembering words not presented in lists. *Journal of Experimental Psychology: Learning, Memory, & Cognition, 21,* 803–814.

Ross, M. (1989). Relation of implicit theories to the construction of personal histories. *Psychological Review, 96,* 341–357.

Ruble, D. N., & Brooks-Gunn, J. (1979). Menstrual symptoms: A social cognition analysis. *Journal of Behavioral Medicine, 2,* 171–194.

Schacter, D. L., & Kilstrom, J. F. (1989). Functional amnesia. In F. Boller & J. Grafman (Eds.), *Handbook of Neuropsychology* (Vol 3: 209–231). Amsterdam, Netherlands: Elsevier.

Snyder, M., Tanke, E. D., & Berscheid, E. (1977). Social perception and interpersonal behavior: On the self-fulfilling nature of social stereotypes. *Journal of Personality and Social Psychology, 35,* 656–666.

Spiegel, D. (1995). Hypnosis and suggestion. In D. L. Schacter (Ed.), *Memory distortions: How minds, brains, and societies reconstruct the past* (pp. 129–149). Cambridge, MA: Harvard University Press.

Tavris, C. (1992). *The mismeasure of woman*. New York: Simon & Schuster.

Walker, W. R., Skowronski, J. J., & Thompson, C. P. (in press). Life is pleasant—and memory helps to keep it that way! *Review of General Psychology*.

MORE TO EXPLORE

Schachter, D. (1999). The seven sins of memory: Insights from psychology and cognitive neuroscience. *American Psychologist, 3,* 182–203.

Wright, L. (1994). *Remembering Satan*. Cambridge, MA: Vintage Books.

3 Taking the Edge Off Adversity: The Psychological Immune System

"There are only two tragedies in life. One is not to get one's heart's desire. The other is to get it."

—Oscar Wilde (1854–1900), Victorian writer and wit

BACKGROUND

You are probably familiar with the story of Aladdin. Going about his daily duties, he stumbles by accident upon a strange-looking lamp. Greatly intrigued, he examines it further. Suddenly, with a great puff of smoke, a magical genie materializes. Grateful for being set free, this genie grants Aladdin three wishes. Aladdin can hardly believe his good fortune. A life of leisure and luxury, once but a distant dream, now seems mere moments away.

Put yourself in Aladdin's shoes. What would you wish for? (Note: clever replies like "an unlimited number of similar wishes" are forbidden!) The three wishes you select will certainly represent things you believe will make you happy. Although you are unlikely ever to get the chance of transforming your life as radically as Aladdin did, you will nonetheless get to make decisions every day that have some bearing on your gladness or sadness. Moreover, when you make such decisions, you necessarily rely on your intuitions about how actions and events will make you feel. For example, you might attend a friend's birthday party, expecting it to be entertaining, but skip a psychology lecture expecting it to be boring.

Unfortunately, our naïve expectations are sometimes mistaken and prompt decisions that we later regret (Nisbett & Wilson, 1977; see chap. 1).

You may possibly find yourself thoroughly bored at your friend's party, or later realize that you would have found that psychology lecture highly entertaining. Indeed, folklore warns about the consequences of misjudging what makes us happy. In some variants of the Aladdin fairytale, for example, the protagonist tragically squanders his once-in-a-lifetime opportunity by making three silly wishes, thereby ending up no better off than when he started.

Can social psychology, then, serve as a reliable source of information about what makes people happy? One would certainly hope so, given that the aim of studying the mind scientifically is to improve upon common-sense. However, psychological research initially had a rather negative focus, trying to find ways of treating mental illness, not ways of enhancing mental wellness. It was eventually realized that any system, including the mind, cannot be understood in terms of its imperfections alone. Just as there is more to physical health than the absence of disease, so there is more to psychological health than the absence of distress.

In recent years, therefore, social psychologists have taken the lead in investigating the whys and wherefores of *subjective well-being* (Diener, Suh, Lucas, & Smith, 1999). In the process, it has been discovered that many of our assumptions about what causes happiness are mistaken (Myers & Diener, 1995). For example, income has little to do with our happiness. Once we earn enough to get by, our bank balance no longer predicts how bright and bubbly we are. True, we have all heard that "money can't buy happiness," but how many of us really believe this? In 1993, three-quarters of incoming U.S. college students reported that "being well off financially" was either a "very important" or "essential" goal for them (Astin, 1997).

So, many of our intuitive theories about the impact of events on our emotional lives are mistaken. However, sometimes they are mistaken in a rather special way. We often hit the nail on the head when it comes to predicting the type of impact an event will have on us and the intensity of that impact. For example, we may correctly predict that winning a lottery would thrill us more than locating a long lost sock, or that the loss of a limb would horrify us more than a run in our nylons. Where we err, however, is in estimating the *duration* of the positive or negative feelings that such events evoke. Research shows, for example, that the thrill of winning the lottery, and the horror of acquiring a physical handicap, both diminish more quickly than expected. Indeed, after only a few months, people who have experienced either one or the other are barely distinguishable in terms of their overall happiness (Brickman, Coates, & Janoff-Bulman, 1978). In technical jargon, our *affective forecasts* exhibit a *durability bias*, for both positive and negative events.

Why do we overestimate how long something will make us feel happy or sad? A number of mental mechanisms may be responsible. First, people may misconstrue an upcoming event, seeing it from only one perspective. For example, a person who considers buying a new Ferrari may only think about how awesome it looks, and forget to think about the hassle and ex-

FIG. 3.1. We get over negative experiences sooner than we expect.

pense involved in maintaining it. Second, people's predictions may undergo motivational distortion. For example, an idler may exaggerate the stress of a prospective job in order to rationalize staying idle. Third, people may focus on a particular event to the exclusion of all others. For example, when people contemplate breaking up with their lover, they may only think of the ensuing heartbreak, rather than of all the joys that will remain in their life, from friends to French fries.

Mechanisms like those previously mentioned can create a durability bias in the forecast of either positive or negative feelings. However, Gilbert, Pinel, Wilson, Blumberg, and Wheatley (1998) sought a mechanism that would create a durability bias specifically in the forecast of negative feelings. These researchers hypothesized that the human mind contains a psychological immune system designed to keep negative feelings at bay, much like the physical immune system is designed to keep dangerous germs at bay. They further hypothesized that the system, like much of our underlying cognitive architecture, operates unconsciously. Having no conscious knowledge of its operation, we do not expect the system to dispel our negative feelings. However, dispel them it does, and our original estimates of the duration of our negative feelings turn out to be pessimistic.

By way of illustration, consider the phenomenon of *post-decisional dissonance* (Brehm, 1956; see also chap. 6). Suppose David is forced to decide between two equally attractive beauties, Cecilia and Patricia. After much deliberation, he selects Cecilia. Having made this decision, however, his psychological immune system starts to justify it. Thus, David finds himself emphasizing both Cecilia's merits and Patricia's shortcomings. Having done so, however, he now feels less regret over rejecting Patricia than he had originally expected to. Note, however, that had David been aware of what his psychological immune system was doing, his regret over rejecting Patricia would not have been able to abate so speedily.

But this is merely a hypothetical example. Gilbert et al. (1998) took it upon themselves to demonstrate that people exhibit a durability bias when forecasting their negative feelings, and that this bias is due to their being unaware of the operation of their psychological immune system.

WHAT THEY DID

In their published paper, Gilbert et al. (1998) reported a total of six studies. Here, we have space to report on just two.

In Study 1, Gilbert et al. (1998) capitalized upon an event likely to have emotional implications for the politically partisan public: the gubernatorial election. The setting was Texas, 1994. All participants had just cast their vote for either George W. Bush (Republican) or Ann Richards (Democrat). They were then asked to fill out a brief 10-item survey. Five bogus items drew attention away from the other five. The genuine items asked participants to report: (a) how happy they currently felt; (b) who their favored candidate was; (c) how happy they would feel 1 month later if their favored candidate won or lost; (d) how good a governor each candidate would make; and (e) what they would think of each candidate 1 month later if he or she were elected. Participants responded to each item on a 7-point scale (e.g., 1 = terrible governor, 7 = excellent governor).

The main purpose of the survey was to measure voters' predictions about how the outcome of the election would affect their happiness. The actual victory or defeat of their favored candidate was expected to have some impact. However, Gilbert et al. (1998) predicted that voters would overestimate how long-lasting that impact would be. They also predicted that this overestimate would be greater if voters' favored candidate lost, because their psychological immune systems would eat away at their resulting negative feelings. In contrast, if participants' favored candidate won, their psychological immune systems would leave their resulting positive feelings unaffected.

To check the accuracy of participants' affective forecasts, an experimenter telephoned the original participants 1 month later, pretending to be conducting an unrelated survey. Of the original 57 voters surveyed, 25 could be reached. The experimenter asked them how happy they were now, and what they now thought of both electoral candidates. Participants' provided responses on the original 7-point scales.

By comparing responses to the two surveys, Gilbert et al. (1998) could also gather circumstantial evidence for the operation of the psychological immune system. One way people deal with negative outcomes, like their favored candidate losing, is to rationalize them in retrospect as not having been so bad. Such a change of heart, if brought about unconsciously, would not be foreseeable. Hence, voters whose favored candidate lost would incorrectly predict, before the election, that their low opinion of the winning candidate would persist. A pattern of results like this would suggest that rationalization—a manifestation of the psychological immune system—was causing the durability bias.

The main goal of Study 1, however, was simply to demonstrate the existence of a durability bias in the forecast of negative feelings. It fell to Study 2 to show that the psychological immune system created this bias, and that people were unaware of its operation.

In Study 2, all participants began by undergoing an acutely upsetting experience. Aspects of this experience were varied to make it either easy or difficult for the psychological immune system to subsequently operate. Gilbert et al. (1998) predicted that, as time passed, participants in the easy condition would start to feel better, whereas participants in the difficult condition would not. They also predicted that, regardless of condition, participants would expect their unhappiness to persist. However, because participants would be unable to tell whether their psychological immune system was operating or not, they would fail to adjust their affective forecasts in light of its operation or nonoperation.

The details of Study 2 are as follows. Participants (91 psychology undergraduates) began by filling out a questionnaire. Only one item on the questionnaire was genuine. It asked participants to rate their current level of happiness. This self-rating served as the baseline against which their subsequent self-ratings of happiness could be compared.

Participants were then presented with an elaborate cover story. The experimenter explained that a number of local businesses were interested in having psychology students evaluate their advertisements and products. In return, students were to receive, in addition to regular course credit, the relatively handsome bonus of $25. However, students first had to pass a test to ensure that they were suitable for the job. Participants were given a written list of 15 questions and allowed several minutes to prepare answers. They then relayed their answers over a microphone to one or more judges allegedly seated in an adjoining room. Participants were told that this procedure would prevent judges' opinions from being biased by their appearance, race, and mannerisms.

In reality, no judges were listening. The purpose of the procedure was to allow Gilbert et al. (1998) to manipulate how well participants' psychological immune systems functioned. To this end, half the participants were told that a single business school student would be evaluating their answers, and would alone decide whether or not to hire them. The remaining participants were told that three business school students would be evaluating their answers, and would hire them unless they all agreed that participants were unsuitable. Gilbert et al. (1998) reasoned that rejection by a single judge would be easier to rationalize than rejection by several judges. Hence, the psychological immune system would be better at relieving hurt feelings in the former condition. To back up this manipulation, the relevance of the questions asked in the many-judge condition was made crystal clear, whereas it was left rather vague in the single-judge condition.

Having relayed their answers, participants were asked to predict how they would feel upon being granted or denied the job, both immediately and 10 minutes later. Eventually, news of the actual decision came through: participants had been rejected. Their egos bruised and pockets empty, participants were now invited by the experimenter to fill out a second questionnaire. Like the first questionnaire, it contained a single genuine item assessing how they felt. At this point, the experimenter left participants alone for 10 minutes, under the pretext that he needed to go photocopy a third questionnaire. The idea was to allow participants' psychological immune systems, if functional, time to alleviate their bad mood. When the experimenter returned with the final questionnaire, it again contained an unobtrusive item asking participants how they felt.

Given the elaborate cover story, and the repeated measurement of happiness, it is understandable that 12 of the original 91 participants later expressed suspicion about the procedures while they were being debriefed. Gilbert et al. (1998) dutifully deleted their data, and conducted their analyses only on the unsuspecting majority.

WHAT THEY FOUND

We begin with Study 1. As a matter of historical record, George W. Bush prevailed over Ann Richards in the 1994 election to become governor of Texas. (A few years later, "Dubya" topped his feat by defeating Al Gore for the presidency, with fewer votes!) Consequently, participants could be categorized either as (Republican) winners or (Democrat) losers on the basis of whom they had voted for. Three questions now arise.

First: How did the election outcome actually affect voters' emotional lives 1 month later? It turned out that changes in participants' happiness levels were not affected by the defeat or victory of their favored candidate. Taking their original levels of happiness into account, winners and losers did not differ in how happy they were 1 month after the election. Perhaps they experienced jubilation or disappointment initially, but by the time they were reinterviewed, any such feelings had subsided. (Interestingly, Democrat voters were happier than Republican voters both before and after the election.)

Second: How did voters expect the election outcome to affect their emotional lives 1 month later? Winners (those whose preferred candidate later won) predicted that a victory for their candidate would make them happier. Losers (those whose preferred candidate later lost) predicted that

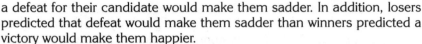

a defeat for their candidate would make them sadder. In addition, losers predicted that defeat would make them sadder than winners predicted a victory would make them happier.

Third: How accurate were voters' expectations in light of their subsequent experience? Winners' forecasts were reasonably accurate. They were only marginally less happy than they expected to be. Losers' forecasts, however, were highly inaccurate. They were much happier than they expected to be. In other words, the results revealed, as predicted, a durability bias mainly in the forecast of negative feelings.

Moreover, an analysis of voters' attitudes toward Bush, pre-election to post-election, suggests that the durability bias observed was partly produced by the psychological immune system. Winners' attitudes toward Bush were consistent. They thought well of him both before and after the election. In contrast, losers' attitudes towards Bush changed. They thought better of him after the election than before (contrary to what they had earlier predicted). This suggests that losers were rationalizing the Bush victory, coming around to the view that Bush, the new incumbent, was not so objectionable after all. However, because they had not anticipated that they would engage in such rationalization, their pre-election forecasts of how they would feel were unduly pessimistic.

Study 2 promised to more definitively implicate the psychological immune system. Recall that participants had been rejected for a lucrative job that they felt they deserved, under conditions that made it either easy or difficult for them to rationalize being rejected. Gilbert et al. (1998) predicted that all participants would feel upset at first, but that, over time, those who found it easy to rationalize their rejection would recover their good spirits. They also predicted that, regardless of how easy or difficult it was to rationalize rejection, participants would expect to remain upset.

Gilbert et al. (1998) first had to rule out a potential complication. Might the mere act of forecasting feelings influence participants' ratings of their happiness? If so, then any findings might be an accidental by-product of their having done so. To check, the researchers ran a parallel group of participants through the same set of experimental procedures, but without having them forecast their feelings. Fortunately, no differences emerged between forecasters and nonforecasters, so the data from both groups were pooled.

The main analyses were performed on scores that represented shifts in participants' happiness levels from baseline. Participants in both the easy and difficult rationalization conditions were roughly equally upset immediately after having been rejected for the job. However, with the passage of time, those in the easy condition started to feel better (about as happy as they had before being rejected), whereas those in the difficult condition ended up feeling even worse. (Note that these effects were due to *manipulated* differences in the functioning of the psychological immune system, unlike in Study 1.)

How did participants predict they would feel immediately after rejection and then again 10 minutes later? Participants generally overestimated how bad they would feel on both occasions. Of greater significance is the fact that participants' forecasts did not differ across easy or difficult conditions. Participants had no idea that their psychological immune systems, when permitted, operated to repair their mood (Fig. 3.2).

SO WHAT?

Chapter 1 showed how people lack insight into the causes of their thoughts and deeds. Chapter 2 went on to show how such mental myopia impairs the accuracy of memory. This chapter shows how it can also impair the accuracy of their mental forecasts. In particular, people seem to be unaware of how their minds act behind the scenes to progressively minimize the impact of unpleasant events. This leads them to underestimate how long those unpleasant events will bother them.

One positive implication of this tendency is that people's mental equilibrium is harder to upset than they are inclined to think. Indeed, research suggests that negative life events occurring more than 3 months ago have little bearing on people's current level of happiness (Suh, Diener, & Fujita, 1996). Moreover, some researchers estimate that, in Western populations, happiness over the life course is as influenced by genetic inheritance as it is by environmental factors (Lykken & Tellegen, 1996). That is,

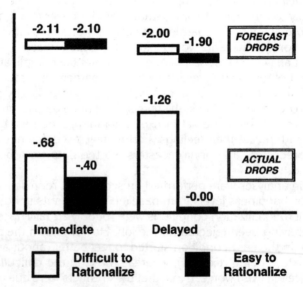

FIG. 3.2. Forecast and actual drops in participants' happiness, immediately or after a delay, after receiving criticism that was difficult or easy to rationalize.

happiness is not only determined by what happens to us; it is also affected by who we are on the inside.

It should not be forgotten that the durability bias is often present in forecasts of positive feelings too. People tend to overestimate how long the happiness caused by pleasant events will last. For example, the delight occasioned by our home team winning can be surprisingly muted the next day when we are desperately cramming for a mid-term exam. The psychological immune system, which negates only negative feelings, cannot induce a durability bias in forecasts of positive feelings. However, earlier in the chapter we mentioned several factors that could, including focalism, the tendency to pay too much attention to one event and to neglect others of equal or greater impact. In one telling study (Wilson, Wheatley, Meyers, Gilbert, & Axsom, 2000), football fans were normally found to overestimate how long the outcome of a game would influence their mood. However, if they first thought about how much time they would spend on various everyday activities, the durability bias was then greatly reduced, proving that a certain narrowness of outlook was prerequisite for its occurrence. Another reason why we overestimate the duration of positive feelings is that we do not realize how quickly we habituate (grow accustomed) to pleasant stimuli. After repeated exposure, the delights that such stimuli bring fade, and often more quickly than expected. As is often said about marriage, it begins when you sink into his (or her) arms, but ends up with your arms in his (or her) sink.

Focalism and habituation help to explain one of the most common but pernicious of human vices: greed. Acquiring something new—a flashy car, a gorgeous lover, a prestigious job—seems like an excellent way to bring about lasting contentment. However, the pleasure of acquisition tends to be shorter-lived than expected. We fail to anticipate that we will grow accustomed to the things that we covet, and that many other factors will conspire to determine our level of well-being. As a result, we often get trapped on an hedonic treadmill. Like hamsters vainly trying to climb up the inside of a spinning wheel, we try to make ourselves happier by bettering our material or social circumstances, only to find our satisfaction levels perpetually slipping back to where they stood before. Perhaps the key to happiness is not getting what you want but fully appreciating what you have.

AFTERTHOUGHTS

An interesting feature of the psychological immune system is that to operate effectively it must operate discreetly. To convince ourselves that we never really wanted that promotion, we must conveniently forget that we spent the previous year working 24/7 and sucking up to superiors. Remaining acutely conscious of these awkward facts might well compromise our ability to deal with our initial disappointment. This raises an interesting question: Is psychological well-being associated with the accurate perception of reality or with a distorted perception of it? The traditional view is that contact with reality is essential for mental health (Jahoda, 1958). As the old one-liner goes, neurotics build castles in the air, psychotics live in them, and psychotherapists collect the rent. The alternative view is that, given how inhospitable reality is, human beings cannot bear too much of it. They must therefore endorse comforting illusions in order to function effectively (e.g., Pyszczynski, Greenberg, & Solomon, 2000). So which is it?

In an influential article, Taylor and Brown (1988) proposed that three classes of positive illusion promote mental health: holding overly flattering views of oneself, overestimating one's personal control, and being unreasonably optimistic about the future. The fact that most normal individuals manifest these illusions, while steering clear of neurosis, suggests that an accurate perception of reality is not a prerequisite for mental health, and may even militate against it.

More specific evidence for the benefit of positive illusions comes from studies in which participants compare where they think they stand on various dimensions to where they think other people stand. On most dimensions most participants rate themselves as superior to their fellows, a state of affairs that cannot statistically be true. The tendency to self-enhance, when assessed in this way, has indeed been found to predict one's ability to cope with stress (Helgeson & Taylor, 1993). On the other hand, the jury remains out on the corollary hypothesis that neurotics are more in tune with reality than normal people. Some research suggests that neurotics, although sadder, are nonetheless wiser. They hold more moderate and accurate views of their personalities, abilities, and prospects. However, other research suggests, however, that their views of the world are just bleaker (Alloy & Abramson, 1988; Dunning & Story, 1991).

One criticism of measuring self-enhancement using self-report ratings is that perceptions of superiority may reflect real superiority. That is, people who self-enhance may do so with justification, being truly above average on several dimensions (Colvin & Block, 1994). To circumvent these problems, researchers have measured self-enhancement in another way: in terms of the discrepancy between someone's view of self and the view that others share of them. When this is done, an odd thing happens. Excessively positive views of self suddenly switch from virtues to vices, being associated with poor social skills and psychological maladjustment (Colvin, Block, & Funder, 1995). Consequently, the practical benefits of self-enhancement are still disputed. For the moment, we advise readers to think well of themselves, but not let anyone else think that they do.

As for illusions of control and unrealistic optimism, the prevailing consensus is that such tendencies are adaptive as long as they are not especially pronounced (Baumeister, 1989) and do not prevail when realistic decisions have to be made (Gollwitzer & Kinney, 1989). Believing that a positive attitude can keep heart disease at bay, or that a pacemaker can greatly improve quality of life, may allow a person to make the most of

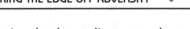

their final years. However, falsely believing that heart disease can be cured by a positive attitude alone, without recourse to medical intervention, is a poor recipe for longevity. A delicate balance between self-deception and reality-testing may be necessary to deal effectively with the demands of everyday living.

REVELATION

Although we are fairly adept at predicting how events will make us feel, we overestimate how long those feelings, especially when unpleasant, will last. One reason for this is that we possess a psychological immune system that, over time and without our knowledge, softens the impact of life's trials and tribulations.

— APG —

CHAPTER REFERENCE

Gilbert, D. T., Pinel, E. C., Wilson, T. D., Blumberg, S. J., & Wheatley, T. P. (1998). Immune neglect: A source of durability bias in affective forecasting. *Journal of Personality and Social Psychology, 75,* 617–638.

OTHER REFERENCES

Alloy, L. B., & Abramson, L. Y. (1988). Depressive realism: Four theoretical perspectives. In L. B. Alloy (Ed.), *Cognitive processes in depression* (pp. 223–265). New York: Guilford Press.

Astin, A. W. (1997). *What matters in college? Four critical years revisited.* San Francisco, CA: Jossey-Bass.

Baumeister, R. F. (1989). The optimal margin of illusion. *Journal of Social and Clinical Psychology, 8,* 176–189.

Brehm, J. W. (1956). Post-decision changes in desirability of alternatives. *Journal of Abnormal and Social Psychology, 52,* 384–389.

Brickman, P., Coates, D., & Janoff-Bulman, R. (1978). Lottery winners and accidents victims: Is happiness relative? *Journal of Personality and Social Psychology, 36,* 917–927.

Colvin, C. R., & Block, J. (1994). Do positive illusions foster mental health? An examination of the Taylor and Brown formulation. *Psychological Bulletin, 116,* 3–20.

Colvin, C. R., Block, J., & Funder, D. C. (1995). Overly positive self-evaluations and personality: Negative implications for mental health. *Journal of Personality and Social Psychology, 68,* 1152–1162.

Diener, E., Suh, E. M., Lucas, R. E., & Smith, H. L. (1999). Subjective well-being: Three decades of progress. *Psychological Bulletin, 125,* 276–302.

Dunning, D., & Story, A. L. (1991). Depression, realism, and the overconfidence effect: Are the sadder wiser when predicting future actions and events? *Journal of Personality and Social Psychology, 61,* 521–532.

Gollwitzer, P. M., & Kinney, R. F. (1989). Effects of deliberative and implemental mind-sets on illusion of control. *Journal of Personality and Social Psychology, 56,* 531–542.

Helgeson, V. S., & Taylor, S. E. (1993). Social comparisons and adjustment among cardiac patients. *Journal of Applied Psychology, 23,* 1171–1195.

Jahoda, M. (1958). *Current concepts of positive mental health.* New York: Basic Books.

Lykken, D., & Tellegen, A. (1996). Happiness is a stochastic phenomenon. *Psychological Science, 7,* 186–189.

Myers, D. G., & Diener, E. (1995). Who is happy? *Psychological Science, 6,* 10–19.

Nisbett, R. E., & Wilson, T. D. (1977). Telling more than we can know: Verbal reports on mental processes. *Psychological Review, 84,* 231–259.

Pyszczynski, T., Greenberg, J., & Solomon, S. (2000). Why do we need what we need? A terror management perspective on the roots of human social motivation. In E. T. Higgins & A. W. Kruglanski (Eds.), *Motivational science: Social and personality perspectives. Key readings in social psychology* (pp. 76–99). Philadelphia: Psychology Press.

Suh, E. M., Diener, E., & Fujita, F. (1996). Events and subjective well-being: Only recent events matter. *Journal of Personality and Social Psychology,* 1091–1102.

Taylor, S. E., & Brown, J. D. (1988). Illusion and well-being: A social psychological perspective on mental health. *Psychological Bulletin, 103,* 193–210.

Wilson, T. D., Wheatley, T. P., Meyers, J. M., Gilbert, D. T., & Axsom, D. (2000). Focalism: A source of durability bias in affective forecasting. *Journal of Personality and Social Psychology, 78,* 821–836.

MORE TO EXPLORE

Lykken, D. T. (2000). *Happiness: The nature and nurture of joy and contentment.* New York: Griffin Trade Paperbacks.

Myers, D. G., & Diener, E. (1995). Who is happy? *Psychological Science, 6,* 10–19.

4 Believing Is Seeing: Partisan Perceptions of Media Bias

"As I am, so I see."
—Ralph Waldo Emerson (1803–1882), American philosopher, essayist, poet

BACKGROUND

It's a brisk Saturday afternoon, late in November of 1951. Crisp autumn leaves blanket the ground. Though the sun is bright, sporadic wind gusts forebode the coming winter. Animated college students (sporting saddle shoes, bobby socks, and V-neck sweaters), their zealous parents, and loyal alumni fill Palmer Stadium on the Princeton University campus. The *Tigers* (the home team) and the Dartmouth *Indians* battle fiercely on the gridiron in the last game of the season. The Tigers are undefeated, thanks in large part to All-American quarterback Dick Kazmaier, who has just appeared on the cover of *Time*.

The game was brutal from the get-go. Penalty whistles blew non-stop. The second quarter saw Kazmaier taken out of the game with a crushed nose. The third quarter saw a Dartmouth player removed from the field with a broken leg. Fights broke out between raucous fans on the two sides. It was a game that will live in infamy.

Princeton won, but not without controversy and a mutual exchange of accusations afterwards. The *Daily Princetonian* protested the opponent's lack of sportsmanship and vicious style of play:

> This observer has never seen quite such a disgusting exhibition of so-called "sport" ... the blame must be laid squarely on Dartmouth's doorstep. Princeton, obviously the better team, had no reason to rough up Dartmouth.

Looking at the situation rationally, we don't see why the Indians should make a deliberate attempt to cripple Dick Kazmaier and other Princeton players. (Hastorf & Cantril, 1954, p. 129)

The *Princeton Alumni Weekly* echoed these sentiments:

Into the record books will go in indelible fashion the fact that the last game of Dick Kazmaier's career was cut short by more than half when he was forced out with a broken nose and mild concussion, sustained from a tackle that came well after he had thrown a pass ... a third quarter outbreak of roughness was climaxed when a Dartmouth player deliberately kicked Brad Glass in the ribs while the latter was on his back ... there was undeniable evidence that the loser's tactics were an actual style of play. (Hastorf & Cantril, 1954, p. 129)

The reaction of Dartmouth's press was scarcely less critical. The *Dartmouth* accused Princeton coach Charley Caldwell of convincing his squad during a half-time pep talk that the Indians were playing dirty. The student newspaper claimed that Caldwell stirred up his charges by insinuating that the Dartmouth team was deliberately targeting their star player, Kazmaier:

His talk got results. Gene Howard and Jim Miller were both injured. Both had dropped back to pass, had passed, and were standing unprotected in

FIG. 4.1.   Fair or foul? Your answer may depend on which team you support.

the backfield. Result: one bad leg and one broken. (Hastorf & Cantril, 1954, p. 129)

The next day, the *Dartmouth* went on to belittle Kazmaier's injury in light of their team's own past injuries:

> As a relatively unprotected passing and running star in a contact sport, he is quite liable to injury. Also, his particular injuries—a broken nose and slight concussion—were no more serious than is experienced almost any day in any football practice ... Up to the Princeton game, Dartmouth players suffered about 10 known nose fractures and face injuries, not to mention several slight concussions. (Hastorf & Cantril, 1954, p. 129)

Spectators and other loyalists—and even news reporters—on the two sides had seemingly tuned into different games.

Enter a pair of social psychologists. A week after the big game, Hastorf and Cantril administered a questionnaire to undergraduates at both universities, to measure the perceptions and opinions on each side. Later, they showed a film of the game to students at both schools, and had the students indicate, while watching the film, any instances of foul play. The results of this classic study indicated that the two groups had, indeed, perceived the game quite differently. Take the Princeton students. A full 90% of them stated that the Dartmouth players had instigated the rough and dirty play. In addition, they deemed Dartmouth players responsible for twice as many infractions as players on their own team. Finally, they saw twice as many flagrant as mild infractions by the Dartmouth players, but three times as many mild as flagrant infractions by members of their own team. For their part, the Dartmouth students saw a more even number of violations. However, they too saw a game that favored their own squad. Separate loyalties, same game, dissimilar perceptions.

Hastorf and Cantril explained what was evident in the news reports and questionnaire responses:

> The "same" sensory impingements emanating from the football field, transmitted through the visual apparatus of the brain ... obviously gave rise to different experiences in different people ... people don't have attitudes about "things" that exist "out there" because the 'thing' is simply *not* the same for different people whether the 'thing' is a football game, a presidential candidate, Communism, or spinach. (Hastorf & Cantril, 1954, pp. 132–133)

So there you have it: People believe certain things and this affects what they experience. We each construct our reality. Believing is seeing.

Partisan perceptions are everywhere. Two children, bloodied noses and in tears, each have a different story to tell about the same fight. Parents and children view the same weekend keg party differently. A husband and wife give different estimates of their respective contributions to household chores. Those for or against stem cell research perceive and respond differently to the same address on the topic. In fact, staunch advocates of a particular social or political cause often see those who do not share their opinions as biased in favor of the other side.

For example, the media, supposedly in the business of objectively reporting events, is often viewed as being biased. Indeed, the discrepant news accounts of the Princeton-Dartmouth game may represent such media bias. And perhaps this is to be expected given the loyal nature of student newspapers. However, the charge is more serious when directed at what should be nonpartisan, nationally syndicated news sources. A biased medium at this level could sway election results by drawing greater attention to particular political issues or by emphasizing certain arguments at the expense of others. It might even influence international relations. For instance, when reporting on events in the Middle East, it might tendentiously portray all Israelis as oppressors, or all Arabs as terrorists.

Why might people regard the media as biased even when they may not be? Perhaps they do so because their perceptions reflect different standards of judgment. They see identical news items but interpret the majority of them as being hostile to their own side. Or they may have selective memory for information that is consistent with their own attitudes (Goethals & Reckman, 1973; see chap. 2). That is, they experience the same content, but recollect it differently afterward. Or finally, they may entertain false theories of media bias, leading them to unwarranted skepticism. Perhaps they believe that the media are controlled by the liberal intellectual elite, or, oppositely, by the religious far right and the military-industrial complex.

WHAT THEY DID

As Hastorf and Cantril had done in 1954, Robert Vallone and his colleagues (1985) sought to investigate the biased perceptions of partisans, as well as the mechanisms underlying such bias. They also wanted to shed light on perceptions of media bias. In other words, their study focused on both biased perceptions and perceptions of bias.

Vallone and his colleagues capitalized on the occurrence of a tragic series of events in the Middle East in 1982. In September of that year, an Israeli invasion of the West Bank culminated in the slaughter of Palestinian refugees in camps at Sabra and Chatilla in Lebanon. Sobering developments were reported nightly on American television. How would research participants who were loyal to either Israeli or Palestinian causes react to this news coverage? Would they view it differently? Detect media bias? Both?

One hundred and forty-four Stanford University students participated in what was described simply as a study of the media coverage of the conflict in Lebanon. The participants included students in introductory psychology classes and members of pro-Israeli and pro-Arab student associations. To start, participants rated their factual knowledge of the Beirut Massacre and indicated their sympathies with respect to Middle East politics. For example, how responsible did they think Israel was for the Beirut Massacre? Three groups of participants were identified—those describing themselves as generally pro-Israeli, generally pro-Arab, or having generally mixed or neutral feelings. These groups assigned different amounts of responsibility to Israel, Lebanese officials, and the soldiers who invaded the camps. For example, whereas pro-Arab participants put 57% of the blame on Israel, pro-Israeli participants put only 22% of the blame on Israel.

The participants then watched a 36-minute video containing six segments of nationally televised news coverage of the Middle East bloodshed. They did so in small groups, each typically a mix of pro-Israeli, pro-Arab, and neutral participants (who were generally not aware of each others' political loyalties). Afterward, they completed a questionnaire containing items about the fairness and objectivity of the news programs, the standards applied to Israel and its adversaries, the amount of attention focused on Israel's role in the massacre, the case made for and against Israel, and the apparent personal views of the news editors. The participants were also asked to estimate the percentage of favorable, unfavorable, and neutral references to Israel in the video and how much initially neutral viewers would be likely to change to more positive or negative positions after watching it.

WHAT THEY FOUND

Vallone et al. (1985) found clear evidence for both perceptions of media bias. Pro-Arab participants perceived a pro-Israel bias in the news programs, whereas pro-Israeli participants perceived an anti-Israel bias. In contrast, neutral participants did not perceive any significant bias in the news programs (Fig. 4.2). Moreover, pro-Arab participants thought the news programs neglected to adequately focus on Israel's role in the massacre, while pro-Israeli participants thought the programs concentrated too much on Israel's involvement. Both groups inferred that the personal views of the creators of the programs were opposite to their own views.

Did the partisan groups perceive the same content in the news reports, and only evaluate the fairness of it differently, or did they actually perceive different content? Findings supported the latter conclusion. Pro-Arabs thought 42% of the references to Israel were favorable, 26% unfavorable. In contrast, pro-Israelis thought that 16% of the references to Israel were favorable, 57% unfavorable. Also, pro-Arabs thought that 32% of neutral viewers would be persuaded to hold a more negative view of Israel's role as

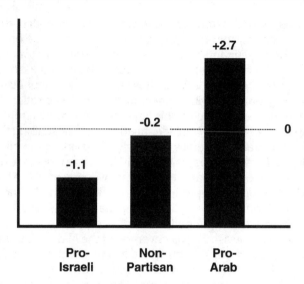

FIG. 4.2.   Perceptions of pro-Israeli bias in television coverage of the 1982 Beirut Massacre among pro-Israeli, nonpartisan, and pro-Arab participants.

a result of watching the programs, whereas pro-Israelis thought that 68% would be so persuaded. An additional analysis revealed that the pro-Israeli versus pro-Arab differences in perception of bias remain significant even when differences in perceived content were statistically held constant. Thus, both of the postulated mechanisms underlying perceptions of a hostile media seemed to operate: partisans saw different content, and they evaluated the same content differently.

Furthermore, within both pro-Israeli and pro-Arab groups, the more knowledgeable the participants believed they were regarding Israeli-Palestinian relations and the Beirut Massacre, the more they were inclined to see media hostility, arguably because they believed they had better grounds for detecting discrepancies between what was presented and what should have been presented. But then, too, participants who rated themselves as more emotionally involved in the overall issue also perceived more media bias, so it is not clear whether motivational or more purely cognitive factors were the driving force behind the perceptions of bias. Finally, Vallone et al. (1985) found evidence that both the pro-Arabs and the pro-Israelis perceived a degree of media bias that was not apparent to more neutral participants.

SO WHAT?

The present study is but one of many that reveal perceptual biases. For example, abundant research has shown how perceptions can easily be swayed by racial stereotypes. In a study by Allport and Postman (1947), White research participants looked at a drawing of a crowded New York City subway. The drawing depicted two men standing and facing each other: a Black man held his hands up and open; a White man wielded an open straight razor in a threatening manner. The research participants then verbally described the scene to others, who did the same in turn. It was found that, from one telling to the next, the razor often shifted from the White to the Black man's hand! In a related study, Duncan (1976) had White college students watch a videotape of two students in a discussion. The discussion got heated and the one student pushed the other student. A Black man's shoving a White man was perceived as violent 75% of the time, playing around or being dramatic 6% of the time. However, a White man's shoving a Black man was perceived as playing around or being dramatic 46% of the time, violent 17% of the time. Such findings raise an important question: do our perceptions reflect reality, or does reality reflect our perceptions?

Other studies have shown how perceptions can be experimentally manipulated. Higgins and his colleagues (1977) had participants complete word search puzzles. Participants in two groups searched for the same words, with a few exceptions. In one group some words were synonyms for *reckless* (e.g., careless or foolish). In the other group, some words were synonyms for *adventurous* (e.g., brave or spirited). Then, in a presumed unrelated study, the participants evaluated a fictitious person, Donald, who was described as having gone white water rafting, having driven in a demolition derby, and as planning to go skydiving. It was found that participants perceived Donald relatively positively if adventurousness had earlier been *primed* (mentally activated so as to make it subsequently more accessible). However, they perceived Donald relatively negatively if carelessness had been primed. (Importantly, activating unrelated schemas, such as neatness or shyness, did not affect perceptions of Donald.)

What is perceived and subsequently remembered can also be subtly manipulated. Cohen (1981) had participants watch a film of a woman at home with her husband. It was mentioned in passing that the woman was either a waitress or a librarian. Weeks later, the participants were asked to recall the contents of the film. Which participants do you think were more likely to remember the woman wearing glasses, eating a salad, drinking wine, and playing the piano, with bookcases in the background? Which do you think were more likely to recall her eating a chocolate birthday cake, with a bowling ball in the corner of the room? The casual mention of the woman's vocation caused participants to recall details that were consistent with that vocation, and to overlook or misremember details that were inconsistent with it.

Perceptions can also be influenced by body language and facial expressions. Even when a news broadcaster's words are impartial, he or she may nonverbally leak personal attitudes. Mullen and ten colleagues (1986) videotaped the evening news on three major American networks (ABC, NBC, and CBS), deleted all sound, and played the tapes for an audience of judges, who rated the good or bad feelings of the newscasters as they were speaking about Ronald Reagan or Walter Mondale prior to the 1984 presidential election (the judges had no idea who or what the newscasters were reporting on). It was discovered that ABC's Peter Jennings (unlike Dan Rather and Tom Brokaw) smiled more and generally appeared happier when talking about Reagan than when talking about Mondale. Perhaps that was what caused people in a random phone survey who reported watching the most ABC newscasts to be the most likely to vote for Reagan.

These and many other studies demonstrate how malleable and often mistaken our perceptions can be. Such studies lead to questions about whether and how we can be accurate. Must perceptions of the same objective reality be so variable? Does every perception need to be so biased and self-serving? If our perceptions are so biased, how do we manage to get by in everyday life? Social psychologists respond to such questions by claiming that people can perceive things accurately when they so desire. They can and do go out of their way to gather extra information, especially when events violate their expectations or when an accurate judgment is critical.

In this regard, it is sometimes helpful for us to be our own devil's advocate. Lord, Lepper, and Preston (1984) had participants read about two studies, one supporting capital punishment (it deters murder and other crimes), the other against capital punishment (it models violence and is not a crime deterrent). Participants judged the study that agreed with their own stand on the issue to be methodologically stronger and more convincing. A second group of participants, however, went through the same procedure, but were informed about perceptual biases beforehand. They were taught that people see things in ways that fit their expectations or motives and were encouraged to try to counter this natural tendency: "be as objective and unbiased as possible." This simple advice did not work. Personal biases still crept in. However, the following directive did reduce bias: "Ask yourself at each step whether you would have made the same high or low evaluations had exactly the same study produced results on the other side of the issue" (Lord et al., 1984, p. 1233). Participants using this strategy gauged the two studies to be equally credible and convincing. Indeed, explaining why something opposite might be true is one of the best ways of perceiving events and issues more objectively and accurately.

Research also finds that we can even negate the power of cultural stereotypes, although the process is effortful and error-prone. Devine (1989) showed that people are generally aware of prevailing stereotypes, even if they deny consciously endorsing them. For example, they readily report that Blacks are supposedly aggressive, athletic, and rhythmic, or that the Irish are supposedly talkative, sentimental, and fond of a pint. Devine found that when one encounters a member of a particular social category—an American Indian, exotic dancer, or college professor—the relevant stereotype is automatically activated (see chap. 12). This causes the group member's ambiguous behaviors to be interpreted stereotypically: "He's lying under the table. That's because he's drunk. The Irish are always drunk."

Devine (1989) showed, however, that it is possible to rein in such automatic responses. Indeed, people who are low in prejudice seem to be those who consciously replace stereotypic thoughts with those that negate the stereotype. In her words: "Inhibiting stereotype-congruent or prejudice-like responses and intentionally replacing them with nonprejudiced responses can be likened to the breaking of a bad habit" (p. 15). Human perception is readily biased, but not necessarily so.

AFTERTHOUGHTS

The studies described in this chapter bring to mind what most social psychologists firmly believe: cognition plays a central role in human behavior. Indeed, a subfield of social psychology, *social cognition* devotes itself to analyzing the nuts and bolts of social thinking. Accordingly, although our response to an event may be a knee-jerk reaction involving little thought, more typically various mental processes—such as *attention* and *perception*—intervene.

For example, something grabs our attention: a provocative dress, a piercing scream, or an inviting smile. Or we attempt to deliberately focus our mind: on our performance before an audience, the arguments of a politician, or the uncertain signs of suicide in a friend. Either way, our attention is partial. We look upon reality as if through a keyhole, attending to a mere fraction of available information. Biased attention then gives way to perception, which is itself potentially biased. We notice someone's body language; we decode it. Someone fails to return our phone call or e-mail; we guess why. A child spends a lot of time alone; we wonder if he or she is painfully ostracized or simply introverted. Our perceptions—innumerable and incessant—are all-important. In fact, psychologists often claim that people do not interact with reality; rather, they interact with their *perception* of reality. We construe the events and dynamics of the world in which we live. We even construe ourselves in the form of our self-concept. Our perceptions and construals feed our decisions, which influence our behaviors, which evoke responses from others that feed back to our perceptions (see chap. 14, on behavioral confirmation).

Is there an objective reality out there, one that we can all agree upon? How can we know things accurately if our perceptions are so biased? If we only see what we want or expect to see, how do we ever know what is real? These are serious epistemological questions. Should we concur with the idealist philosopher George Berkeley, who argued that reality is a mere idea? (If a tree falls in a forest and no one is around to hear it, does it make a sound?) Should we accept the claim, made by extreme skeptics, that we can never know anything for sure?

Religion, philosophy, and the science of psychology rely upon different methods for knowing things. Religion relies on divine revelation and mystical insights, philosophy on reason and logic, and psychology on empirical methods—observation, experimentation, and replication. Indeed, psychologists and other scientists believe that the best way of knowing the truth about everyday things—what size dam is needed to hold back a river, how to vaccinate against a disease, and whether the two hemispheres of the brain serve different functions—is by empirical methods. Using such methods, psychologists are able to slice through the very biases they detect. Although psychology and other sciences are not completely free of biases, the give-and-take of scholarly criticism and the demand for replication ensure a reasonable degree of objectivity. Of course, even if science can provide us with reliable knowledge about our selves and the world, it still has its limits. There may be some knowledge— such as why anything exists at all, how to best live one's life, or whether there is life after death—that science is not equipped to provide.

At any rate, perceptions will never cease being important. As we write this chapter, tensions between Israelis and Palestinians are peaking yet again, with many on either side seeing no peaceful end to the cycle of violence they believe is being pedaled by their enemies. Could it be that biased perceptions and perceptions of bias are fueling the flames of this long standing conflict?

REVELATION

Our group loyalties and preconceptions cause us to perceive events and other stimuli in a biased manner. One consequence of this is that partisans on both sides of an issue tend to overestimate bias in media reports.

— KPF —

CHAPTER REFERENCE

Vallone, R. P., Ross, L., & Lepper, M. R. (1985). The hostile media phenomenon: Biased perception and perceptions of media bias coverage of the "Beirut Massacre." *Journal of Personality and Social Psychology, 49,* 577–585.

OTHER REFERENCES

Allport, G. W., & Postman, L. J. (1947). *The psychology of rumor.* New York: Henry Holt and Company.

Cohen, C. E. (1981). Person categories and social perception: Testing some boundaries of the processing effects of prior knowledge. *Journal of Personality and Social Psychology, 40,* 441–452.

Devine, P. G. (1989). Stereotypes and prejudice: Their automatic and controlled components. *Journal of Personality and Social Psychology, 56,* 5–18.

Duncan, B. L. (1976). Differential social perception and attribution theory of intergroup violence. Testing the lower limits of stereotyping of blacks. *Journal of Personality and Social Psychology, 34,* 590–598.

Goethals, G. R., & Reckman, R. F. (1973). The perception of consistency in attitudes. *Journal of Experimental Social Psychology, 9,* 491–501.

Hastorf, A. H., & Cantril, H. (1954). They saw a game: A case study. *Journal of Abnormal Social Psychology, 49,* 129–134.

Higgins, E. T., Rholes, W. S., & Jones, C. R. (1977). Category accessibility and impression formation. *Journal of Experimental Social Psychology, 13,* 141–154.

Lord, C. G., Lepper, M. R., & Preston, E. (1984). Considering the opposite: A corrective strategy for social judgment. *Journal of Personality and Social Psychology, 47,* 1231–1243.

Mullen, B., Futrell, D., Stairs, D., Tice, D. M., Baumeister, R. F., Dawson, K. E., Riordan, C. A., Radloff, C. E., Goethals, G. R., Kennedy, J. G., & Rosenfeld, P. (1986). Newscasters' facial expressions and voting behavior of viewers: Can a smile elect a president? *Journal of Personality and Social Psychology, 51,* 291–295.

MORE TO EXPLORE

Giner-Sorolla, R., & Chaiken, S. (1994). The causes of hostile media judgements. *Journal of Experimental Social Psychology, 30,* 165–180.

Paul, R., & Elder, L. (2002). *How to detect media bias and propaganda in national and world news.* Dillon Beach, CA: Foundation for Critical Thinking.

5 Frames of Mind: Taking Risks or Playing Safe?

"The optimist believes that this is the best of all possible worlds. The pessimist fears that this may be true."
> Robert Oppenheimer (1904–1967), father of the atomic bomb

BACKGROUND

If ever you feel bored, try this neat experiment at home. Take three glasses. Fill the first with ice water, the second with hot water, and the third with lukewarm water. Now place your left hand in the first glass and your right in the second. Wait for about a minute. Finally, transfer both of your hands to the third glass. The result: the same water will feel, at the same time, warm to your left hand but cool to your right. What does this odd perceptual anomaly indicate? It indicates that perceptions of intensity do not depend on the *absolute* strength of a stimulus, but rather upon its *relative* strength. Otherwise stated, perceptual experience is influenced by its context. In this chapter, we review research showing that what is true of our perceptual experience is also true of judgments and decisions more generally.

Suppose someone made you the following offer, call it offer X. You must choose between either (a) receiving either $15,000 for certain, or (b) having an equal chance of receiving $10,000 or $20,000. What would you do? It turns out that most people prefer to take the guaranteed $15,000. However, from a strictly rational point of view, it should make no difference how someone chooses: the *expected value* of each alternative is the same.

Let's explain the jargon. The expected value of an alternative is the likelihood that it will happen multiplied by the desirability of its happening. Likelihood is represented by a value between 0 (impossible) and 1 (inevitable), desirability by some quantity measured in numerical units (typically monetary ones). In the previous example, the likelihood of the first alternative is 1, and its desirability is $15,000. Multiplying, this yields an expected value of $15,000. The likelihood of the second alternative is the sum of its two possible outcomes: a likelihood of 0.5 times a desirability of $10,000, plus a likelihood of 0.5 times a desirability of $20,000. This also yields an expected value of ($10,000 × 0.5) + ($20,000 × 0.5) = $15,000.

Suppose now a different offer were on the table, call it offer Y. After receiving a handsome $20,000, you must choose between either (a) definitely returning $5,000, or (b) taking a 50-50 chance of having to return either $10,000 or $0. How would you choose this time? Most people, it turns out, prefer to take their chances (Kahneman & Tversky, 1979).

A little careful reflection reveals that offers X and Y are in fact equivalent, but differently stated. Returning $5,000 after receiving $20,000 (offer Y) is the same as receiving $15,000 outright (offer X); and receiving $20,000 and then risking having to return either $10,000 or $0 (offer Y) is the same as receiving either $10,000 or $20,000 outright (offer X). Yet the manner in which these equivalent offers are *framed* tends to make people plumb for one over the other. Why?

Prospect theory (Kahneman & Tversky, 1981) provides an answer. It proposes that we see gains or losses as, respectively, advantageous or disadvantageous departures from an assumed status quo. The magnitude and direction of these perceived departures depends on how the human

FIG. 5.1.   Perceptions of risk depend on how choices are framed.

mind transforms expected values into subjective impressions. Prospect theory assumes that the transformation is lawful and attempts to characterize it in terms of four basic postulates. We describe three of these now, and the fourth in the "So What?" section later.

The first postulate of prospect theory is this: As gains increase, the perceived benefit of each subsequent unit gain will decrease. For example, if you earn $10,000 a year, then getting a raise of $1,000 will be cause for celebration. However, if you earn $1,000,000 a year, then the same raise will seem trivial.

The second postulate is the mirror image of the first: As losses increase, the perceived costliness of each subsequent unit loss will decrease. For example, a loss of $1,000 at roulette will distress you more if you just lost $10,000 on the last throw than if you just lost $1,000,000.

The third postulate of prospect theory is the one most pertinent to the present study: People's preferences will undergo a reversal depending on whether they are envisaging potential losses or gains. Specifically, when a potential gain beckons, people will be more likely to avoid risk, but when a potential loss looms, they will be more likely to court risk.

Prospect theory thus clarifies why people typically prefer $15,000 up front to a 50-50 chance of receiving either $10,000 or $20,000. With the payoff being framed in terms of gains, the certain outcome is preferred. The theory also clarifies why, after the initial receipt of $20,000, people typically prefer a 50-50 chance of losing either $10,000 or $0 to a guaranteed loss of $5000. With the payoff now being framed in terms of losses, the uncertain outcome is preferred.

The fact that framing a choice in terms of losses or gains can influence how people choose has implications for, among other things, how persuasive a message is. Traditionally, one major branch of social psychology has concerned itself with establishing what causes or prevents attitude change (Petty & Wegener, 1998; see chap. 16). It turns out that prospect theory can be usefully extended to suggest how to enhance the persuasiveness of messages—in particular, messages advocating healthful behaviors.

Just as financial choices can be framed as gains or losses, so too can healthful behaviors. They can be framed in terms of the probable gains that will result from performing them, or the probable losses that will result from failing to perform them. For example, the statement "If you quit smoking, your health will benefit" is *gain-framed* because it praises the virtues of kicking the habit. In contrast, the statement "If you keep smoking, your health will suffer" is *loss-framed* because it decries the vice of continuing to indulge.

It is further possible to distinguish two distinct categories of healthful behaviors: those that involve the *detection* of physical disease (e.g., brain scans) and those that involve the *prevention* of physical disease (e.g., exercise). These categories of behavior tend to be perceived in distinct ways. Disease-detecting behaviors, because they sometimes reveal the presence of disease, are typically seen as risky to perform. Thus, a brain scan may be dreaded for fear an inoperable tumor may be discovered. Disease-preventing behaviors, on the other hand, because their goal is to maintain health, are typically seen as safe to perform. Thus, exercise is mentally linked to keeping you fit and trim, not to uncovering your ailments.

What has all this got to do with prospect theory? It could be argued that the safe–risky distinction closely corresponds to the certain–uncertain distinction. In everyday parlance, safety and certainty go together (sure things, safe bets), as do risk and uncertainty (dicey deals, iffy prospects). Consequently, the predictions of prospect theory for outcomes varying in certainty–uncertainty may also hold for outcomes varying in safety–risk.

On the basis of this reasoning, Rothman, Martino, Bedell, Detweiler, and Salovey (1999) derived the following hypothesis: disease-preventing behaviors, being linked to safe and certain outcomes, ought to be more influenced by gain-framed messages, whereas disease-detecting behaviors, being linked to risky and uncertain outcomes, ought to be more influenced by loss-framed messages. In other words, the effectiveness of adopting one framing strategy over another should depend upon the type of healthful behavior being advocated.

Prior research had already yielded findings broadly consistent with this hypothesis. For example, loss-framed messages had proven superior to gain-framed ones in convincing women to undertake mammograms—a disease-detecting behavior (Banks et al., 1995), whereas gain-framed messages had proven superior to loss-framed ones in promoting the use of sunscreen—a disease-preventing behavior (Detweiler, Bedell, Salovey, Pronin, & Rothman, 1999). However, it is not clear whether the results of the two studies were attributable to their use of different framing manipulations or of different healthful behaviors. The researchers needed to track down a single behavior that could be convincingly described in terms of either disease-prevention or disease-detection. They settled on a promising (if unglamorous) candidate: dental rinsing.

Two types of dental rinse exist: antibacterial rinse, which prevents plaque accumulation, and disclosing rinse, which reveals their presence. Both types of rinse are similarly deployed. The use of antibacterial rinse is clearly a disease-preventing behavior, the use of disclosing rinse, a disease-detecting behavior. Rothman et al. (1999) predicted that, in accordance with prospect theory, messages highlighting gains would be better at convincing participants to use an antibacterial rinse, whereas messages highlighting losses would be better at convincing them to use a disclosing rinse.

WHAT THEY DID

One hundred twenty undergraduates from the University of Minnesota, mostly female, served as participants. On arriving at the lab, they were told that the purpose of the study was to evaluate the effectiveness of pamphlets aimed at promoting dental hygiene. The precise hypothesis under investigation was concealed to avoid biasing participants' responses. Participants were then handed a professional-looking pamphlet four pages in length. It contained much general information about dental health that did not differ across different experimental conditions. However, the pamphlet did differ in two critical respects: in terms of which dental hygiene measure was recommended, and in terms of how it was framed. Specifically, half the 120 participants read a message recommending the use of antibacterial rinse, half, a message recommending the use of disclosing rinse. In addition, for half the participants in each of these groups, the messages were gain-framed, for the other half, loss-framed. Thus, there were four experimental conditions in all, each featuring 30 participants, arranged into what is called a 2 × 2 between-groups design.

For participants encouraged to use the antibacterial rinse, the gain-framed recommendation read, "People who use [an antibacterial] rinse are taking advantage of a safe and effective way to reduce plaque accumulation," whereas the loss-framed recommendation read, "People who use [an antibacterial] rinse are failing to take advantage of a safe and effective way to reduce plaque accumulation." For participants encouraged to use a disclosing rinse, the gain-framed recommendation read, "Using a disclosing rinse before brushing enhances your ability to detect areas of plaque accumulation," whereas the loss-framed recommendation read, "Failing to use a disclosing rinse before brushing limits your ability to detect plaque accumulation." Such differences in wording may seem trivial. However, prospect theory predicts that they will have an impact on the persuasiveness of the recommendations.

The researchers were primarily interested in the impact of the pamphlets on participants' behavior. At the very end of the study, participants were given a stamped postcard that they could later mail in to receive a free sample of either antibacterial or disclosing rinse (depending on the condition to which they had been assigned). The researchers predicted that, in the days that followed, more participants would request samples of antibacterial rinse when the benefits of using it had been emphasized, whereas more participants would request samples of disclosing rinse when the costs of not using it had been emphasized.

For thoroughness, self-report measures of the pamphlets' persuasiveness were also administered (prior to the distribution of postcards). Participants were asked to indicate: (a) their attitude towards using the rinses (by rating their effectiveness, benefit, importance, and desirability), (b) their intentions to buy and use the rinses, and (c) how much they would be willing to pay for the rinses. The researchers also assessed how interesting, involving, and informative participants found the pamphlets to be overall (though no difference between conditions was expected here).

Participants also filled out several ancillary self-report measures. Prior to reading the pamphlet, they provided background details about themselves and their dental history, so that the researchers could make sure that these details had no bearing on the effect of the framing manipulation. Then, after reading the pamphlet, participants completed two further measures designed to reveal how they had reacted to and processed the information contained in the pamphlet. The idea was to get a handle on some of the psychological mechanisms that might have mediated (been instrumental in bringing about) any effects of the message framing. Participants were instructed to indicate both the feelings that had they experienced while reading the pamphlet and the thoughts that had occurred to them.

Participants also rated, both before and after reading the pamphlet, how likely they thought they were to develop gum disease given their current dental practices, as well as how severe a problem gum disease would be for them if they ever developed it. By taking these ratings both beforehand and afterwards the researchers were able to estimate how each participant's perceptions of the risk and severity of gum disease changed as a result of reading the pamphlet.

Finally, a brief check on their framing manipulation was included. Participants were asked to rate the overall tone of the pamphlet and whether the pamphlet emphasized the benefits of rinsing or the costs of not rinsing.

WHAT THEY FOUND

Based on an extension of prospect theory, the researchers predicted that persuasion would be greater when messages recommending a disease-preventing behavior were framed in terms of potential gains and when messages recommending a disease-detecting behavior were framed in terms of potential losses. The pattern in which participants mailed in postcards to obtain a dental rinse clearly supported this hypothesis. Of those participants who read pamphlets advocating the use of antibacterial rinse (to prevent plaque accumulation and gum disease), a greater number mailed in postcards when a gain frame was employed. However, of those participants who read pamphlets advocating the use of disclosing rinse (to detect plaque accumulation and gum disease) a greater number mailed in postcards when a loss frame was employed. A comparable crisscross pattern emerged with respect to participants' intentions to purchase and use dental rinses (Fig. 5.2).

Confidence in the validity of these findings was bolstered by two additional findings. First, manipulation checks suggested that the messages had been framed appropriately: gain-framed messages were reported as emphasizing benefits and as being positive in tone, whereas loss-framed messages were reported as emphasizing costs and as being negative in tone. Second, none of the background variables measured, such as dental history, affected the results to any significant degree.

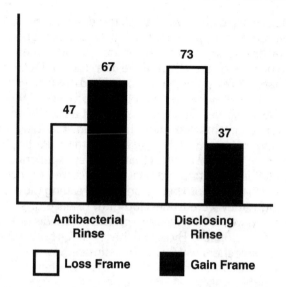

FIG. 5.2. Percentage of participants who used antibacterial or disclosing rinse after reading loss-framed or gain-framed health messages.

Having obtained a clear confirmation of their main hypothesis, the researchers went on to investigate the question of psychological mediation. What changes in participants' mental states lay behind the impact of the framing manipulation? Rather than exhaustively review the findings for each of the measures, we outline one interesting account of how the framing manipulation might have worked, comment on its viability, and then assess the evidence obtained for mediation in general.

The more readily an event comes to mind the more likely its occurrence is judged to be (Tversky & Kahneman, 1973). Hence, people overestimate the probability of graphic or newsworthy causes of death, such as plane hijacks, and underestimate the probability of hidden and banal causes of death, such as blood clots (Coombs & Slovic, 1979). This availability bias may have also played a role in the present study. Specifically, messages advocating the use of disclosing rinse may have mainly brought to mind thoughts about the disadvantages of not rinsing (gum disease), thereby increasing the perceived likelihood of those disadvantages. If so, then loss-framed messages, by capitalizing on participants' aversion to those disadvantages, would have had the persuasive edge over gain-framed messages. Conversely, messages advocating the use of antibacterial rinse may have mainly brought to mind thoughts about the advantages of rinsing (healthy gums), thereby increasing the perceived likelihood of those advantages. If so, then gain-framed messages, by capitalizing on the appeal of those advantages, would have had the persuasive edge over loss-framed messages.

If this account were true, then perceived likelihood of gum disease, and expressed worries about dental health, should both have been greater in the disease-detecting conditions than in the disease-preventing conditions. However, no evidence of this pattern emerged, thereby casting doubt on the account put forward previously. In fact, rather damaging to any mediational account of the framing manipulation, no overall connection was found between participants' attitudes towards dental rinsing and their postcard-mailing propensities.

There are several possible explanations for this odd disjunction between attitude and behavior. First of all, the appropriate mediators may not have been sought. For example, participants were not asked to rate the likelihood of their contracting or avoiding gum disease given their use or nonuse of dental rinse, only the likelihood of their contracting or avoiding gum disease in general. A more specific inquiry may have worked better. Second, participants' self-reports may have been compromised by response biases. For example, their attitudes towards dental rinsing may have reflected whether they felt they should rinse rather than whether they felt inclined to rinse. Finally, it may have been that the psychological causes of participants' behavior were simply not available to self-report. Often the causes of our behavior elude identification through introspection (Nisbett & Wilson, 1977; see chap. 1).

Despite the failure to locate mediating variables (not everything works out smoothly in social psychological research) the present study nonetheless offered clear evidence that message frame and content could be manipulated to enhance the efficacy of health-promoting messages. It is also worth noting that Rothman and his colleagues (1999) ran an additional study in which participants read a message, again either gain- or loss-framed, advocating the detection or prevention of a hypothetical viral infection. Its findings dovetailed those of the present study.

SO WHAT?

If we wish to act rationally, we ought to make decisions by weighing the probability and desirability of the various outcomes that would result from deciding one way or the other. The manner in which those outcomes are portrayed should make no difference. The water in a glass that is described as half-full or half-empty will quench our thirst to an equal degree. However, the human mind turns out to be significantly swayed by how potential outcomes are portrayed. Logically speaking, telling someone that the engaging in act X promotes outcome Y, or that not engaging in act X fails to promote outcome Y, provides the same objective information: Y (partly) depends on X. However, the way in which that information is presented—in particular, whether the emphasis is placed on losses or gains—influences the decision-making process. Hence, we seem to make judgments about things in the world, not as they are in themselves, but as they are relative to other things.

There are many other examples of how the framing of alternatives can influence our decisions. One is our use of *psychic budgets* (Thaler, 1980). Our readiness to part with our money often depends on how we categorize our forthcoming expenditure. For example, if buying a new house, we might be prepared to spend more on sundries like garden gnomes than we would if the house were already ours. The reason is that, before the house is bought, the cost of the gnomes falls under the generous budget for the entire house, and so seems comparatively trivial. However, after the house is bought, the cost of the gnomes falls under the tighter budget of everyday expenses, and so seems comparatively extravagant. Needless to add, sales professionals are happy to exploit our budgeting biases, craftily inflating the asking price for accessories to a major purchase.

Another example of framing effects involves presenting alternative options as either maintaining the status quo or as altering it. Suppose you have a zero chance of developing a fatal disease. How much would you pay to avoid having a 1 in 1,000 chance of developing it? Most people say that they would be prepared to pay several thousand dollars. However, now suppose that you already have a 1 in a 1,000 chance of developing that disease. How much would you now pay to reduce that risk to zero? Inconsistently, most people say that they would be prepared to pay only a few hundred dollars. Why is this?

An answer is provided by the fourth and final postulate of prospect theory: The loss of a benefit is considered more disadvantageous than the gain of that benefit is considered advantageous. One implication of this postulate is that, to induce people to accept a gamble involving an equal chance of winning or losing, it is necessary to award them more for winning than to penalize them for losing. For example, only a third of people accept an equal chance of winning $200 or losing $100, even though the expected value of the gamble is positive: $(0.5 \times \$200) - (0.5 \times \$100) = \$50$ (Tversky & Shafir, 1992). Findings like this strongly suggest that people have a bias towards maintaining the status quo, at the expense of foregoing likely benefits.

The existence of this bias in favor of the status quo can explain why people pay more to avoid potential risks than they do to eliminate preexisting ones. Potential risks strike people as disrupting the status quo. Hence, running them seems costly, not running them just par for the course. In contrast, preexisting risks strike people as reflecting the status quo. Hence, running them seems par for the course, not running them beneficial.

But why do costs psychologically outweigh benefits? Perhaps it is just a brute fact that our potential for experiencing suffering exceeds our potential for experiencing joy. Bad experiences do appear to have a more powerful effect on us than good experiences (Baumeister, Bratslavsky, Finkenauer, & Vohs, 2001). Hence, prudence may serve us better than pluckiness overall.

Another possibility is that the tendency to weigh costs more heavily than gains may have evolved over time because it conferred a survival benefit on our forefathers. Our hazardous ancestral environment may have happened to suit risk-averse cave-dwellers better than the risk-seeking ones, so that the former reproduced in greater numbers, thereby making us what we are today. This is not to deny that people vary considerably in their penchant for risk-taking. For example, people with high self-esteem take more risks on average than people with low (Baumeister, Tice, & Hutton, 1989). It is merely to affirm that risk-aversion is, on the whole, characteristic of the human race.

At this point, an astute reader may be wondering: If prospect theory is true, then why is gambling such a popular pastime? Why do people commonly throw caution to the wind in defiance of the objective odds? The answer is that most amounts gambled are psychologically trivial. If only very large bets (relative to one's income) could be laid, gambling would disappear overnight. Prospect theory properly applies only when significant amounts of money are involved.

AFTERTHOUGHTS

Once we understand how the framing of a particular problem undermines the rationality of our judgments we may find ourselves in a curiously divided mental state. On the one hand, we can see how our judgment ought to remain unaffected. On the other hand, we can still feel our judgment being swayed one way or the other. It is as if two distinct levels of understanding co-exist, or at least alternate in quick succession. A smart one that grasps the irrationality, and a dumb one that falls for it hook, line, and sinker.

This kind of mental duality also emerges when people are alerted to other cognitive biases, in particular those that involve probability judgments. Consider a lottery in which the winning 6 numbers are to be chosen at random from a pool of 36 numbers. There are two tickets for sale. One features the numbers "1,2,3,4,5,6," the other, "2,18,17,29,4,35." Which ticket would you buy, given the choice? You probably feel an instinctive preference for the second ticket. The odds of a ticket with haphazard numbers winning certainly seem better than the odds of a ticket with consecutive numbers winning. Of course, a little reflection reveals that a preference for one ticket over another is irrational, because any set of six numbers, regardless of its composition, is equally likely to be chosen in a truly random lottery. The mistake is to think that, because, as a class, haphazard combinations are more likely to occur than consecutive combinations, any single haphazard combination is more likely to occur than any single consecutive combination. This is one example of the *representativeness bias* in operation. The ticket featuring the haphazard numbers is chosen on the basis of its similarity to past winning tickets, not on the basis of correct statistical logic (Kahneman & Tversky, 1972). Nonetheless, despite finding this explanation rationally convincing, you may still find that your preference for tickets featuring nonconsecutive numbers remains.

How can we make sense of the fact that half our mind can understand something while the other half cannot? One way to view the matter is by analogy with perceptual illusions (Piattelli-Palmarini, 1996). Have you ever been gazing out of the window of a train, only to notice, when it comes to a halt, the train nonetheless appears to be moving in reverse? You can prove that the train is in fact stationary by aligning any point on the window with a point on the platform and confirming the absence of relative motion. Nevertheless, despite this conclusive visual test, the train still appears to be moving backward. Perceptual illusions of this sort cannot be eliminated from consciousness because our brains are physiologically hard-wired to produce them (Bruce, Green, & Georgeson, 1996). No amount of effort can reason them out of existence. Their illusory quality can only be abstractly pondered. The same may be true of many of our cognitive biases.

REVELATION

People avoid risks when they stand to gain, but take risks when they stand to lose. Consequently, how a choice is framed, in terms of loss or gain, can influence how people choose, over and above the objective consequences of choosing one way or the other.

— APG —

CHAPTER REFERENCE

Rothman, A. J., Martino, S. C., Bedell, B. T., Detweiler, J. B., & Salovey, P. (1999). The systematic influence of gain- and loss-framed messages on interest in and use of different types of health behavior. *Personality and Social Psychology Bulletin, 25,* 1355–1369.

OTHER REFERENCES

Banks, S. M., Salovey, P., Greener, S., Rothman, A. J., Moyer, A., Beauvais, J., & Epel, E. (1995). The effects of message framing on mammography utilization. *Health Psychology, 14,* 178–184.

Baumeister, R. F., Bratslavsky, E., Finkenauer, C., & Vohs, K. D. (2001). Bad is stronger than good. *Review of General Psychology, 5,* 323–370.

Baumeister, R. F., Tice, D. M., & Hutton, D. G. (1989). Self-presentational motivations and personality differences in self-esteem. *Journal of Personality, 57,* 547–579.

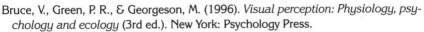

Bruce, V., Green, P. R., & Georgeson, M. (1996). *Visual perception: Physiology, psychology and ecology* (3rd ed.). New York: Psychology Press.

Coombs, B., & Slovic, O. (1979). Newspaper coverage of causes of death. *Journalism Quarterly, 56,* 837–843.

Detweiler, J. B., Bedell, B. T., Salovey, P., Pronin, E., & Rothman, A. J. (1999). Message framing and sunscreen use: Gain-framed messages motivate beach-goers. *Health Psychology, 18,* 189–196.

Kahneman, D., & Tversky, A. (1972). Subjective probability: A judgment of representativeness. *Cognitive Psychology, 3,* 430–454.

Kahneman, D., & Tversky, A. (1979). Intuitive prediction: Biases and corrective procedures. *TIMS Studies in Management Science, 12,* 313–327.

Kahneman, D., & Tversky, A. (1981). The framing of decisions and the rationality of choice. *Science, 221,* 453–458.

Nisbett, R. E., & Wilson, T. D. (1977). Telling more than we can know: Verbal reports on mental processes. *Psychological Review, 84,* 231–259.

Petty, R. E., & Wegener, D. T. (1998). Attitude change: Multiple roles for persuasion variables. In D. Gilbert, S. Fiske, & G. Lindzey (Eds.), *The handbook of social psychology* (4th ed., pp. 323–390). New York: McGraw-Hill.

Piattelli-Palmarini, M. (1996). *Inevitable illusions: How mistakes of reason rule our minds.* New York: Wiley.

Thaler, R. (1980). Towards a positive theory of consumer choice. *Journal of Economic Behavior and Organization, 1,* 39–60.

Tversky, A., & Kahneman, D. (1973). Availability: A heuristic for judging frequency and probability. *Cognitive Psychology, 5,* 207–232.

Tversky, A., & Shafir, E. (1992). The disjunction effect in choice under uncertainty. *Psychological Science, 3,* 305–309.

MORE TO EXPLORE

Belsky, G., & Gilovich, T. (1999). *Why smart people make big money mistakes—and how to correct them: Lessons from the new science of behavioral economics.* New York: Simon & Schuster.

6 Clashing Cognitions: When Actions Prompt Attitudes

"The most merciful thing in the world ... is the inability of the human mind to correlate all its contents."
—H. P. Lovecraft (1890–1937), American writer of cult fiction

BACKGROUND

The expression "sour grapes" is commonly employed to describe the ungracious attitude of a sore loser toward a worthy winner. However, the dictionary definition of sour grapes differs. It can be traced all the way back to a classic fable by the Greek storyteller Aesop, entitled "The Fox and the Grapes." Aesop tells of a ravenous fox rummaging about for scraps of food. Glancing up, the fox catches sight of a mouth-watering bunch of grapes. He valiantly tries to climb the tall tree around which the supporting vine coils. Alas, his limbs are poorly suited to scaling tree trunks, and he keeps sliding back to the ground. In the end, exhausted by his fruitless endeavors, the fox grumpily gives up. As he scampers away he consoles himself with the following thought: "I bet those grapes weren't ripe anyhow!"

Sour grapes, then, seem to have less to do with wrath and more to do with *rationalization*. Aesop's fable suggests that, when matters turn out badly as a result of our own action, we tend to minimize how bad they actually were to make ourselves feel better.

A vivid real-life example of this tendency comes from an in-depth field study of a doomsday cult (Festinger, Riecken, & Schachter, 1956). Led by a charismatic housewife from Minnesota, one Mrs. Marian Keech, members

64

of this cult came to the conclusion that the world as we know it would end on December 21, 1954. Apparently, at God's behest, all dry land would be deluged, and all earthly creatures drowned. On the eve of the apocalypse, however, the faithful few would be transported by flying saucer to another planet, where they would take up residence until the terrestrial flood waters had subsided.

The cult's dire predictions were, of course, disconfirmed. The question that intrigued the researchers (who had infiltrated the group in search of the answer) was how cult members would react to the disconfirmation. Would they sensibly begin to doubt the doctrines of the cult? Many did. They walked away disillusioned, forever skeptical of suburban saviors. However, many more cult members stoutly maintained their faith. Having committed themselves to the cause for many months, and having renounced all worldly possessions, they preferred to explain away the unexpected denouement. At the last minute, they decided, God had spared the wayward world, in recognition of the piety and fidelity shown by cult members themselves. Buoyed by this ingenious (not to mention flattering) rationalization, cult members set about proselytizing unbelievers harder than ever. Their renewed zeal seems to have been motivated by a need for social validation. If only they could get other people to agree with them, then they could obtain reassurance that their beliefs had been right all along.

Of course, people do not only rationalize when farfetched prophecies fail, but also under less dramatic circumstances. For example, people tend, after choosing between different alternatives, to increase their preference for the one they have just chosen (Brehm, 1956); to regard activities at which they have performed poorly as of little significance (Crocker & Major, 1989); and to justify a prior lack of charity towards victims by blaming them for their plight (Lerner, 1980).

Now suppose that you were a social psychologist seeking to develop a general theory of rationalization, one capable of making sense of all the findings previously listed. How would you proceed? You might choose to focus on the fact that rationalization is always, at some level, the making of later thoughts and deeds consistent with earlier ones. For example, continuing to proselytize on behalf of a doomsday cult whose prophecies have been disconfirmed, although it makes little logical sense, makes plenty of psychological sense if people have already spent several months proselytizing on the cult's behalf. Persevering allows them to avoid the embarrassment of admitting how wrong they were in the first place. Hence, understanding rationalization in terms of consistency gives social psychologists a way of analyzing its many manifestations.

Several theories of psychological consistency have been proposed over the years. However, the theory of *cognitive dissonance*, set forth by Leon Festinger (1957), remains unrivaled in scope and influence. Festinger (1957) proposed that pairs of cognitions (an inclusive term for thoughts and feelings) can be consonant, dissonant, or irrelevant with respect to one other. In particular, consonant cognitions are those that psychologically imply one another. For example, "I helped the old lady across the street" and "I am a helpful person" are consonant beliefs. Dissonant cognitions, on the other hand, are those that psychologically imply the reverse of one other, as do the beliefs "I refrained from helping the old lady across the street" and "I am a helpful person." Irrelevant cognitions, finally, are those that carry no psychological implications for one another, as with "I helped the old lady across the street" and "I am good at math."

According to Festinger, the presence of dissonant cognitions gives rise to a state of unpleasant psychological tension. Moreover, the greater the number of dissonant cognitions, and the greater their importance to the individual, the more intense the resulting tension will be. Once the tension has been aroused, the individual is motivated to alleviate it. In particular, he or she tries to find ways to reduce the magnitude of the underlying cognitive dissonance responsible for the tension. Several tactics are available, all of which involve rationalization in one form or another (Abelson, 1963).

Festinger never went so far as to stipulate how dissonance reduction was to be achieved in different settings. He merely stipulated that it would be achieved, one way or another. Nonetheless, he did make one very specific prediction concerning the preconditions for arousing cognitive dissonance. This prediction applies in settings where people are induced to be-

FIG. 6.1. Asserting one thing, but doing another, arouses cognitive dissonance.

have in a manner that contradicts one of their important attitudes, that is, when they are induced to perform a *counter-attitudinal* act.

Suppose that Miguel liked a movie, but then told Maria, who was considering going to see it, that the movie was rubbish. The act of lying would be counter to Miguel's true attitude. The thought associated with this act, "I told Maria that the movie was rubbish," would then clash with Miguel's pre-existing thought, "I liked the movie."

Festinger's (1957) prediction was that performing a counter-attitudinal act would arouse cognitive dissonance only if the incentive for performing it was just sufficient to get the job done. For example, Miguel might well experience cognitive dissonance if, in a moment of selfishness, he voluntarily told Maria that the movie was rubbish so she would attend a different movie with him, one he hadn't seen already. However, if some mafia don had bundled Miguel into the back of a car and had threatened to rub him out unless he told Maria that the movie was rubbish (beginning to sound like a Woody Allen movie?), then no cognitive dissonance would result.

Now, one way people can reduce cognitive dissonance is to shift their attitudes so that they better accord with their behavior. For example, Miguel might conclude, after lying to Maria about not liking the movie, that he had not really liked the movie after all. This revision of opinion would serve to clear his conscience. Festinger predicted that, whenever people strive to reduce cognitive dissonance by shifting their attitudes, their attitudes will shift more when they are given a smaller incentive to behave counter-attitudinally than when they are given a larger one.

This flies in the face of what one might intuitively expect. Indeed, the received wisdom in Festinger's time was that the principles of reward and punishment that govern how animals behave should also govern how humans think. On this view, a larger incentive, known to produce more behavior change in animals, ought also to induce more attitude change in humans. The theory of cognitive dissonance suggested, however, that the human mind did not operate like this. On the contrary, a smaller incentive should produce more attitude change, as it implied that a person was freely undertaking a counter-attitudinal act.

Putting matters to the empirical test, Festinger joined forces with an undergraduate student of his, Merrill Carlsmith, to conduct an ingenious experiment (1959) in which participants were persuaded to do something inconsistent with their attitudes after being given either a large or small incentive to do so.

WHAT THEY DID

Festinger and Carlsmith began by having their participants—71 male psychology undergraduates at Stanford University—perform a pair of mind-numbingly boring tasks. After being told they were taking part in a study involving measures of performance, participants spent the first half hour diligently filling a tray with spools, then emptying it, then filling it once more, again and again, using only one hand. The next half hour brought no relief. They spent it repeatedly rotating 48 square pegs on a board a quarter turn clockwise, one after the other. To compound their tedium, participants were not even given any specific performance goal, but simply told to work at their own pace. As they yawned their way through both tasks, an experimenter with a stopwatch sat in the background, busying himself taking notes.

When they had turned their last peg, participants no doubt breathed a sigh of relief. In actuality, however, the study was only just beginning. The researchers had no interest in participants' ability to manipulate spools or pegs. They simply wanted to make participants regard the study—that is, the initial stage of the real study—in a negative light. What they were really interested in was how participants' attitudes toward this "study" would change in response to experimental manipulations.

To reinforce the impression that the study had indeed concluded, the experimenter reset his stopwatch, and began debriefing participants about its purpose. As part of an elaborate cover story, the experimenter claimed that the study was about how the presence or absence of positive expectations affected fine motor coordination. He went on to say that participants had been assigned to the no-expectation condition, in which they had received no information about the study before taking part. He alleged that additional positive-expectation condition also existed, in which participants, prior to taking part, were informed (falsely) that the study was interesting and fun. The experimenter further claimed that this information was imparted by an experimental confederate, pretending to be a student who had just completed the study himself. The pretense was necessary, argued the experimenter, because participants would be more likely to accept the testimony of a fellow student than the assurances of a professor.

Keep in mind that the entire debriefing was fake. The real study had nothing to with expectations, and there were no such confederates. The elaborate deception merely served to make subsequent experimental manipulations look sensible.

At this point, the experimenter, who had up until now come across as confident and fluent, affected an air of hesitancy and worry. He explained, with evident embarrassment, that his confederate had failed to turn up. The confederate's absence had left him in the lurch because the next participant, who was assigned to the positive expectation condition, was now waiting to begin. He now humbly asked participants for a favor: Would they mind filling in for the absent confederate? And would they be available on future occasions to do the same?

If participants showed any signs of reluctance the experimenter reassured them that the favor would not take very long, and that they would need to be available in the future only rarely. With these reassurances, all participants volunteered their services. The experimenter then explained that their role would involve striking up a causal conversation with the other participant, and conveying the impression that the study was interesting and fun. A sheet of paper detailing what to say in this regard was provided. The experimenter then escorted participants to the office where the other participant, a female undergraduate, was waiting.

This "participant" was actually a confederate of the experimenter. In the conversation that ensued, she responded in a preplanned way. She began by letting participants do most of the talking. When the subject of the study came up, and participants began singing its praises, she indignantly expressed surprise. A friend of hers, she claimed, had already taken part in the study, and had found it exceedingly dull, and had advised her to get out of it if at all possible. In response to this challenge, participants had been instructed to reaffirm their conviction that the study was a veritable barrel of laughs, and that the confederate would be sure to enjoy it. To verify that these conversations proceeded as planned, the researchers secretly recorded them on tape for later inspection.

Given that this study had more twists and turns than a boardwalk rollercoaster, let's take stock for a moment. Participants had taken part in a very boring study. They had come away with a very negative impression of it. Yet they now found themselves voluntarily misleading a participant of the opposite sex into believing that the study had been interesting and fun. Clearly, what participants privately believed ("I disliked the study") and what they publicly did ("I claimed the study was enjoyable") were at odds with one another. In short, cognitive dissonance had been created, and as a consequence participants would have experienced an unpleasant inner tension. Festinger and Carlsmith predicted that participants would attempt to relieve this tension by bringing the clashing cognitions that were causing it back into harmony. One way to do this was to adopt a more favorable attitude towards the study.

Inducing cognitive dissonance in an experimental setting would have been no small achievement in itself. However, Festinger and Carlsmith also wished to test whether they could also prevent cognitive dissonance from occurring by manipulating the magnitude of the incentive offered to participants for behaving contrary to their attitudes. They predicted that a large incentive would reduce or eliminate cognitive dissonance because it would provide participants with an additional cognition consonant with their deceptive behavior, namely, "I am doing this because of the large incentive I will receive." The large incentive would give them a justification for having misled the confederate.

Thus, the experimenter promised one group of participants a generous $20, and another group a paltry $1, for trying to convince the female confederate that the study was interesting and fun. (One should bear in mind that this was back in the 1950s, when $20 was a considerable sum of money, even for well-to-do Stanford undergraduates!) A third group of participants, after enduring the tedium of the initial study, did not have to deceive a female confederate afterward. This group's results provided a baseline against which results from the other two could be compared.

The experimental manipulations over, the researchers needed to measure participants' final attitudes toward the study. However, there was a difficulty. How could they be sure that what participants reported reflected their true feelings and not simply what they felt they should report? Suppose you did a boring experiment and then had to tell the next participant that it was interesting. You might then report to an experimenter that you too had found it interesting simply to avoid an embarrassing scene, or out of gratitude for the money he had given you for helping him out. To safeguard against such possibilities, the experimenter did not attempt to measure participants' attitudes himself. Instead, he delegated this responsibility to a second confederate, seemingly unassociated with the prior proceedings. The experimenter mentioned in passing that some psychology students down the hall were conducting surveys. The supposed purpose of these surveys was to assess how the quality of studies conducted in the department of psychology could be improved. Hence, if participants had any complaints to make about the study in which they had participated, here was the perfect opportunity for them to do so.

The experimenter escorted participants down to the interviewer's office, commenting along the way that the study had, in general, been well received. This comment was to help participants persuade themselves that the study was indeed enjoyable, if cognitive dissonance was already pushing them in that direction. After the experimenter bade them farewell, the second confederate, posing as a student interviewer, proceeded to ask participants how interesting they had found the study, how much they had learned from it, how scientifically important they had thought it was, and how eager they would be to take part again in a similar study. He instructed them to respond aloud before committing their answers to paper. Participants expressed their attitudes, in both cases, using rating scales that ranged from −5 (not at all) to +5 (extremely).

Here the study truly ended. Participants were questioned afterwards about whether they had suspected its true purpose. On these grounds, five participants were eliminated. Six more suffered the same fate for failing to comply with instructions. This left 60 participants, with 20 in each experimental group.

WHAT THEY FOUND

As predicted, participants paid $1 to misrepresent the study ended up with significantly more positive attitudes toward the study than baseline participants did. These $1 participants changed their attitudes to be more consistent with what they had openly declared to be true, presumably to reduce cognitive dissonance. However, the attitudes of the participants paid $20 to do the same did not show a similar shift. The provision of a larger incentive evidently headed cognitive dissonance off at the pass. In sum, both of the researchers' main predictions were clearly confirmed (Fig. 6.2).

The same pattern of results emerged for participants' ratings of their willingness to participate in a similar experiment, although here the pattern was less pronounced. This is to be expected given that the manipulation of cognitive dissonance was principally designed to influence attitudes, not behavior. The remaining two measures, which assessed the perceived educational value and scientific importance of the study, differed little across the study's three conditions. This is also to be expected given that these measures tapped attitudes that were at best peripherally related to how participants behaved. Changing these attitudes would not, in consequence, have allowed participants to reduce the cognitive dissonance induced by their behavior.

SO WHAT?

First of all, the study shows how rationalization can be profitably understood in terms of cognitive consistency. Festinger and Carlsmith (1959) engineered a situation in which uncomfortably dissonant cognitions were created and then showed that participants' response was to take advantage of an available means of harmonizing them, namely by changing their attitudes. This finding supports the hypothesis that keeping cognitions consonant is a primary human motivation and one that can have a powerful impact on our beliefs and feelings. Indeed, keeping cognitions consonant may be more important than fulfilling other wishes. The French

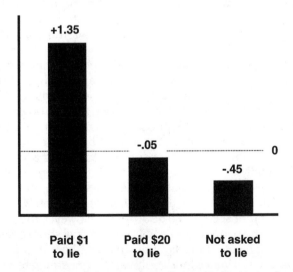

FIG. 6.2. Participants' ratings of how much they liked a boring "study," when paid $1 or $20 to lie that the study had been interesting, or when not asked to lie.

wartime leader Charles de Gaulle once publicly declared that he would give up smoking for good, and duly did so. When asked how he had managed to resist his subsequent nicotine cravings, he replied, "De Gaulle cannot go back on his word!" Public commitments of this sort keep people honest because if they renege on them the dissonance they experience will be especially acute.

The study also demonstrated that it is not only attitudes that give rise to actions, but also actions that give rise to attitudes. In many cases, it may even be easier to change people's minds by inducing them to perform a counter-attitudinal act than by having them carefully consider persuasive arguments. Do you think the participants in the present study could have been talked into regarding the boring tasks that they had performed as interesting? It seems unlikely. Demonstrations of cognitive dissonance, then, highlight the potential irrationality of the persuasive process. Our attitudes are changed not only by objective facts but also by subjective motivations.

Indeed, cognitive dissonance has been used as a deliberate instrument of indoctrination. For example, during the Korean War, Chinese communists took charge of many prison camps. There, they set about inducing captive American soldiers to engage in what might be called trivial acts of defection. For example, they had them publicly endorse mildly pro-communist statements like, "America is not perfect." As you might expect, such tactics did not initially create much cognitive dissonance or attitude change. However, their Chinese captors were only just getting started. They proceeded to increase by barely noticeable degrees the magnitude of the pro-communist gestures that the American soldiers performed. Bit by bit, these prisoners of war found themselves doing more and more pro-communist things, like drafting Maoist tracts, with only minimal inducement. The eventual result was a substantial pro-communist shift in ideology (Schein, 1956).

Finally, Festinger, and Carlsmith's study showed that, when trying to get people to change their minds, the subtle approach is superior to the blatant. The larger the incentive, the smaller the dissonance. This finding has practical implications for, among other things, how to effectively manage children's behavior. Suppose, for example, that little Lamprini dislikes the taste of spinach and refuses point blank to eat it. What should you do? Your best move may be to induce her to eat just a little (that is, engage in some mildly counter-attitudinal behavior), thereby allowing cognitive dissonance to bring about a more pro-spinach attitude. But how should you motivate Lamprini to take that very first bite? Promising her chocolate cake might seem like a good tactic. However, the present study suggests that such an in-your-face bribe would only short-circuit any useful cognitive dissonance that might be created. Lamprini would instead learn that spinach is a yucky food, only worth consuming to get a yummy dessert. (The motivation-sapping properties of overt reward are pursued in chap. 8.)

A superior tactic would be to give Lamprini an inducement that was just enough to get her to taste her spinach—a little gentle encouragement perhaps. She would then be more likely to conclude that she is eating the spinach because she likes it. The same lesson applies to the stick as to the carrot: the milder the punishment, the greater its persuasiveness. If children are severely warned, as opposed to softly told, not to play with a forbidden toy, they later come to like that toy more, and are more likely to play with it when adults are not around (Aronson & Carlsmith, 1963; Freedman, 1965). This effect may be due either to their inclination to express their autonomy in defiance of restrictive authority (Brehm & Brehm, 1981) or to their understanding that what is forbidden is usually attractive (Bushman, 1996). At any rate, such inverse correlations between cognitive dissonance and consequence size highlight the pitfalls of trying to explain human behavior and attitudes in terms of simple learning principles.

AFTERTHOUGHTS

The theory of cognitive dissonance gives us a way of making sense of many aspects of human thinking and behavior that might otherwise remain perplexing. Nevertheless, the theory has been criticized and revised over the years (Harmon-Jones & Mills, 1999). We now briefly touch on some of these developments in order to give the reader a sense of how social psychological theories evolve over time as research progresses.

Soon after the present study appeared in the literature, a few researchers questioned whether its findings were genuine. They either pointed out various confounds that might have compromised the study's validity (Chapanis & Chapanis, 1964) or else conducted other studies whose findings seemed at odds with dissonance theory (Rosenberg, 1965). However, 40 years later, countless studies have soundly confirmed that dissonance effects are real and can be reliably replicated.

Convinced that they were dealing with real phenomena, social psychologists then began debating how best to interpret them. Festinger (1957) proposed, as we have seen, that counter-attitudinal acts give rise to unpleasant arousal, and that attitude change is one way to eliminate that arousal. Bem (1967) disagreed with this account, proposing that the underlying dynamics were far simpler. He contended that we come to know our own attitudes in the same way that we come to know the attitudes of other people, namely, by observing behavior. He argued that we do not so much peer inside our own souls to discover how we feel, as watch what we do and then make an informed guess. On this view, the knowledge that I dislike spinach would come from the innumerable times I have complained about it, refused to eat it, and so on, rather than from any perception of my own feelings. Counter-attitudinal behavior causes attitude change by leading people to calmly infer that they hold attitudes that match their counter-attitudinal behavior. Participants in the Festinger and Carlsmith study were well aware of telling the female confederate that the study was interesting. This, according to Bem, led them to conclude that they too also found the initial tasks interesting (or at least more interesting than they otherwise would have). In other words, attitudes change through simple self-perception, without any motivational fuss.

Both Festinger and Bem's theories make intuitive sense. Which then is correct? The contemporary consensus is that both are correct, but under different circumstances. Cognitive dissonance is believed to occur when people perform extremely counter-attitudinal acts, whereas self-perception is believed to occur when people perform mildly counter-attitudinal acts (Fazio, Zanna, & Cooper, 1977). So if I hate pizza, and you subtly induce me to eat some, then I will come to like pizza more as a way of resolving the dissonance created internally. However, if I only slightly dislike pizza, and you subtly induce me to eat some, then I will come to like pizza more by noting my pizza-eating behavior and inferring a pizza-loving disposition. But how can we be sure that unpleasant arousal *ever* plays a role in dissonance? The definitive proof comes from studies in which attitude change is eliminated after participants have been given another way to explain where their unpleasant arousal has come from (Losch & Cacioppo, 1990; Zanna & Cooper, 1974).

Researchers have also tried to clarify the conditions necessary for cognitive dissonance to occur. Festinger (1957) had established already that people respond better to nudges than shoves, but later research established that they must also (a) freely perform the counter-attitudinal act; (b) foresee that the act will have negative consequences; and (c) experience the unpleasant arousal that they attribute to the act itself (Goethals, Cooper, & Naficy, 1979; Linder, Cooper, & Jones, 1967; Zanna, Higgins, & Taves, 1978). All these conditions were met in the original Festinger and Carlsmith study (1959).

However, these findings also inspired Cooper and Fazio (1984) to radically reformulate Festinger's theory. They argued that cognitive inconsistency per se was irrelevant to the production of dissonance effects. The phenomena attributed to cognitive inconsistency only occurred, they claimed, when people believed that they had freely chosen to bring about unwanted consequences that they had foreseen.

By way of illustration, imagine a mirror-image version of the Festinger and Carlsmith study. Here participants begin by performing two enjoyable tasks. They then voluntarily tell a female confederate that these tasks were boring. Will these participants now go on to develop less positive attitudes toward the tasks? We suspect not, or at least, not to the same degree. The fact that the anticipated consequences of telling the lie are not negative (a nice, as oppose to nasty, surprise now awaits the confederate) removes the need for rationalization. Nonetheless, the level of cognitive inconsistency is no less than it was in the original study; its polarity has merely been reversed. The results of such thought experiments are backed up by actual research showing that if an act, freely undertaken, has foreseeable unwanted consequences, then attitude change occurs, even if that act is consistent with one's original attitudes (Scher & Cooper, 1989).

However, Festinger may have the last laugh. More recent research implicates cognitive consistency after all. For one thing, cognitive dissonance effects appear to be confined to people who value consistency as a personality trait (Cialdini, Trost, & Newsom, 1995). In addition, shifts in attitude occur even when people perform acts that do not have any immediate negative consequences. For example, persuading participants to freely write down, on a later discarded piece of paper, that they like an unpleasant tasting beverage, leads them to rate that beverage more favorably later (Harmon-Jones, Brehm, Greenberg, Simon, & Nelson, 1996). Moreover, if participants are induced to make a private speech in favor of condom use, and are then reminded about their past failures to use condoms, they then purchase more condoms later, by way of atonement (Stone, Aronson, Crain, Winslow, & Fried, 1994). Festinger's (1957) original theory can accommodate such findings; Cooper and Fazio's (1984) reformulation cannot. Ironically, studies of cognitive consistency have themselves yielded inconsistent findings!

However, if we assume that some valued aspect of the self is threatened by all manipulations of cognitive dissonance, and that people then take steps to restore their damaged self-esteem, then a degree of theoretical integration may be possible. The desire to maintain a positive self-image is a primary human motivation (Sedikides & Gregg, in press). Evidence that it lies behind cognitive dissonance comes from studies in which participants are given the opportunity to affirm their self-image. Suppose for the sake of argument that participants in the Festinger and Carlsmith study had been allowed to contribute to their favorite charity immediately after lying to the female confederate. It is likely that this act would have sufficed to make them feel better about themselves, thereby removing any motivation to affirm their self-image by revising their opinion of the boring study (proving that they are not just shameless liars). In actual studies run along similar lines, the shifts of attitude usually following manipulations of cognitive dissonance are eliminated by an opportunity to perform a good deed or affirm an important value (Steele, 1988). Hence, the underlying motivation seems not so much about resolving inconsistency as about maintaining a positive self-image.

Moreover, a neat compromise viewpoint is also available. Cognitions are not so much mutually consonant or dissonant with one another (as Festinger originally claimed) as they are consonant or dissonant with some valued aspect of the self, such as honesty, competence, personal consistency, or whatever (Aronson, 1969). On this view, the dissonant cognitions in the Festinger and Carlsmith study were not so much "I disliked the study" and "I claimed the study was enjoyable," but rather "I am a truthful person" and "I lied by claiming the study was enjoyable." The advantage of this formulation is threefold: first, it retains the elegant cognitive algebra of Festinger's original theory; second, it broadens that theory to cover cases where inconsistencies are not resolved; and third it specifies what makes cognitions important in the first place: self-relevance.

Yet the role of the self in cognitive dissonance remains unclear. There is no direct evidence, for example, that performing counter-attitudinal acts makes people temporarily think ill of themselves. Instead, they merely seem to experience a generalized sense of uneasiness or discomfort (Elliot & Devine, 1994; Harmon-Jones, 2000). Furthermore, one curious extension of the Festinger and Carlsmith study found that, if participants attempted to convince a confederate, truthfully, that the original task had been boring, they later rated the task as having being more enjoyable than if tried to convince a confederate, falsely, that the original task had been enjoyable (Girandola, 1997). If compromised moral principles are the ultimate source of cognitive dissonance, then why should truthfulness lead to greater attitude change than deceit?

So there we have it. Oscar Wilde's remark that truth is rarely pure and never simple certainly applies to cognitive dissonance theory. However, there is no denying that successive incarnations of the theory have thrown progressively more light on our understanding of human motivation, and that social psychologists will continue to unravel the mysteries that remain for many years to come.

REVELATION

If you wish to change somebody's opinion, subtly induce them to act at odds with it while letting them think they did so of their own free will. This tactic works because people readily rationalize objectionable actions for which they feel responsible by adjusting their attitudes to match them.

— APG —

CHAPTER REFERENCE

Festinger, L., & Carlsmith, J. (1959). Cognitive consequences of forced compliance. *Journal of Abnormal and Social Psychology, 58,* 203–10.

OTHER REFERENCES

Abelson, R. P. (1963). Computer simulation of "hot cognition." In S. Tomkins & S. Messick (Eds.), *Computer simulation of personality.* New York: Wiley.

Aronson, E. (1969). The theory of cognitive dissonance: A current perspective. In L. Berkowitz (Ed.), *Advances in experimental social psychology* (Vol. 4, pp. 1–34). New York: Academic Press.

Aronson, E., & Carlsmith, J. M. (1963). Effects of the severity of threat on the devaluation of forbidden behavior. *Journal of Abnormal and Social Psychology, 12,* 16–27.

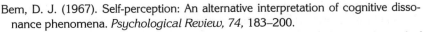

Bem, D. J. (1967). Self-perception: An alternative interpretation of cognitive dissonance phenomena. *Psychological Review, 74*, 183–200.

Brehm, J. W. (1956). Post-decision changes in desirability of alternatives. *Journal of Abnormal and Social Psychology, 52*, 384–389.

Brehm, S. S., & Brehm, J. W. (1981). *Psychological reactance*. New York: Academic Press.

Bushman, B. J. (1996). Forbidden fruit versus tainted fruit: Effect of warning labels on attraction to television violence. *Journal of Experimental Psychology: Applied, 2*, 207–226.

Chapanis, N., & Chapanis, A. (1964). Cognitive dissonance: Five years later. *Psychological Bulletin, 61*, 1–22.

Cialdini, R. B., Trost, M. R., & Newsom, J. T. (1995). Preference of consistency: The development of a valid measure and the discovery of surprising behavioral implications. *Journal of Personality and Social Psychology, 69*, 318–328.

Cooper, J., & Fazio, R. (1984). A new look at dissonance theory. In L. Berkowitz (Ed.), *Advances in experimental social psychology* (Vol. 17, pp. 229–267). New York: Academic Press.

Crocker, J., & Major, B. (1989). Social stigma and self-esteem: The self-protective properties of stigma. *Psychological Review, 96*, 608–630.

Elliot, A. J., & Devine, P. G. (1994). On the motivational nature of cognitive dissonance: Dissonance as psychological discomfort. *Journal of Personality and Social Psychology, 67*, 382–394.

Fazio, R. H., Zanna, M. P., & Cooper, J. (1977). Dissonance and self-perception: An integrative view of each theory's proper domain of application. *Journal of Experimental Social Psychology, 13*, 464–479.

Festinger, L. (1957). *A theory of cognitive dissonance*. Stanford, CA: Stanford University Press.

Festinger, L., Riecken, H. W., & Schachter, S. (1956). *When prophecy fails*. New York: Harper Torchbooks.

Freedman, J. L. (1965). Long-term behavioral effects of cognitive dissonance. *Journal of Experimental Social Psychology, 1*, 145–155.

Girandola, F. (1997). Double forced compliance and cognitive dissonance theory. *Journal of Social Psychology, 137*, 594–605.

Goethals, G., Cooper, J., & Naficy, A. (1979). Role of foreseen, foreseeable, and unforeseeable behavioral consequences in the arousal of cognitive dissonance. *Journal of Personality and Social Psychology, 37*, 1179–1185.

Harmon-Jones, E. (2000). Cognitive dissonance and experienced negative affect: Evidence that dissonance increases negative affect even in the absence of aversive consequences. *Personality and Social Psychology Bulletin, 26*, 1490–1501.

Harmon-Jones, E., Brehm, J. W., Greenberg, J., Simon, L., & Nelson, D. E. (1996). Evidence that the production of aversive consequences is not necessary to create cognitive dissonance. *Journal of Personality and Social Psychology, 70*, 5–16.

Harmon-Jones, E., & Mills, J. (1999). *Cognitive dissonance: Progress on a pivotal theory in social psychology*. Washington, DC: American Psychological Association.

Lerner, M. J. (1980). *The belief in a just world: A fundamental delusion*. New York: Plenum.

Linder, D., Cooper, J., & Jones, E. (1967). Decision freedom as a determinant of the role of incentive magnitude in attitude change. *Journal of Personality and Social Psychology, 6,* 245–254.

Losch, M. E., & Cacioppo, J. T. (1990). Cognitive dissonance may enhance sympathetic tonus, but attitudes are changed to reduce negative affect rather than arousal. *Journal of Experimental Social Psychology, 26,* 289–304.

Rosenberg, M. (1965). When dissonance fails: On eliminating evaluation apprehension from attitude measurement. *Journal of Personality and Social Psychology, 1,* 28–42.

Schein, E. (1956). The Chinese indoctrination program for prisoners of war: A study of attempted "brainwashing." *Psychiatry, 19,* 149–172.

Scher, S. J., & Cooper, J. (1989). Motivation basis of dissonance: The singular role of behavioral consequences. *Journal of Personality and Social Psychology, 56,* 899–906.

Sedikides, C., & Gregg, A. P. (in press). Portraits of the self. In M. A. Hogg & J. Cooper (Eds.), *Sage handbook of social psychology.* London: Sage Publications.

Steele, C. M. (1988). The psychology of self-affirmation: Sustaining the integrity of the self. In L. Berkowitz (Ed.) *Advances in experimental social psychology* (Vol. 21, pp. 261–302). New York: Academic Press.

Stone, J., Aronson, E., Crain, A. L., Winslow, M. P., & Fried, C. B. (1994). Inducing hypocrisy as a means for encouraging young adults to use condoms. *Personality and Social Psychology Bulletin, 20,* 116–128.

Zanna, M. P., & Cooper, J. (1974). Dissonance and the pill: An attribution approach to studying the arousal properties of dissonance. *Journal of Personality and Social Psychology, 29,* 703–709.

Zanna, M. P., Higgins, E., & Taves, P. (1978). Is dissonance phenomenologically aversive? *Journal of Experimental Social Psychology, 12,* 530–538.

MORE TO EXPLORE

Cialdini, R. (1993). Commitment and consistency. In R. Cialdini (Ed.), *Influence: Science and practice* (pp. 50–93). New York: Harper Collins.

Harmon-Jones, E. (2000). An update on cognitive dissonance theory, with a focus on the self. In A. Tesser, R. B. Felson, & J. M. Suls (Eds.), *Psychological perspectives on self and identity* (pp. 119–144). Washington, DC: American Psychological Association.

7 Baptism of Fire: When Suffering Leads to Liking

"Fanaticism consists in redoubling your effort when you have forgotten your aim."
—George Santayana (1863–1952), Spanish-American philosopher

BACKGROUND

Chapter 6 showed that, when we are led, with minimal inducement, to behave in a manner inconsistent with our attitudes, our attitudes often shift to become more consistent with our behavior (Festinger & Carlsmith, 1959). This is one way of reducing the unpleasant cognitive dissonance that comes from knowing we have willingly done something embarrassing or immoral. Because the deed cannot be denied, nor responsibility for it evaded, we preserve our dignity or integrity by adopting an attitude that justifies the deed, and by believing that we held that attitude all along.

However, cognitive dissonance can also arise, and be resolved, by other means. Consider the identical twins, Jess and Tess. Normally inseparable, the pair happened to attend different showings of the same movie. Whereas Jess paid an extravagant $20 for an advance screening, Tess paid a paltry $5 for a bargain matinee. Unfortunately the movie they watched turned out to be rather disappointing—at least, that was the subsequent consensus of movie-goers and critics alike. Some days later Jess and Tess got around to discussing their respective cinematic experiences. Although they usually agreed about everything, they found that they disagreed about the merits of the movie. Whereas Tess echoed the misgivings of the majority, Jess was fulsome in her praise.

The twins' difference of opinion can be explained by the difference in how much each spent. Jess prided herself on being a sensible spender. Hence, the admission that she had willingly wasted a sizeable sum on a lousy movie was too much for her to bear. The most convenient way to avoid making this admission was to regard the movie in retrospect as better than it had been. Tess too prided herself on being a sensible spender. However, having spent a much smaller sum to see the movie, she did not feel any great need to revise her opinion of it afterwards.

Cognitive dissonance theory can explain why Jess came to like the movie more than Tess did. However, note that the counter-attitudinal behavior creating the dissonance (forking out $20) took place *prior* to the formation of the attitude (the impression of the movie), not after it, as happened in the study reported in chapter 6. This inverted sequence of events points to the operation of a different class of dissonance effect. It boils down to this: If we first attain something at considerable cost we later become biased toward evaluating it favorably. For Jess and Tess, the cost was financial. But other costs can also arouse dissonance—effort exerted, trouble taken, pain suffered. In all cases, the greater the hardship endured, the greater the subsequent change in attitude.

This conclusion may strike you as plausible enough. Perhaps you have already observed a correlation between the amount of work people put into something and how much they value the result. For instance, someone who has worked diligently to get a degree is liable to prize it more than someone who has worked only half-heartedly to get it. However, such correlations on their own are not enough to prove the *effort-justification* effect. This is so for two reasons. First, the amount of work people put in often determines the quality of the result. For example, if a student works hard on a term paper, his or her favorable opinion of the finished product may reflect its true quality, rather than any attempt on his or her part to justify the effort exerted. Second, people who strive harder to attain a result are likely to have initially placed greater value on attaining that result. So suppose that Chun-Ju does her level best to make the school volleyball team but that Yi-Ying barely tries at all. Both girls nontheless make the volleyball team thanks to their innate skill. It turns out that Chun-Ju later appreciates being on the team more than Yi-Ying does. Was this due to the greater effort Chun-Ju put in? Not necessarily. Chun-Ju might have originally liked the idea of being a team member more, and then tried harder to make the team as a consequence. Hence, observation alone can provide only circumstantial evidence for an effort-justification effect.

What is a social psychologist to do? He or she needs to conduct an experiment in which the cost of attaining an outcome is varied while everything else—including the quality of the outcome attained and the intensity of the original desire to attain it—is held constant. Under such circumstances, differences in outcome evaluation can be confidently attributed to differences in initial cost, and to nothing else.

Eliot Aronson and Judson Mills (1959) set about obtaining the relevant data. They concentrated on a common but often significant social event: that of joining the ranks of an established group. Realizing that becoming a new group member can sometimes be a challenging experience, the researchers predicted that the more severe a person's initiation into a group, the more they would come to like that group and value being a member.

WHAT THEY DID

To test their hypotheses cleanly, the researcher had to artificially create a social group that satisfied two conditions. First, it had to afford a suitable pretext for an initiation procedure whose severity could be varied. Second, it had to be interesting enough for participants to want to join even after they learned about the initiation procedure.

To meet these challenges, the researchers created a group whose alleged purpose was to discuss on a weekly basis a most intriguing topic: the psychology of sex. Sixty-three female college students volunteered to become members.

The initiation procedure consisted of an embarrassment test that was supposed to determine whether participants felt comfortable talking openly about sex. Across the study's three conditions, the magnitude of the embarrassment that participants experienced during the initiation was systematically manipulated. In the severe-initiation condition, participants had to say aloud 12 highly obscene words (including some four-letter ones) and then read aloud two passages of prose depicting lurid sexual activity. To make matters worse, they had to do this in front of the male experimenter, who was closely monitoring them for any signs of hesitation or blushing. In the mild-initiation condition, participants were given the far less daunting task of reading aloud five mildly sex-related words (e.g., virgin, petting). In a final condition, the initiation procedure was omitted completely. In both mild-initiation and severe-initiation conditions, the experimenter explained that the embarrassment test was necessary in order to ensure that all participants would contribute in equal measure to the group discussion. The reason, he claimed, was that the dynamics of the discussion process were under scrutiny, and that reluctance to speak would distort these dynamics. Importantly, the experimenter emphasized that participants were under no obligation to take the test, although they could not become group members without doing so. This ensured that participants only took the test voluntarily (a known necessary condition for cognitive dissonance to occur; Linder, Cooper, & Jones, 1967). The fact that there was no pressure placed on participants to undergo the initiation may ease some of the reader's ethical concerns about the study. One participant did indeed exercise her prerogative not to take the embarrassment test.

The experimenter also explained to participants that, in an effort to reduce the embarrassment caused by discussing sex face to face, he had opted to put all participants in separate rooms and have them communicate over an intercom system via microphone and headphones. However, this was merely an elaborate deception aimed at keeping an important fact under wraps, namely, that the discussion group did not actually exist! In reality, all participants listened through their headphones to the same recorded discussion taking place between supposed group members.

Why the elaborate deception? Why not just use a real group? The answer is that the researchers were trying to cut down on irrelevant variation in their experiment. Such irrelevant variation would make the effects of the manipulation harder to detect, much as the background hiss on a radio makes a channel harder to hear. If participants had interacted in person, then the ensuing discussion would have been difficult to regulate, and would have introduced much irrelevant variation into the experiment. However, with all participants listening to the same discussion, all such variation was removed in a single stroke.

Of course, to maintain the clever deception, the researchers had to keep participants from joining in the discussion. To achieve this, they first asked participants whether or not they had ever read a book called *Sexual Behavior in Animals*. All replied in the negative. The experimenter then explained to participants that they could not join in the current discussion because the other group members had already read the book, and introducing someone who hadn't could distort the dynamics of the discussion. (Remember, participants were earlier told that the discussion group had been meeting for several weeks, so this revelation did not strike them as odd.) Nevertheless, participants were told that they could still listen in on the group discussion to get a feel for what the group was like.

Participants were led to believe that the group had already begun meeting. The experimenter interrupted the group over the microphone, and explained to them that a new member (whose name he gave) would be listening. At the precise moment when participants donned their headphones, three prerecorded voices introduced themselves, and then settled back into their discussion.

So what juicy topics did these fictitious group members address? Participants hoping to deepen their understanding of sexuality were in for a monumental disappointment. The researchers' own description of the recording illustrates why:

> The recording ... was deliberately designed to be as dull and as banal as possible ... participants spoke dryly and haltingly on secondary sex behavior in lower animals, inadvertently contradicted themselves and one another, mumbled several non sequiturs, started sentences that they never finished,

hemmed, hawed, and in general conducted one of the most worthless and uninteresting discussions imaginable. (Aronson & Mills, 1959, p. 179)

When the discussion finished participants were asked to fill out a questionnaire about what they thought of both the discussion and of the other group members. They were told that everybody in the group had done the same. The main prediction was that participants in the severe-initiation condition, because they had experienced more dissonance, would come to think more highly of the group discussion, and of the group members themselves.

The cover story proved remarkably successful. Only one participant, when questioned afterwards, expressed any definite suspicions about the nonexistence of the discussion group (her data were discarded). It is also noteworthy that, when the real purpose of the study was at last revealed to participants, none were dismayed either at having been deceived or at having been put through the initiation procedure. In fact, the researchers reported that most participants were intrigued by the study, even returning at the end of the term to learn about the results.

WHAT THEY FOUND

The results were clear-cut: compared to participants in the mild-initiation and no-initiation conditions, participants in the severe-initiation condition rated both the discussion and the discussants more favorably, providing powerful evidence for the effort justification effect (Fig. 7.1). As predicted, the more severe participants' initiation into a group, the more they said they liked that group. Why? Most likely because of the cognitive dissonance they experienced. Specifically, participants' knew that (a) they had freely submitted to an unpleasant initiation procedure; and (b) that group membership was a disappointment. Unable to deny the freedom of their actions or the unpleasantness of the initiation, they instead looked back on group membership through rose-tinted glasses, and concluded that being part of the group was a worthwhile experience. (See chap. 4, for more on perceptual bias, and chap. 2, for more on retrospective bias.)

Two other experimental findings deserve comment. First, there were no differences between the mild-initiation and no-initiation conditions with regard to how participants rated the discussion and the discussants. It seems that the mild-initiation condition caused participants hardly any embarrassment, with the result that little cognitive dissonance was created. The researchers might have preferred liking for the group to rise in step with severity of initiation, but it was difficult for them to predict in advance what increment in severity would correspond to what increment in liking. Second, initiation severity had a greater influence on participants' opinions about the quality of the discussion than on their opinions about the likability of the group members. This may have been because derogating the quality of the

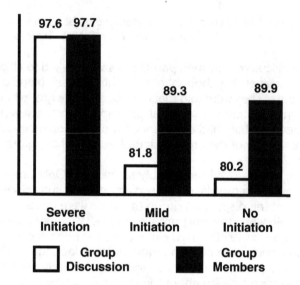

FIG. 7.1. Participants' ratings of the group discussion, and of other group members, after undergoing a severe or mild initiation into the group, or neither.

discussion was more crucial to reducing dissonance. Alternatively, participants may simply have been reluctant to directly criticize fellow students.

It has been pointed out that other psychological mechanisms could perhaps have accounted for the findings obtained in the present study. For example, participants in the severe-initiation condition might have formed a more positive impression of the group discussion because it seemed decidedly pleasant in comparison to the mortifying test they had just been put through. Or again, these participants, despite experiencing embarrassment, might still have had their interest in sexual topics piqued, and thus looked upon the tedious discussion of animal courtship more favorably. Happily, subsequent research has ruled out even these alternative explanations. In a rigorous replication study (Gerard & Mathewson, 1966), initiation severity was manipulated by varying levels of (safe but unpleasant) electric shock. The merit of this new manipulation was that the content of the initiation procedure was no longer related to the content of the discussion group. This permitted several possible confounds to be simultaneously eliminated. In addition, the researchers manipulated whether participants did or did not believe that they were part of the group whose members and discussion they later evaluated. This permitted the researchers to tease apart the effects of otherwise identical negative experiences— one linked to group initiation, the other not—on later attitudes toward the group. Several other precautions were also taken. Despite this extra degree of rigor, the results obtained were strongly consistent with an effort-justification effect.

SO WHAT?

The study demonstrated that the overcoming of painful obstacles en route to becoming a group member makes people value group membership more, not less. This helps us to understand why, in everyday life, loyalty to a group can increase over time even in the face of seemingly substantial and repeated incentives to leave.

Commonsense holds that the way to make people join a group, and ensure that they remain members, is to remove all possible obstacles to joining, and to generously reward long-term fidelity. In one sense, this is obviously true. If I do not have to do anything special to join a group, and am paid handsomely for being a member, why should I not join it? Yet, although such powerful incentives are effective at shaping our behavior, they do not necessarily lead us to internalize feelings of loyalty to a group. That is, you can bribe people into belonging to a group but you cannot bribe them into feeling committed to it. If you want to transform how people truly feel, you would be wise to adopt a more indirect approach. The present study documents one tactic that someone in a position of power can employ: Induce people to willingly undergo some hardship as a precondition for joining a group. Cognitive dissonance will then ensure that people's private attitudes toward the group shift in a positive direction. Hence, group membership need not be maintained through the provision of incentives; the process of self-justification ensures that people come to value group membership for its own sake.

The problem, of course, is how to motivate people to take the first big step toward membership. Sometimes the allure of the group is sufficient on its own. The promise of a pay raise, status boost, or unique opportunity can inspire would-be members to endure any preliminary hardships they encounter. Ironically, it is precisely those who are originally more motivated to join a group who will be prepared to endure initiations of greater severity, thereby reinforcing their already positive attitude toward group membership. This is an example of how social conditions can conspire to make preexisting attitudes more extreme, creating a self-reinforcing loop (Abelson, 1995). Consider also, in this connection, the case of a prospective group member called upon at first to make a small sacrifice for the privilege of group membership, but then gradually seduced into making much larger sacrifices. Each increment along the way is so small that it is never possible, having made the previous sacrifice, not to justify making the next one also. Such a slippery slope may snare even people who were not initially so keen to become model group members. (See chap. 21 for how a slippery slope has also been used to explain obedience to authority.)

There is evidence to suggest that the slope need not even be so slippery for commitment to take root. Making a token concession at first can lead a person to a more consequential concession later. In one study, for example, undergraduate participants were asked whether they would turn up at seven in the morning to take part in research on thinking processes. Half the participants were immediately informed of the early starting time, whereas the other half were informed of it only after first agreeing to take part in the research itself. This trivial difference in the wording of the request made a substantial difference to the number of participants who complied with it. Whereas less than a quarter of those immediately informed of the early starting time turned up, more than half of those who first verbally committed to the research did (Cialdini, Cacioppo, Bassett, & Miller, 1978).

Salespeople often use similar techniques to get customers to part with their hard-earned cash. One of the authors (APG), thanks to an acquaintance with an investigative journalist, gained inside knowledge about how a car finance company used compliance techniques to sweeten deals for themselves at the expense of their customers. As a matter of sales policy, for example, they had customers unnecessarily wait for hours while their finance deal was supposedly being negotiated upstairs. Can you see how this might up their level of commitment to the final settlement offered?

Given the various subtle means by which commitment can be strengthened, can you now begin to appreciate how people can get sucked into unsavory organizations whose practices and beliefs strike outsiders as absurd and extremist? Nonetheless, we must not lose sight of the fact that effort-justification phenomena are not limited to fringe organizations: they abound in mainstream society too. Think of all the social institutions that require sacrifices as a precondition for joining their ranks. College fraternities haze new members in fiendish ways; the military puts new recruits through training of purgatorial intensity; and bleary-eyed interns slave night and day before becoming medical doctors. The rationale for such harsh preconditions on group membership is unclear until one realizes their potential for arousing cognitive dissonance. That dissonance can be resolved by members adopting a more positive attitude toward the group, which in turn facilitates greater loyalty, obedience, and esprit de corps, all of which promote group integrity.

An analysis of 19th-century utopian cults by Kanter (1972) underscored the central roles of effort-justification and commitment in keeping groups together. She found that cults requiring their members to make significant sacrifices were more successful. For example, cults that had their members surrender all their personal belongings lasted much longer than those that did not. Hence, the experimental findings of Aronson and Mills are nicely borne out by historical data.

AFTERTHOUGHTS

In concluding our discussion of the effort justification effect, let us once more consider the plight of Jess, who spent all that money to see such a disappointing movie. Suppose that Jess had sufficient acquaintance with dissonance theory not to let the $20 she paid influence her judgment. Half-

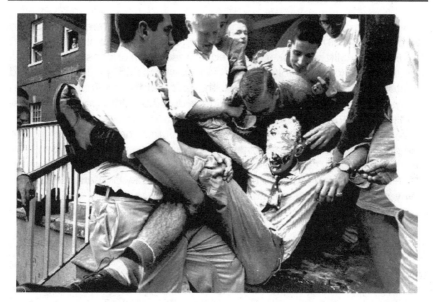

FIG. 7.2.   Welcome to the fraternity!

way through the movie, she bravely admitted to himself that she had made a mistake. What, rationally, should she do now? Stay or leave? You might suspect that, having paid so much, she would be better off staying. However, a little thought makes it clear that Jess should leave as soon as she can. After all, she cannot get a refund no matter what she does. However, if she leaves, she will at least no longer have to sit through a boring movie. With the money already spent, the only thing that matters is the quality of Jess's life from now on. Hence, she should walk out of the movie immediately. She would thereby avoid a common behavioral trap called the *sunk cost error*—the irrational tendency to honor an irrevocable loss to the detriment of one's present and future welfare. In experimental tests, for example, people tend to keep investing well past the break-even point, even when the investment climate has obviously become unfavorable (Rubin & Brockner, 1975).

Irrationally sitting through a boring movie because you paid for the privilege of doing so is a relatively minor instance of the sunk cost error. Matters start to get more serious when high-ranking officials persist in squandering public funds on pointless projects to justify all the public funds they have already squandered. For example, take the infamous Tennessee-Tombigee Waterway. Costing $2 billion to build, and requiring more earth to be displaced than the Panama Canal, it today stretches 234 miles from Alabama to Mississippi. Midway through construction, however, it became apparent that the estimated value of the waterway would be far less than the amount required to complete it. Nonetheless, Alabama Senator Jeremiah Denton had these words to say in defense of forging ahead: "To terminate a project in which $1.1 billion has been invested represents an unconscionable mishandling of taxpayers' dollars" (cited in Dawes, 1988, p. 23). The good Senator appears to have overlooked the fact that the original $1.1 billion was gone forever, and that spending another $0.9 billion would only mishandle taxpayers' dollars further.

We should not base any of our future decisions, whether made in public or in private life, on prior investments that have proven fruitless. Rather, we should deliberately cut our losses and move on. This can be difficult, given our relative aversion to incurring sure losses (Tversky & Shafir, 1992). But now you know why you should make the effort!

REVELATION

When people voluntarily undergo an unpleasant experience to achieve something, they come to value that something more, not less. This helps explain why people become committed members of groups even when membership entails considerable initial sacrifice and offers scant subsequent reward.

— APG —

CHAPTER REFERENCE

Aronson, E., & Mills, J. (1959). The effect of severity of initiation on liking for a group. *Journal of Abnormal and Social Psychology, 59,* 177–181.

OTHER REFERENCES

Abelson, R. P. (1995). Attitude extremity. In R. E. Petty & J. A. Krosnick (Eds.), *Attitude strength: Antecedents and consequences* (pp. 25–41). Hillsdale, NJ: Lawrence Erlbaum Associates.

Cialdini, R., Cacioppo, J., Bassett, R., & Miller, J. (1978). Low-ball procedure for producing compliance: Commitment then cost. *Journal of Personality and Social Psychology, 36,* 463–476.

Dawes, R. M. (1988). *Rational choice in an uncertain world.* San Diego, CA: Harcourt Brace.

Festinger, L., & Carlsmith, J. (1959). Cognitive consequences of forced compliance. *Journal of Abnormal and Social Psychology, 58,* 203–210.

Gerard, H. B., & Mathewson, G. C. (1966). The effects of severity of initiation on liking for a group: A replication. *Journal of Experimental Social Psychology, 2,* 278–287.

Kanter, R. M. (1972). *Commitment and community: Communes and utopias in sociological perspective.* Cambridge, MA: Harvard University Press.

Linder, D., Cooper, J., & Jones, E. (1967). Decision freedom as a determinant of the role of incentive magnitude in attitude change. *Journal of Personality and Social Psychology, 6,* 245–254.

Rubin, J. Z., & Brockner, J. (1975). Factors affecting entrapment in waiting situations: The Rosenkrantz and Guildenstern effect. *Journal of Personality and Social Psychology, 31,* 1054–1063.

Tversky, A., & Shafir, E. (1992). The disjunction effect in choice under uncertainty. *Psychological Science, 3,* 305–309.

MORE TO EXPLORE

Larrick, R., Nisbett, R., & Morgan, J. (1993). Who uses the normative rules of choice? Implications for the normative rules of microeconomic theory. *Journal of Organizational Behavior and Human Decision Processes, 56,* 331–347.

Sutherland, S. (1994). *Irrationality: The enemy within* (pp. 92–104). London, UK: Penguin.

8 Taking the Magic Out of the Markers: The Hidden Cost of Rewards

"Work is more fun than fun."

—Noel Coward (1899–1973), lyricist and playwright

BACKGROUND

There is a heartwarming tale about an elderly gentleman who, while feeding pigeons from his favorite park bench, is one day confronted by a mob of surly teenagers. For several minutes, they cruelly make fun of him. He endures the episode stoically, hoping that it will soon be over, and never repeated. Alas, when he returns to his bench the following day, the mob is there again. Indeed, their taunts start to become a regular feature of his visits to the park. The elderly gentleman eventually decides that enough is enough, and hatches a clever plan to put an end to their mischief. The next time they make fun of him, he does something wholly unexpected. He pays each of them a dollar for their trouble. The astonished teenagers conclude that the old guy must be going senile. He continues to show the same unaccountable generosity day after day, and no matter how badly the teenagers treat him, they still get paid. Then one day, without a word of explanation, he abruptly stops distributing cash. His tormenters are outraged. Why should they bother to taunt somebody who pays them nothing for the privilege? With a disdainful air, they part company with him forever. Smiling, the elderly gentleman returns to feeding his pigeons.

Readers may recognize in this anecdote some familiar themes. Remember how smaller incentives can cause larger shifts in opinion (see chap. 6),

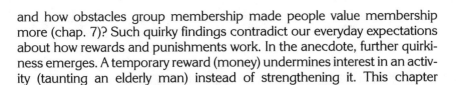

and how obstacles group membership made people value membership more (chap. 7)? Such quirky findings contradict our everyday expectations about how rewards and punishments work. In the anecdote, further quirkiness emerges. A temporary reward (money) undermines interest in an activity (taunting an elderly man) instead of strengthening it. This chapter unpacks this paradoxical point and describes an experiment that tests its validity in an important applied setting.

According to pop psychology gurus, the main problem with human motivation is that it is in such short supply (e.g., Durand, 2000). If only people could get sufficiently motivated, the argument runs, all manner of social and personal ills could soon be overcome. Bulging waistlines would recede, flagging test scores would soar, and the homeless masses would acquire luxury penthouses. Finding effective ways to cultivate desirable motivations is therefore a top priority. How should this be accomplished?

Motivations can be divided into two basic types. On the one hand, we can wish to do something for its own sake, for the joy and satisfaction that the activity itself affords. On the other hand, we can wish to do something as a means to an end, for its desirable consequences it promises. In the former case, we are said to be *intrinsically* motivated, in the latter, *extrinsically* motivated. For example, if the authors of the present volume wrote out of sheer intellectual and literary enthusiasm, their motivation would be intrinsic. However, if they wrote with a view to lining their pockets with royalties, their motivation would be extrinsic. Now, if you wished to encourage somebody to do something, you could focus on increasing either their intrinsic or extrinsic motivation. The question is: Which strategy would serve you best?

Consider the issue in practical terms. Imagine you are a piano teacher whose task it is to turn giddy youngsters into competent musicians. If you chose to motivate your pupils intrinsically, you would try to make your lessons as engaging as possible. You might, for example, teach them a series of popular tunes, or use musical games to educational effect. Your goal would be to stimulate pupils' enthusiasm, capitalizing upon their inborn desire to make music.

If, however, you chose to extrinsically motivate your pupils, you would adopt an altogether different approach. Your first step would be to perform a behavioral analysis of piano instruction, that is, to find out what rewards promote, or what punishments impede, behaviors associated with making musical progress (e.g., practicing regularly, turning up on time, hitting the right note). Your guiding assumption would be that the motivation to perform any behavior depends on external contingencies, that is, on the objective consequences of performing it. If doing something has pleasant consequences, people will tend to do it more often, whereas if doing something has unpleasant consequences, people will tend to do it less often (Skinner, 1953). So, in terms of our piano-playing example, if Ashok gets candy every time he practices, he will likely practice more diligently; or, if

Madhumita gets scolded every time she arrives late, her punctuality will likely improve. By implementing and adjusting contingencies with sufficient rigor, Ashok and Madhumita can be made to do, and made to want to do, most of what is required of them as novice musicians. Their motivation can be maintained by the deft use of carrots and sticks.

Some *behaviorists* (as those who advocate this carrot-and- stick approach are called) contend that only reward should be used as a motivator because punishment has several drawbacks. First, punishment is ineffective: The pain and anxiety that it creates disrupt the overall learning process. Second, punishment is inefficient: It gets rid of unwanted behaviors but does not establish specific new ones. Third, punishment is unethical: It hurts, and therefore should only be used as a last resort. Thus, rapping Ashok or Madhumita on the knuckles for playing the wrong note does not help them to concentrate, nor does it teach them how to play the right note, nor does it respect their rights as individuals.

By comparison, rewarding people for doing the right thing seems to be a far more enlightened and constructive approach. Rewards motivate effectively; they are nice to receive; they are a fitting recompense for hard work. Indeed, the received wisdom in Western culture is that rewards are marvelous inventions. Look around and you will see incentive systems everywhere—gold stars for perfect scores, bonuses for working overtime, Nobel prizes for inspired research.

However, are rewards as beneficial as they are made out to be? Indisputably, they work. When contingencies that deliver rewards are implemented, people want to get the job done and they work toward doing so. So where is the problem? Consider again our pair of fledgling pianists, Ashok and Madhumita. The purpose of teaching them is not only to get them to follow instructions while they are being taught, but also to instill in them a desire to keep playing piano after instruction has ceased. Which motivational approach, intrinsic or extrinsic, is best suited to achieving this long-term goal? The intrinsic approach, trying to get pupils to play piano for its own sake, seems to be a promising one, given that its intent is to sow seeds of interest that will later bear fruit. But what about the extrinsic approach? If pupils are initially given rewards for, say, playing "Boogie-Woogie," and those rewards are then withdrawn, will pupils thereafter be more likely to play Boogie-Woogie than if they had never been rewarded for doing so? It seems possible. The rewards might get pupils into the swing of things, to provide them with the motivational momentum they need to get started and to keep going. The only trouble is that exactly the opposite seems to be true.

WHAT THEY DID

Lepper, Greene, and Nisbett (1973) suspected that conditionally rewarding people for engaging in an activity would not only not promote their interest in it, but would actually *undermine* their interest in it. To test this hypothesis experimentally, the researchers adopted the following strategy. First, they identified an activity, X, that people engaged in spontaneously. Second, they measured how often people engaged in X when the opportunity arose (an indirect measure of interest). Third, they provided some people, but not others, with a reward for engaging in X. Half the time, this reward was expected (they were told they would receive it), whereas half the time, it was unexpected (its receipt came as a surprise). The impact of these manipulations on how often people subsequently engaged in X was then assessed.

Lepper et al. (1973) predicted that people in the expected-reward condition would engage in X less often than they had originally. They reasoned that such people would attribute engaging in X to the forthcoming reward rather than to any personal inclination. This self-perception would then undermine their motivation for engaging in X. In contrast, Lepper et al. (1973) predicted that people in both the no-reward condition and the unexpected-reward condition would engage in X as often as they had before. Interest would not be lost because participants would believe they had engaged in X because they wanted to (i.e., they would not attribute their behavior to some external factor). The inclusion of the unexpected-reward condition was important because it allowed the researchers to test whether it was the expectation of a reward, and not just the receipt of a reward, that undermined motivation.

The study was conducted in a nursery school, a practical setting appropriate for testing the effects of conditional rewards. The 51 participants were children from middle-income families between the ages of 3 and 5. Two-thirds were girls. The classroom format was such that the children were free throughout the day to engage in any one of a number of recreational activities. One of these was the target activity: playing with magic markers. It was chosen because (a) children found it interesting, (b) their level of interest could be easily measured (in terms of time spent playing with the markers), and (c) the activity did not look out of place alongside other classroom activities.

The experimental set-up was as follows. Several magic markers, together with a sheaf of drawing paper, were placed on a table to the side of the classroom. Two observers, neatly hidden behind a one-way mirror, recorded the length of time that children spent at the table playing with the markers. If these grown-up observers had been visible, the children's behavior might have been inadvertently influenced, and the results of the study compromised. Both observers were kept unaware of the experimental condition to which the children had been assigned, to guard against possible recording bias.

The children's baseline (initial) interest in magic markers was assessed by how often they played with them for the first hour of class on three consecutive days. This was followed by an interval of 3 to 4 weeks, during which the experimental manipulations were administered. Children's eventual interest in playing with magic markers was then assessed on three further consecutive days. Their eventual interest thus reflected the impact of the experimental manipulations.

These manipulations ran as follows. In the expected-reward condition, children received an award for the quality of their drawings, having been told in advance that they would. In the unexpected-reward condition, children received the same award, but without being told beforehand that they would. In the no-reward condition, children did not receive any reward, nor were they told that they would. Note that the actual quality of their drawings was not taken into account. Children were assigned to one of the three conditions at random.

Implementing the manipulations involved a little theater. One by one, the children were approached by a friendly experimenter who chatted and played with them for a while. This experimenter then invited each child to come to a surprise room with him. Although several children refused his invitation (perhaps justifiably—he was, after all, a stranger) the majority accepted. On arriving at this surprise room, each child was told to sit down at a small table on which magic markers and drawing paper had been placed. The experimenter then told children that another grown-up would shortly be coming by to see what kinds of pictures young children liked to draw.

It was here that the differences between the conditions were introduced. Children in the expected-reward condition were told that the grown-up would be giving out "Good Player Awards" for good quality drawings. The awards were designed to look highly appealing to youngsters. They took the form of colorful 3 × 5 inch cards, decorated with a flashy gold star and red ribbon, with a space for the child's name and that of the school. The experimenter showed children a sample award, and asked whether they would like to win it. Children in the unexpected-reward and no-reward conditions were not shown this award; they were merely asked whether they would like to draw a picture for the grown-up who would shortly be arriving.

The grown-up then arrived to play his part. Dismissing the first experimenter, he sat down across the table from the children, and invited them to start drawing. Throughout the 6 minutes of allotted drawing time the grown-up attempted to show interest in, though not necessarily approval of, children's performance.

Once they had finished drawing, children in the no-reward condition were immediately sent back to class, reassured they had done a good job. However, children in both the expected and unexpected reward conditions stayed on to receive their Good Player Award, to much fanfare and applause. The second experimenter proudly inscribed their names and the name of their school on each award. The children were then invited to pin their coveted awards on an Honor Roll board (which featured a display of similar awards) so that everyone would know what a good player they were.

WHAT THEY FOUND

What effect did these manipulations have on the children's behavior a few days later? Children who drew with the magic markers—in the hope of earning the Good Player Award—were subsequently less interested in those markers than children who were either given the award unexpectedly, or given no award at all. The effect was quite pronounced. Children in the expected-reward condition ended up playing with the markers only about half as often as children in the other two conditions (Fig. 8.2).

Given that children's baseline interest in playing with magic markers had also been assessed, it was possible to analyze whether, within each of the three conditions, their interest rose or fell as a consequence of the manipulation. Again in line with predictions, children in the expected-reward condition showed a significant decrease in interest, whereas children in the other conditions showed no real change.

Some interesting secondary findings also emerged. First, when children in the unexpected-reward condition were split into those who had, and had not, originally been interested in playing with magic markers, those who had not been became more interested in playing with them. Perhaps receiving the Good Player Award out of the blue had left them with a favorable

FIG. 8.1. Children like to draw, until they are rewarded for doing so.

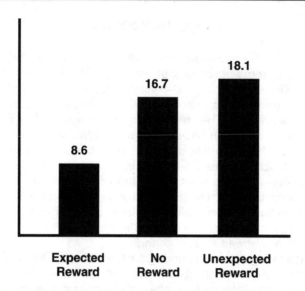

FIG. 8.2. Percentage of time that child participants played with magic markers after being given an expected reward, no reward, or an unexpected reward.

impression of the activity. In contrast, when children in the expected-reward condition were split in the same way, those who had originally been particularly interested in playing with magic markers became less interested in playing with them (though the interest of both declined). This result suggests that the more interesting the activity, the more extrinsic rewards undermine intrinsic interest in it. However, the fact that participants with less intrinsic interest also had scope for losing further interest complicates interpretation.

One final striking finding emerged. The manipulation also affected the quality of the pictures that the children drew (as judged by three raters unaware of the condition to which they had been assigned). In the expected-reward condition, children drew poorer quality pictures than in both other conditions. Apparently, the ill effects of extrinsic reward were not limited to undermining interest, but also extended to compromising performance.

SO WHAT?

This study shows that making the receipt of a reward conditional on the performance of an activity ultimately reduces people's interest in performing that activity. Rewards do alter behavior effectively in the short-term. In the long-term, however, they have the side effect of making people weary of activities that they would otherwise continue to enjoy.

The researchers determined that extrinsic rewards could undermine preschoolers' motivation to engage in a fun activity. Does this effect generalize? Indeed it does: Literature reviews confirm that many kinds of incentives reduce enthusiasm for many kinds of tasks (Deci, Koestner, & Ryan, 1999). Moreover, the young and the old alike are susceptible (although tangible incentives affect the young to a greater degree). We describe below two concrete examples of how extrinsic rewards can prove to be motivationally counterproductive.

The first concerns smoking. In one large study, the effectiveness of different methods for helping people kick the habit was tested (Curry, Wagner, & Grothaus, 1991). Some participants received a prize for turning in weekly progress reports; some received personalized feedback to help them abstain; some received both; and some received neither. A week later, it was the participants in the prize alone (reward) condition who were doing best. However, 3 months later the picture had radically changed. Now, participants in the prize alone condition were doing the worst, puffing away even more often than those who had received neither prize nor feedback. Moreover, saliva tests revealed that these extrinsically rewarded participants lied twice as often as everyone else about how much they were smoking.

The second example concerns good behavior in children. Conscientious parents strive to raise their sons and daughters who are cooperative and caring. However, if extrinsic rewards undermine intrinsic motivation, then the use of bribery and flattery for this purpose may ultimately backfire, spawning little devils rather than darling angels. Indeed, the empirical evidence bears out this suspicion. For example, children who receive tangible rewards from their mothers are less likely to help both at home and in the lab, and children frequently praised for doing the right thing become less likely to do it as time passes (Fabes, Fultz, Eisenberg, May-Plumlee, & Christopher, 1989; Grusec, 1991). Although interpretation of these studies is complicated (maybe troublesome kids get rewarded more) other research does indicate that rewarding people for doing good deeds makes them less likely to see themselves as likely to perform them spontaneously (Kunda & Schwartz, 1983).

Which brings us neatly to our next question: Why do extrinsic rewards undermine intrinsic motivation? Three different answers to this question, not mutually exclusive, have been proposed. The first, sketched out earlier, and supported by the previous Kunda and Schwartz study, has to do with self-perception. When we receive a reward for doing X, we infer that we are doing X for that reward and not for its own sake. In the absence of the reward, we cannot see why we would do X. Once the reward is taken away, therefore, we act in accord with our self-perception, and stop doing X. Lepper et al. (1973) dubbed this process overjustification, because the extrinsic reward provides, as it were, too much reason for doing X.

A second possibility is that whenever some X is portrayed as a means to an end, it comes to be regarded as undesirable because means generally are undesirable. We know this from everyday life. We brush and floss to avoid tooth decay, we dust and vacuum to keep our house clean, and we grunt and sweat to stay fit. Consequently, whenever we do X to get a reward, we are implicitly reminded of all the other times we did something undesirable to get a reward, and X automatically conjures up negative connotations. Lepper, Sagotsky, Dafoe, and Greene (1982) conducted a clever follow-up study to test this possibility. They noted first that preschool children loved to play, not only with magic markers, but also with pastel crayons. They then set up two reward contingencies. Half the children were told that, in order to play with the markers, they would first have to play with the crayons; the other half were told the opposite. The result? Two weeks later, children spent less time playing with the drawing utensil that had previously been made a precondition for playing with the other.

A third possibility is that extrinsic rewards are perceived as unpleasantly controlling. Unlike lower animals, we do not just blindly respond to carrots and sticks. We also understand and respond to the contingencies that govern their delivery. Suppose, for example, that Jasmine kisses her dog, Duke, only when Duke eats the food that Jasmine has prepared for him. This is liable to train Duke to eat such food, in accordance with well-established principles of instrumental conditioning. Duke, obedient mutt that he is, will raise no objection to this arrangement. However, suppose that Jasmine now kisses her boyfriend Jerome only when he eats the food that she has prepared for him. It is unlikely that Jerome will respond with the same dog-like docility. He will almost certainly resent the fact that Jasmine is so ungracious as to make her kisses conditional on the consumption of her food, however tasty. As a consequence, Jerome's intrinsic motivation for kissing Jasmine is likely to wane.

The example is facetious, but the principle is not. To the extent that a situation is perceived as undermining our autonomy, we will tend to withdraw from it or rebel against it (Brehm & Brehm, 1981). Whenever we work in order to obtain rewards, it feels like something outside of ourselves is determining what we do, not our inner being. We feel like pawns rather than persons. According to self-determination theory (Ryan & Deci, 2000) this amounts to a failure to satisfy one of our fundamental needs. Extrinsic rewards therefore fall into the same category as threats, deadlines, inspections, and evaluations. All have a corrosive impact on intrinsic motivation (Kohn, 1999).

In fairness to extrinsic rewards, it should be pointed out that they are not only controlling. They also provide valuable feedback about people's level of performance. This could conceivably promote intrinsic motivation, assuming that people are keen on developing their skills. However, given that such feedback could also be given in the absence of extrinsic rewards, it is hardly a compelling defense of their use.

In addition, it is often urged that praise is a better motivator than tangible reward because it is less obvious, expected, and coercive. However, to the extent that this is true, praise is no longer a bona fide incentive because it is no longer truly conditional; rather, it is an interpersonal means of acknowledging and encouraging competence. There is surely a world of difference between a mother who adamantly refuses to compliment her daughter unless she passes an exam and a mother who encourages her daughter to do so and congratulates her when she does. Indeed, part of the problem with conditional rewards is that they impair the quality of relationships, driving a wedge between the person who grants them and the person who works to receive them.

AFTERTHOUGHTS

The harmful consequences of extrinsic rewards are not, unfortunately, limited to undermining intrinsic motivation. Recall that, in the present study, children hoping to receive a Good Player Award also drew poorer quality pictures. The effect is no fluke. For example, in another study the ability of student journalists to think up catchy headlines was monitored over time. Some were paid for each headline they produced, others not. It transpired that paid students quickly reached a point at which they stopped improving, whereas unpaid students continued to improve (Deci, 1971). Indeed, whenever people perform a variety of tasks that require creative input, the result is less original and inspired when rewards have been promised in return (Amabile, Hennessey, & Grossman, 1986).

Extrinsic rewards also impair one's ability to solve problems. In one classic study, participants were presented with a box of matches, a box of thumbtacks, and a candle, and asked to mount the candle on a wall using only these materials. (Can you do it? Hint: Use *all* the materials!) Participants offered incentives of varying magnitudes to solve this problem took nearly one-and-a-half times as long as participants offered nothing (Glucksberg, 1962). Another study found that the offer of incentives interfered with participants' ability to discover a nonobvious rule (in this study, a particular sequence of key presses) and that participants were reluctant to abandon incorrect rules that had secured them rewards earlier (Schwartz, 1982).

This undermining of creativity and problem-solving presumably occurs because people are preoccupied with the prospect of receiving the reward. Tunnel-vision makes people think and act greedily and inflexibly, thereby impairing their performance in settings that call for the cool-headed consideration of complex possibilities. Indeed, when rewards are at stake, people generally choose the task that will secure those rewards most easily (Pittman, Emery, & Boggiano, 1982).

We could keep telling cautionary tales about the ill effects of incentives. However, it is better to light a candle than to curse the darkness. The pragmatic question is: How can intrinsic motivation be enhanced? In particular, what would make students approach their studies with a curious and enthusiastic mindset? This is an especially crucial question given that good grades are probably one of the most demotivating of incentives. (Just ask any college student how interested they are in learning something that will not appear on an exam!)

One promising approach is to add features to a prescribed learning activity in order to satisfy a students' underlying needs for stimulation, mastery, and autonomy. For example, take an activity as potentially offputting as learning how to use arithmetical operators in their correct hierarchical order, and how to insert parentheses that suspend the hierarchy where necessary. Cordova and Lepper (1996) had grade school children play a computer game in which success depended on optimizing the use of numbers and operators made available to them. In brief, the children had to generate the biggest number they could on each turn so that they would advance as quickly as possible toward a target number. Although the game as it stands is already appealing enough (and certainly an improvement over teaching arithmetic conventions verbally) the researchers added three features to the task in an attempt to make it more appealing still. First, they personalized the game. Rather than make general announcements, the computer addressed children by name at various key junctures (e.g., "May the force be with you, Commander Constantine!"). Second, the game was contextualized by embedding it in a fantasy scenario called *Space Quest*. Now the goal was not only to attain an arbitrary numerical target, but rather to reach the planet Ektar and pick up precious titanium deposits before the aliens did, thereby saving the Earth from a global energy crisis. Third, incidental aspects of the game were made more controllable. For example, the children could choose the type of spacecraft they would travel in (e.g., Starship) and what its name would be (e.g., Enterprise NCC 1701). Results showed that each of these embellishments powerfully enhanced children's intrinsic motivation. Thanks to their greater involvement with the task, children attempted to formulate more complex expressions, which in turn increased their rate of learning. Furthermore, children who played the embellished games showed higher levels of aspiration, and greater feelings of competence, than children who played unembellished equivalents. If comparable adaptations could be made to educational curricula across the board, taking into account what students at each stage are interested in, formal tuition would become less of a chore and strict discipline less of a necessity.

We have so far spent this chapter being critical of extrinsic motivation. However, before closing, we should mention two arguments that might be made in its favor. First, it provides an economical way of making people behave in desirable ways. A well-meaning person in a position of power may use carrots (and sticks) to pursue laudable goals when those under him or her have a preference for pursuing questionable ones. For example, a novice teacher faced with a class of pupils who enjoy misbehaving may need to establish order by dishing out rewards and punishments in a systematic fashion. Once that basic goal has been achieved, he or she can move on to nurturing their academic interests—*reculer pour mieux sauter*, as the

French say. Second, and implied by the previous point, not all intrinsic aspirations are worthy of being nurtured. For example, some people may get a kick out of bad-mouthing others behind their back, committing criminal offences, or cheating on their partner. Such activities are unlikely to afford either them or others lasting happiness. It seems right, therefore, that extrinsic controls on such behavior should be applied, either formally or informally.

REVELATION

Receiving a reward for doing something makes people want to do it more. However, when the reward is withdrawn, people want to do it even less than they did before receiving the reward.

— APG —

CHAPTER REFERENCE

Lepper, M., Greene, D., & Nisbett, R. E. (1973). Undermining children's intrinsic interest with extrinsic reward: A test of the "overjustification" hypothesis. *Journal of Personality and Social Psychology, 28,* 129–137.

OTHER REFERENCES

Amabile, T. M., Hennessey, B. A., & Grossman, B. S. (1986). Influences on creativity: The effects of contracted-for reward. *Journal of Personality and Social Psychology, 50,* 14–23.

Brehm, S. S., & Brehm, J. W. (1981). *Psychological reactance: A theory of freedom and control.* New York: Academic Press.

Cordova, D. I., & Lepper, M. R. (1996). Intrinsic motivation and the process of learning: Beneficial effects of contextualization, personalization, and choice. *Journal of Educational Psychology, 88,* 715–730.

Curry, S. J., Wagner, E. H., & Grothaus, L. C. (1991). Intrinsic and extrinsic motivation for smoking cessation. *Journal of Consulting and Clinical Psychology, 58,* 310–316.

Deci, E. L. (1971). Effects of externally mediated rewards on intrinsic motivation. *Journal of Personality and Social Psychology, 18,* 105–115.

Deci, E. L., Koestner, R., & Ryan, R. M. (1999). A meta-analytic review of experiments examining the effects of extrinsic rewards on intrinsic motivation. *Psychological Bulletin, 125,* 627–668.

Durand, D. (2000). *Perpetual motivation.* New York: ProBalance Inc.

Fabes, R. A., Fultz, J., Eisenberg, N., May-Plumlee, T., & Christopher, F. C. (1989). Effects of rewards on children's prosocial motivation: A socialization study. *Developmental Psychology, 25,* 509–515.

Glucksberg, S. (1962). The influence of strength of drive on functional fixedness and perceptual recognition. *Journal of Experimental Psychology, 63,* 34–41.

Grusec, J. E. (1991). Socializing concern for others in the home. *Developmental Psychology, 27,* 338–342.

Kohn, A. (1999). *Punished by rewards.* Boston: Houghton Mifflin.

Kunda, Z., & Schwartz, S. H. (1983). Undermining intrinsic moral motivation: External reward and self-presentation. *Journal of Personality and Social Psychology, 45,* 763–771.

Lepper, M. R., Sagotsky, G., Dafoe, J. L., & Greene, D. (1982). Consequences of superfluous social constraints: Effects on young children of social inferences and subsequent intrinsic interest. *Journal of Personality and Social Psychology, 42,* 51–65.

Pittman, T. S., Emery, J., & Boggiano, A. K. (1982). Intrinsic and extrinsic motivational orientations: Reward-induced changes in preference for complexity. *Journal of Personality and Social Psychology, 42,* 789–797.

Ryan, R. M., & Deci, E. L. (2000). Self-determination theory and the facilitation of intrinsic motivation, social development, and well-being. *American Psychologist, 55,* 68–78.

Schwartz, B. (1982). Reinforcement-induced behavioral stereotype: How not to teach people to discover rules. *Journal of Experimental Psychology: General, 111,* 23–59.

MORE TO EXPLORE

Deci, E. L., & Flaste, R. (1995). *Why we do what we do: Understanding self-motivation.* New York: Penguin.

Sansone, C., & Harackiewicz, J. M. (2000). *Intrinsic and extrinsic motivation: The search for optimal motivation and performance.* San Diego, CA: Academic Press.

Skinner, B. F. (1953). *Science and human behavior.* New York: Free Press.

9 The Calvinist's Conundrum: Unconsciously Engineering Good Omens

"… [God] has mercy on whomever He chooses, and He hardens the heart of whomever He chooses." (Romans 9:18, NRSV)
—Saint Paul (?–67 C.E.), Apostle to the Gentiles

BACKGROUND

In 16th-century France, a religious reformer named John Calvin broke away from the Catholic Church. He founded a Protestant faith whose roots lay in the teachings of Saint Paul and Saint Augustine. These saints had emphasized the absolute sovereignty of God and the need for His grace. Calvin duly took on board these views and then pushed them as far as they would go. The result was an austere and uncompromising creed, capable of instilling much fear and trembling in its adherents.

Calvin preached that people were so inherently corrupt that nothing in their nature could possibly incline them toward God. He did accept, however, that some people were genuinely devout. How was this possible? The answer, according to Calvin, was that God had predetermined that this would be so. God had, before creating the world, elected to grant a special minority of people a grace that would redeem them from Original Sin, and so make it inevitable that they worship God during their brief spell on Earth. So redeemed, these favored few, God's Elect, would enjoy a wonderful future: an eternity in heaven with their beloved Creator. However, the majority of their fellows, denied God's saving grace, would remain incapable of righteousness. Left to wallow in their wickedness, a fearsome fate would await them: everlasting agony in the fiery depths of hell.

What reasons did God have for deciding in advance who would be saved and who would be damned? Calvin was content to plead ignorance on this point. All that mattered, he claimed, was that God was God. Whatever He willed was good by definition. Still, Calvin did at least specify what God did *not* take into account: the efforts people made to live ethically. Whether or not they strove to live a life of virtue or vice had absolutely no bearing on their ultimate destiny. If people had not already been chosen by God their attempts to lead a virtuous life would come to nothing—they would roast regardless. According to Calvin, this was not unfair, because human beings were despicable to begin with, and therefore deserved to be damned. Only the receipt of God's grace could render them worthy of salvation.

Calvin's God had not seen fit to reveal to His earthly subjects whether heaven or hell awaited them. Yet he had not left them completely in the dark either. Certain signs were rumored to foretell your likely location beyond the grave. One indication of beckoning bliss was the tendency to lead an upright life. It was grounds for believing that you had already received the grace to be good, a privilege only God's Elect could receive. Calvin and his followers observed with satisfaction that they were the ones leading eminently upright lives: temperate, industrious, and frugal.

You may already sense the potential that Calvinism had to tie its adherents up in mental knots. Suppose that, as a devout Calvinist, you notice in yourself an urge to sin. Should you try to resist it? From one point of view, it should not even matter whether you do or do not. Your fate has already been decided, so you might as well give in to your ungodliness. Yet what if you gallantly strive to overcome that sinful urge anyway? No good either. As mentioned earlier, Calvinism holds that willpower is irrelevant to salvation. Even worse, God's Elect should not even be tempted to sin, because God's grace should make righteousness in both thought and deed inescapable. Hence, the experience of temptation alone should bring beads of sweat to the brows of sincere Calvinists.

How did Calvinists cope with the temptations they surely felt? George Quattrone and Amos Tversky (1980) suggested that, although Calvinists did try to resist temptation, they denied that they were doing so. That is, they strove to be virtuous unconsciously. This psychological trick allowed them to interpret their virtue as a comforting sign of salvation rather than as a chilling sign of damnation.

The researchers saw this trick as one example of a general form of self-deception: the tendency to perform, without admitting it, actions *diagnostic* of (indicating), but *causally unrelated* to (unable to influence), desired outcomes. In order to test whether this form of self-deception existed, the researchers reproduced a clever small-scale variant of the Calvinist's predicament in the experimental laboratory.

WHAT THEY DID

Participants in Quattrone and Tversky's study underwent a bogus medical exam, the results of which supposedly indicated their future medical status. The results of that exam could, of course, in no way influence their medical status. Participants' underlying condition would remain the same regardless of the exam's results. However, by making the results of the exam behavioral in nature, the researchers hoped to show that participants would alter its results so as to predict that their health prospects were promising. The researchers also hoped to show, by asking participants why they had behaved as they did, that they had no awareness of altering their exam results. This would be consistent with participants engaging in motivated self-deception, convincing themselves that the results of the exam were diagnostic of a favorable future medical status, even when they had fixed its results.

It happened like this. Thirty-eight undergraduate students signed up to take part in a study on the psychological and medical aspects of athletics. The female experimenter who greeted them explained that the purpose of the study was to investigate how, after a session of vigorous exercise, abrupt changes in body temperature would affect the cardiovascular system. Athletes sometimes take a cold shower immediately after working out. Could this refreshing activity nonetheless stress the heart, possibly damaging it in the long term? To add to the credibility of the cover story, the

FIG. 9.1. John Calvin,
preacher of predestination.

study was run in the physiology wing of the psychology department, where hi-tech equipment and bottled chemicals were much in evidence. The experimenter also wore the obligatory white lab coat.

Participants began with a so-called cold pressor test. They placed both their forearms in a cooler full of ice water and kept them submerged for as long as they could. Though physically harmless, the cold pressor test proved challenging. The majority of participants felt compelled to withdraw their forearms in less than a minute. Nonetheless, for as long as they kept their forearms submerged, they rated their degree of discomfort every 5 seconds in response to prompts by the experimenter. These prompts took the form of letters, spoken aloud in alphabetical order. Participants replied to these prompts by saying aloud a number between 1 and 10, where 1 reflected no problem tolerating the cold, and 10 an inability to tolerate it further. The reason for prompting participants with ascending letters of the alphabet was to allow them to keep track of how long they had kept their hands submerged. This information would later enable them to make a crucial comparison.

So far as participants were concerned, the purpose of this phase of the study was to get a baseline measure of heart rate following an abrupt change in body temperature. The apparent purpose of the next phase was to determine whether a period of vigorous exercise would change these results. After finishing the cold pressor test, therefore, participants pedaled an exercise bicycle as hard as they could for 60 seconds. Then, after a short break, they completed a second cold pressor test. To ensure that participants remained convinced of the cover story, the experimenter went through the motions of measuring their pulse at appropriate intervals.

The true purpose of study, of course, was not to measure the impact of temperature and exercise on heart rate, but rather to permit a test of the hypothesis that participants would alter their behavior unconsciously in order to make it diagnostic of some desired outcome. The behavior the researchers chose to focus on was participants' performance on the second cold pressor test. They made participants' performance on this task appear relevant to their future health prospects by persuading them during the break period that the ability to endure cold following a period of exercise had implications for cardiovascular fitness. The expectation was that participants would alter their performance on the second cold pressor test in the direction that implied greater coronary fitness.

How were participants led to believe that their performance on the second cold pressor test had a bearing on their future health prospects? During the break period, the experimenter gave participants a complimentary lecture. Participants assumed that this lecture was merely to occupy them to good pedagogical purpose while they were waiting for the next phase of the study to begin. However, its real purpose was to convey bogus medical information that would motivate participants to engage in outcome-diagnostic behavior.

It was claimed in the lecture that the cold pressor test was used to study the psychophysics of pain. (Psychophysics is the branch of experimental psychology that investigates how the objective properties of stimuli relate to subjective perceptions of them.) Participants were shown a graph illustrating the relation between forearm immersion time and levels of subjective discomfort. It was explained that this relation differed from person to person as a function of skin type and heart type. With respect to the heart type, participants were informed that everyone possessed either one or another cardiovascular complexes, referred to, for the sake of brevity, as Type I or Type II hearts. A Type II heart was allegedly associated with a longer life span than a Type I heart, a fact vividly illustrated by another graph. The experimenter explained that, although people with Type I and Type II hearts did not normally differ in how much pain they could tolerate, a prior period of vigorous exercise could bring out the difference. The idea was to persuade participants that their performance on the second cold pressor test would have implications for how long they would live.

Then came the neat point in the experimental design. Half the participants were told that people with a Type II heart would be more tolerant of cold pressor pain after exercise, whereas half were told that such people would be less tolerant of it (in both cases, relative to people with a Type I heart). It was predicted that participants in the former condition would alter their behavior to show an increased tolerance for pain, whereas participants in the latter condition would alter their behavior to show a decreased tolerance for pain. Such shifts in tolerance would indicate that participants were motivated to manufacture evidence that an auspicious future lay in store for them.

The seemingly odd way in which participants reported their levels of discomfort can now be seen to make sense. The alphabetized prompts, administered every 5 seconds, permitted them to compare how much time they spent tolerating pain during the first cold pressor test to how much time they spent tolerating it during the second. If they were motivated to unconsciously adjust their performance during the second test, they would have guidelines for how to do it.

A different experimenter administered the second cold pressor test. This was done for two reasons. First, it was necessary to guard against the possibility that the experimenter, familiar with participants' earlier performance, might inadvertently influence their later performance, or record participants' responses with bias. Second, it was necessary to guard against the possibility that shifts in participants' performance would occur merely to please the experimenter, thereby complicating interpretation of the results. Participants were openly told that each experimenter would not know about the results collected by the other, so that neither would have the two pieces of information needed to infer their likely heart type. To reinforce this impression, the replacement experimenter dressed in casual clothing, suggesting that he was there solely for the purposes of adminis-tering the second test.

After the second cold pressor test had been completed, the experi-menter gave participants a brief questionnaire to complete which con-tained two critical items. The first asked participants whether they believed they had a Type I or a Type II heart. The second asked them whether they had purposely tried to alter the amount of time they kept their forearms in the water during the second cold pressor test.

WHAT THEY FOUND

Did participants shift their level of pain tolerance in the direction they be-lieved was correlated with having a robust Type II heart? Yes. Participants told that people with a Type II heart were more tolerant of cold kept their forearms submerged for a longer time during the second cold pressor test. Conversely, participants told that people with a Type II were less tolerant of cold kept their forearms submerged for a shorter time during the second cold pressor test (Fig. 9.2). Individual analyses revealed that roughly two-thirds of participants in both conditions showed the predicted shift, with the remaining third showing no shift at all (except for one who showed a shift in the opposite direction, enigmatically described by the research-ers, without further elaboration, as a suicidal type). Participants were evi-dently altering their behavior to make it diagnostic of favorable health prospects, even though this alteration obviously could not influence what sort of heart, Type I or Type II, they already had.

Were participants aware of changing the amount of time they kept their forearms submerged? By and large they were not: 29 of the 38 participants denied attempting any change. (Interestingly, deniers and admitters did not differ in terms of their actual behavior. In both conditions, roughly the same proportion of participants altered their behavior, and to roughly the same extent.) The fact that most participants were unconscious of altering their behavior on purpose, in conjunction with the fact that their behavior really did alter in the direction linked to better health prospects, suggests that they were guilty of unconscious self-deception. Such results are in line with the hypothesis that people will suppress awareness that they have de-liberately performed an action whose results tend to be a sign of some de-sired outcome. The deliberate performance of the action, of course, means that the action is no longer a sign of that outcome.

Participants who showed the predicted shift in pain tolerance were also verbally asked why they had shifted. The typical response given was that the temperature of the water had changed. This is consistent with self-decep-tion, attributing behavior to an external stimulus rather than an internal motivation. However, it might be argued that participants were simply re-luctant to publicly admit that they had deliberately modified their behavior.

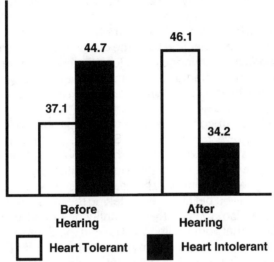

Before Hearing	After Hearing

☐ Heart Tolerant ■ Heart Intolerant

FIG. 9.2. The number of seconds that participants kept their forearms in ice water, before and after hearing that a healthy heart is tolerant or intolerant of cold.

This contention, however, is less plausible in the light of a final set of findings. Of the 29 participants who denied intentionally altering how long they kept their hands immersed in the water, 20 of them (69%) also privately reported inferring that they had a Type II heart. In contrast, only two of the nine participants (22%) who admitted intentionally altering their responses also privately reported that inference. In other words, the majority of deniers privately inferred that their future health prospects were good whereas the majority of admitters privately inferred that their future health prospects were poor. Thus, denial went hand in hand with comforting beliefs, and admission with disquieting ones. This suggests that participants' reports of their intentions were the result of genuine self-deception rather than superficial self-presentation.

SO WHAT?

It is often claimed in casual conversation that people deceive themselves with regard to their motives. Though this claim may be plausible in principle, the evidence for it in particular cases is often weak. The great achievement of the present study was to demonstrate that self-deception exists in one particular form: not admitting to yourself that you have purposefully altered some sign to make it appear that some desired outcome is likely.

It is easy to think up real-world examples where this form of self-deception might operate. Suppose, for example, that you suspect you might be suffering from a serious disease one symptom of which is a loss of appetite. As matters stand either you have the disease or you do not—nothing you can do now is going change that. Nevertheless, do you not find yourself eating a little more than usual? Does not the knowledge that you are managing to eat a hearty dinner provide you with a measure of illusory reassurance?

Unfortunately, the unconscious steps that people take to reassure themselves can have grave repercussions. Suppose again that you suspect yourself of having a serious disease, but that the only way to know for sure is to undergo further medical testing. Unaccountably, you procrastinate, make excuses, go about your daily business as usual. Why? Could it be because at some level you believe that not taking the tests is not only a sign of good health, but also a factor that can influence good health? In other words, do you feel that your likelihood of having the disease is increased by your taking the test or decreased by your not taking it? Rationally, this makes no sense at all, but the false logic can prove intuitively seductive. You kid yourself by refusing to admit that you are avoiding the medical tests out of concern for what they might reveal. To make such an admission, however, would prevent you from irrationally regarding not taking the tests as an indication of good health. The irony is that, although procrastination may provide some temporary psychological benefit, it may fatally delay the administration of life-saving medical treatment.

Our tendency to fabricate good omens expresses itself in other ways. Consider, for example, a second study conducted by Quattrone and Tversky (1980), published alongside the one reported here. In that study, the researchers attempted to provide an answer to a classic conundrum: Why do people bother to vote at all? Any individual vote has near zero chance of exerting a decisive impact in an election, so why turn out at all? Various explanations for this irrational behavior have been suggested. Typically, these appeal to a sense of civic duty or democratic idealism. However, Quattrone and Tversky (1980) put forward a different hypothesis. They argued that people vote because they believe that how they vote is a sign of how like-minded others will vote, and hence (by the twisted logic of self-deception) is an influence over how like-minded others will vote. Their results supported this curious hypothesis.

We conclude this section by describing another phenomenon that involves self-deception: *defensive self-handicapping* (Jones & Berglas, 1978). Oddly enough, people sometimes deliberately harm their chances of performing well on an important test. The reason? Fearing that failure is in the cards, but unwilling to conclude that they cannot succeed, people unconsciously prearrange circumstances so that they favor failure. This allows them to attribute failure, if it occurs, to those circumstances, and to deny responsibility for prearranging it. A prime example would be a student who lets his friends talk him into going drinking the night before a test, and who then blames his poor test performance on his hangover, which, of course, he never "meant" to cause. It seems that if people cannot change their performance to make it signify a desirable state of affairs (as participants in the present study did) they may try to change circumstances so that their performance at least does not signify an undesirable state of affairs. In the case of defensive self-handicapping, the undesirable state of affairs is the shame of admitting incompetence.

AFTERTHOUGHTS

The present study documented one way that people deceive themselves with regard to their motives. Yet a puzzling question remains. How exactly does self-deception operate? How can people intend to do something yet be unaware that they are intending to do it?

Classic accounts of self-deception resolve the paradox by splitting the mind in two. An unconscious mind is postulated to possess an intelligence comparable to, or greater than, that of the conscious mind. This unconscious mind knows the true reasons for a person's behavior; indeed, it makes a person behave in those ways. Moreover, this unconscious mind keeps the conscious mind blissfully ignorant of all its activities. According to this view, the unconscious minds of participants in the present study knew that varying forearm immersion time would invalidate the cold pressor test. Nonetheless, these unconscious minds made the participants vary it anyhow, secure in the knowledge that their conscious minds would never find out.

This sort of account is highly problematic. It implies that there are two people inhabiting your head, one of whom is fooling the other. It boils down to invoking multiple personality disorder to explain self-deception, a rather drastic ploy. There is little evidence for such a sophisticated arrangement, but even if there were, it would in any case raise more questions than it answers. For example, if the unconscious mind deceives the conscious mind, why does it do so? Does it have a naturally deceitful character? And does the unconscious mind knowingly deceive the conscious mind? If so, would not that imply it was itself conscious? In addition, might there even be yet another unconscious mind deceiving it? The more one thinks about, the more the split-mind account of self-deception seems to miss the essence of the phenomenon.

Greenwald (1988) provided a more plausible model of self-deception. The central contention of the model is that it is possible to avoid threatening information without exhaustively analyzing it first. An analogy to junk mail, of all things, makes this clear. When junk mail arrives, you do not need to open the envelope and read its contents in order to identify it. The telltale signs are already plain to see: bulk postage rates, low-quality paper, a flurry of exclamation marks. As a result, perfunctory inspection is enough to identify junk mail as such. The same is true of threatening information. It can be recognized as uncongenial on the basis of superficial cues. Moreover, once it has been so recognized, evasive mental maneuvers can be taken. If one has noticed the information, one can opt not to pay further attention to it; or, if one has paid attention to it, one can avoid trying to understand it; or, if one has understood it, one can refuse to draw logical inferences from it. In every case, one steers clear of realizations that create unpleasant feelings. Note how this solves the paradox of self-deception. If information perceived at a lower level of awareness has a negative ring to it then further processing at a higher level is avoided. The mechanism behind self-deception therefore involves not dwelling on information that shows signs of being uncongenial (Frey, 1986; Taylor, 1991).

Consider participants in the present study again. After the lecture, they presumably wanted to keep their forearms immersed in the ice water for a longer or shorter period of time. The likely result was a subtle strengthening or weakening of their resolve (see chap. 13 for how goals can be unconsciously triggered). At some point thereafter, participants may have become dimly aware of a temptation to alter their results. However, they may have suppressed this awareness, let it pass out of their mind naturally, or chose not to elaborate upon its implications, because they realized that succumbing to this temptation would invalidate the test. Yet, the strength of their underlying resolve had perhaps already been influenced after hearing the lecture. Hence, participants may have found themselves, by the time they had their hands in the cooler, possessing or not possessing the resolve to continue. Given that people are not experts on the origins of their own mental processes (Nisbett & Wilson, 1977; see chap. 1) it is no surprise that they would be unable to tell that it was the lecture that had affected their resolve rather than the temperature of the water itself. Certainly, many psychological processes must come together for self-deception to occur, but the avoidance of threatening information is a key component.

In conclusion, self-deception is not the result of one center of intelligence hoodwinking the other. Rather, it is the result of a low-level screening process that banishes suspicious-seeming cognitions before they have the opportunity to be fully entertained by the conscious mind.

REVELATION

People deceive themselves by acting so as to create signs that everything is well even when they cannot make everything well. They then deny that they have acted in this way, because admitting as much would imply that those signs are bogus.

— *APG* —

CHAPTER REFERENCE

Quattrone, G. A., & Tversky, A. (1980). Causal versus diagnostic reasoning: On self-deception and the voter's illusion. *Journal of Personality and Social Psychology, 46,* 237–248.

OTHER REFERENCES

Frey, D. (1986). Recent research on selective exposure to information. In L. Berkowitz (Ed.), *Advances in experimental social psychology* (Vol. 19, pp. 41–80). New York: Academic Press.
Greenwald, A. G. (1988). Self-knowledge and self-deception. In J. S. Lockard & D. L. Paulhaus (Eds.), *Self-deception: An adaptive mechanism?* (pp. 113–131). Englewood Cliffs, NJ: Prentice Hall.
Jones, E. E., & Berglas, S. (1978). Control of attributions about the self through self-handicapping strategies: The appeal of alcohol and the role of underachievement. *Personality and Social Psychology Bulletin, 4,* 200–206.
Nisbett, R. E., & Wilson, T. D. (1977). Telling more than we can know: Verbal reports on mental processes. *Psychological Review, 84,* 231–259.
Taylor, S. E. (1991). Asymmetrical effects of positive and negative events. The mobilization-minimization hypothesis. *Psychological Bulletin, 110,* 67–85.

MORE TO EXPLORE

Giannetti E. (2000). *Lies we live by: The art of self-deception.* London: Bloomsbury.
Greenwald, A. G. (1980). The totalitarian ego: Fabrication and revision of personal history. *American Psychologist, 35,* 603–618.

10 Pitfalls of Purpose: Ironic Processes in Mood Control

"The best-laid schemes of mice and men / Often go astray / And leave us nought but grief and pain / For promised joy!"
—Robert Burns (1759–1796), Scottish poet

BACKGROUND

As the hit movie *Ghostbusters* careers toward its conclusion, its four reluctant heroes—Spengler, Venkman, Stantz, and Widdemore—find themselves facing off against an evil demigod. In a rasping voice, the demigod addresses them:

> Subcreatures! Gozer the Gozerian, Gozer the Destructor, Volguus Zildrohar, the Traveler, has come! Choose and perish!

The Ghostbusters wonder what these ominous words might mean. Spengler is the first to catch on. He explains to the others that Gozer is about to bring about a calamity of cosmic proportions. However, the precise form this calamity will take depends on whatever they are currently thinking about. Frantically, the Ghostbusters yell at one another not to think of anything. A moment later, however, Gozer declares:

> The choice is made! The Traveler has come!

With matters going from bad to worse, Venkman angrily demands to know who thought of something. Both Spengler and Widdemore protest their innocence. All eyes turn slowly to Stantz. He whimpers in self-defense:

I couldn't help it! It just popped in there!

In the background, booming footsteps can be heard, growing louder with each passing moment. Then, out of the metropolitan night, the dreaded Agent of Destruction emerges. A terrifying colossus, he towers above the city streets. Yet there is something distinctly odd about him. His entire body is white and pudgy. He wears a dinky sailor's hat and a smart blue scarf. The Agent of Destruction is—no, it can't be!—*Mr. StayPuft*, the Marshmallow Man! Contemplating this 300-foot tall mass of malevolent goo, the deadpan Venkman comments: "Good job, Ray!"

The above is a salutary (if reassuringly fictional) reminder of how our mental control can break down under precisely those circumstances where it is most crucial to maintain it. You will probably recall times when your own attempts to master your mind failed. You tried to forget your cares and fall asleep but stayed awake worrying. You tried to study for an exam but could not help fantasizing about your lover. But equally, you may recall times when your attempts to master your mind succeeded. You were irked by a casual insult but still managed to stay cool. You lost a large sum of money but did not let that spoil your evening. Such varied outcomes raise an interesting question. Why do some of our attempts at mental control succeed but others fail?

FIG. 10.1.   Delicious yet malicious: The Marshmallow Man.

A partial answer to the question is provided by research on willpower. Consider for a moment how a muscle works. When vigorously exercised, it loses strength, but when allowed to relax, its strength returns. Research shows that the human will operates in a similar way. Its strength is expended through use but replenished by rest. The expenditure of willpower is technically known as *ego depletion*.

In one memorable study (Baumeister, Bratslavsky, Muraven, & Tice, 1998) participants were seated in front of two plates. One was filled with scrumptious freshly baked cookies, the other with unappetizing raw radishes. The experimenter instructed participants to consume items from one plate only (either cookies or radishes). He then left them alone for a few minutes. When he returned, he had them complete a problem-solving task that required them to copy two geometrical figures, without lifting pen from paper. Unbeknown to participants, the task was impossible to complete. The point, however, was to measure how long they persisted in the face of certain frustration. It turned out that participants who had eaten the radishes (i.e., avoided eating the cookies) gave up sooner than participants who had eaten the cookies. Thus, resisting temptation uses up some willpower so that less of it is available for use on subsequent tasks. Additional studies showed that willpower could also be depleted by bottling up feelings or by making choices repeatedly. Is it any wonder, then, that we sometimes blow our top after a succession of small annoyances, or that we are as exhausted by a shopping expedition as by a vigorous hike? The moral of the story is that willpower is a limited resource. Mental control succeeds when it is available but fails when it is not.

However, failures of mental control are due to more than just ego depletion. Our minds also have a built-in kink that can confound even a will of iron. This kink comes to light when attempts at mental control not only fail but backfire. Familiar examples include becoming more wakeful while trying to fall asleep, or collapsing in a fit of giggles when trying to keep a straight face. How can such obviously unintended outcomes be explained? According to Wegner (1994), they are best understood as the result of an interaction between two psychological processes.

The first of these is the *intentional operating process*, or intender for short. It consists of the conscious, deliberate, and effortful attempt to seek out mental contents that match some desired mental state. For example, to improve our mood, the intender steers our attention toward cheery thoughts and diverts it away from gloomy ones.

Although the intender is in charge of exerting mental control, it often acts on information gathered by its undercover accomplice, the *ironic monitoring process*, or monitor for short. Behind the scenes, invisible yet all-seeing, the monitor checks that no unwanted intruders have penetrated the psychological fortress. If they have, it dispatches the intender to deal with them. Cloak-and-dagger metaphors aside, the monitor's role is to signal failures of mental control to the intender so it can act upon them.

Matters work in reverse too. The intender can also trigger the monitor. In particular, whenever the intender attempts to realize a particular mental state, the monitor looks for specific failures to realize it. For example, if your intender sought not to think of Mr. StayPuft, your monitor would be on guard specifically for thoughts of Mr. Staypuft.

A key feature of the monitor is that it operates covertly. If news of every little mental mishap reached consciousness, the resulting brouhaha would bamboozle the conscious mind, making self-control quite impossible. In that sense, the monitor really does resemble a spy. If its cover is blown, it cannot do its job.

How does all of the aforementioned help to explain why mental control sometimes backfires? The key point is that the intender and monitor place different demands upon the mind. The first, being conscious and effortful, makes heavy use of available mental resources; the second, being automatic and efficient, makes much lighter use of them. So, if mental resources are taxed by some secondary task, thereby imposing a *cognitive load*, the functioning of the intender will be impaired relative to the functioning of the monitor. However, although distractions undermine the capacity of the intender to control mental content, they do not undermine the capacity of the intender to trigger the monitor. The mere intention to exert control is enough. Taken together, these two facts set the stage for the occurrence of ironic reversals under cognitive load.

Suppose that, as Síobhan studies for an upcoming statistics exam, her conscious mind is focused on thoughts of means, modes, and medians. However, somewhere at the fringes of her consciousness is the thought that her period is late. Her monitor dutifully signals to her intender that an unwanted thought is lurking. However, because she is devoting most of her available mental resources to studying, her intender is hamstrung, and unable to banish the worrisome thought. The intender repeatedly attempts to banish the thought, but the only effect is to prompt further vigilance on the part of the monitor, which now signals with greater insistence that this particular unwanted thought is present. In desperation, the intender redoubles its resolve to suppress the thought. Unfortunately, this merely initiates a self-reinforcing loop, in which ever more effortful attempts at mental control result in ever more frustrating failures to achieve it. Soon, Síobhan's consciousness is awash with the very thought that her intender sought to banish, thanks to all the attention that her monitor has drawn to it. Her determined concentration on means, modes, and medians gives way to a resigned preoccupation with potential pregnancy. Note that these dynamics would not have occurred if sufficient mental resources had been available, if Síobhan had, for example, been relaxing on her study break. In that case, the intender would have had a good chance of successfully suppressing the unwanted thought.

Ironic process theory, which we have been describing, applies across a wide range of psychological phenomena. In this chapter, we focus on how it applies to a single phenomenon: mood. Wegner, Erber, and Zanakos (1993) predicted that attempts to deliberately alter mood, though normally successful, would backfire when people were placed under cognitive load. Moreover, they predicted that this would occur both when people tried to improve their negative moods and when they tried to worsen their positive ones. Admittedly, trying to worsen a positive mood is a rather perverse undertaking. However, it made good sense as an experimental goal because it allowed a surprising implication of ironic process theory to be tested, namely, that deliberately trying to feel worse, under cognitive load, makes you feel better.

WHAT THEY DID

Mood control can obviously only be attempted when people are actually *in* a mood. So the first step for Wegner et al. (1993) was to induce moods in their experimental participants. To this end, they asked 184 female and 105 male undergraduates to think back to a significant event in their life and to recall the concrete details of that event as vividly as they could ("picture the event happening to you," "think of what was going through your mind at the time"). Some participants were told to recall a happy event, others a sad one.

The experimenter then said aloud one of several phrases with a view to manipulating what participants did with their self-induced moods. Some participants in the happy memory condition were told to relive the happiness associated with the remembered event, others to avoid reliving it. Similarly, some participants in the sad memory condition were told to relive their sadness, others not to. In addition, to provide a baseline against which the effects of the mood-control instructions could be evaluated, the experimenter did not give any mood-control instructions to another group, whose members included participants from both the happy and sad memory groups.

Note that trying to feel happy, and not to feel sad, represent attempts to improve mood, while trying to feel sad, and not to feel happy, represent attempts to worsen mood. The reason that the researchers included both kinds of instruction was to test a subtle secondary hypothesis, namely, that deliberate attempts to induce a mood under cognitive load would produce weaker ironic effects than deliberate attempts to suppress it. The researchers' reasoning was as follows. When mental suppression—trying not to think or feel something—backfires under cognitive load, the ironic result will be specific, that is, consciousness will be flooded with precisely that mental content that the intender is trying to eliminate (e.g., happy for sad, sad for happy). However, when mental induction—trying to think or feel something—backfires, the result will be nonspecific, that is, a mix of contents will flood consciousness (happy and neutral for sad, sad and neutral for happy). So, if you tried not to feel sad under cognitive load you would end up more ironically sad than if you simply tried to feel happy. Similarly, if you tried not to feel happy under cognitive load you will feel more ironically happy than if you simply tried to feel sad.

Returning to the details of the procedure, the researchers further subdivided participants on the basis of the cognitive load imposed upon them. Half of them were required to remember until the end of the study a nonrepeating 9-digit number (e.g., 175263948).

To summarize the experimental design: All participants were asked to recall memories that either put them in a happy or a sad mood. While recalling these memories, some participants tried to worsen their mood (by trying to be sad if recalling happy memories, or trying not to be happy if recalling sad memories) while others tried to improve their mood (by trying to be happy if recalling sad memories, or trying not to be sad if recalling happy memories). Still other participants did not try to change their mood at all. In each of these three conditions, half the participants were saddled with a cognitive load, the other half not.

After 7 minutes of reminiscence, participants provided a report of their final mood. This was the main dependent variable on which ironic effects were predicted to emerge. Participants rated how happy or sad they felt along a series of scales. Extra scales assessing levels of tension or relaxation were also included to verify that the experimental manipulations had affected feelings of happiness and sadness specifically.

Participants were also asked to write down whatever thoughts came to mind while recalling happy or sad events from their lives. During the period in which they did so, the experimenter absented himself so as to avoid potentially biasing their reports. The written protocols that participants produced were then given to two trained assistants to code for mood-relevant content.

One final detail is worth remarking on. The study had been advertised as an investigation into how doing one mental task affects performance on another. In keeping with this cover story, the researchers had participants engage in a period of free writing prior to beginning the study proper. The purpose of including this initial phase was to encourage participants to draw the erroneous inference that the purpose of the study was to assess how free writing influenced subsequent measures and manipulations. Throwing participants off the scent ensured that the experimental hypotheses would not be inadvertently confirmed or refuted by savvy participants trying to please or peeve the experimenter.

WHAT THEY FOUND

The first noteworthy finding of the study was that the mood control instructions had no overall impact on mood. That is to say, participants told to improve their mood (by trying to be happy or not to be sad) were no happier on average than participants told to worsen their mood (by trying to be sad or not to be happy). The mood of participants in either condition was equal to that of participants who were given no mood control instructions. Does this mean, then, that the mood control manipulation was simply ineffective?

A closer look at the data reveals not. Participants' attempts at mood control produced diametrically opposite results depending on whether or not they were under cognitive load. When participants had no digits to remember, they successfully improved or worsened their mood just as they intended. However, when they did have digits to remember, their attempts at mood control backfired. Trying to improve their mood only made their mood worse, while trying to worsen their mood only made their mood better. This is a clear confirmation of the predictions of ironic process theory. The contrary trends obtained, in the presence and absence of cognitive load respectively, were about equal in magnitude. The mood control manipulation had no overall effect only because the intended and ironic effects, both substantial, canceled one another out (Fig. 10.2).

The researchers also obtained some evidence that attempting to suppress a mood produced stronger ironic effects than attempting to induce a mood. Participants under cognitive load who tried to suppress a mood failed miserably in the attempt, whereas participants who tried to cultivate a mood did not fail quite so miserably. However, the differential failure rate was not particularly large. One reason might have been that, in the absence of strict warnings to the contrary, participants instructed to cultivate a mood might sometimes have tried to suppress its opposite, while partici-

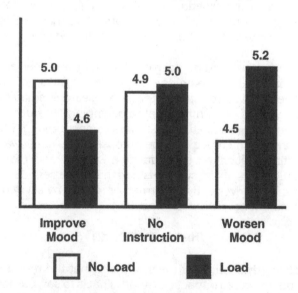

FIG. 10.2.   Happiness of participants instructed to improve their mood, worsen their mood, or do neither, when they were under, or not under, cognitive load.

pants instructed to suppress a mood might sometimes have tried to culti-vate its opposite. This would have undermined the difference between the suppression and cultivation conditions.

The researchers also analyzed participants' thought-listings for positive or negative content. It was expected that the results here would mimic those for self-reported mood. Sure enough, in the absence of cognitive load, participants instructed to improve their mood wrote down more posi-tive thoughts than participants instructed to worsen their mood (with par-ticipants given no mood-control instructions falling in between). However, under cognitive load, ironic reversals did not emerge: there was no signifi-cant difference in the positivity of participants' listed thoughts across the three conditions. Only when mental control succeeded did participants' thoughts match their eventual mood, not when mental control backfired.

What accounts for the curious discrepancy? One possibility is that the re-quirement of remembering a 9-digit number may have interfered with partic-ipants' ability to write down meaningful thoughts capable of taking on a positive or negative character. Instead, participants may have limited them-selves to expressing brief, scattered thoughts, and noting them down dryly.

However, a final study by Wegner and his colleagues (1993) again found clear-cut ironic effects. In that study, the index of interest was the accessi-bility of positive and negative thoughts, or the degree to which those thoughts are active in the mind. Mental accessibility can be measured by how distracted people are by relevant stimuli, or by how they interpret am-biguous stimuli. Results showed that suppressing mood, though it nor-mally reduced the accessibility of mood-related thoughts, ironically increased it when participants were placed under cognitive load.

SO WHAT?

The present study demonstrated that deliberate attempts to control mood backfire when mental resources are scarce. This may help to explain the or-igin and persistence of some forms of depression and anxiety. Due to exter-nal demands, or poor multitasking skills, some people may find themselves continually under cognitive load. As a result, their best efforts to cheer up or calm down may only make their symptoms worse.

On the bright side, however, the present study also suggests three strat-egies that people might use to improve psychological performance. First: Take steps to minimize ongoing cognitive load so that mental resources are freed up. Second: Stop trying to obsessively control your mind, as Eastern religions like Buddhism and Taoism have long recommended (Smullyan, 1992). Note that both of these strategies would also protect against ego-depletion, mentioned in the Background section. Third: Deliberately try to induce unwanted symptoms in order to take ironic advantage of the cognitive load, and thereby alleviate those symptoms.

The idea that the deliberate cultivation of unwanted psychological states could be psychologically beneficial is not new. The existential psychologist Frankl (1963) recommended the use of *paradoxical intention* as a therapeutic technique. Take people who suffer from alektorophobia, a morbid dread of chickens. Frankl would have recommended that, instead of trying to escape their fear (by mentally tuning out every time chickens are mentioned) they should instead try to intensify it by deliberately calling to mind flapping feathers and squawking beaks. This would force patients to face their fear and allow them to reclaim their psychological autonomy. However, the idea of using cognitive load to unlock the power of paradoxical intention is a theoretical innovation unique to ironic process theory.

In this regard, consider a symptom that plagues many of us from time to time—insomnia. As we settle down to sleep, worries can no longer be diluted by external distractions. As a consequence, we must rely on purely internal means of keeping worries at bay. This can be difficult, especially if our mind is already tired, and ego-depletion has set in. The very worries that monopolize our attention can impose their own cognitive load. Is it any wonder, then, that our determined attempts to fall asleep sometimes result in persistent wakefulness?

In a test of whether insomnia could be ironically engineered, participants were told either to fall asleep or to stay awake when they were or were not under cognitive load (Ansfield, Wegner, & Bowser, 1996). Given the impropriety of burdening participants with real worries, the researchers manipulated cognitive load in another way. They had half the participants listen to upbeat attention-grabbing music (John Philip Sousa marches) and the other half listen to soothing background music (New Age vibes). In the soothing condition, where cognitive load was low, participants who tried to fall asleep predictably nodded off more quickly than participants who tried to stay awake. However, in the upbeat condition, where cognitive load was high, the reverse occurred. Participants who tried to stay awake actually nodded off more quickly than participants who tried to fall asleep. The practical implication is clear. If your noisy neighbors are throwing a party late at night you should struggle to stay awake.

The significance of ironic process theory extends beyond explaining psychiatric symptoms. Have you ever found yourself, to your great embarrassment, saying exactly the opposite of what you intended to say? Freud (1914) famously drew attention to such slips of the tongue. He argued that they reflected unconscious impulses erupting into everyday speech. However, more mundane explanations are possible. Verbal slips may reflect a combination of syntactic mix-ups and situational priming, as when a male traveler mistakenly asks a busty ticket clerk for "a picket to Titsburgh." Nonetheless, given that slips of the tongue are certainly unintended acts, it would be surprising if ironic process theory did not throw some light on them.

Ironic process theory predicts that slips of the tongue will occur when people try hard to avoid saying something. Take, for example, sexist language. Closet chauvinists must watch their words and intentionally avoid making potentially insulting remarks about the, ahem, strength-impaired sex. Could being mentally busy interfere with their efforts at self-censorship? In a test of this hypothesis (Wegner, 1994), student participants were asked to say aloud a number of sentence fragments that could be completed in either a sexist or nonsexist manner (e.g., women who go out with a lot of men are extroverts–shameless). Given no special instructions, participants made slightly fewer sexist completions when mentally busy than when not. However, when explicitly instructed to avoid being sexist, participants made a far greater number of sexist completions when mentally busy than when not. Interestingly, the tendency to show this effect was unrelated to participants' attitudes toward women. These findings imply that a genuine feminist trying hard not to be sexist would be as prone to stereotypical slips as a chauvinist pig trying to please his liberal audience. In other words, slips of the tongue are evidence, not of unconscious sentiments, but of conscious attempts at mental control.

Ironic process theory nicely explains and correctly predicts a range of paradoxical intentional phenomena. It is proof that scientific psychology can address the same puzzling quirks of motivation that Freudian psychoanalysis did and provide more plausible and empirically grounded accounts of them. Nonetheless, like all medium-range psychological theories, it still leaves a number of important questions unanswered. For example, even in the absence of mental load, suppressed thoughts rebound back into consciousness (Wegner, Schneider, Carter, & White, 1987). This suggests that mental control is intrinsically imperfect. One intriguing study found that participants who spent time suppressing a negative stereotype of skinheads later sat further away from a chair that had been temporarily vacated by a skinhead (Macrae, Bodenhausen, Milne, & Jetten, 1994). Apparently, compressing our mental springs only makes them decompress with greater force when we release them. Second, although mental state and cognitive load can be operationally distinguished in the laboratory, they tend to get mixed up in everyday life. Suppose I have a persistent worry that I wish to control. Does that worry, in virtue of preoccupying my thoughts, not impose a cognitive load by itself? Complications like this muddy the conceptual waters a bit.

AFTERTHOUGHTS

Ironic process theory is a scientific account of how the mind exerts control over itself. It seeks to explain self-control causally, by specifying, for example, how two mental systems, the intender and monitor, interact with one another. Although many readers would accept that an unconscious system like the monitor could run like clockwork, enmeshed in a web of causes and effects, fewer would accept that a conscious system like the intender could operate in the same way. This is because what our intender does—what we intend to do—does not seem inevitably determined by impersonal factors; instead, it seems that it is we who do the determining. In other words, we are powerfully persuaded, by our own subjective experiences, that we possess *free will*.

A hard-nosed social psychologist might here voice skepticism. How much credence, she might ask, can we give to our subjective impressions? Research shows that being self-conscious does not give us special insight into how our minds work (Nisbett & Wilson, 1977; see chap. 1). Research also shows that stimuli outside our awareness can subtly influence what we think and do (Bargh, Chen, & Burrows, 1996; see chap. 13). Could it be, then, that factors of which we are unaware are the real causes the actions that we believe ourselves to be performing freely?

One famous study highlights this stark possibility (Libet, 1985). Participants were instructed to flex their wrists several times over the course of a 30-minute session, the precise moment of each wrist-flexion being left up to them. Electrodes, placed on participants' scalps, continuously monitored their brain activity. Results showed that half a second before participants flexed their wrists, the electrodes picked up a distinctive electrical signal, a so-called readiness potential. Results also showed, however, that participants' decision to flex occurred only one-fifth of a second before their wrist-flexion. (The moment of decision was determined by having participants note the time on a nearby clock, with an adjustment being made for the time needed to note it.) In other words, the readiness potential preceded participants' decision to flex. This implies an unsettling conclusion. Participants' brains appeared to know that they were about to voluntarily act before they did.

If the real causes of voluntary action are hidden from us, then feelings of voluntary agency must be based on something else, some set of judgmental criteria. If so, then it should be possible, by manipulating those criteria, to trick people into believing that they are doing something when they actually are not, or that they are not doing something when they actually are. Sound impossible? Well, consider the bizarre phenomenon of *facilitated communication*. Some years ago, a group of therapists claimed to have discovered that autistic children, normally mute and unresponsive, could type eloquently when their hands were obligingly held over a computer keyboard. Unfortunately, this discovery turned out to be entirely bogus. The therapists were, in fact, guiding their patients' hands to keys in line with what they expected them to type (Burgess et al., 1998). Inadvertent action projections of this sort have been recreated in the psychological laboratory (described in Wegner & Wheatley, 1999).

The reverse of action projection also occurs. In one experiment (Wegner & Wheatley, 1999), participants manually moved a computer mouse around so that the arrow it controlled traveled from one icon to another. A confederate, in an adjacent seat, helped them to move the mouse around. When the arrow landed on particular icons the confederate brought the mouse to a prearranged halt. Yet, about half the time, participants believed that they were the ones who had deliberately brought the mouse to a halt.

The experiment contained additional elements. Participants wore headphones through which words were continuously played. When the words named the icon that the arrow landed on, and did so just before the arrow landed, participants were especially likely to believe they had deliberately brought the mouse to a halt. This suggests that, whenever people have a thought related to an action, and have it just before the action occurs, they will tend to regard themselves as having intended that action, assuming no alternative explanation is available.

Is free will, then, just an illusory feeling? On this question, the studies cited, though suggestive, are hardly conclusive. First, free will is more likely to characterize intentional acts performed for a reason than intentional acts carried out on a whim (such as wrist flexion). Second, the fact that people are sometimes mistaken in identifying the locus of an action does not prove that they always are, any more than the existence of occasional visual illusions proves that people cannot normally see. Still, such studies should make us more wary of taking our intuitions of free will at face value.

Free will matters for two reasons. First, in its absence, praise and blame can never be truly deserved. Unless people could have acted otherwise they cannot be morally responsible for their actions. They can, of course, be *held* responsible for their actions; but merely holding people responsible, in the interests of regulating society, does not *make* them responsible. Second, if free will is an illusion, then all events must unfold in a wholly predestined manner, except perhaps for a dash of quantum uncertainty. Our conscious decisions would then be nothing more than nature blindly working through us. If so, cherished notions of human autonomy and morality would be under threat. Nonetheless, many scientists feel intellectually compelled to accept psychological determinism on the grounds that free will would amount to some sort of ghost in the machine. Whatever the ultimate truth of the matter, there is no denying that the findings of social psychological research have some bearing on the question, and sharpen appreciation of the critical points of debate.

REVELATION

Attempts to bring about a desired mental state tend to backfire if people are distracted or preoccupied. Under such circumstances, they would be well advised to abandon the attempt, or, even better, to try not to bring about that mental state, as this will ironically tend to bring it about.

— APG —

CHAPTER REFERENCE

Wegner, D., Erber, R., & Zanakos, S. (1993). Ironic processes in the mental control of mood and mood-related thought. *Journal of Personality and Social Psychology, 65*, 1093–1104.

OTHER REFERENCES

Ansfield, M. E., Wegner, D. M., & Bowser, R. (1996). Ironic effects of sleep urgency. *Behaviour Research and Therapy, 34*, 523–531.

Bargh, J. A., Chen, M., & Burrows, L. (1996). Automaticity of social behavior: Direct effects of trait construct and stereotype activation on action. *Journal of Personality and Social Psychology, 71*, 230–244.

Baumeister, R. F., Bratslavsky, E., Muraven, M., & Tice, D. M. (1998). Ego depletion: Is the active self a limited resource? *Journal of Personality and Social Psychology, 74*, 1252–1265.

Burgess, C. A., Kirsch, I., Shane, H., Niederauer, K. L., Grahman, S. M., & Bacon, A. (1998). Facilitated communication as an ideomotor response. *Psychological Science, 9*, 71–74.

Frankl, V. E. (1963). *Man's search for meaning.* New York: Pocket Books.

Freud, S. (1914). *The psychopathology of everyday life.* New York: Macmillan.

Libet, B. (1985). Unconscious cerebral initiative and the role of conscious will in voluntary action. *Behavioral and Brain Sciences, 8*, 529–566.

Macrae, C. N., Bodenhausen, G. V., Milne, A. B., & Jetten, J. (1994). Out of mind but back in sight: Stereotypes on the rebound. *Journal of Personality and Social psychology, 67*, 808–817.

Nisbett, R. E., & Wilson, T. D. (1977). Telling more than we can know: Verbal reports on mental processes. *Psychological Review, 84*, 231–259.

Smullyan, R. M. (1992). *The tao is silent.* New York: Harper.

Wegner, D. M. (1994). Ironic processes of mental control. *Psychological Review, 101*, 34–52.

Wegner, D. M., Schneider, D. J., Carter, S., & White, T. (1987). Paradoxical effects of thought suppression. *Journal of Personality and Social Psychology, 53*, 5–13.

Wegner, D. M., & Wheatley, T. P. (1999). Apparent mental causation: Sources of the experience of will. *American Psychologist, 54*, 480–492.

MORE TO EXPLORE

Libet, B., Freeman, A., & Sutherland, K. (1999). *The volitional brain: Towards a neuroscience of free will.* Exeter, England: Imprint Academic.

Wegner, D. M. (1989). *White bears and other unwanted thoughts: Suppression, obsession, and the psychology of mental control.* New York: Viking/Penguin.

11 Familiarity Breeds Liking: The Positive Effects of Mere Exposure

"The song is best esteemed with which our ears are most acquainted."
—William Byrd (1543–1623), English composer

BACKGROUND

Which of the following Turkish words do you imagine mean something positive and which something negative: *Iktitaf, Jandara, Afworbu, Biwojni, Civadra*? Well, to be honest, they are not really Turkish words. They are made-up words used by Robert Zajonc (1968) in a classic demonstration of the *mere exposure effect*—the tendency to like stimuli better the more one encounters them. Zajonc (whose name is improbably pronounced "Zcience") flashed such words to participants 1, 2, 5, 10, or 25 times, having them pronounce each one as they went along. Afterward, they rated how positive or negative they thought the meaning of each word was. He found, as expected, that participants rated the more frequently presented words more positively. He also tested for the same effect using other stimuli, such as those that look to the untrained eye like Chinese calligraphy. He flashed each for 2 seconds a variable number of times, and again found that those presented more often were preferred. Ever the enthusiastic experimentalist, Zajonc also helped to conduct a logistically more complicated study that involved people as stimuli (Saegart and others, 1973). Participants moved from one room to another tasting a variety of liquids, from yummy Kool-Aid concoctions to yucky mixtures of vinegar,

127

quinine, and citric acid. In the process, each participant met each of the other participants more or less frequently (none had known each other previously). The interactions involved brief, face-to-face contact with no talking. Following these room-to-room migrations, the participants evaluated each other. Their evaluations were more favorable for others they had met frequently, less favorable for those they had met rarely (regardless of how pleasant or unpleasant the liquids they had tasted were). This is another example of the mere exposure effect. Whether stimuli are nonsense words, abstract patterns, ideographs, or facial photos, the more they are encountered, the more they tend to be liked.

A shortcoming of these earlier studies, however, is that they each represented a *within-participants design*. In such a design, each participant experiences more than one level of a particular variable. For example, they might work on a frustratingly difficult crossword puzzle in an uncomfortably hot room and then later work on a different, yet equally challenging, crossword puzzle in a comfortable air-conditioned room (the dependent variable in each case might be how long they persist in working on each puzzle). Another example is the study described earlier, in which participants were exposed to different alleged Turkish words more or less frequently. A major concern of either study is that the results might have been due to participants' intuitions about its purpose. Participants' hunches may have led them to produce results they believe were expected by the experimenters. (Suspicions about a study's purposes can also cause participants to work against expected results, either deliberately or unwittingly.) Indeed, previous research had found that participants reported liking stimuli more even if they simply *imagined* having seen them more frequently. This suggests that the mere exposure effect could have been an artifact of participants' suspicions about the purpose of the study and what it should reveal.

It is now well-recognized that certain cues in an experiment, referred to as *demand characteristics*, can indeed prompt guesses and motives in participants that influence their behavior and bias research results (Orne, 1962). Demand characteristics are a vexing and ever-present problem in experimental research. Fortunately, there are several ways to guard against them. A credible *cover story* (stated rationale for the study) helps. It prevents participants from feeling any need to figure out the real purpose of the experiment. Also, postexperimental inquiries serve to reveal demand characteristics, allowing researchers to eliminate them from future studies. Such inquiries often begin with broad, open-ended questions ("Do you have any thoughts or questions about this study?") and proceed to more pointed questions ("When indicating which of the Turkish words you liked best, were you aware that some had been presented to you more times than others? Did you believe that they were Turkish words?"). Yet another way to help purge a design of demand characteristics is to change the design altogether, from a within-participants design to a *between-participants design*. In a between-participants design, each group of participants is exposed to only one set of conditions. They are unaware of what other participants are exposed to (or even that there are other groups of participants), and are therefore less inclined to imagine that the experimenter is making comparisons across conditions.

For example, in order to study the effects of light intensity on ping-pong performance, one might, in a within-participants design, have each participant play one game under full illumination and another under greatly reduced illumination (randomly switching the order for different participants). Unfortunately, in this design, participants would easily realize that illumination is the main focus of the study, and might alter their behaviors accordingly. In contrast, in a between-participants design, each group of participants would play a game under either high *or* low illumination (not both). This arrangement would prevent them from suspecting that light intensity is being manipulated. Again, a good cover story would also prevent suspicion: "This study is a product analysis of a newly designed ping-pong ball. Simply play the best you can while we videotape your performance." Only a telepathic participant would then surmise: "Hey, this study is really about the effect of light intensity on ping-pong performance" and therefore attempt to play better or worse.

The point is that there was a need in the 1970s for research that would render implausible any explanations for the mere exposure effect that implicate demand characteristics. Social psychologists interested in this issue wanted to be sure that it was the number of exposures, and not participants' suspicions, that were affecting liking for stimuli. Theodore Mita and his colleagues (1977) came up with an ingenious way of doing just that. They succinctly described the purpose of their study: "… to test the mere-exposure hypothesis so that there was virtually no possibility of sensitizing participants to the frequency-affect hypothesis" (p. 597). They capitalized on two facts that many people would consider trivial, if they considered them at all. First, when people view their own faces, they usually do so in a mirror, whereas others normally see their faces directly. Second, there are subtle asymmetries in a person's face: one eyebrow is slightly bushier than the other, or one side of the chin bears an unsightly pimple. As a result, the mirror image of a person's face is subtly different from the image other people see. Mita and his colleagues (1977) incorporated these apparently trivial facts into their ingenious study.

WHAT THEY DID

Even with the hints we have provided, it might be difficult for you to imagine a study that would demonstrate the mere exposure effect while eliminating demand characteristics. It often takes a good bit of experience and creativity to come up with the clever, if sometimes quirky, methodologies found in social psychology. Mita and his colleagues (1977) conducted two experiments. We will only describe the second, a more rigorous replication of the first. Replications are often necessary if one wants to publish one's research in a premier journal. They also help to establish the *reliability* (repeatability) and *boundary conditions* (limits) of a particular research finding.

At the University of Wisconsin, 38 women participated in a study on self-perception. Each was asked to bring along her boyfriend. (Each woman had indicated earlier that she was dating or living with someone whom she believed was in love with her.) As it happened, 10 of the women failed to bring a partner to the experiment, mostly because the partners were out of town, so they could provide only partial data (it's usually not easy to recruit couples into a study). In a preliminary session, a photo was taken of each woman. The film was then developed into two portrait-sized, black-and-white photographs that were the mirror images of one another. The two photos were subtly different, due to the fact that people's faces are not perfectly symmetrical, as mentioned previously. The *mirror print* was of how the woman appeared to herself in a mirror, whereas the *true print* was of how the woman appeared to others.

In the second session each woman brought along her boyfriend. He waited in another room while she was being tested, and was then tested himself while she waited (the two were not allowed to communicate while changing rooms). The woman sat at a table upon which the photographs of her were displayed. She was shown the two photos five different times (she was asked to look away each time they were displayed, and nothing was said on each trial about whether a photo was the same as one previously shown). The left-right positioning of the mirror print and true print photos was randomized on each trial for each woman. The experimenter was not told which of the photos was the mirror print and which was the true print (a precaution that had not been taken in the first study). This was to ensure that he was not unduly influencing her responses. On each trial, the woman's task was to simply indicate which of the photos she liked better, even if her decision was based on trivial or inexplicable differences. The women were not told the real purpose of the study or that the photographs were, in fact, mirror images of each other. After stating preferences on five different trials, each woman was asked to provide reasons for her choices, in order to assess demand characteristics and determine how well she understood the instructions. She was also asked what she thought the purpose of the study was (these various responses were tape-recorded). She then changed rooms with her partner, who went through an identical procedure of indicating photo preferences and being interviewed.

The design of the study was simple, as were its hypotheses. Mita and his fellow researchers predicted that the women would tend to prefer the mirror prints (which would present a likeness they would be most familiar with), whereas their partners would tend to prefer the true prints (which to them would be most familiar).

WHAT THEY FOUND

On the first trial alone, 20 of the 28 women indicated that they preferred the mirror prints, while 17 of their 28 boyfriends indicated that they preferred the true prints. The first effect (women generally preferred the mirror print) was statistically significant, while the second effect (the majority of the boy-friends said they preferred the true print), although in the expected direc-tion, was not. (This essentially replicated the results of the first study.) Moreover, the joint prediction—that the women would prefer the mirror prints *and* the boyfriends would prefer the true prints—was corroborated in 43% of the couples (significantly more than the 25% predicted by chance).

When Mita and his colleagues analyzed participants' responses across all five trials, they found even stronger confirmation of their hypotheses. Twenty of the 28 women preferred the mirror prints, whereas 19 of their 28 boyfriends preferred the true prints. Both results are statistically significant (Fig. 11.1). Thus, when aggregating across trials, a boyfriend-preference effect finally emerged. Furthermore, in 50% of the couples, both the woman-preference and the boyfriend-preference predictions were con-firmed (double what chance would predict).

What reasons did participants give for their preferences? Did they come close to mentioning that they thought the two photos were mirror images of each other, that one of the photos was more familiar, and that it was for this reason that they preferred it? They did not. Instead, they seemed to in-vent reasons, mentioning that the photo they preferred was "more natu-ral," had "better head tilt," "better eyes," a "straighter part," or looked "less mean." None of the participants mentioned anything about being exposed to either photograph more or less frequently. And only two participants re-ported noticing that the photos were mirror images of each other, and even then they reported no knowledge of the study's hypotheses. In other words,

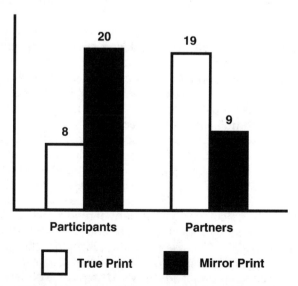

FIG. 11.1. The number of participants, and their partners, who most often preferred, over a series of trials, true or mirror prints of participants' faces.

Mita and his colleagues found no evidence of demand characteristics when probing for them.

SO WHAT?

Mita and his colleagues (1977) provided an elegantly simple test of the mere exposure hypothesis. The design of their study traded on a unique difference between conditions: The true and mirror images were almost indistinguishable, except that the two groups of participants (the women and their boyfriends) would have been exposed to each of them more or less frequently. Participants had no clue as to why they preferred certain photos or as to what the experiment was about. In fact, this experiment was so neatly done that even a trained social psychologist could probably have been a participant without figuring out its true purpose.

Several follow-up studies have illuminated conditions that *moderate* (affect the magnitude of) the mere exposure effect. For example, for at least some stimuli there seems to be an optimal range of exposure. Greater exposure improves liking up to a point, but beyond that point, liking drops and the stimulus becomes increasingly aversive. At first, one cannot get enough of Celine Dion's *My Heart Will Go On* (love theme from *Titanic*), but after hearing it 373 times, enough already! Also, if one doesn't like something to begin with, then repeated exposure tends to render it increasingly less likeable. The unsightly artificial plant that one mildly dislikes eventually becomes wholly hated. Or, repeated conversations with someone at the opposite end of the political spectrum can amplify one's antipathy for that person. In addition, relatively complex stimuli, like Bach's labyrinthine organ works or Picasso's jigsaw-puzzle-like paintings, can be experienced often without producing jadedness. In addition, children seem to show less of a mere exposure effect than do adults, maybe because children have shorter attention spans or find such predictability reassuring. However, aside from these and a few other limiting conditions, the mere exposure effect is quite robust (Bornstein, 1989). That is, it is easy to replicate using a variety of stimuli and procedures.

The mere exposure effect finds its place in the real world. For example, it is partly due to mere exposure effects that well-known, incumbent politicians (or politicians who are not well-known but spend oodles of money on media exposure) are preferred to unfamiliar ones. For example, Grush and his colleagues (1978) predicted 83% of the winners in a U.S. congressional election primary by calculating the amount of media coverage devoted to each candidate. Evidently, repeated names and sound bites win the political day (see chap. 16). Consider also the Olympian efforts companies make to be the proud sponsors of the Olympic Games. Their goal, of course, is to have their product ads televised to millions of viewers ad infinitum. Not only does the mere exposure effect occur naturally in our re-

FIG. 11.2.   Which photo do you prefer?

sponses to songs on the radio and people we encounter in the elevator, it can also be wielded for political or financial gain.

AFTERTHOUGHTS

Social psychology investigates how people perceive and influence one another. A common starting point is to examine the merest of human interactions. This chapter demonstrates how being exposed to a stimulus repeatedly affects liking for it. Chapter 22 investigates what happens to a person when he or she is immersed in a crowd, and chapter 24 explores what happens to one's performance on a task when others are present. Such minimal situations—in which exposure but little if any interaction occurs—are important because they underlie and interact with more involving and complex social psychological processes. They also reveal some of the automatic, non-conscious processes that govern human behavior.

About 25 years ago, following decades of waning respect for Sigmund Freud's theory of unconscious motivation, there occurred a resurrection in psychology of belief in nonconscious influences on human behavior. It was once again becoming clear that people often do not know what influences their thoughts, feelings, and behaviors. For example, they often cannot explain their choices (Nisbett & Wilson, 1977; see chap. 1). Of course, many of our behaviors are quite deliberate and conscious, and we have a pretty good understanding of what provokes them. A friend invites us to a party, so we go. Someone insults us, and we plot revenge. However, it is also the case that much of what we do is an automatic, unconscious response to environmental stimuli. As such, we often do not understand our own responses or the very operation of our own minds. We circle the words *ocean* and *moon* in a word search puzzle, and then an hour later, for reasons we cannot fathom, "Tide detergent" pops into our minds. Mere exposure effects also seem to occur relatively automatically and unconsciously, but nonetheless exert a powerful effect on human sentiments. In fact, such effects may even occur in animals. Research by Cross and his colleagues (1967) found that rats who heard pieces by Mozart during infancy favored new pieces by Mozart over others by Schoenberg later on, whereas rats not exposed to Mozart did not show this preference! (See chaps. 12 and 13 for more about automatic social psychological processes.)

What explains such rudimentary influences upon our perceptions? Why does the mere exposure effect occur? Sociobiologists, who interpret social behavior in evolutionary terms, have suggested that there is a deep-rooted tendency in people to assume that what is familiar is *safe*, and that what is unfamiliar is dangerous. Liking familiar and seemingly safe stimuli, and avoiding unknown and unpredictable stimuli, is said to increase one's chances of survival. Bornstein (1989) asked this question:

> Who was likely to live longer, reproduce, and pass on genetic material (and inherited traits) to future generations, the cave dweller who had a healthy fear of the strange and unfamiliar beasts lurking outside, or the more risk-taking (albeit short-lived) fellow who, on spying an unfamiliar animal in the distance, decided that he wanted a closer look? (p. 282)

However, one might object to such an explanation by pointing out that curiosity about the unfamiliar and unknown, and the risk-taking that might follow, are likely to be adaptive traits as well. Nothing ventured, nothing gained. Would the human race have advanced or even survived without taking brave steps into the unknown? Furthermore, if everything familiar is liked, why does the word "new" generally have such positive connotations, and "old" such negative ones?

Social psychological explanations have suggested that frequent exposure leads to a sense of *familiarity*. This, in turn, might lead to an assumption of *similarity*, and plenty of research confirms that we like others who are similar to us (see Newcomb, 1961, for a classic demonstration of this). Cognitive explanations have pointed to the role of *recognition*. Frequent exposure makes objects more recognizable, which makes them more attractive. In other words, the conscious recognition of a stimulus *mediates* (is a necessary link in the causal chain) between exposure to a stimulus and one's emotional response to it. Studies have shown, however, that mere exposure can also occur subliminally—outside of conscious awareness—and still be efficacious (Bornstein & D'Agostino, 1992). Thus, conscious recognition seems not to be a necessary mediator of the mere exposure effect.

These competing explanations suggest that, with regard to the mere exposure effect, the *why* question has proven more intractable than the *when* question. This often happens. Determining when an effect occurs is part of describing it, whereas ascertaining why it occurs amounts to explaining it, a more difficult task. Psychology attempts to explain the causes of things by conducting experiments. Mita and his collaborators did conduct an experiment (deliberately manipulating an independent variable and controlling extraneous variables), and so were in a position to infer causation. They could say that more frequent exposure to a stimulus causes one to like it more. What they could not determine from their design, however, is what, if anything, mediates the causal link between exposure and liking.

A final afterthought: There is something reassuring about the mere exposure effect. Within limits, the more we're exposed to something initially ordinary, the more we tend to like it. In particular, the more often we encounter common decent folk, the more appealing they are to us. Mere repeated contact with someone is sufficient to increase our attraction to him or her. Contrary to what cynics would say, familiarity tends to breed liking, not contempt. This is quite a comforting thought, and all the more so the more one contemplates it!

REVELATION

How we feel about a person (or any other stimulus) is influenced by a host of factors, but most basically, it is governed by mere exposure. We tend to like people more the more often we encounter them.

— KPF —

CHAPTER REFERENCE

Mita, T. H., Dermer, M., & Knight, J. (1977). Reversed facial images and the mere-exposure hypothesis. *Journal of Personality and Social Psychology, 35,* 597–601.

OTHER REFERENCES

Bornstein, R. F. (1989). Exposure and affect: Overview and meta-analysis of research, 1968–1987. *Psychological Bulletin, 106,* 265–289.

Bornstein, R. F., & D'Agostino, P. R. (1992). Stimulus recognition and the mere exposure effect. *Journal of Personality and Social Psychology, 63,* 545–552.

Cross, H. A., Halcomb, C. G., & Matter, W. W. (1967). Imprinting or exposure learning in rats given early auditory stimulation. *Psychonomic Sciences, 7,* 233–234.

Grush, J. E., McKeough, K. L., & Ahlering, R. F. (1978). Extrapolating laboratory exposure research to actual political elections. *Journal of Personality and Social Psychology, 36,* 257–270.

Newcomb, T. M. (1961). *The acquaintance process.* New York: Holt.

Nisbett, R. E., & Wilson, T. D. (1977). Telling more than we can know: Verbal reports on mental processes. *Psychological Review, 84*, 231–259.

Orne, M. T. (1962). On the social psychology of the psychology experiment: With particular reference to demand characteristics and their implications. *American Psychologist, 17*, 776–783.

Saegart, S. C., Swap, W. C., & Zajonc, R. B. (1973). Exposure, context, and interpersonal attraction. *Journal of Personality and Social Psychology, 25*, 234–242.

Zajonc, R. B. (1968). Attitudinal effects of mere exposure. *Journal of Personality and Social Psychology Monographs, 9*(2, part 2), 1–27.

MORE TO EXPLORE

Moreland, R. L., & Beach, S. R. (1992). Exposure effects in the classroom: The development of affinity among students. *Journal of Experimental Social Psychology, 28*, 255–276.

Zajonc, R. B. (1980). Feeling and thinking: Preferences need no inferences. *American Psychologist, 35*, 151–175.

12 Beneath the Mask: Tools for Detecting Hidden Prejudice

"He who has eyes to see and ears to hear can convince himself that no mortal can keep a secret. If his lips are silent, he chatters with his fingertips; betrayal oozes out of every pore."
—Sigmund Freud (1865–1939), pioneer of psychoanalysis

BACKGROUND

When we, the authors of this volume, mention that we are (social) psychologists, we almost always receive one of two replies. The first is: "That must be *so* interesting!" We certainly think so, and hope readers of this volume agree. The second reply we get is: "I'd better watch out—you might start analyzing me!" When we hear this, we react in two ways. First, we are wryly amused that others believe we can so easily peer into their minds. Second, we are a little frustrated that others misunderstand how we do our science. We find ourselves in the position of having to gently refute people's widely held misconceptions about what (social) psychologists do, or are capable of doing.

For example, people commonly believe that psychologists can figure them out simply by making a few shrewd observations. In this regard, psychologists supposedly resemble Sherlock Holmes, the famous detective who drew astounding inferences from clues that lesser mortals overlooked. A speck of dust here, a muddy footprint there, and Holmes could deduce that Moriarty had stolen the Princess's emerald. Similarly, a nervous gesture here, a slip of the tongue there, and your neighborhood psychologist can supposedly deduce that nobody really loved you as a child.

Sherlock Holmes was, of course, a fictional character, so it is hardly surprising that his investigative methods would have come to grief in the real

137

world. In fact his so-called deductions were little more than wild guesses based on slender evidence. Holmes's creator, Conan Doyle, made sure that his hero's guesses were always on target, but flesh-and-blood sleuths cannot count on Conan Doyle for assistance. Consequently, everyday detective work is mundane and methodical. Specialized techniques and tools are used to gather evidence (e.g., profiling, forensics, surveillance) and different individuals pool their expertise to crack a case. It is not just a matter of some genius investigator turning up one day and single-handedly solving crimes that left the rest of the criminal justice system perplexed.

The stereotypical psychologist who unerringly sizes people up at a glance turns out to be as fictional as Sherlock Holmes. Take the pioneer of psychoanalysis himself, Sigmund Freud. Although he clearly regarded himself as a brilliant diagnostician, his case histories, when looked at objectively, tell a very different story. Freud boldly maintained that an accurate analysis would lead to the permanent remission of neurotic symptoms. However, his claims to have cured any patient have since been discredited, calling into question the soundness of his original interpretations (Crews, 1995).

Indeed, it may well be impossible for anyone to acquire the diagnostic powers claimed by Freud. Our understanding of other people is compromised by perceptual biases. For example, we all too readily infer the existence of personality traits from isolated behaviors (Gilbert, 1998; see chap. 23), failing to see how such behaviors can be influenced by social context (Darley & Batson, 1973; chap. 19) or by our own presence (Snyder, Tanke, & Berscheid, 1977; chap. 14). Perhaps the most clear-cut sign of our mind-reading limitations is our near inability to tell whether other people are lying. Although liars may give themselves away by subtle nonverbal cues (e.g., a shrill voice), numerous studies show that laymen and professionals alike are almost no better than chance at identifying them, even with training (Vrij, 2000).

To discover how the human mind works, then, what is needed is not so much an individual with superior insight but rather a community of scientists who put forward theories and test them. Indeed, you can think of social psychologists (and their colleagues in related fields) as a squad of hard-working detectives, each of whom is trying to solve a piece of an incredibly complex case. Like detectives, social psychologists depend, not on unaided intuition, but on specialized techniques and tools. Their preferred technique is experimentation because it clarifies what causes what (see the Introduction to this volume). However, they also use an array of measurement tools to assess people's mental states and underlying dispositions.

Much of the time, the measurement tool of choice is the questionnaire, given its versatility and convenience. Note, however, that questionnaires must be carefully assembled and pretested. It is not merely a matter of cobbling together items that look right. A questionnaire must contain items that form a coherent whole, yield results that replicate over time, and predict outcomes that make theoretical sense. These virtues are what distinguish the questionnaires that social psychologists employ from those that appear in popular magazines.

Yet, even the best-validated questionnaires can only shed so much light on the workings of the mind. This is so for three reasons. First, people sometimes do not wish to reveal to others what they really think and feel. This is particularly true when sensitive topics are being researched. For example, a closet male chauvinist will be reluctant to reveal his sexist attitudes in a survey administered by a woman (even with anonymity guaranteed). Second, people may not wish to admit to themselves how they really think and feel. A liberal White, for instance, may refuse to acknowledge, much less express, his underlying racial prejudice. Third, people may simply not know what they really think or feel, due to unawareness, uncertainty, or disinterest.

In light of all this, how can social psychologists delve deeper into the workings of the human mind? They can do so by employing measurement tools that go beyond the limitations of self-report. Several such tools are available, but here we focus on just one: the *sequential priming task* (Chartrand & Bargh, 2000).

The way it works is best illustrated by example. Imagine that you are seated in front of a computer and that your task is to classify words that appear on the screen one by one. Each of these target words is either a male pronoun (e.g., he) or a female pronoun (e.g., she). To classify male pronouns, you press a key on the left, to classify female ones, a key on the right. You go as quickly as you can without making errors.

Now comes the interesting part. On each trial, a prime word is flashed briefly just before each target word appears. This prime is either the name of a traditionally male job (e.g., doctor) or the name of a traditionally female job (e.g., nurse). During the task, all the primes systematically precede all the targets. This means that, in terms of gender stereotypes, some of the primes and targets match (doctor–he, nurse–she) whereas others mismatch (doctor–she, nurse–he). Research shows that this makes a difference: People go faster on trials containing stereotypical matches than trials containing stereotypical mismatches (Banaji & Hardin, 1996).

The explanation for this effect is that each prime word activates a meaning. In other words, it prepares you to think and act in accordance with its semantic connotations (Djiksterhuis & van Knippenberg, 1998; see chap. 13). Consequently, you get a head-start when responding to matching targets. However, when responding to mismatching targets, you are handicapped, because you have to overcome your initial inclination to respond in the opposite way.

A key feature of the sequential priming task is that the primes and targets follow one another in rapid succession. As a result, differences in your speed of response from trial to trial cannot be attributed to any conscious strategy on your part. Rather, these differences reflect how your mind operates spontaneously. The sequential priming task can therefore be seen as indicating the automatic associations that exist in your mind between the primes and the targets.

Alternative versions of the task are easy to construct. For example, suppose that Black and White faces were substituted as primes, and pleasant and unpleasant words as targets. If White participants now responded more rapidly on Black–unpleasant and White–pleasant trials than on Black–pleasant and White–unpleasant trials, then the existence of an automatic race bias could be plausibly inferred.

Many studies have been conducted in which participants' responses to conventional questionnaires and sequential priming tasks have been compared to one another (Blair, 2001). Curiously, the two generally correlate poorly, if at all. That is, participants' automatic associations cannot be readily inferred from what they say about themselves. Exactly what this means is a matter of debate. The most intriguing possibility is that sequential priming tasks reflect underlying social attitudes that people are unwilling or unable to express, publicly or privately. If true, then social psychologists would have a technological means of getting inside people's heads. They might even be able to predict people's behavior in settings where self-reports prove uninformative.

Dovidio, Kawakami, Johnson, Johnson, and Howard (1997) decided to put the matter to the test, focusing on the touchy subject of racial prejudice.

WHAT THEY DID

In their original article, Dovidio et al. (1997) reported three studies in which racism against U.S. Blacks was the topic of investigation. We focus on the last of these, in which 31 White undergraduates served as participants.

Dovidio et al. (1997) began by noting that discrimination—the behavioral outcome of racial prejudice—could take more or less extreme forms. It could either be *deliberate*, involving the intentional mistreatment of minorities, or *spontaneous*, involving their inadvertent mistreatment. An example of deliberate discrimination would be a bigot hurling a racial slur at a Black man; an example of spontaneous discrimination would be a nonbigot crossing the street to avoid an interracial encounter.

On the basis of the previous distinction, Dovidio et al. (1997) put forward two complementary hypotheses. The first was that prejudice assessed by questionnaire, or *self-reported prejudice*, would predict deliberate discrimination. This is not too surprising. Someone who is prepared to state that they dislike members of minority groups is also more likely to intentionally mistreat them. In both cases people are aware of what they are doing. The second hypothesis was that prejudice assessed by the sequential priming task, or *implicit prejudice*, would predict spontaneous discrimination. People who engage in spontaneous discrimination often do so without intending to or without even realizing it. Yet this is precisely how people respond during the sequential priming task. In both cases people are reacting automatically and unconsciously.

The measure of implicit prejudice employed was a variant of sequential priming tasks described earlier. Across 96 trials (randomly sorted) Black and White men appeared as primes, and words with pleasant or unpleasant meanings as targets. The primes took the form of computer-generated faces, prerated to ensure that they all looked equally attractive. The targets took the form of traits used to describe people (e.g., kind, cruel), and were deliberately selected so as not to carry any racial connotations. If participants responded faster on some trials (Black face/unpleasant trait or White face/pleasant trait) than on others (Black face/pleasant trait or White face/unpleasant trait) then an automatic race bias could be inferred.

The priming task had some added intricacies that, while not essential to understanding its results, do bear mention in the interests of accurate representation. Impatient readers may leapfrog over the next four paragraphs.

The decision that participants had to make was not, as in an earlier task, whether the target words were pleasant or unpleasant, but rather whether target words were consistent with a cue. This cue was a letter, either P or H, that appeared between each prime and target. P stood for person, and H for house. Person targets (e.g., cruel, kind) were the traits previously mentioned; house targets (e.g., drafty) were another set of adjectives. If a house target followed H or a person target followed P, participants then pressed a key for yes. If a house target followed P or a person target followed H, participants then pressed a key for no.

The purpose of introducing these irrelevant house/person categorizations was to make the sequential priming task as indirect as possible. Under this arrangement, participants did not even have to consciously evaluate whether the target adjectives were pleasant or unpleasant. Any variation in response speed produced by different combinations of primes and targets would therefore be purely automatic and unconscious. The last remnants of conscious evaluation had been purged from the paradigm.

Additional features of the task served to conceal its purpose. Each face prime was flashed a few centimeters left or right of where participants were looking, and only then for a few short milliseconds. As a consequence, the face primes stood little chance of being consciously recognized. They became, in effect, subliminal. This made it very unlikely that participants would figure out the true purpose of the task and attempt to manipulate their responses.

We point out these technicalities to illustrate how much care social psychologists must take in order to make valid measurements. The methodologies they employ can be no less sophisticated than those employed by so-called hard scientists.

Next, a measure of self-reported prejudice was administered. Participants filled out two questionnaires: the Old-Fashioned Racism Scale, and its successor, the Modern Racism Scale. As you might expect, the former featured rather brazen items like: "It is a bad idea for Blacks and Whites to marry one another," whereas the latter featured a more understated one like: "Blacks are getting too demanding in their push for equal rights." The researchers surmised that the Modern Racism Scale, in virtue of tapping racist sentiments more obliquely, might evoke more honest responding, and therefore correlate better with the results of the sequential priming task.

Participants were then escorted to another room to take part in an apparently unrelated exercise. Its alleged purpose was to help other students develop their skills as interviewers. In reality, these trainee interviewers were confederates, playing a prescribed role. The point of the cover story was to create a situation in which tendencies to discriminate against Blacks could be assessed without arousing suspicions.

Participants were interviewed by two women, one White and one Black. In the course of both interviews, participants were asked a pair of questions designed to elicit lengthy and discursive answers. Their reactions to each interviewer were then assessed. A less positive reaction to the Black interviewer would have reflected racial discrimination, everything else being equal.

However, the researchers needed to be confident that everything else was in fact equal. They wished to ensure that the findings of the study could not be plausibly attributed to some factor apart from race. To this end, they took several precautions. First, they instructed the female interviewers to ask questions, and respond to answers, in a standard manner. In particular, they told them to maintain eye contact with participants, acknowledge their answers with polite nods, and gently prompt them if their answers were too short. Second, the researchers used alternate pairs of White and Black interviewers, rather than just a single pair. Third, several features of the study were systematically counterbalanced (done different ways around). These included which question in a pair was asked first, which pair of questions was asked by each interviewer, and which interviewer saw participants first.

Participants' reactions to the interviewers were assessed in two ways. First, participants were asked to rate each interviewer for her likability and sincerity. These ratings reflected participants' *conscious assessments* of how well the interviewers had performed at their job. A more favorable assessment of the White than the Black interviewer was deemed evidence of deliberate racial discrimination. Participants also rated themselves on the same two dimensions.

Second, participants' nonverbal behavior during the interview was scrutinized. A video camera, pointed at participants, provided footage of their behavior throughout the whole interview. To maintain the cover story, a second camera was pointed at the interviewers too. Two trained assistants, blind to the purpose of the experiment, independently sifted through this footage for two specific nonverbal behaviors: levels of eye contact (reflecting liking, respect, and intimacy) and rates of blinking (reflecting feelings of discomfort or anxious arousal). These behaviors, easy to identify and quantify, served as indicators of the *interpersonal warmth* that participants showed toward the interviewers. Showing greater interpersonal warmth toward the White than the Black interviewer was deemed evidence of spontaneous racial discrimination.

WHAT THEY FOUND

We begin with participants' self-reported prejudice. Did they show evidence of being overt racists? Very little: They chalked up mean scores of only 1.28 and 1.67 on the Old-fashioned Racism Scale and Modern Racism Scale respectively, even though both scales ranged from 1 to 5. So, if we take participants' word for it, they were largely free of racial prejudice. But might the validity of their self-reports have been compromised by a desire to be, or to appear, unprejudiced?

This brings us to participants' implicit prejudice. Their performance on the sequential priming task told a different story. On average, participants responded more rapidly when Black faces primed unpleasant adjectives than when White ones did. This pattern (replicated in both companion studies) indicates that, at the level of automatic associations, participants tended to evaluate Blacks more negatively than Whites. Hence, the sequential priming task seems to have tapped into a deep-rooted prejudice that at least some participants were either unwilling or unable to express.

This possibility is consistent with an additional finding. Participants' self-reported prejudice was unrelated to their implicit prejudice. Specifically, participants' scores on both the Old-fashioned Racism Scale and the Modern Racism Scale failed to correlate with their scores on the sequential priming task (although one companion study did find such a correlation).

Now the key question: did participants' self-reported and implicit prejudice predict different kinds of racial discrimination? They did. As expected, the higher participants scored on either of the racism questionnaires, the more their conscious assessments were biased in favor of the White interviewer (rating her as more likeable and sincere). Also as expected, the higher participants' scored on the sequential priming task, the more inclined they were to show greater interpersonal warmth toward the White interviewer by looking at her longer and blinking less. In sum, participants' self-reported prejudice indicated how likely they would be to deliberately discriminate, and their implicit prejudice indicated how likely they would be to spontaneously discriminate (Fig. 12.1).

Note too that participants' questionnaire scores did not predict their interpersonal warmth during the interview, nor did their scores on the sequential priming task predict their ratings of the interviewers. In other words, self-reported and implicit prejudice each predicted an outcome that the other did not.

Finally, what about participants' conscious assessments of their own likability and sincerity during the interviews? Interestingly, participants' self-ratings bore no relation to the interpersonal warmth they actually showed towards the interviewers. Their self-ratings also bore no relation to their performance on the sequential priming task. Only their scores on the Modern Racism Scale (and to a lesser extent, those on the Old-Fashioned Racism Scale) were significantly related to their self-ratings.

SO WHAT?

The present study illustrates how, with a clever piece of technology—the sequential priming task—social psychologists can take a peak inside the human mind and discover important facts that conventional questionnaires do not reveal. In particular, social psychologists can get a handle on hidden stereotypes and prejudices that exist as automatic associations between attributes and social groups. These hidden stereotypes and prejudices often stand at odds with their self-reported equivalents, suggesting that people are not as unequivocally unbiased as they think or say they are. The added virtue of the present study is that it proves that automatic associations are not just idle curiosities. It shows that it is possible to predict what people will do from them. Moreover, it shows that it is possible to predict kinds of behavior that self-report questionnaires do not. In the present study, the prejudice that White participants reported against Blacks did not predict how warmly they behaved toward a Black interviewer. However, participants' automatic negative associations toward

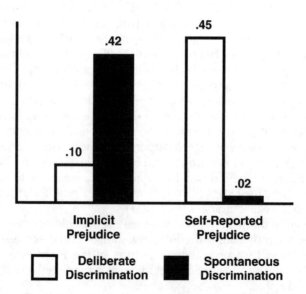

FIG. 12.1.   Correlations between racial prejudice, in its implicit and self-reported forms, and discrimination, in its spontaneous and deliberate forms.

Blacks did. It may be that, on encountering Blacks, people who are implicitly prejudiced against them experience an automatic and unconscious tendency to withdraw from their company that reveals itself in interpersonal uneasiness. Although people's moral scruples may ensure that they do not engage in deliberate discrimination, they cannot so effectively regulate their nonverbal behavior. As a result, people can wind up spontaneously discriminating without knowing it.

Other studies have yielded conceptually similar findings. For example, Fazio, Jackson, Dunton, and Williams (1995) found that although scores on the Modern Racism Scale predicted White participants' opinions about the infamous 1992 race riots in Los Angeles, only a measure of implicit prejudice predicted how friendly participants later behaved toward a Black confederate. In a follow-up study, the same researchers found that the more strongly White participants' reported inhibiting their racism, the greater the disagreement between their implicit and self-reported racism became. This shows that the Modern Racism Scale is not immune to motivational biases as Dovidio et al. (1997) had suspected it might be.

At this point, some readers may be thinking: "Okay, perhaps implicit prejudice does predict spontaneous discrimination. But isn't deliberate discrimination a much greater social evil, and doesn't explicit prejudice predict it? So why bother with fancy technologies like the sequential priming task?"

Deliberate discrimination is indeed a more serious matter than spontaneous discrimination. However, this does not mean that spontaneous discrimination is innocuous. A vivid example of the potential harm it can do was provided by Word, Zanna, and Cooper (1974). After finding that White interviewers gave off more negative nonverbal signals to Black job candidates than to White candidates, they trained a second batch of White interviewers to impart those same negative signals to a second batch of White job candidates. This produced a marked decrement in these candidates' performance, no doubt due to the lack of enthusiasm or approval being subtly conveyed. Similar processes may operate in real life to jeopardize the employment opportunities of minorities. Moreover, because nonverbal behavior is largely unconscious, people may unknowingly instigate self-fulfilling prophecies based on the bad vibes they give out (Synder et al., 1977). It is surely no accident that interpersonal warmth has been identified as a far stronger mediator of self-fulfilling prophecies than explicit feedback (Harris, 1989).

Although a minority of U.S. citizens still express old-fashioned bigotry, most racism against Blacks today seems to be of the spontaneous variety (Dovidio & Gaertner, 1998). If so, then the measures of implicit prejudice may be especially valuable in characterizing how truly egalitarian modern Western society has become, above and beyond what it has become politically correct to reveal.

FIG. 12.2.   Subtle discrimination can express itself through non-verbal behavior.

AFTERTHOUGHTS

A variety of measurement tools that go beyond the limitations of self-report are available to the contemporary social psychologist. These range from techniques for detecting emotion in face muscles, to equipment for monitoring brain waves, to reaction-time tasks of all shapes and sizes (Cacioppo, Petty, Losch, & Crites, 1994). One powerful technique that has recently become popular is the *Implicit Association Test*, or IAT (Greenwald, McGhee, & Schwartz, 1998). Here, respondents have to classify stimuli (words or pictures) into one of four categories via computer. They press one key if a stimulus falls into two of the categories, and another if it falls into the other two. When the categories paired with each key match (e.g., flower–good, insect–bad) respondents tend to classify stimuli more rapidly than when those categories mismatch (e.g., flower–bad, insect–good). By assessing difference in respondents' speed under the matching and mismatching configurations, the extent to which one dimension (e.g., flower–insect) is automatically associated with the another (e.g., good–bad) can be inferred. The IAT yields strong effects, and readers can try out sample IATs for themselves at the following website: http://buster.cs.yale.edu/implicit/.

   Much research currently focuses on figuring out what, theoretically speaking, indirect measurement tools pick up, and what, practically speaking, they can predict. Social psychologists thus share the passion of other scientists for developing and refining their investigative methods. They are in the same boat as physicists who construct ever more energetic particle accelerators, astronomers who construct ever more powerful telescopes, and microbiologists who construct ever more sensitive assays. Such diverse measurement tools all have one thing in common: they are objective. That is, they provide results that everyone can agree on even if their meaning is debated. This is in contrast to the methods used by traditional psychoanalysts, which depend almost entirely on intuitive observation and guesswork. Even the tools-of-the-trade that clinicians typically employ, such as ambiguous inkblots and picture cards, still allow for a great deal of subjectivity. The result is that such tools tend to tell more about the clinician who uses them than about the client on whom they are used (Lilienfeld, 1999).

We conclude by examining the pros and cons of perhaps the most well known technique for trying to determine what people are really thinking: the so-called lie detector. Currently, two main types of lie detector exist. The first is the *polygraph* test. Suspects to a crime are asked a series of questions. Their physiological reactions while replying to them are measured. Three sets of questions are asked: those having to do to the crime itself (relevant); those that have nothing to do with the crime (irrelevant); and those that, while having nothing to do with the crime, are nonetheless designed to upset innocent suspects more than the relevant questions (control). If all goes according to plan, guilty suspects should react more strongly to relevant than to control questions, whereas innocent suspects should show either the reverse pattern or no difference. Irrespective of guilt, irrelevant questions should elicit the weakest reactions of all.

The main problem with the polygraph test is that circumstantial factors can easily conspire to make innocent suspects exhibit a guilty profile (Lykken, 1998). For example, a genuine rape victim accused of making up charges against her assailant may react most strongly to relevant questions simply because any reference to her rape evokes traumatic memories. Alternatively, a man mistakenly accused of rape may react in the same way because relevant questions evoke possibly legitimate anxiety over false prosecution. In such cases, control questions, which are typically broad in scope and concerned with misdemeanors past, simply cannot compete impact-wise with relevant questions. Polygraph administrators cannot always be trusted to accurately judge the effects of relevant and control questions on innocent suspects. Hence, the polygraph is, in principle, a fallible instrument. Moreover, field studies confirm its fallibility in practice. One of the most rigorous found that, although three-quarters of guilty suspects were correctly identified, between one-third and one-half of innocent suspects were falsely identified (Patrick & Iacono, 1989). An instrument with such a margin of error is simply not suitable for making decisions about the guilt or innocence of individuals.

A sounder way of distinguishing the guilty from the innocent is to probe them for knowledge of a crime. In the Guilty Knowledge Test, or GKT (Lykken, 1998), suspects are asked a series of questions about a crime that only a guilty party could be expected to know. After each question is asked, a number of multiple-choice answers are stated aloud. Only one of these answers is correct. However, all are designed to strike an innocent suspect, unaware of the details of the crime, as equally plausible. Suspects' physiological reactions to each answer are measured. If the information conveyed by an answer is recognized then a stronger physiological reaction results. Hence, guilty suspects will yield a pattern of reactions that reflects knowledge of the crime, whereas innocent suspects will show a random pattern. With enough questions and answers, a reliably clear-cut discrimination can be made.

In addition, note that, because no answers stand out for innocent suspects, the problems that dog the polygraph do not arise. The only limitation of the GKT is that suitable questions can be difficult to construct if the details of the crime have been widely publicized or if innocent suspects have witnessed the crime for themselves. Yet, for all its merits, the GKT has not been widely employed in the criminal justice system, nor has it been a target of much field research, perhaps because it treads on polygraphers' traditional turf. This is a pity because, in available field studies, the GKT misclassifies only 3% of innocent suspects, while classifying 76% of guilty ones correctly (Elaad, Ginton, & Jungman, 1992).

In conclusion, clever technologies can help us peel away the superficial layers of the mind when our native powers of discernment fail us. However, we must remain mindful of their pitfalls. If there is any royal road to the unconscious mind (a claim Freud made of dreams) it is strewn with obstacles that need to be carefully negotiated.

REVELATION

Social psychologists use technical tools, not subjective interpretation, to tell more about people than they are willing or able to say about themselves. Using such tools, they can detect underlying prejudice in people who explicitly deny it, and predict subtle forms of discrimination.

— APG —

CHAPTER REFERENCE

Dovidio, J. F., Kawakami, K., Johnson, C., Johnson, B., & Howard, A. (1997). On the nature of prejudice: Automatic and controlled processes. *Journal of Experimental Social Psychology, 33,* 510–540.

OTHER REFERENCES

Banaji, M. R., & Hardin, C. D. (1996). Automatic stereotyping. *Psychological Science, 7,* 136–141.

Blair, I. V. (2001). Implicit stereotypes and prejudice. In G. Moskowitz (Ed.), *Cognitive social psychology: The Princeton symposium on the legacy and future of social cognition* (pp. 359–374). Mahwah, NJ: Lawrence Erlbaum Associates.

Cacioppo, J. T., Petty, R. E., Losch, M. E., & Crites, S. L. (1994). Psychophysiological approaches to attitudes: Detecting affective dispositions when people won't say, can't say, or don't even know. In S. Shavitt & T. C. Brock (Eds.), *Persuasion: Psychological insights and perspectives* (pp. 43–69). Boston: Allyn & Bacon.

Chartrand, T. L., & Bargh, J. A. (2000). Studying the mind in the middle. A practical guide to priming and automaticity research. In H. Reis & C. Judd (Eds.), *Handbook of Research Methods in Social Psychology* (pp. 253–285). New York: Cambridge University Press.

Crews, F. (1995). *The memory wars: Freud's legacy in dispute.* New York: A New York Review book.

Darley, J. M., & Batson, C. D. (1973). "From Jerusalem to Jericho": A study of situational and dispositional variables in helping behavior. *Journal of Personality and Social Psychology, 27,* 100–108.

Dijksterhuis, A., & van Knippenberg, A. (1998). The relation between perception and behavior, or how to win a game of Trivial Pursuit. *Journal of Personality and Social Psychology, 74,* 865–877.

Dovidio, J. F., & Gaertner, S. L. (1998). On the nature of contemporary prejudice: The causes, consequences, and challenges of aversive racism. In J. L. Eberhardt & S. T. Fiske (Eds.), *Confronting racism: The problem and the response.* Thousand Oaks, CA: Sage.

Elaad, E., Ginton, A., & Jungman, N. (1992). Detection measures in real life guilty knowledge tests. *Journal of Applied Psychology, 77,* 757–767.

Fazio, R. H., Jackson, J. R., Dunton, B. C., & Williams, C. J. (1995). Variability in automatic activation as an unobtrusive measure of racial attitudes: A bona fide pipeline? *Journal of Personality and Social Psychology, 69,* 1013–1027.

Gilbert, D. T. (1998). Ordinary personology. In D. T. Gilbert, S. T. Fiske, & G. Lindsey (Eds.), *The Handbook of Social Psychology* (4th ed., pp. 89–150). New York: McGraw-Hill.

Greenwald, A. G., McGhee, D. E., & Schwartz, J. L. K. (1998). Measuring individual differences in implicit cognition: The implicit association test. *Journal of Personality and Social Psychology, 74,* 1464–1480.

Harris, M. J. (1989). Controversy and cumulation: Meta-analysis and research on interpersonal expectancy effects. *Personality and Social Psychology Bulletin, 17,* 316–322.

Lilienfeld, S. O. (1999). Projective measures of personality and psychopathology: How well do they work? *Skeptical Inquirer, 23,* 32–39.

Lykken, D. (1998). *A tremor in the blood: The uses and abuses of the lie detector.* Reading, MA: Perseus Books.

Patrick, C. J., & Iacono, W. G. (1989). Psychopathy, threat, and polygraph test accuracy. *Journal of Applied Psychology, 74,* 347–355.

Snyder, M., Tanke, E. D., & Berscheid, E. (1977). Social perception and interpersonal behavior: On the self-fulfilling nature of social stereotypes. *Journal of Personality and Social Psychology, 35,* 656–666.

Vrij, A. (2000). *Detecting lies and deceit.* New York: Wiley.

Word, C. O., Zanna, M. P., & Cooper, J. (1974). The nonverbal mediation of self-fulfilling prophecies in interracial interaction. *Journal of Experimental Social Psychology, 10,* 109–120.

MORE TO EXPLORE

Crosby, F., Bromley, S., & Saxe, L. (1980). Recent unobtrusive studies of Black and White discrimination and prejudice: A literature review. *Psychological Review, 87,* 546–563.

Greenwald, A. G., & Banaji, M. R. (1995). Implicit social cognition: Attitudes, self-esteem, and stereotypes. *Psychological Review, 102,* 4–27.

13 I Think, Therefore I Act: Priming Intelligence With Social Stereotypes

"The definition of genius is that it acts unconsciously; and those who have produced immortal works, have done so without knowing how or why. The greatest power operates unseen."
                                        —William Hazlitt (1778–1830), English essayist

BACKGROUND

One day, a young man drives past a giant billboard. On it is a colorful advertisement for vacations in Iceland. The most eye-catching feature is an elegant Nordic lady provocatively sipping a chilled cocktail. The man pays hardly any attention—a week in the frozen tundra is just not his idea of an exotic getaway. Some weeks later, however, he finds himself quite unaccountably on a plane bound for Reykjavík. How could the advertisement, so briefly sighted, have prompted such a drastic change in attitude? The answer becomes apparent on closer inspection. The glass in the lady's hand contained a number of ice-cubes. Within these ice-cubes, obscured by patterns of refracted light, lay the sultry image of a naked woman. The man unconsciously perceived this woman as he drove by. She then lodged in his mind, and became permanently linked to all things Icelandic. Thereafter, every time his restless libido stirred, he felt the North Atlantic calling to him like a siren. Eventually he felt compelled to buy a flight ticket.

According to Key (1981), such subliminal seduction is rife. Advertising agencies everywhere deliberately embed sexual images in their ads to beguile us into purchasing their products. Knowing that our conscious minds will likely reject their pitch, they seek to win over our unconscious minds. And, because our unconscious minds ultimately cause everything we do, those agencies have the ultimate mind-control tool at their disposal. Western consumers, bombarded by media images from cradle to grave, do not therefore belong to a free market. They merely acquiesce to the impulses that the master manipulators have instilled in them.

Before ditching our television sets, however, we might do well to query the premises on which such extravagant claims rest. Why should the unconscious mind, when it allegedly dominates the conscious mind, be itself so easy to control? Why should the unconscious mind be better at discerning embedded images than the conscious mind? Why should the embedded image of a naked woman be more alluring than the visible image of a scantily clad one? And wouldn't the embedded images of rival companies ultimately cancel each other out? The more you think about it, the more fears of being unknowingly coerced into buying stuff seem exaggerated.

However, if rational arguments fail to allay our anxieties, there is the empirical evidence to fall back on. Overall, subliminal advertisements either have very small effects on consumer choice or none at all (Trappey, 1996). Other research calls into question the power of subliminal material to exert other types of influence. Take self-help tapes, alleged to contain potent words of inspiration just out of audible range. Consumers often spend considerable sums on them in the hope of listening their way to mental health or academic success. However, large-scale tests indicate that such tapes neither raise self-esteem nor enhance memory, even though users convince themselves that they do (Greenwald, Spangenberg, Pratkanis, & Eskenazi, 1991). And for readers worried about the corrupting influence of satanic messages recorded backwards on heavy metal soundtracks, here is the good news: No evidence exists that the meaning of

FIG. 13.1.   Can you spot the "subliminal" message?

these messages can be detected by, or has any influence on, those who listen to them (Begg, Needham, & Bookbinder, 1993).

It seems, then, that subliminal influence is a myth readily refuted by sound research and clear thinking. Yet, there is another side to the story. While social psychologists have been busy debunking the wilder claims of the lunatic fringe, they have also been showing how material presented outside of awareness actually can have profound effects on people's thoughts, feelings, and behavior.

Consider, for example, the *mere exposure effect* (Bornstein, 1989; see chap. 11). This denotes our tendency to like stimuli better the more often we encounter them (at least until boredom sets in). What is noteworthy is that the effect occurs even for stimuli presented for only a few milliseconds, below the threshold for conscious perception. Indeed, the effect appears to be stronger, not weaker, for very briefly presented stimuli.

However, a stimulus does not have to be subliminal for it to have an unsuspected influence. Indeed, that was precisely the point of chapter 1. We are remarkably poor even at identifying how recent known events have shaped our attitudes (Nisbett & Wilson, 1977). In other words, a stimulus that we process consciously at Time 1 can affect us unconsciously at Time 2. Higgins, Rholes, and Jones (1977) provided a classic demonstration of this phenomenon. They asked participants to form an impression of a man named Donald on the basis of a short description of his personality and behavior. His most striking trait was his appetite for dangerous sports. As part of a supposedly unrelated task, participants had earlier seen a list of words. When this list had contained positive adjectives like *adventurous*, participants formed a favorable impression of Donald. However, when the list had contained negative adjectives like *reckless*, they formed an unfavorable impression of Donald. Participants were, unbeknown to themselves, judging Donald in terms of recently activated mental schemas. Importantly, the priming effect held only for terms that were readily applicable to Donald. Other positive and negative adjectives, like *neat*, and *listless*, had no effect on participants' impressions of him.

However, it is not only our impressions that can be primed: our behavior can be too. According to the principle of *ideomotor action*, first put forward by William James in his classic book *The Principles of Psychology* (1890), the mere contemplation of a thought automatically prepares us to act on it. It follows that if we can be primed to think something, then we also can be primed to do it.

Ideomotor effects have been demonstrated in a number of remarkable studies (Bargh, Chen, & Burrows, 1996). In one, researchers primed participants with either the trait rude or the trait polite. They did this by embedding words related to these traits in sentences that participants had to unscramble. Afterward, they measured how long participants took to interrupt an experimenter who kept on talking to a confederate. Those who had been primed with the trait rude took less time to interrupt, and those primed with the trait polite more time to interrupt, than participants who had not been primed at all. Bargh et al. (1996) then followed up this study with another showing that behavior could also be indirectly primed by activating stereotypes associated with a particular trait. They subliminally primed participants either with neutral words or with words having to do with unflattering stereotypes of the elderly (e.g., forgetful, frail). They then measured how long it took participants to walk down a hallway. Despite the fact that the word *slow* itself was not shown, participants primed with the elderly stereotypical words took longer to complete the short journey. Apparently, thoughts activated outside of awareness are capable of automatically triggering behaviors to which they are stereotypically related.

The phenomena we have described have a startling, rabbit-out-of-a-hat quality that makes them difficult to believe. Nonetheless, they have been reliably replicated across a variety of settings. However, the examples we have reported so far have involved modifications of relatively simple thoughts and behaviors, such as global judgments or impulsive actions. Is it possible that more complex thoughts and behaviors—requiring conscious deliberation and effort—could also be primed? For example, could something as elaborate as intellectual performance—which draws upon an individual's powers of concentration, inference, and memory—be altered simply by mentally activating material that relates to the trait intelligence?

Intent on probing the limits of automatic influence, Ap Dijksterhuis and Ad van Knippenberg (1998) conducted a study to find out. This dynamic Dutch duo primed participants with social groups that were stereotypically associated with the trait of intelligence to a greater or lesser degree. They then examined whether this had an effect on how well participants performed on a general knowledge test.

WHAT THEY DID

Dijksterhuis and van Knippenberg (1998) conducted a total of four studies. We focus on the first of these, and restrict ourselves to briefer comments on the other three.

In developing their priming manipulation, Dijksterhuis and van Knippenberg capitalized on a familiar stereotype: that of the university professor. Pretests had confirmed that participants regarded professors as smart and knowledgeable people. Consequently, thinking about professors was an excellent way of mentally activating the trait of intelligence for them. Following this reasoning, participants in one condition were instructed to spend 5 minutes imagining a typical professor, writing down what sort of appearance he might have, what sort of lifestyle he might lead, and what sort of things he might do. Participants in a second condition were instructed to do the same, but this time for secretaries, people whom undergraduates had earlier rated as being neither particularly smart nor particularly dumb. Thinking about secretaries was therefore an excellent way of not activating the trait of intelligence, but of imitating the first condition in every other respect. In a third condition, participants were not instructed to think about any social group at all, but were merely asked to skip on to the next part of the study. This final condition served as a check on whether the mere act of imagining any social group might unexpectedly impair or improve their intellectual performance by mentally tiring them out, or getting their cerebral juices flowing, respectively. The researchers did not expect the results of the last two conditions to differ.

To summarize, there were three conditions in all: professor-prime, secretary-prime, and no-prime, with 20 participants (university undergraduates) being randomly assigned to each. Participants were told (in the first two conditions) that the information they provided would be used in future studies conducted by the Department of Social Psychology. This was merely a ruse to put them off the scent.

Next, participants were informed that they would be doing an unrelated task. They were directed to open an envelope on the table in front them. It contained a booklet featuring 42 questions drawn from the popular board game Trivial Pursuit. The questions appeared in a multiple-choice format, with one correct and three incorrect alternatives. An example: "Who painted *La Guernica?*—a. Dali, b. Miró, c. Picasso, d. Velásquez." (The answer is c. Picasso.)

The researchers deliberately selected difficult questions in order to intellectually challenge participants. In pretests, other undergraduates had succeeded in getting on average only half the answers in the booklet correct. Random guessing would have resulted in a quarter being correct on average. Moreover, to ensure that participants flexed their mental muscles to the fullest, they were allowed to take as much time as they wished to answer the questions.

To give the impression that the quiz was completely unrelated to the first task, participants were led to believe that the Department of Personality (note the name change) was attempting to put together a general knowledge scale for future use. Participants were informed that their data would be used to gauge the difficulty of different subsets of questions within the scale. In line with this cover story, the questionnaire was divided into five bogus sections, which ranged from very easy (1) to very hard (5). In reality, however, there was no relationship between the difficulty of the questions and where they appeared in the questionnaire.

It was important that the researchers employ these mild deceptions in order to make absolutely sure that participants would not guess the hypothesis under investigation. In this regard, they were successful. No participant mentioned afterward having entertained any suspicions. Indeed, participants remarked during debriefing that they found it hard to believe telling stories about people would influence their performance on a general knowledge test.

WHAT THEY FOUND

Dijksterhuis and van Knippenberg predicted that participants in the profes-sor-prime condition would outperform participants in the two other condi-tions on the general knowledge test. Did the results bear out this prediction? They did. Participants who had spent time thinking about uni-versity professors got approximately 10% more of their answers right than participants who had either spent time thinking about secretaries or who had not thought about any social group. The 3% difference in performance between the secretary-prime and no-prime condition was no more than what would have been expected by chance. It seems, then, that activating the mere idea of a social group widely regarded to be intelligent is enough to get people to engage in more intelligent behavior (Fig. 13.2).

To explore how long the priming effect lasted, the researchers divided participants' overall score into three scores, corresponding to the propor-tion of correct answers they gave in the first, second, and third portions of the general knowledge test. No indication was found that the impact of the priming manipulation decayed over the course of the test, which took, on average, 8 minutes to complete. Moreover, two companion studies also failed to find any evidence of decay, even though one of them featured a test that lasted a quarter of an hour. Thus complex behavior, like test perfor-mance, can be quite durably primed, at least when no competing influ-ences are present.

Moreover, the companion studies conducted by Dijksterhuis and van Knippenberg (1998) convincingly replicated and expanded their primary finding. In one study, for example, a dose–response relationship was identi-fied. The longer participants spent thinking about professors the more their intellectual performance was enhanced. This strongly suggests that the priming of complex behavior is a lawful phenomenon, not a capricious chimera. In another study, participants spent time thinking about soccer hooligans prior to taking the general knowledge test. This impaired their performance, in keeping with the stereotype of soccer hooligans as stupid. A final study showed that directly priming the traits of intelligence and stu-pidity (by having participants list behaviors characteristic of one or the other) had the same effect as indirectly priming those traits (by activating stereotypes of professors and hooligans).

SO WHAT?

Our current thoughts and deeds are not as self-contained as they seem. Recent events, which at first blush seem incapable of influencing us, none-theless do, and without our realizing it. Dijksterhuis and van Knippenberg demonstrated that even something as elaborate as intellectual perfor-mance is sensitive to earlier activities as seemingly irrelevant as recalling the content of stereotypes. Moreover, their findings were no fluke. Wheeler,

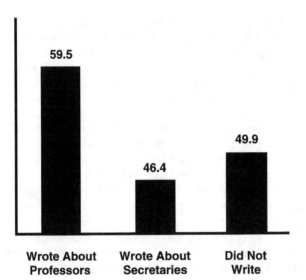

59.5

49.9

46.4

Wrote About   Wrote About   Did Not
Professors   Secretaries   Write

FIG. 13.2.   Percentage of correct answers given by participants on a quiz, having written about professors, about secretaries, or having not written anything.

Jarvis, and Petty (2001) had White participants write an essay about a day in the life of a student named either Tyrone or Eric. These names strongly implied, of course, that the student was either Black or White. Afterward, participants completed a portion of the mathematical section of the Graduate Record Examination (like the SAT, only more difficult). It turned out that those who had written about Tyrone performed significantly worse. The stereotype of Blacks having been activated, they inadvertently verified one of its negative implications: academic underachievement.

How does mentally activating the notion intelligence, whether directly or indirectly, affect performance? What are the mental links in the chain? At the time of writing, this is a matter of debate. Consider again the present study in which thoughts of brainy professors improved performance on a general knowledge test. Obviously, priming did not make participants suddenly more knowledgeable. However, it may have allowed them to access their current knowledge more effectively by prompting the use of better strategies for recalling or inferring answers. Alternatively, it may have provided participants with motivation to think harder.

But there is an interesting twist to the regular behavioral priming effect. When a prime denotes a specific individual, as opposed to a social category, a contrast effect tends to occur. That is to say, the prime tends to lead people to think or act in ways contrary to the implication of the prime. So, although priming participants with stereotypes of professors makes them more intelligent, priming them with Albert Einstein makes them less so. In addition, although priming participants with stereotypes of supermodels make them less intelligent, priming them with Claudia Schiffer makes them more intelligent (Dijksterhuis et al., 1998). (Now you know whose picture to pin up above your study desk!) Such turnabout findings suggest that people spontaneously compare themselves, favorably or unfavorably, to individuals who exemplify traits, and a sense of increased or decreased competence results that improves or impairs performance.

Sometimes it is remarkable how little priming is needed to modify intellectual performance. For example, Steele and Aronson (1995) found that simply reminding high-achieving Black students of their race was enough to impair their performance on a test of mental ability. In such cases, the distracting fear of confirming the stereotype that Blacks are academically inferior is enough to undermine performance, and may help explain the achievement gap between Blacks and Whites. There is a positive flipside to such *stereotype threat* however. Shih, Pittinsky, and Ambady (1999) found that Asian women who were reminded of their race before taking a math test did better than those who were not. Mentally activating a positive racial stereotype, namely that Asians are good at math, proved to be empowering—a form of *stereotype enhancement*. Similar reminders of gender, however, made Asian women do worse. In both studies, the complicating factor is that the activated stereotype also forms part of participants' personal identity. This may amplify the power of the subtle primes on performance.

AFTERTHOUGHTS

Given all of these weird and wacky priming effects, readers might legitimately wonder whether Key's paranoia about subliminal seduction is not partly justified. Have social psychologists ultimately succeeded in showing that, when it comes to unconscious influences, we are puppets on strings after all? Again, rational argument and empirical evidence come to our rescue. Our autonomy is not quite as undermined as might first appear.

First, the priming effects described were experimentally engineered. In an experiment, researchers deliberately arrange matters so as to maximize the chances of obtaining the desired result. They do this by cutting out all irrelevant influences, paring down a phenomenon of interest to its bare essentials. The real world, however, is abuzz with influences of every sort. Hence, effects that emerge cleanly in the laboratory only emerge messily in everyday life.

By way of illustration, consider the study described earlier in which priming stereotypes of the elderly slowed participants' walking pace. The study was set up so that the only critical influence on participants was the priming manipulation and the only behavior in which they were likely to engage was walking. Strolling down your local Main Street however, matters rapidly become more complicated. Suppose you bump into an elderly gentleman and exchange a few words with him. This event is liable to mentally activate the trait *slow*, leading you to walk away from the encounter somewhat sluggishly. But suppose that, the very next moment, you catch sight of a gorgeous stranger, looking quite enchanting, across a crowded street. This would then presumably put the pep back in your step. Or suppose that, after bidding the elderly gentleman farewell, you instead entered a bookstore and started browsing. Because browsing is something you do at a leisurely pace anyhow, the mental activation of the trait slow would be irrelevant.

The upshot is that a sneaky hidden persuader would be hard pressed to plant a prime capable of permanently shaping your behavior. The ebb and flow of everyday life ensures that the effects of one prime are continually overridden by the effects of others, and that some behaviors will be unaffected by some primes.

Experimental research confirms that priming only occurs under favorable conditions. Aspects of the situation can keep it in check. In one study, for example, participants were primed with the trait *helpfulness*. Under normal circumstances, this made them more likely to pick up a pen that a confederate had accidentally dropped. However, when the pen was leaky, or when participants had a pressing appointment, the effects of the prime disappeared. That is, priming occurred only in situations where there was no added cost to helping and where there was no competing goal to pursue (Macrae & Johnstone, 1999; see also chap. 18).

Characteristics of the person can also put the lid on priming. For example, people differ in the extent to which they automatically associate a social category, such as the elderly, with a stereotypical trait, such as slowness. When you test for the presence or absence of such an association (see chap. 12 for how to do this) you find that behavioral priming effects occur only in people in whom it is present (Dijksterhuis, Aarts, Bargh, & van Knippenberg, 2000).

What all this suggests is that conditions both inside the person and outside in the situation must be coordinated for behavioral priming to occur. This will prevent any unscrupulous party from taking overwhelming advantage of priming effects. Nonetheless, we should be attentive to those rare circumstances in which person and situation are coordinated. This may allow us to develop ways of preventing stereotype threat and even promoting stereotype enhancement.

REVELATION

Although the hidden persuaders are the stuff of fiction, stimuli presented outside of awareness can nonetheless have surprisingly profound effects on thoughts, feelings, and behavior. In particular, merely calling to mind thoughts about social groups can improve or worsen intellectual performance.

— *APG* —

CHAPTER REFERENCE

Dijksterhuis, A., & van Knippenberg, A. (1998). The relation between perception and behavior, or how to win a game of Trivial Pursuit. *Journal of Personality and Social Psychology, 74,* 865–877.

OTHER REFERENCES

Bargh, J. A., Chen, M., & Burrows, L. (1996). The automaticity of social behavior: Direct effects of trait concept and stereotype activation on action. *Journal of Personality and Social Psychology, 71,* 230–244.

Begg, I. M., Needham, D. R., & Bookbinder, M. (1993). Do backward messages unconsciously affect listeners? No. *Canadian Journal of Experimental Psychology, 47,* 1–14.

Bornstein, R. F. (1989). Exposure and affect: Overview and meta-analysis of research, 1968–87. *Psychological Bulletin, 106,* 265–289.

Dijksterhuis, A., Aarts, H., Bargh, J. A., & van Knippenberg, A. (2000). On the relation between associative strength and automatic behavior. *Journal of Experimental Social Psychology, 36,* 531–544.

Dijksterhuis, A., Spears, R., Postmes, T., Stapel, D. A., Koomen, W., van Knippenberg, A., & Scheepers, D. (1998). Seeing one thing and doing another: Contrast effect in automatic behavior. *Journal of Personality and Social Psychology, 75,* 862–871.

Greenwald, A., Spangenberg, E., Pratkanis, A., & Eskenazi, J. (1991). Double-blind tests of subliminal self-help audiotapes. *Psychological Science, 2,* 119–122.

Higgins, E. T., Rholes, W. S., & Jones, C. R. (1977). Category accessibility and impression formation. *Journal of Experimental Social Psychology, 13,* 141–154.

James, W. (1890). *The principles of psychology.* New York: H. Holt and Company.

Key, W. B. (1981). *Subliminal seduction: Ad media's manipulation of a not so innocent America.* New York: Signet.

Macrae, C. N., & Johnstone, L. (1999). Help, I need somebody: Automatic action and inaction. *Social Cognition, 16,* 400–417.

Nisbett, R. E., & Wilson, T. D. (1977). Telling more than we can know: Verbal reports on mental processes. *Psychological Review, 84,* 231–259.

Shih, M., Pittinsky, T. L., & Ambady, N. (1999). Stereotype susceptibility: Identity salience and shifts in quantitative performance. *Psychological Science, 10,* 80–83.

Steele, C. M., & Aronson, J. (1995). Stereotype threat and the intellectual test performance of African-Americans. *Journal or Personality and Social Psychology, 69,* 797–811.

Trappey, C. (1996). A meta-analysis of consumer choice and subliminal advertising. *Psychology and Marketing, 13,* 517–530.

Wheeler, S. C., Jarvis, W. B. G., & Petty, R. E. (2001). Think onto others: The self-destructive impact of negative stereotypes. *Journal of Experimental Social Psychology, 37,* 173–180.

MORE TO EXPLORE

Steele, C. M. (1997). The threat in the air: How stereotypes shape intellectual identity and performance. *American Psychologist, 52,* 613–629.

Wheeler, S. C., & Petty, R. E. (in press). The effect of stereotype activation on behavior: A review of possible mechanisms. *Psychological Bulletin.*

14 What Did You Expect?: The Behavioral Confirmation of the Physical Attractiveness Stereotype

"Imaginations which people have of one another are the solid facts of society."

—Charles Horton Cooley (1864–1929), American sociologist

BACKGROUND

In George Bernard Shaw's celebrated play, *Pygmalion,* a raffish flower girl, Eliza Dolittle, is transformed as she lives up to the expectations of her snobby tutor, Professor Henry Higgins. In social psychology, this "Pygmalion effect" is more commonly called the *self-fulfilling prophecy.* According to Merton (1948):

> The self-fulfilling prophecy is, in the beginning, a false definition of the situation evoking a new behavior which makes the originally *false* conception come true. The specious validity of the self-fulfilling prophecy perpetuates a reign of error. For the prophet will cite the actual course of events as proof that he was right from the beginning. (p. 195)

The dynamics of the self-fulfilling prophecy typically involve *behavioral confirmation*, which Darley and Fazio (1980) described as a sequence that begins when a perceiver forms an expectation about a person, then acts toward that person based on the expectation. The target person next interprets the perceiver's actions, and responds in a way that is consistent with the perceiver's expectation. Finally, the perceiver, based on the target's actions, continues to harbor the expectation, apparently confirmed. (Whew!) A chain reaction, one that occurs in a variety of social contexts.

For instance, introduce a guest speaker (without his knowledge) as "warm and friendly" and you will motivate the audience to express interest, which will then inspire the speaker to give a more animated, flamboyant talk. But introduce him as "a bit cold and unfriendly" and you would produce an unsympathetic and reserved audience, which will, in turn, cause the speaker to give a cautious, lackluster talk. This is basically what Kelley (1950) found.

Or, randomly pull the names of some 1st and 2nd graders out of a hat and tell a teacher (who does not know them) that, based on results from the "Harvard Test of Inflected Acquisition" (there really is no such test), those particular kids are on the verge of a substantial IQ spurt (even though the children are actually no different from other children). The teacher will then be likely to give them more emotional support, challenging work, attention in class, and detailed feedback on their performance. Eight months later they will show greater progress than their peers, in terms of improved schoolwork (as appraised by the teachers) and higher IQ gains (on objective tests). In some cases their IQs will jump as many as 30 points. This is basically what Rosenthal and Jacobson (1968) found.

Or, while interviewing a job applicant, whose ethnic background would "blend in nicely" with the rest of the company, sit close to and make attentive eye contact with her, and ask questions that probe for positive information, and she will duly perform in a self-assured, bubbly manner, leading you to confidently announce that "She's just right for the position!" But, perhaps because her ethnicity would "stand out like a sore thumb," sit at a more professional distance, let her do the talking (after all, she's the one being interviewed), and ask questions that will turn up uncomplimentary information, and she will perform in a nervous, uninspired manner. This is similar to what Word and his colleagues (1974) found.

Word and his colleagues had White participants interview White and Black job applicants. The applicants were actually trained *confederates* (individuals cooperating with the experimenter) who behaved according to a set script. Their verbal and nonverbal behaviors were practiced so as not to vary. The participants thought the researchers were studying the behaviors of the applicants, when in fact it was the interviewers (the participants themselves) who were being analyzed. Interviewers were found to lean more toward, make more eye contact with, and say nicer things to White than Black applicants. They gave briefer interviews to, and sat further away from, the Black candidates. Having demonstrated this effect, Word and colleagues then trained interviewers to act accordingly—either warmly or coolly—toward White research participants playing the role of job applicants. Ratings by independent judges found that the applicants performed more competently if they had received the warm treatment, and less competently if they had been treated as the Black applicants had previously been treated.

In all of these examples, behavior is reciprocated. Positive acts prompt positive responses and negative acts prompt negative ones. As a result, the perceiver retains his or her impression of the target person. Moreover, the target person may even come to internalize the perceiver's evaluation, especially if the perceiver is important to the target. "It's true what they think of me."

Mark Snyder and his colleagues (1977) provided a classic experimental demonstration of behavioral confirmation. Surveying the field in the mid-1970s, they noticed that much of the theorizing done by cognitively oriented social psychologists left the individual about whom they were theorizing "lost in thought." Investigators had learned a lot about the machinery of social cognition. They had discovered a lot about how one attributes a cause to another person's behavior, or how one infers a person's traits from his or her acts. Yet so far they knew very little about the social consequences of attributions, impressions, expectations, and the like. Although research had documented how we cognitively bolster or protect the stereotypes we possess—overestimating the frequency of supportive examples, filling in informational gaps, interpreting ambiguous information as being consistent with our generalizations—not enough research had investigated how our perceptions shape our behaviors in encounters with others, and their behaviors in turn. Therefore, Snyder and his colleagues sought to investigate people's responses to others' expectations and behaviors.

In order to do this, they focused on the *physical attractiveness* stereotype: Beautiful people are good people (Dion and others, 1972). If you show people three photos, one of a very attractive person, one of a so-so person, and one of an unattractive person, you will find that they tend to rate them quite differently. Physically attractive people are generally judged to be on the winning end of almost every dimension. They are believed to possess more positive personality traits, hold more prestigious jobs, and be happier in their professional and social lives. (Forget the fact that they are also judged to be more vain, narcissistic, and unfaithful to their spouses.) Snyder and his colleagues chose the physical attractiveness stereotype because it is potent and because it is based, like gender, age, and race stereotypes, on superficial features that are easy to experimentally manipulate and present to others incidentally.

WHAT THEY DID

Snyder and his colleagues sought to design a study that would mirror the way impressions are spontaneously formed and come to influence others' behaviors in everyday life. That is, they wanted their study to have *ecological validity*—to mimic the sorts of things people do and experience daily.

One hundred and two University of Minnesota students (an equal number of males and females) participated in the study, described as focusing on how people become acquainted through interactions that either do or do not involve nonverbal communication. This cover story provided a rationale for having unacquainted males and females arrive at separate rooms and have a telephone conversation that they agreed could be recorded. As part of this ruse, participants provided information about themselves, such as their academic major. They were each told that a folder of such information would be given to their partner to help jumpstart their conversation. Inserted unobtrusively into the folder given to each male was a Polaroid snapshot allegedly of the female. Importantly, this photo was not really of the female partner. In addition, a photo was taken of the male, consistent with the false claim that it would be given to his female partner. However, nothing about photos was ever mentioned and no photo was ever shown to her.

The photo that each male participant received was drawn from a set of photos provided by young women from nearby colleges who had posed to the tune of 5 dollars. These photos had been rated by a separate group of college-age men as being very attractive (average rating of 8.1 on a 10-point scale) or very unattractive (average rating of 2.6). (Although the women providing the photos agreed, in writing, to have their pictures used for research purposes, they were never told of the attractiveness ratings they received.) Thus, each male was tricked into believing that he would be conversing with either a highly attractive or highly unattractive woman. In order to determine how much the photos shaped stereotypic impressions, Snyder and his colleagues had each male rate the particular female he was about to converse with on each of 27 traits (such as friendliness, enthusiasm, and trustworthiness). Keep in mind that their impressions would be based on the totality of information they had received in the folder, including the experimentally manipulated photograph.

The male and female of each pair then engaged in a 10-minute, get-acquainted conversation, speaking though microphones and listening through headphones from separate rooms. (Three of the 51 conversations had to be interrupted and the participants immediately debriefed, because the males started commenting on the photos, perhaps saying "I'm noticing your big beautiful eyes and nice smile ... like to 'go out' sometime?") Afterward, the males again indicated their impressions of their partners on various trait dimensions, while the females rated themselves on the same dimensions and also indicated how comfortable they felt during their conversations, how physically attractive they believed their partners thought they were, and how much they thought their partners treated them the way males typically do. Finally, the male and female participants were carefully debriefed—an especially important step since the experimenter had deceived them.

Following this phase of the study, independent judges—who did not know the physical attractiveness of the males, the actual or perceived physical attractiveness of the females, or the hypotheses of the study more generally—listened to the tracks of the tape-recorded conversations containing only the females' voices or only the males' voices. The judges rated how animated and enthusiastic the women and men each were, how intimate and personal their conversations were, and so on, allowing Snyder and his collaborators to examine, in detail, the process of behavioral confirmation.

WHAT THEY FOUND

The males did indeed associate physical attractiveness with desirable personality characteristics (based on their ratings after being exposed to the photos, but before the actual conversations). The alleged attractive women were imagined to be relatively friendly, socially skilled, poised, and humorous. In contrast, the alleged unattractive women were assumed to be unfriendly, socially inept, awkward, and serious. So far, so good: the experimental manipulation created the expected impressions (ones consistent with the physical attractiveness stereotype).

Furthermore, the men who talked with presumed attractive women were judged by those examining the tape-recorded conversations to be more sociable, sexually warm, bold, humorous, confident, and animated than were their counterparts who chatted with presumed unattractive women.

Finally, the most striking result: the judges rated the alleged attractive women as being more poised, sexually warm, animated, and sociable than they did the alleged unattractive women. (Remember, there were no actual average attractiveness differences between the women in the two experimental conditions.) Importantly, on trait dimensions that are unrelated to the physical attractiveness stereotype, such as intelligence or sensitivity, no differences were found across the two conditions (Fig. 14.1). Thus, all the elements of behavioral confirmation were found. Erroneous initial impressions and generalizations on the part of the males led to changes in their behaviors, and to corresponding changes in the females' behaviors.

Snyder and his colleagues attempted to isolate *mediators* (more specific causal factors) of the behavioral confirmation they found. They surmised that the degree of friendliness displayed by the male perceivers was the key factor in evoking reciprocal friendliness in the target women. To what else could differences in the women's phone behaviors be due, besides differences in the men's phone behaviors? The ratings they obtained revealed that women thought to be attractive regarded their partners' images of them as being more accurate (even though they had no knowledge that those images were being influenced by photos). Alleged attractive women also indicated that they regarded their partners' manner of interacting with them as being more typical of how men usually treated them. These perceptions help to explain why the women believed to be attractive responded so warmly to their male partners' friendly overtures. The pre-

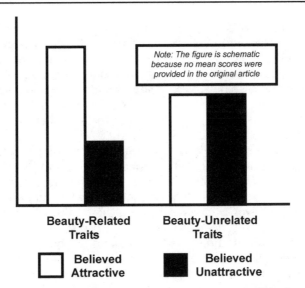

FIG. 14.1. Judges' ratings of women speaking over an intercom to male participants who had been led to believe the women were attractive or unattractive.

sumed homely women had a cooler, more aloof reaction probably because it seemed to them that their partners had misperceived them and treated them in an unusually standoffish manner.

SO WHAT?

Snyder et al. (1977) demonstrated important potential outcomes of stereotypic impressions. The young men's expectations governed their self-presentations, which in turn encouraged females to behave accordingly. The men created the very behaviors they expected to encounter! This dynamic was engineered with very little effort. A photo was inconspicuously slipped into an information folder that males glanced through before striking up a phone conversation. Of course, the process would be more complicated in the "real world." There, expectations and behaviors would occur in both directions. The women would have expectations of their own, generating behaviors that would mold the behaviors of the men as well. Behavioral confirmation would occur in a back-and-forth manner. The physical attractiveness stereotype would also normally overlap with other stereotypes, such as those pertaining to gender, age, social class, race, or ethnicity. In everyday life, it is often a confluence of impressions that evoke behaviors and responses to those behaviors.

Snyder et al. (1977) demonstrated that beliefs can create their own reality. Social perceivers possess a wide range of expectations that can operate with little effort but great effect. This effect can be negative.

Believing females to be passive followers rather than active leaders, it would be easy, without intention or awareness, to elicit acquiescent behaviors from them. Believing that men are callous and unemotional, it would be easy to discourage any signs of tenderness or emotionality on their part. It would also be easy to render an elderly person helpless, simply by believing that and behaving as if he or she truly is helpless. Negative expectations are insidious in their power to make of their victims exactly what they are accused of being.

Snyder and Swann (1978) demonstrated a similar dynamic in a study involving conversations between strangers. One member of each pair was led to believe that the other member was either hostile (likes contact sports; is insensitive and cruel) or nonhostile (likes poetry and sailing; is kind and cooperative). Judges evaluating the conversations found that partners randomly described as hostile ended up showing more hostility. Furthermore, when the presumed hostile and nonhostile persons conversed with new partners, who had no set expectations of them, the chain of events continued—persons previously presumed to be hostile maintained such a manner.

Indeed, behavioral confirmation is obtained in a variety of circumstances. A study by Curtis and Miller (1986) showed that if you merely believe that another person likes you, you will try to validate his or her reasons for liking you by behaving in a likable manner, which will cause him or her to, in truth, like you. But believing that someone dislikes you can easily lead to the opposite: giving him or her good reasons to actually dislike you. If the process seems circular, that's because it is.

Moreover, Miller and his colleagues (1975), noticing what litter bugs children can be, admonished those in a particular class to be neat and clean. The admonition did increase the percentage of litter that children put into wastebaskets, but only temporarily. However, when the researchers praised the children, on 8 consecutive days, for being neat and tidy, environmental conscientiousness soared and persisted. "They think we're neat and clean—well, we'll show them that they're right!" Although we sometimes surrender, behaviorally, to negative labels, we also try to live up to positive ones.

Several of the foregoing studies provide good examples of what is referred to as schematic processing. A *schema* is an organized, structured set of cognitions that exerts influence over its possessor's perceptions and behaviors (it partly overlaps with the intuitive theories referred to in chaps. 1, 2, and 3). Schemas influence how one handles new information or responds to particular stimuli. One sees a pit bull, and all of his or her various thoughts about pit bulls spring to mind (including, hopefully, some that suggest caution). We have schemas related to the members of certain groups: Australians, TV evangelists, spelling bee champions, and so on. We also have schemas for individual people (like the schema you might have of a favorite aunt or uncle). We have schemas for particular occupations or social roles (prison guard or shaman). We even have schemas for social events, often called *scripts*: wedding scripts, restaurant scripts, first date scripts, job interview scripts, and so forth. Scripts generally include information about what events occur, and in what sequence they occur, in given social situations. These manifold types of schemas influence questions we ask, inferences we draw, information we remember, and our expectations about the future. They also influence our behaviors. In the present study, the men's expectations—regarding target women's physical attractiveness—served as schemas, influencing their behaviors, and the women's behaviors too.

When we encounter a person—a Hare Krishna devotee with orange robe and shaven head, say—our perceptions and behaviors are influenced both by our minds, filled as they are with myriad beliefs and expectations (including those pertaining to Krishna devotees), and by what we actually experience in our interaction with that person (who may not appear naive or brainwashed at all). In other words, what is outside in our environment interacts with what is inside our mind. Our preexisting thoughts do not completely determine our perceptions of reality (at least not normally), nor does reality typically influence us in a direct, unadulterated way. However, at times one or the other is dominant, as when our preconceptions hold sway. This can be problematic. Though we cannot stop ourselves from believing things and thinking in generalities, we also cannot afford to harbor fallacious convictions that have no chance of being amended by incontrovertible experiences.

To be sure, schematic processing saves us a lot of time and energy. You see someone that fits your street person schema, and that is pretty much all you think you need to know. You are driving in a procession of cars in a funeral, and that is pretty much all you think you need to know. A script tells you what to do and how to be. You are on automatic pilot. No need to think a lot. Yet there are potential liabilities of schematic thinking, in the form of biases, errors, and inflexible modes of behavior. We may think that a person is lazy because, after all, he is "one of them" (though, in fact, he may be exceptionally hardworking). We may think someone cannot handle a particular job because she is a woman (even though she may be eminently qualified for the position). We may refrain from mentioning to someone our love of the opera because that person works as a supermarket butcher (when in fact he or she is an avid patron of the fine arts). And so on: ignored information, wrong interpretations, and inaccurate predictions.

Perhaps the greatest import of the study by Snyder et al. (1977) lies in its more general demonstration of how much thoughts influence behaviors and how much one person's behaviors influence those of others. Being told that someone is a knockout or drop-dead handsome will turn our mental wheels and affect our behavior (at least until we see the person for ourselves). Hearing that a particular person is secretive or delusional may channel our behavior so as to elicit sneaky or neurotic behavior from him or her. Of course, we are just as much the objects as we are the subjects of behavioral confirmation. How much of our own behavior, and who we are more generally, has been shaped by others' impressions and expectations?

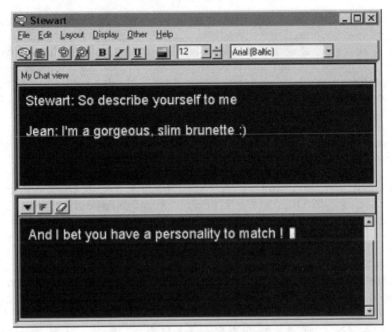

FIG. 14.2. Will Jean now behaviorally confirm Stewart's stereotypical expectations?

AFTERTHOUGHTS

It should be pointed out that in everyday life, unlike in the experimental laboratory, expectations are often rooted in reality (Jussim, 1991). For example, if little Johnny has done poorly all semester, and his teacher develops warranted negative expectations about his academic capacity, it will hardly be surprising if her negative expectations end up coinciding with his future poor performance. That is, expectations can reflect reality as well as shape. That said, performance tends to improve, and motivation goes up, if students are encouraged to operate under the assumption that their abilities are malleable and capable of incremental improvement, rather than fixed and permanently tied to current levels of performance (Dweck, 1999).

It is also important to recognize that perceivers do not always shape the behaviors of targets. There are limits to the influence expectations have. Behavioral confirmation is far from assured in every context. You find that someone has cast you in a negative light so you try to prove him or her wrong. You disagree with what you perceive is someone's impression of you, so you try to change it. Behavioral *dis*confirmation. For example, fervent Yvgeny expects tasty Tatyana to be "easy," and makes her an indecent proposal. Offended by his expectations, Tatyana kicks him in the groin, showing just how "difficult" she can be!

Nonetheless, genuine instances of behavioral confirmation remind us of two complementary themes running through social psychology. One theme is that people are quick to attribute traits to others. Ample research has demonstrated people's fairly automatic tendency to assume that each person possesses stable, enduring traits that cause him or her to behave in a predictable manner, even across varied situations (Carlston & Skowronski, 1994; Gilbert, 1998). The other theme, iconoclastically articulated by personality psychologist Walter Mischel (1968), is that there is scant empirical evidence for pervasive cross-situational consistency in people's behavior, nowhere as much as we intuitively think there is. People are not always the same in different situations; they are not as trait-like as we imagine. Extroverts have their solitary days, and introverts occasionally come out of their shells. The so-called *fundamental attribution error* involves unjustifiably attributing a person's behaviors to personality traits when situational constraints explain them better (Ross, 1977).

However, what is interesting about the fundamental attribution error is that it is self-perpetuating. As Snyder et al. (1977) pointed out, our believing that others possess certain traits causes us to behave in certain consistent ways toward them. This causes them, via behavioral confirmation, to behave in consistent ways in our presence. It is we, through our behaviors, who are producing the consistencies in their behaviors. In others words, traits we believe exist in others may be largely due to the consistency of our own expectations and behaviors!

Finally, behavioral confirmation suggests a simple experiment you might try. Start by thinking the worst of the people you meet today. Believe that they are basically rotten, even if they pretend otherwise. See them as having malevolent ulterior motives. Give them the hard time they deserve. Let us know how they respond.

Tomorrow, reverse your approach. Treat each person you meet as your best friend, someone you have not seen for a long time, and deeply miss. Put each one on a pedestal; lavish him or her with love and respect. Expect them to impress you with charm and goodness. Let us know what happens. Your findings should convince you—just as do the experimental demonstrations of social psychology—of the ready occurrence and significance of behavioral confirmation.

REVELATION

Although our expectations of people are based on their behavior, it is likewise true that their behavior is the result of our expectations. Simply believing that someone is attractive will lead to their actually being attractive.

— KPF —

CHAPTER REFERENCE

Snyder, M., Tanke, E. D., & Berscheid, E. (1977). Social perception and interpersonal behavior: On the self-fulfilling nature of social stereotypes. *Journal of Personality and Social Psychology, 35,* 656–666.

OTHER REFERENCES

Carlston, D. E., & Skowronski, J. J. (1994). Savings in the relearning of trait information as evidence for spontaneous inference generation. *Journal of Personality and Social Psychology, 66,* 840–856.

Curtis, R. C., & Miller, K. (1986). Believing another person likes or dislikes you: Behaviors making the beliefs come true. *Journal of Personality and Social Psychology, 51,* 284–290.

Darley, J. M., & Fazio, R. H. (1980). Expectancy confirmation processes arising in the social interaction sequence. *American Psychologist, 35,* 867–881.

Dion, K. K., Berscheid, E., & Walster, E. (1972). What is beautiful is good. *Journal of Personality and Social Psychology, 24,* 285–290.

Dweck, C. S. (1999). *Self-theories: The role in motivation, personality, and development.* Philadelphia: Psychological Press.

Gilbert, D. T. (1998). Ordinary personalology. In D. T. Gilbert, S. T. Fiske, & G. Lindzey (Eds.), *The handbook of social psychology* (4th ed., pp. 89–150). New York: McGraw-Hill.

Jussim, L. (1991). Social perception and social reality: A reflection-construction model. *Psychological Review, 98,* 54–73.

Kelley, H. H. (1950). The warm-cold variable in first impressions of persons. *Journal of Personality, 18,* 431–439.

Merton, R. (1948). The self-fulfilling prophecy. *Antioch Review, 8,* 193–210.

Miller, R. L., Brickman, P., & Bolen, D. (1975). Attribution versus persuasion as a means of modifying behavior. *Journal of Personality and Social Psychology, 31,* 430–441.

Mischel, W. (1968). *Personality and assessment.* New York: Wiley.

Rosenthal, R., & Jacobson, L. (1968). *Pygmalion in the classroom: Teacher expectation and pupils' intellectual development.* New York: Holt, Rinehart, & Winston.

Ross, L. (1977). The intuitive psychologist and his shortcomings: Distortion in the attribution process. In L. Berkowitz (Ed.), *Advances in experimental social psychology* (Vol. 10, pp. 174–221). New York: Academic Press.

Snyder, M., & Swann, W. B., Jr. (1978). Behavioral confirmation in social interaction: From social perception to social reality. *Journal of Experimental Social Psychology, 14,* 148–162.

Word, C. O., Zanna, M. P., & Cooper, J. (1974). The nonverbal mediation of self-fulfilling prophecies in interracial interaction. *Journal of Experimental Social Psychology, 10,* 109–120.

MORE TO EXPLORE

Harris, M. J., Milch, R., Corbitt, E. M., Hoover, D. W., & Brady, M. (1992). Self-fulfilling effects of stigmatizing information on children's social interactions. *Journal of Personality and Social Psychology, 63,* 41–50.

Rosenthal, R. (1994). Interpersonal expectancy effects: A 30-year perspective. *Current Directions in Psychological Science, 3,* 176–179.

15 Good Vibes: Insights Into Belief in Mental Telepathy

"I almost had a psychic girlfriend, but she left me before we met."

—Anonymous

BACKGROUND

Our responses to social situations depend on how we interpret or *construe* them (see chap. 4). Interpretations of events around us are ordinarily accurate enough to get us through our daily lives. But sometimes, especially when a situation is unfamiliar or ambiguous, our understanding of it can be flawed, or at least at odds with others understanding of it.

A nice example, albeit a fictional one, comes from the movie *E.T.* The extraterrestrial creature in the movie became the beloved playmate of the trusting, lonely boy who discovered him. By contrast, the adult authorities in town, being suspicious by nature, saw only a sinister, ugly thing.

Or consider the following nonfictional account, told to one of us (RPA) by a Peace Corps volunteer just back from a remote Indian village in the Andes mountains of Chile. The hardworking Indians, living simple lives in their isolated village, had rarely seen people eager as the volunteers, who showed up suddenly offering to help improve their schools, roads, farming, and sewage system. The Indians suspected that it was all a clever trick by missionaries seeking to convert them to alien beliefs. Having arrived at this conclusion, the villagers acted reverently in the presence of these "ministers" but doggedly opposed any measures they recommended. This behavior was extremely puzzling to the volunteers and their supervisors. The misunderstanding was finally corrected, just when it was time to leave. At many Peace Corps sites, a great deal of time is wasted in trying to correct false perceptions. (On the other hand, our concept of wasting time and the Third World concept are sharply different, and it may after all be necessary to waste time getting familiar with one another's ways.)

When faced with a puzzling, unfamiliar situation for which there is no readily available explanation, one approach is to think of familiar situations encountered or heard about in the past, and consider how well they map onto the present one. This may suggest plausible interpretations of what one is presently facing, and what to think and do about it. Some phenomena are intrinsically mysterious, like UFO rides, palm reading, and how your not-so-smart friend got into Yale. In this chapter, we analyze yet another mysterious phenomenon: mental telepathy.

Whether or not people are capable of mental telepathy is a fascinating question, one about human potential and the very nature of reality. But equally intriguing to psychologists is the question of why people believe that telepathic powers exist, or that they themselves possess it. Fred Ayeroff and Robert Abelson (1976) referred to this as *extrasensible belief* (ESB), and surmised that such belief depends, at least in part, on the similarity of the telepathy experience to a familiar and successful *social experience*.

What social experiences might seem similar to mental telepathy? Imagine a typical telepathic scenario: two physically separated individuals have no known means of communication, but the sender exerts mental energy on his image of some stimulus—an object or idea—and the receiver is then able to recognize the projected image. The upshot is that the receiver gets information from the sender, without any natural explanation for how that information was transmitted.

The experience of sending or receiving invisible messages is not totally unfamiliar. In social interaction, people sometimes know that they are influencing each other, but don't really know how they manage it. Two people may be able to finish each other's sentences, instinctively know each other's thoughts, hit it off wonderfully, etc. Love at first sight and the sense that one has found one's soulmate may be the most vivid example of this experience. This sense of inexplicable communion with the loved one can be strong, and is popularly taken to be beyond objective, scientific analysis (although a number of social psychologists interested in this topic would beg to differ—see chap. 27). In other arenas—business or sports, for example—the same magical feeling may be experienced when two people readily agree to a deal or play well together. We label such mysterious interpersonal connections, and the magical feelings they produce, *good vibes*.

The author of this chapter, joined by his undergraduate research assistant, Ayeroff, predicted that if he could experimentally manipulate this experience of good vibing within a mental telepathy situation, he would be able to show that belief in ESP hinges on such an experience. Yet he was also aware of other factors that influence belief in ESP or, more specifically, belief in one's ability to control essentially random events. Ellen Langer (1975) argued that the more similar a chance situation is to a skill situation, the more one tends to believe that one has control over the chance situation. Langer demonstrated that increasing the role of one's involvement in a chance situation increases one's sense of efficacy therein. For example, research participants who were given a *choice* of lottery tickets were more apt to believe that they would win than were those who were simply given a ticket. Others had similarly found that involvement contributed to a greater sense of personal efficacy in the realm of luck. For example, Strickland and his colleagues (1966) found that research participants placed more daring bets before rolling dice than after rolling them (with the outcome hidden, of course). The opportunity to toss the dice presumably reminded them of skill situations in which they had managed to bring about a certain outcome.

Thus, Ayeroff and Abelson (1976) independently manipulated both good vibing and involvement in order to make a case for the role of the first, and to replicate findings regarding the importance of the second, in promoting ESB.

WHAT THEY DID

Thirty-two college undergraduates, a mix of males and females, participated in the study. The sample included firm believers in ESP, outright skeptics, and open-minded fence-sitters. In briefing participants, the experimenter claimed that he was agnostic about the possibility of telepathy, and he urged participants to be so too. The present experiment was said to be capable of providing better evidence than had heretofore been available due to a number of improvements in design. Participants were screened so that good friends were never paired together. When a pair came into the lab, they drew lots to determine which member would begin as the sender and which as the receiver.

The setup consisted of two soundproof rooms separated by a corridor. The experimenter sat at a table in the corridor, and could see, through one-way mirrors, the sender sitting at a table in one room and the receiver doing the same in the other. The sender and receiver could not see or hear each other however. The experimenter had access to a switch that could open a channel of communication between the two. Also, on the sender's desk was a switch that controlled a light on the receiver's desk. The receiver was to turn this light on during the few seconds in which he or she was mentally projecting an impression. The sender also possessed a deck of cards; each card depicted a single concrete object.

The participants were told that each trial would consist of an attempt by the sender to transmit by concentrated thought the symbol on a card, after which the receiver would decide which of five possible symbols had been sent. There would be four blocks of 25 telepathy trials for each pair of participants, with an intermission after 50 trials to permit the sender and receiver to switch rooms and roles, and to read the instructions applicable to their new roles.

After this general briefing, each pair of participants was randomly assigned to one of four conditions in what is referred to as a 2 × 2 design (meaning that there were two levels of each of two variables). The two factors manipulated were involvement and good vibing, as previously defined. The instructions that defined these different conditions were presented in a booklet given to the senders. The use of a booklet ensured that the experimenter would not know which condition a pair of participants was in. It also helped to ensure constancy across conditions.

Involvement was manipulated as follows. Participants were told that previous telepathy experiments had almost always used a deck of Zener cards, each featuring a simple, common symbol—a circle, square, triangle, plus sign, or three parallel squiggles. They were told, however, that such stimuli were probably not rich or vivid enough to produce high task motivation or good telepathic outcomes. Livelier, new symbols would therefore be tried—a top hat, fried egg, knife, Egyptian pyramid, bumble bee, and so on. Participants typically found this idea credible and worth testing. Cards from the mixed deck were turned over one by one to define the sequence of stimuli that the sender would attempt to communicate telepathically.

In the high involvement condition, the experimenter presented the participants with an assortment of 10 symbols, and asked the sender, in the presence of the receiver, to select 5 of the 10 symbols, and then make up a 50-card deck with 10 occurrences of each of the 5 symbols. Thus, the sender and receiver jointly selected the target symbols that they agreed would be most sendable. The receiver was told that he or she would also have the opportunity to select, in cooperation with his or her partner, any 5 of the 10 symbols on later trials after a switch of roles. The sender in this condition also had the opportunity to shuffle the cards before turning over and transmitting the symbol on each one. In contrast, participants in the low involvement condition were *told* (via written instructions) which 5 of 20 displayed symbols they had to use, and did not have an opportunity to shuffle the cards prior to attempting to transmit what was on them. Thus, half the participants selected symbols for telepathic transmission and shuffled the cards displaying those symbols, while the other half did neither.

Good vibing was manipulated as follows. Half the participants were put through a warm-up of five trials with the intercom on between the rooms. The sender was instructed to transmit each of the five designated symbols, first naming it, and then describing for the receiver the particular visual or verbal impressions he or she was getting during the presumed mental transmission. At the same time, the receiver was instructed to respond to the sender's narration on each trial. Thus, the sender might say: "I'm going to focus on a bumblebee. I'm imagining the black and yellow stripes on its body, its black eyes and tiny antennae, and the way it is hovering and darting about above a bed of marigolds. I'm concentrating all my mental energy on the bumblebee." The receiver might then respond: "I'm picking up an image of a bumble bee—its black and white stripes and the way it is hovering above and in and out of flowers. Of the symbols to choose from, I'm guessing that you are communicating a bumble bee." "That is correct!" the sender might then reply, before the two went on to discuss strategic ways of enhancing their telepathic success. Indeed, this procedure was billed as an opportunity for the partners to hook up their impressions and establish what visual imagery they should use.

Ayeroff and Abelson noted that this condition involved not only the exchange of task-related impressions but also an accompanying pseudo-success experience. That is, because a sender announced during these practice trials which symbols he or she was about to transmit, the receiver would have then imagined the symbol and might easily have attributed whatever mental impression he or she had to something that had been telepathically transmitted. In other words, because they were told which symbol was incoming, they couldn't fail to correctly recognize it. The researchers predicted that participants might mistake this success for their own telepathic prowess.

Participants in an opposite condition were denied this opportunity to tune in to one another before the real telepathy task started. Although the intercom was left on during the warm-up trials, participants were here only allowed to say a word or two to indicate their readiness to send or receive messages. There was no detailed discussion of intuitive impressions, nor subsequent simulation of telepathic success. Participants merely noted, in private, the images they saw before their mind's eye. Under such circumstances, they had little chance of picking up good vibes from one another.

To measure *estimated* success trial-by-trial, the participants were told to give their most sincere feeling as to whether or not they had scored a hit after each trial—in other words, whether or not the symbol reported by the receiver matched the one actually intended by the sender. To convey these judgments of success or failure, both sender and receiver were to hold up one of two cards—hit or no hit—so that the experimenter in the corridor could see the two cards through the pair of one-way mirrors. The participants could not see or hear each other; they had no way of knowing what card the other held up on each trial.

The researchers tallied the number of hits claimed by sender and by receiver, as well as the actual number of hits. Again, Ayeroff and Abelson hypothesized that the introduction of either factor—involvement or good vibing—would lead participants to exaggerate their estimates of success in the telepathy trials, and all the more so when both factor were present. Having either some amount of control over the task or a good-vibing experience beforehand was predicted to produce an illusion of telepathic communication.

WHAT THEY FOUND

One obvious question to ask about the results of this study concerns the actual success of the participants. Did they demonstrate ESP? They did not. Ayeroff and Abelson (1976) found that the average percentage of correct hits over all 16 pairs of participants (a total of 1,600 trials) was 19.25, which is unremarkably worse than the pure chance level of 20% (recall that the receivers were attempting to intuit which one of five symbols had been sent on each trial). Of course, it might have been the case that only one or a few of the pairs performed remarkably better than guessing, an effect that might not show up if one only looked at averages. However, none of the individual pairs stood out in any statistically remarkable way either. Also worth noting is that neither of the experimental manipulations had an effect on actual hit rates. Ayeroff and Abelson (1976) thus concluded that the overall hit rates gave no evidence supportive of ESP.

But what about ESB? Were participants' beliefs in their abilities exaggerated? They were, and in ways that were consistent with Ayeroff and Abelson's predictions. In particular, claims of hits were quite sensitive to the experimental manipulations. In the condition in which involvement and successful communication were both present, the mean hit rate claimed by the participants was a remarkable 56% (while the actual hit rate when these two features were present was only 21%). Participants in this condition evidently believed that mental telepathy was quite possible (although they never actually said so). However, a subjective hit rate of nearly three times the objective hit rate is wildly out of touch with reality. In addition, if one but not the other of the two manipulations was present, judged success hovered around 50%, which is still more than twice the actual hit rate. In the condition in which neither rewarding communication nor high involvement was present, confidence in hits dropped to near chance levels: 26% (Fig. 15.1).

Additionally, the sender and receiver appeared to be independently judging successes, as the assessments of hits by the sender showed no trial-by-trial relation to the assessments of the receiver. In other words, although both sender and receiver tended to overestimate their hits, they did not agree on when those hits occurred. Furthermore, Ayeroff and Abelson (1976) found that there was no relationship between trial-by-trial confidence and accuracy. Thus, it was obvious participants were essentially guessing during the task and that they were guessing about when their guesses were correct.

One final result was obtained that Ayeroff and Abelson (1976) did not anticipate, but which is consistent with the notion that involvement will lead to overestimates of success. Senders judged hits to have occurred more often than did receivers. The difference was about 5%, modest but noteworthy.

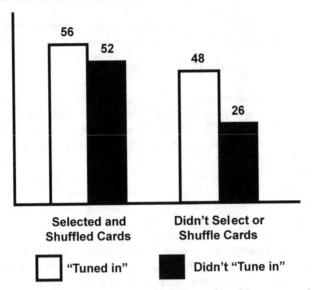

FIG. 15.1. Participants' judgments of their telepathic success, in percent, when they had selected and shuffled their cards, "tuned in" to one another, both, or neither.

SO WHAT?

Generally, knowledge of psychological causation is quite poor (Nisbett & Bellows, 1977; chap. 1). As a result, it is relatively easy for a person to mistake one situation for another and erroneously simplify matters. People may believe that they have mystically picked up on the occurrence of distant events when in fact they have only subtly sensed ordinary cues in their environment.

A lack of insight, leading to errors of judgment, is not particular to psychology. Knowledge of the basic principles of other disciplines is also poor. Physics is a case in point, as the following thought-experiment illustrates (McCloskey and others, 1983). Imagine an airborne spy with instructions to drop a packet of secret documents inside a red circle on the ground. At the exact moment the plane passes over the circle, the spy releases the packet. Is this the right moment to do so? Many people think that it is, but in thinking this they fail to take into account how the motion of the plane is transferred to the packet. The packet does not fall directly downwards, but rather follows a curved trajectory, remaining under the plane.

Many years ago, one of us interviewed individuals who had a strong belief in ESP (they were recruited through a newspaper ad). One woman, married to a construction worker, had an eerie suspicion at lunchtime that her husband, who was working on a job just two blocks away, had just been killed in a terrible accident. Sure enough, at 11:58, a crane had fallen and crushed him. The wife took her premonition to be a genuine psychic experience. Nevertheless, an alternative, mundane explanation is that she subconsciously registered the sound of the crash, and misread it as a clairvoyant signal of her husband's demise. The additional fact that she and her husband had been arguing violently for several days may have predisposed her to wish him dead.

Explanations of mysterious phenomena tend to be rooted in everyday analogs. Exercising extrasensory powers amounts to giving a demonstration of being extraordinarily sensitive to weak signals. For example, a sentry may detect some suspicious movement in the dark, or a conductor may detect a single wrong note played by one member of an orchestra. The author of this chapter would find claims of psychic abilities more credible if the explanations involved were not so reminiscent of explanations of ordinary sensitivity to the physical environment. Indeed, most social psychologists are skeptical of extrasensory perception. Unlike many hard scientists, they are occupationally familiar with the types of confounds that can creep into ESP experiments with people.

AFTERTHOUGHTS

The research literature on parapsychology is large, puzzling, and subject to intense debate. It is hard, in general, to produce a repeatable, coherent set of relationships between and within various domains of extrasensory perception. The believer in ESP tends to welcome any data that are better than what would be achieved by chance. He or she believes that such data require an occult explanation. The skeptic, however, says: "But it doesn't add up. What is your theory? What does it mean? Would some other investigator find the same pattern?" There are, nonetheless, a handful of empirical results that are not easy for skeptics to explain unless they are willing to claim fraud and connivance (Hansel, 1980). Debate also rages over several exceptional cases, where the usual methodological weaknesses have been ironed out (Bem & Honorton, 1994; Hyman, 1994).

Nevertheless, as a skeptic once wryly remarked, mental telepathy will never replace the telephone. Whatever effects are found tend to be small and inconsistent. That said, if a small but genuine psychic effect were definitively established it would shake the foundation of our understanding of human capability. One problem is that it has not yet been possible to classify individuals into those with predispositions for better or worse psychic performance. Indeed, manifestations of ESP tend to be disconcertingly erratic. Even Uri Geller, king of the spoon-benders, can only work his magic at select times and in select places, for example when no magicians or skeptics are on hand. Finding a psychic who can perform consistently is much like identifying a magic electoral precinct that always votes with the party that wins nationally. The list of such perfect bellwether precincts grows successively shorter and shorter with each election, until no precincts remain. This implies that such precincts never existed in the first place. Could the same be true of psychics?

While the question of the existence of psychic phenomena remains unresolved, it is still possible to analyze factors associated with *belief* in ESP. Belief in ESP is generally not swayed by the results of controlled experimental research. The total body of data tends to be quite ambiguous, and people on both sides of the debate are much in the habit of rationalizing results they find disagreeable (Ditto & Lopez, 1992; see chap. 4). Furthermore, there is no well-supported literature on differences in personality between believers and skeptics. Hints of difference tend to be interpreted along an artist-versus-scientist dimension (Parker and others, 1998). Higher scores are expected from sensitive, artistic types, whereas low scores are laid at the feet of cold, critical personalities. This is not too interesting a distinction, however, as it doesn't really explain what is going on in the psychic process.

As social psychologists, we are more concerned with stimulus situations that promote belief in extrasensory experiences. Situations that are ambig-

FIG. 15.2. Unlikely to replace the telephone. Copyright © 2002 by Daniel Leighton.

uous, weird, and spooky—but which retain elements in common with normal situations—are good candidates for suggesting the presence of occult forces. Any situation that cannot be unambiguously interpreted is very likely to be misinterpreted in the direction congruent with an individual's past experience. For example, everybody knows what it is like to be tempted to do something that, on reflection, seems like a bad idea. Imagine a friend inviting you to go bar hopping the night before an exam, or a shady acquaintance inviting you to go in on an illegal scheme (in this regard, see chap. 23!). Now suppose that one day you feel an unaccountable desire to do something impulsive when nobody else is around. The experience is unsettling because you are unable to identify the source of the desire. The impulse seems to come out of nowhere. However, your previous experience suggests that there should be someone somewhere who is responsible for creating that desire (a friend or shady acquaintance). Perhaps being of a religious persuasion, you conclude that there is indeed somebody tempting you, but that this person is some sort of hidden spirit or demon.

Sometimes prior experiences can give rise to enduring preoccupations, and people come to see the world primarily in terms of those preoccupations. There is an old joke about a patient who inspects a series of inkblots and then tells his psychiatrist what he thinks each one represents. (Each inkblot might resemble something specific, say, two men dancing, or nothing in particular. What one sees is supposed to be psychologically revealing.) The patient responds to the first card by saying "I see a naked woman." He responds to a second card similarly: "It's a naked woman." His response to the third card: "More of the same, doc—two naked women." Without showing more cards, the clinician concludes that the man has a pathological obsession: "I notice that you seem to have a special interest in naked women—can you tell me more about that?" "Don't ask me, Doc," the man complains, "You're the one who's showing all the dirty pictures!"

Tomkins (1962) hypothesized that such preoccupations (*nuclear scenes*, he called them) have their roots in early traumatic experiences that are revived by later similar experiences. Many clinicians also refer to *pre-emptive metaphors* that guide ongoing interpretations of social relationships by treating the present as an extension of the past. Only recently, however, have such phenomena become the target of empirical investigation. Andersen and Berenson (2001) reviewed a substantial body of experimental research showing that our experiences of people in the past shape our appraisal of and reactions to new people. A typical study runs as follows. Participants begin by describing in a few sentences a person who matters to them—a significant other. After a delay and a distraction, participants learn about a target person, described in terms of some, but not all, of the sentences which participants generated, as well as several new sentences. At the end of the study, participants are shown both types of sentences, and asked to identify which were used to characterize the target person. They tend to falsely identify sentences that were *not* used to characterize the target person, but that *were* used to characterize their significant other. That is, on the basis of some similarities between a significant other and a new target person, participants tend to mistakenly extrapolate additional similarities. Further studies along the same lines show that people react emotionally to other people as if they resembled preexisting significant others more than they actually do. It is a clear case of reality being *assimilated* (made to conform) to preexisting schemas (sets of expectations), a case of *top-down* processing (Higgins and others, 1977; see chap. 14).

Bottom-up processes, in contrast, involve people *accommodating* (fitting) their schemas to reality, as when a detective diligently seeks out evidence that might eliminate a suspect, or a conscientious person questions the accuracy of prevalent stereotypes. Top-down processing is more likely when a person's intellectual curiosity and resources are in short supply, bottom-up processing when they are willing and able to think carefully. We spend our days flipping between these two modes of processing depending on the demands of the social situation (Stevens & Fiske, 1995).

REVELATION

We make sense of ambiguous novel situations by using superficially similar past experiences as a guide, often making unwarranted inferences as a result. For example, belief in personal telepathic ability can be mistakenly engendered by a recent experience of close rapport (good vibes) with others.

— RPA —

CHAPTER REFERENCE

Ayeroff, F., & Abelson, R. P. (1976). ESP and ESB: Belief in personal success at mental telepathy. *Journal of Experimental Social Psychology, 36,* 240–247.

OTHER REFERENCES

Andersen, S. M., & Berenson, K. R. (2001). Perceiving, feeling, and wanting: Experiencing prior relationships in present-day interpersonal relations. In J. P. Forgas & K. D. Williams (Eds.), *The social mind: Cognitive and motivational aspects of interpersonal behavior* (pp. 231–256). New York: Cambridge University Press.

Bem, D. J., & Honorton, C. (1994). Does psi exist? Replicable evidence for an anomalous process of information transfer. *Psychological Bulletin, 115,* 4–18.

Ditto, P. H., & Lopez, D. F. (1992). Motivated skepticism: Use of differential decision criteria for preferred and nonpreferred conclusions. *Journal of Personality and Social Psychology, 63,* 568–584.

Hansel, C. E. M. (1980). *ESP and parapsychology: A critical reevaluation.* New York: Prometheus Books.

Higgins, E. T., Rholes, W. S., & Jones, C. R. (1977). Category accessibility and impression formation. *Journal of Experimental Social Psychology, 13,* 141–154.

Hyman, R. (1994). Anomaly or artifact? Comments on Bem and Honorton. *Psychological Bulletin, 115,* 19–24.

Langer, E. (1975). The illusion of control. *Journal of Personality and Social Psychology, 32,* 311–328.

McCloskey, M., Washburn, A., & Felch, L. (1983). Intuitive physics: The straight-down belief and its origin. *Journal of Experimental Psychology: Learning, Memory, & Cognition, 9,* 636–649.

Nisbett, R. E., & Bellows, N. (1977). Verbal reports about causal influences on social judgments: Private access versus public theories. *Journal of Personality and Social Psychology, 65,* 1093–1104.

Parker, A., Grams, D., & Pettersson, C. (1998). Further variables relating to psi in the ganzfeld. *Journal of Parapsychology, 62,* 319–337.

Stevens, L. E., & Fiske, S. T. (1995). Motivation and cognition in social life: A social survival perspective. *Social Cognition, 13,* 189–214.

Strickland, L. H., Lewicki, R. J., & Katz, A. M. (1966). Temporal orientation and perceived control as determinants of risk-taking. *Journal of Experimental Social Psychology, 3,* 143–151.

Tomkins, S. (1962). *Affect, imagery, consciousness.* New York: Springer.

MORE TO EXPLORE

Langer, E. J. (1983). *The psychology of control.* Beverly Hills, CA: Sage.

Gilovich, T. (1993). *How we know what isn't so: The fallibility of human reason in everyday life.* New York: Free Press.

Rao, K. R. (2001). *Basic research in parapsychology.* Jefferson, NC: McFarland & Co.

16 The Eye Is Quicker Than the Mind: Believing Precedes Unbelieving

"Man is a credulous animal, and must believe something; in the absence of good grounds for belief, he will be satisfied with bad ones."
—Bertrand Russell (1872–1970), British philosopher

BACKGROUND

As we discussed in chapter 15, when someone construes an ambiguous new experience in terms of an old familiar category a false impression can result. This can often be seen in the way people's view of history shapes their view of the present. The traces of a powerful emotional event can persist for centuries, recruiting new examples that seem to fit a familiar pattern. When two groups are in conflict, for example, cultural lore reminds their respective members who their enemies are, what historical grievances they have, and why their cause is just. Thus, every new Palestinian suicide bombing is yet another instance of Arab lawlessness and treachery, every new Israeli military incursion yet another instance of Zionist oppression and expansionism.

There is another process by which people can be led to false impressions. Consider someone who wants to deceive members of an audience about a particular idea, political candidate, or commercial product. When might audiences accept falsehoods as truths? Daniel Gilbert's (1992) answer is "Always—at first." People believe everything they read or hear—whether truth, fiction, or outright lie—when they first read or hear it. It is only afterward that they may come to disbelieve it.

Gilbert (1992) was interested in the sequence by which someone comprehends a statement and assesses its truth value (accepts it as true or rejects it as false). The usual assumption, apparently commonsensical, is that people first comprehend the meaning of a given statement, and then decide whether it is true or false. Gilbert traced this account back to René Descartes, the 17th-century mathematician and philosopher who devised the *Cartesian coordinate* system that has dropped generations of students into the maze of analytic geometry. Descartes also famously addressed the question of what, if anything, can be known for certain. Can we even be sure of our own existence? His answer was: "I think, therefore I am." (Subtle joke: One day, René Descartes woke at noon with a bad hangover. His head throbbing, he went to a nearby restaurant. The waitress asked if he would like his usual decanter of wine. "I think not!" he exclaimed, and vanished.)

Gilbert was skeptical of Descartes' assumption that the truth of an assertion is assessed only after that assertion is comprehended. He was more sympathetic to an alternative model of belief developed by Baruch Spinoza, a Dutch philosopher and Descartes' younger contemporary. According to Spinoza, the process of comprehension cannot be separated from the process of acceptance. More specifically, we initially accept everything we hear or read. We may, however, *un*accept some of it at a later time, when by one means or another we become aware of features that are suspect or false. We will heretofore refer to this surprising (if not seemingly goofy) idea as the Gilbert-On-Spinoza-Hypothesis, or "GOSH" for short. Consider this: in the case of pictures (instead of verbal statements) we do not make a distinction between comprehension and acceptance. They are one and the same. We 'see' things automatically, and almost always take what we see to be what is there. This accords with common sense, and is linguistically embedded in such phrases as "Seeing is believing" and "I saw it with my own eyes." Or, as famed baseball star Yogi Berra once quipped, "You can see a lot just by looking."

There is good reason to believe what we see. In confrontations with danger, it is vital to act quickly. We do not stand around weighing the evidence for and against the belief that the animal we have comprehended 100 yards away is a real—as opposed to a paper—tiger. We have a greater chance of survival if we take it to be real, and get the heck out of there. The earliest humans (and other primates) must have faced a number of life-threatening situations, and therefore the evolutionary advantage was with the development of fast, relatively uncritical perceptual systems. No physical harm results from fleeing two comedians in a tiger suit.

However, there is something of a conceptual leap from visual perception to verbal processing. The analogy alone doesn't prove that comprehension of a statement is the same thing as acceptance of the statement as true. An experiment needs to be conducted that can distinguish between the afore-mentioned Cartesian and Spinozan possibilities.

There are important differences in the predictions of these two models. If we spontaneously accept a statement the very moment we read or hear it in its entirety, and don't have the opportunity to scrutinize it afterward, then Gilbert predicts the statement will remain accepted. We thereby run the risk of being misled. In contrast, the commonsense Cartesian model predicts that this will not happen. We will defer accepting or rejecting a statement until after it has been understood and we have weighed any evidence for or against it. These different predictions gave Gilbert et al. (1993) the hook they needed to tell the two models apart.

WHAT THEY DID

Two things were needed: a mixture of true and false statements, and a pro-cedure for interrupting the processing of those statements. The most woodenheaded, straightforward way to assemble a set of trues and falses is to collect facts from the real world and distort some of them. For example, "Germany, Italy, and Japan were the three powers that fought against the U.S. and its allies in World War II" is true. "Madrid is the capital of Mexico" is false. The truth value of these statements is determined by information that often has been learned by rote from teachers or school books. This means, however, that the statements are not useful for testing the GOSH, which is essentially concerned with the processing of new statements or informa-tion more generally.

To avoid well-learned facts, a seemingly promising strategy is to invent facts, using made-up concepts, such as "greebles eat mung." The experi-menters could then tell the participants which of these assertions were true and which false (on Planet Zorg, or in some other fictional setting where the use of strange words might be reasonable). Psychologists have used non-sense words for many different experiments for more than 100 years. Ebbinghaus (1885/1964) used nonsense stimuli in his pioneering studies of memory and forgetting.

However, Gilbert et al. (1993) didn't like these hypothetical statements either. They wanted statements that—if accepted—would have important consequences (assertions about greebles do not, unless one happens to be a greeble). If, for example, false testimony in a jury trial tended to be one-sidedly favorable or unfavorable to the defendant, it could alter the ver-dict from guilty to innocent, or vice versa. Short of that, it could affect the severity of the sentence if the defendant were found guilty. Indeed, Gilbert's group settled on such statements, couched in a consequential account.

In the first of their three studies (for simplicity, the only one we will de-scribe in detail), participants (71 female college students) read aloud two unrelated crime reports presented as lines of text crawling across a com-puter monitor. One report was about a man named Tom who was accused of robbing a stranger who had given him a ride. The second report was about a man named Kevin who was charged with robbing a convenience store. Each of the reports contained both true statements (displayed in black) and false statements (displayed in red). The participants were told that the statements in red were false—details taken from unrelated police reports and mixed in with the facts, much as false testimony is often mixed in with true testimony during a trial. The participants were asked to consider the crime reports and play the role of trial court judges, determining the prison sentences of each of the two defendants.

One neat experimental point was this. Half the time, the false statements were favorable to the defendant in the first trial and unfavorable to the defendant in the second trial. In other words, the false statements made the first crime seem less serious and the second more serious. The remainder of the time it was the other way around. The false statements made the first crime seem more serious and the second less serious. This counterbalancing ensured that the results of the experiments could not be attributed to differences between the two crimes as any results obtained would be averaged across both crimes.

A second manipulation was necessary to test the GOSH. It involved either interrupting or not interrupting participants' processing of the statements, either by creating a distraction or refraining from doing so. Thus, in one condition, participants performed a digit-search task while reading about the crimes. A string of blue digits crawled across the screen just below the text they were asked to read aloud—they had to push a certain button every time they encountered the digit 5. In the other condition, participants did not perform a digit-search task—they could focus all of their cognitive resources on the text describing the two crimes, including the false statements printed in red.

Thus, for each of the two crime cases, this was a 2 × 2 design. False statements were either favorable or unfavorable to the perpetrator of the crime, and the participants were either distracted by a digit-search task or not.

Then, after reading the two reports, participants were asked to recommend a prison term, between 0 and 20 years, for each of the defendants. This recommended prison term was the main dependent variable, although Gilbert and his colleagues collected additional data, such as participants' ratings of how much they liked each of the perpetrators, and how dangerous they believed each of them to be.

Gilbert and his colleagues predicted that the addition of the digit-search task would prevent participants from being able to unaccept false statements they had initially accepted. Participants would therefore continue to accept these statements as true, which would bias the prison terms they recommended. Among participants who were distracted, therefore, false statements supportive of a defendant would prompt more lenient sentencing, and false statements critical of a defendant more severe sentencing. For participants who were not distracted, however, the false statements would have little if any impact on judgments, because those false statements would be appropriately rejected or ignored.

WHAT THEY FOUND

This is precisely what Gilbert and his colleagues found. Interrupted participants rendered more lenient jail terms (on average, about 6 years) when the false statements made the crime seem less serious, and more severe jail terms (on average, about 11 years) when the false statements made the crime seem more serious. (Notice that the recommended jail time was almost double in the latter condition.) However, when participants were not mentally burdened by the digit-search task, the false statements had a negligible influence on the sentence they rendered (about 6 and about 7 years, respectively) (Fig. 16.2). Participants' ratings of the perpetrators' likableness and dangerousness followed the same pattern. False statements favorable to the defendant rendered him more likable and less dangerous, and false statements unfavorable to the defendant rendered him less likeable and more dangerous, but only when, crucially, participants were interrupted by the digit-search task.

Taken together, these results indicate that participants who were overloaded by the digit search acted as though many of the false statements were true. Evidently, they had initially believed most of those statements, but had no opportunity to unbelieve them. (If you were an unscrupulous lawyer trying to persuade a jury that your client was innocent, you might find in such results good reasons to tell even implausible lies, supposing that you could at the same time keep jurors' minds occupied with irrelevant complexities in the evidence.)

FIG. 16.1. Especially when my mind is busy.

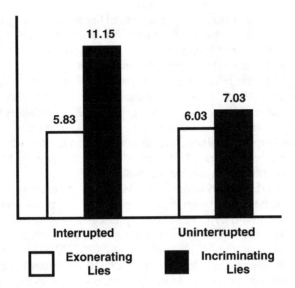

FIG. 16.2.   Years in prison that participants recommended for defendants, after reading, while being interrupted or not, exonerating or incriminating lies
about them.

At this point, the astute reader may raise a possible objection. Perhaps
being interrupted by the digit-search task did not so much prevent participants from disbelieving the false statements as confuse them about
which statements were true and which were false. This could, under certain assumptions, have led to the pattern of results actually obtained.
(Specifically: if the false exacerbating statements had been more negative
than the true statements about the crime, then the overall impression of
the defendant would have been more negative. Similarly, if the false ex-
tenuating statements had been more positive than the true statements
about the crime, then the overall impression of the defendant would have
been more positive.)

Gilbert et al. (1993) were alert to this potential alternative explanation. To
test its validity, they had wisely included a recognition memory task at the
end of their experiment. Participants had to indicate whether some of the
statements they had previously seen were true or false. Now, if participants
had simply been confused by the digit-search task, then they would have
misremembered as many true statements as false as they had false statements as true. However, if the digit-search task had made them specifically
unable to disbelieve false information, then they would only have misremembered false statements as true. The pattern of recognition observed
was asymmetrical in precisely this way, consistent with the GOSH.

Worth mentioning briefly are the results of the second study by Gilbert et al. (1993), which focused on the durability of the affects of false statements. Recognition memory after about 20 minutes showed that 54% of interrupted false statements were recalled as true. In contrast, when not interrupted, 29% of the false statements were recalled as true. Thus, the interruption manipulation almost doubled the number of false statements miscategorization as true ones. The substantial 29% of falses taken to be true in the noninterrupted condition was perhaps the result of self-interruption. Many participants' minds may have wandered after reading particular statements. By comparison, true statements were very rarely recalled as false—only 4% and 5% in the two conditions.

Gilbert et al. (1993) had begun by revisiting an unresolved philosophical debate over the nature of belief. From there, they had proceeded to formulate a tentative working hypothesis: "Acceptance ... may be a passive and inevitable act, whereas rejection may be an active operation that undoes the initial passive acceptance" (Gilbert et al., 1993, p. 222). Then, in a series of elegant studies, they experimentally manipulated how mentally busy participants were, by having them do or not do concurrent tasks that undermined their ability to process information normally. As we have seen, this allowed them to test whether rejection is indeed an active operation, one that can be prevented. Their compelling results allowed them to conclude with a bold statement: "People do have the power to assent, to reject, and to suspend their judgment, but only after they have believed the information to which they have been exposed" (Gilbert et al., 1993, p. 230).

SO WHAT?

One might be tempted to pooh-pooh the debate between the Cartesian and Spinozan positions as trivial intellectual posturing. However, Gilbert's data have huge consequences. We would argue that the laboratory situation, even with its fussy details and short time scale, maps well onto the real world with all its uncontrolled happenings. What is required to make this leap from the lab to life is the realization that critical incidents can take place on a short time scale in the real world too. A remark may be overheard just prior to having one's attention diverted by any of a number of things. Indeed, a colleague of the authors once used this device to political effect. Disliking John Lindsay, then a candidate for mayor of New York City, he arranged for like-minded students to converse with each other while standing in a subway car next to one target person after another. Just before stopping at a station, one student gossiped to the other: "Did you hear about that Lindsay scandal? One of Lindsay's men had his hand in the till. And Lindsay ain't talkin'!" There was a confusion of people going in and out after the train stopped—the distraction served to undermine capacity for doubt. Beyond that, in every domain there are people who are somewhat gullible because they don't have enough knowledge and confidence to reject an incoming belief ("You can fool all of the people some of the time ...").

In the real world the GOSH effect is nothing less than a systematic formula for getting away with telling lies, and a prescription for massive public misinformation. There are an astonishing number of wrong-headed beliefs in mass circulation in the United States, and elsewhere (Gilovich, 1993; Schermer, 1997). Beyond the penchant for members of the public to fall prey individually to misinformation, there is a *polluted well effect* (terminology ours). Circulating falsehoods have contaminated the well of public opinion. People convey medical advice picked up from general gossip—for example, they declare the good health benefits of drinking eight full glasses of water a day, even though there is absolutely no good evidence for this. Or someone sends an embellished e-mail message, tells a revealing joke at a business luncheon, or reports some hearsay to the editor of the local paper. Then a second set of media sources gets hold of what seems to be an interesting item, and passes it along, typically without attribution. Then come a third layer, and a fourth, and so on. Now the item is in the public domain. Almost nobody knows the original source, and after passage through several generations, it becomes too difficult to trace the source, and no one seems to care. When the item is issued in several disparate outlets, it carries much more weight than it would have deserved had the possibly biased or unreliable source been identified at the time the message was received. And if it comes from all parts of the ideological spectrum, one cannot reasonably attribute blame to the communicators' biases (unless one has a well-developed conspiracy theory about all available sources of communication).

The polluted well effect is not strictly a GOSH effect. It is closely related, however, in that the message is presumed true in the absence of further specification. Consider a few vivid examples.

The Good Old Days

Surveys show that problems in our school environments have turned gravely worse in the last 40 years. In the 1950s, teachers listed the three most serious problems in school as running in the halls, chewing gum, and making too much noise. The three most serious problems in the 1990s, by contrast, were rape, pregnancy, and drugs. O'Neill (1999), in an investigative tour de force, located the originator of the survey of the school problems legend. You guessed it—there never were any surveys yielding such comparative results over time. The conclusions were made up by a man named T. Cullen Davis of Fort Worth, Texas, a Christian fundamentalist who defended his thesis of moral decay by stating that he had talked to teachers personally, who told him how bad things were in the 90s, and who remembered how much better they had been in the 50s. (See chap. 2 for a discussion of the pitfalls of retrospective memory.) The job of locating Mr. Davis was monumental. O'Neill likened it to peeling an onion with a million layers.

Love, Oh Love, Oh Proven Love!

Did you hear about the Yale study that discovered the 12 most persuasive words in the English language: 'love,' 'beauty,' 'proven,' etc.? At the Yale Communication and Attitude Change Project throughout the 1950s and 1960s, we would get a letter every two months or so, asking who ran this study, and whether we had the data. During this period, the results appeared in a widely read airline magazine, among many other publications. One of the authors was part of the Yale Project, and remembers other members asking everybody they knew who the author of the study was. It sounded like a pretty silly thing to waste time on, but in any case, no indication was ever found that anyone connected with Yale had done such a study. We suspected that it was a Madison Avenue project. Or perhaps a research assistant who had once been a Yale undergraduate put a misleading Yale imprimatur on the story.

Your Elevator or Mine?

In November of 1976, a power outage knocked out electricity from New York to Montreal. Manhattan was especially hard hit when the juice went off. Thousands of people were marooned between floors in dark elevators. Thousands more gamely staggered down many flights of stairs in the dark. Once outside, they discovered that there were no streetlights, and that, although navigating Manhattan's streets in the dark might be adventurous, crossing the Brooklyn or Queensboro bridges would be sheer madness. Those who weren't stuck in elevators were often parked at the curb, waiting hours for the outage to be fixed. When things returned to normal early the next day, there was a great deal of conversation about what people had done during those lost hours. Exactly 9 months later, a local reporter happened to be in a big New York hospital, where he thought he saw a great volume of activity in the maternity ward. He checked with a passing nurse, and also called other New York hospitals. He was consistently told that the number of births was clearly above average that day. His newspaper then printed his "proof" that a substantial number of the men and women who had spent long hours in darkness the night of the blackout had done what men and women are prone to do during long hours of darkness. The story was picked up by many other papers and magazines, helped along by wire service coverage. Years later, virtually everybody who had heard of the blackout believed that one of its consequences was an increase in sexual activity.

A modicum of thought about the matter should at least raise some doubts. It is unlikely that the groups trapped in the elevators would have been sympathetic to one or more couples mating on the floor in their midst. Imagine the stress the blackout victims were under: not knowing if and when they would get home, worrying about friends and family but having no way to contact them, having no dinner, and so on. Meanwhile, couples at home suddenly thrown into darkness would have been more worried about batteries, candles, and dead refrigerators than their own libidos.

In fact, the data are subject to a little-known artifact; there is a weekly cycle of delivery dates (including Cesarian deliveries) with its peak on Monday, so that had the reporter sent in the figures for the day a week later or earlier, or three or seven weeks later, the result would have been the same. The human gestation period had nothing to do with the case. This example is discussed in further detail in Abelson (1995).

AFTERTHOUGHTS

If other people can be fooled by false appearances then so too can one fool oneself. An everyday example is the common practice of intentionally setting one's watch or clock a few minutes fast. According to strict logic, this practice is absurd: One knows that the timepiece is fast. However, the time-setter is cleverly capitalizing on the seductive nature of appearance. In glancing at one's watch, one will get the immediate impression that the false time on the watch is true, so that one will be induced to hurry faster to get to one's destination. Seeing is believing.

A similar, albeit more confusing, example is Daylight Savings Time. Clearly time is not saved—the light hours are merely moved up along the arbitrary scale of clock time. The idea of Daylight Savings Time was to make the long days of spring and summer seem even longer. Suppose that sunset is at 7 p.m. You can lengthen the apparent afternoon by calling 7 p.m. 8 p.m. Now the sun sets later. All the changed clocks around the country tell us that it is really 8 p.m., even though we know that we used to call this very moment 7 p.m. The change amounts to a societal collusion to promote the fiction that the afternoons are even longer than what is ordained by earth and sun.

One other example of group collusion comes from a Yale faculty poker group that met regularly to play table stakes poker. In this version of poker there is essentially no limit on the size of bets. The amounts won and lost in an evening often ran in the $100–$200 range, and various attempts were made to decrease these unacceptably large amounts while still maintaining the same level of excitement. Almost all the fixes we tried failed. Finally, somebody got a crazy idea, and it worked. The chips were given double values. Each player got $20 worth of chips for $10 of real money. At the end of the game, the chips were cashed, with players getting $10 for each $20 of chips. There were no other changes in the game.

Logically, this doubling-and-halving maneuver is vacuous. The players all realize that when they make a bet of $50 with the cheap money, they are really only betting $25. Why, then, should the 2 for 1 procedure make any difference? Well, when a player says, "I bet $50!" it sounds like a big, bold bet. It is really only worth $25, but his words are taken at face value, just as the GOSH would predict.

There was some recognition that when a player would normally bet $25, the double-value chip game would lead him to bet somewhere between $25 and $50. Often such a bet might come out to be $35 or $40, which would respectively represent $17.50 and $20 in real money, in comparison to the $25 we supposed that he would bet in the standard-value chip game. The net result was that less money was won and lost by the biggest winner and loser. Everybody fumbled for an explanation for this seemingly childish self-deception. Gilbert's research helps to clarify the matter: the value of the chips is perceived true unless further reflection reveals its inflated value. Yet the players are too involved in the game to remind themselves of this on every bet. The chip inflation effect may not have been rational, but it worked.

There are many other phenomena that depend on the immediately distinctive features of a stimulus to create audience gullibility. Economists puzzle over the *money illusion* (Levin and others, 1981), whereby the face value of the money involved in a decision-making situation is taken to be more important than other factors that can matter a great deal. The archetypal illustration of the money illusion is that a majority of workers would prefer a $10 a month raise in an era of 7% inflation to a raise of $5 a month in an era of 1% inflation. It is considered irrational to choose the first option, because the increase in real wages is only 3% net, compared to 4% for the second option. This is not an exact case of the GOSH effect, but it broadly relates in that people tend to focus on the size of the raise, and neglect to consider the inflation factor.

There has been much research on the so-called *primacy* versus *recency* variable in persuasion. If there are two sides to a story, debate, or impression of a person, which side dominates, the first side to be heard (primacy) or the last (recency)? If, for example, you were a trial lawyer, would you rather be the first to sum up the case to the jury, or the last?

There is no universal answer to such a question. It depends on such factors as how hard people are thinking about the information they receive (Haugtvedt & Wegener, 1994). Yet it is not an unfair summary to say that what comes first is generally advantaged, unless something in the situation calls attention to, or sets apart, what comes second. Primacy wins, unless its advantages are undone. How like the GOSH effect that sounds! One way to undo primacy is to be sure the audience understands that each side will have its turn. This helps the audience to suspend their judgment until they have heard both sides of the story.

We think that there is great psychological generality to the formula of doing the simplest thing in a situation unless some factor warns us away. Thus, people will believe what they hear or are told unless there is reason to be suspicious. They will accept their first impressions in the absence of contrary information. Among computer scientists, the term for a standard response to any stimulus not otherwise categorized is the default value. We are claiming here that persons have default responses to situations, and under ordinary circumstances, use these defaults. Overriding a default requires one of several active processes. This is a general statement, which includes the case at hand. Namely, that the default in reading or hearing some information is acceptance, and subsequent unacceptance requires overriding that default.

What methods can a person use to reject something he or she would otherwise accept? Resistances can arise either on-line or off-line. The latter refers to the possibility of the target person having been predisposed to reject the message. Gilbert et al. (1993) do not consider this possibility, but it certainly deserves consideration. Often people say things like: "I don't believe a word that guy says." For example, at a public meeting on school busing in New Haven, as a liberal local priest came to the microphone to speak in favor of a busing plan, a woman in the audience whispered audibly: "What does he know? He never had any children!" The most common cases of this sort of resistance are probably those arising from quarrels over territory, ideology, rights, or morality, where each party regards the other as chronically misguided or lying, and tells each other so. Both observation and experimental research suggest that in these circumstances, the outcome is negative persuasion, where both sides are driven farther and farther from each other's positions (Abelson & Miller, 1967).

When resistance has been established prior to the communication, it would seem that a reject response must occur immediately, contrary to the GOSH effect. Yet this is not necessarily so. A participant primed for resistance need not exercise it immediately. There is, in fact, some experimental evidence for the phenomenon of delayed resistance. McHugo and others (1991) chose video clips from the more emotional passages of political speeches, and then had participants rate their own feelings at certain key moments of the tapes. The researchers found a general tendency for participants' emotions to mimic those of the speaker, particularly with regard to fear or anger. When the candidate knitted his brows or looked worried there was an immediate echo of a worried expression on audience members' faces. In general, participants' ratings during the speech of their own feelings were consistent with the facial expressions they showed. However, there was one curious exception. When Ronald Reagan spoke with the intention of reassuring his audience, virtually all participants' spontaneous responses showed the echo effect. They looked reassured and relaxed, and many smiled. A few seconds later, however, Democrats rated their own feelings as negative, not as relieved and reassured. It was as though they couldn't help but smile at a smiling face, no matter whose, but then realized they were smiling at Ronald Reagan, enemy of Democrats! They must have said to themselves: "Whoa! Why am I smiling at that guy?" whereupon they gained control of themselves and reported negative feelings, as the GOSH would predict.

REVELATION

Although commonsense suggests that we suspend belief or disbelief until after we have understood a message, research shows that, initially, belief accompanies understanding, and that doubt follows later only if mental resources and motivation are sufficient.

— RPA —

CHAPTER REFERENCE

Gilbert, D. T., Tafarodi, R. W., & Malone, P. S. (1993). You can't not believe everything you read. *Journal of Personality and Social Psychology, 65,* 221–233.

OTHER REFERENCES

Abelson, R. P. (1995). *Statistics as principled argument.* Mahwah, NJ: Lawrence Erlbaum Associates.

Abelson, R. P., & Miller, J. C. (1967). Negative persuasion via personal insult. *Journal of Experimental Social Psychology, 3,* 321–333.

Ebbinghaus, H. (1964). *Memory.* New York: Dover. (Original work published 1885)

Gilbert, D. T. (1992). How mental systems believe. *American Psychologist, 46,* 107–119.

Gilovich, T. (1993). *How we know what isn't so: The fallibility of human reasoning in everyday life.* New York: Free Press.

Haugtvedt, C. P., & Wegener, D. T. (1994). Message order effects in persuasion: An attitude strength perspective. *Journal of Consumer Research, 21,* 205–218.

Levin, I. P., Faraone, S. V., & McGraw, J. A. (1981). The effects of income and inflation on personal satisfaction: Functional measurement in economic psychology. *Journal of Economic Psychology, 1,* 303–318.

McHugo, G. J., Lanzetta, J. T., & Bush, L. K. (1991). The effect of attitudes on emotional reactions to expressive displays of political leaders. *Journal of Nonverbal Behavior, 15,* 19–41.

O'Neill, B. (1999). *Honor, symbols, and war.* Ann Arbor: University of Michigan Press.

Schermer, M. (1997). *Why people believe weird things: Pseudoscience, superstition, and other confusions of our time.* New York: W. H. Freeman.

MORE TO EXPLORE

Allingham, M. (1999). *Rational choice.* New York: St. Martin's Press.

Wegner, D. M., Wenzlaff, R., Kerker, R., M., & Beattie, A. E. (1981). Incrimination through innuendo: Can media questions become public answers? *Journal of Personality and Social Psychology, 40,* 822–832.

17 Going Along to Get Along: Conformity to Group Norms

"Social man is a somnambulist."
—Gabriel de Tarde (1843–1904), French sociologist and criminologist

BACKGROUND

Human social life is structured by *norms*: rules, shared by a group of people, about what beliefs and behaviors are appropriate. Norms prescribe certain practices (you should think or do this) and proscribe others (you should not think or do that). Most social situations are governed by norms: a job interview, a first date, dining at a classy restaurant, a college lecture, a wedding or funeral, even riding in an elevator. Crammed into one recently, I simply announced: "14 please," and someone in the opposite corner (whom I could not see) pushed 14. This simple rule greased the wheels of social interaction. In my mind I counted at least four or five other elevator norms.

Norms can exist at the level of entire nations or cultures, and some are almost universal. The norm of *social responsibility* stresses one's duty to help people in desperate need: a crying child, apparently lost or hurt, is everyone's responsibility. The norm of *reciprocity* requires one to repay others' gifts or favors: being mailed a packet of personalize address labels by the Paraplegic Society makes it hard to not send back a requested donation. However, although there are some universal norms, cultures differ, often greatly, in what they expect or accept from their members. One group values promptness ("come on time or don't come at all"), while another values spontaneity ("come when you get here"). One accepts premarital sex, another places a

199

premium on virginal brides. Romantic love is a norm here, arranged marriages there. In one culture women cover themselves from head to toe, while in another they wear hardly anything (in *National Geographic* fashion). Here you eat with silverware, there with chopsticks, and somewhere else with fingers. In one culture a firm handshake is admired, while in another a gentle handshake is preferred. In some countries it is an insult to face the soles of one's feet or shoes toward another person; in another, who cares? People in different corners of the world have different personal spaces and conversational distances. Without knowing these, a foreigner might be perceived as cold and unfriendly, or too intimate or pushy. Thus, norms define social sins of commission (doing what one should not be doing) and sins of omission (failing to do what one should be doing).

Even what we eat is normatively influenced. It has been said: "Americans eat oysters but not snails. The French eat snails but not locusts. The Zulus eat locusts but not fish. The Jews eat fish but not pork. The Hindus eat pork but not beef. The Russians eat beef but not snakes. The Chinese eat snakes but not people. The Jale of New Guinea find people delicious." This lengthy saying, though it indulges stereotypical exaggeration, highlights cultural differences with respect to diet.

Differences in sexual norms have often fascinated, if not titillated, anthropologists and other social scientists. It is normative among the Tiwi people of Melville Island (off the northern coast of Australia) for young girls to have sexual intercourse with their much older future husbands, because doing so is believed to stimulate the onset of puberty (Goodall, 1971). The Sambia of New Guinea believe that young boys also need sexual stimulation. They swallow semen (supplied by local men) in order to achieve manhood (Herdt, 1981). Operating under a different set of norms, the Mehinaku of central Brazil give no encouragement to sexual stimulation of children. However, they believe that fathering a child through sexual intercourse is a group project. Multiple men each ejaculate into a woman's vagina, contributing collectively (they believe) to conception (Gregor, 1985).

Norms can occur in groups of all sizes and shapes: a religion, profession, gang, audience, or family. Norms are even found in personal relationships. A close relationship is said to represent a *reich der zwei*—country of two—replete with its own dyadic norms. Each friendship or love relationship develops its own modus operandi. She cooks; he clears the table and washes the dishes. She says: "I'm going up for a nap"; he says: "Me too!"

Observing norms in everyday life reveals how ubiquitous and consequential they are. We usually abide by them automatically and without question. Group members, almost without exception, conform to the norms of their collectives. In many ways, we are all somnambulists, sleepwalking our way through the normative influences of our social world.

An experiment by Langer and her colleagues (1978) illustrated just how mindless people can be in everyday social situations. A research confederate asked unsuspecting participants whether she could skip to the front of the line at a photocopier in order to copy five pages, making her request in one of three ways. She either gave a legitimate reason for the request (she needed to make copies for a looming deadline), a pseudo-reason for it (she asked to use the photocopier because she wanted to make copies), or no reason at all (she simply asked to use the photocopier). As you might expect, compliance was high when the confederate gave a legitimate reason (94%), and relatively low when she gave no reason at all (60%). However, the surprise was that compliance was as high in the pseudo–reason condition (93%) as in the legitimate reason condition. Merely hearing someone going through the motions of supplying a reason was enough to automatically activate the social norm that one should defer to others who make a request with a justification attached. Importantly, however, when the research assistant asked to be able to jump to the front of the line to make 20 copies, compliance was lower, especially and equally so in the pseudo and no reason conditions (in both cases it was 24%, whereas it was 42% in the legitimate reason condition). Evidently, when confronted with the turbulence of larger demands on our time or energy, we go off automatic pilot. (For more on the automatic nature of social behavior, see chaps. 12 and 13.)

Muzafir Sherif (1936) was one of the first social psychologists to investigate the emergence and perpetuation of norms—in this case perceptual norms—in the laboratory. He presented participants with a stationary dot of light for 2 seconds in an otherwise dark room. This created an optical illusion known as the *autokinetic effect*: the stationary dot appeared to jump about. When participants were asked to judge how much the light had moved, they typically gave an estimate of between 1 and 10 inches (although one participant claimed that the dot had moved 80 feet!). When groups of participants were asked to announce their estimates out loud on consecutive days, a norm emerged. Their estimates gradually converged. Once such a norm was established, and group members were replaced with new members, their estimates quickly fell into line with the previously established norm. Research by Jacobs and Campbell (1961) found that when a *confederate* (someone associated with the experimenter), posing as a participant, gave an extreme estimate, this too affected the perceptual norm of the group. When the confederate was then replaced with an actual participant, and that participant replaced with another participant, and so on, the inflated norm persisted through as many as five generations of changing group members.

In Sherif's study, participants could not be sure how much the light moved. The estimates of others therefore provided valuable information, which it was rational to incorporate into their own judgments. Thus, the privately emerging norm was most likely the result of participants internalizing (agreeing with) the others' estimates. Indeed, Jacobs and Campbell (1961) demonstrated that participants did, indeed, internalize the norms and abided by them when tested alone after several months.

Two decades later, Solomon Asch (1955) revisited the issue. What would happen if stimuli were less ambiguous, he wondered. What if others mistakenly disagreed with one's judgment of something obvious? To what extent might one conform to their opinions then, and what factors might influence the degree of compliance shown?

WHAT HE DID

Asch (1955) presented a group of seven college students, sitting around a large table, with a series of pairs of large white cards. On one card was a single vertical black line (a standard). On the other card, there were three vertical black lines of different lengths (comparisons). One comparison line was exactly the same length as the standard, the other two were of different lengths. One by one, the participants announced which of the three lines (*a*, *b*, or *c*) was the same length as the standard. This process was repeated over 18 trials, with the standards and comparison lines varying on each trial. Simple question: how often did participants choose the correct comparison line?

Under normal circumstances, individuals would state the correct line over 99% of the time; the correct match was always obvious. Yet there was something unusual about this situation—only one of the group members was a true participant! This lone participant was blissfully unaware that the other group members were confederates, coached beforehand to give unanimously wrong answers on prearranged trials.

On the first trial, everyone, including the true participant who sat in the sixth position around the table, chose the correct matching line. The same thing occurred on the second trial after a new pair of cards was displayed. On the third trial, however, each of the first five confederates (whom, again, the participant had every reason to believe were also actual participants in the study) casually, but confidently, stated the wrong answer. Surprised and a bit unnerved, the participant then gave his answer. Finally, the sixth confederate gave the same wrong answer as did the five others. On 10 of the next 15 trials, the other group members again all gave wrong answers. Asch subjected each participant to this same procedure.

Pause for a moment. What goes through the mind of someone who finds himself in a minority of one? What would you have done in this situation? Perhaps you would have ignored the majority and have stated the obviously correct answer. Maybe you would have had steadfast confidence in your own judgments, thinking that the other group members were docile sheep following a myopic first responder or that they were all victims of some optical illusion. Maybe you would have viewed the majority as probably correct but still feel obliged to give your own answer. Perhaps you would have ignored the evidence of your senses and gone along with the majority, maybe even interpreting your dissimilar perceptions as shameful, something to hide. Asch's participants reported just such an assortment of reactions in follow-up interviews.

Asch took his basic paradigm in several directions. For example, he sought to determine which mattered more in producing conformity, the *size* of the majority or whether or not it was *unanimous*. So, to begin with, he varied the number of group members present. Sometimes there was only one other group member, sometimes there were as many as 15. Would the number determine a participant's inclination to go along with the group? In addition, Asch planted a dissenter in the group, to disturb the majority's unanimity. This ally was either another actual participant or a confederate instructed to always give correct answers. What effect would a dissenter have on the participant's degree of compliance with the majority? Would his presence undermine the group's influence? However, then Asch wondered if any effect of a dissenter would be due to his dissenting or to his being correct, so in some conditions he arranged for the dissenter to give a different wrong answer from the majority, sometimes more erroneous, sometimes less. He also examined the effect of having a dissenter cross over to the side of the majority or leave the group altogether (because of a supposed appointment with the dean) midway through the experiment. Finally, Asch systematically manipulated the discrepancy between the standard line and the other lines to see if there was a point at which the majority would be perceived as being so flagrantly mistaken that the participant would in no way parrot a wrong answer. Whew! Don't these researchers ever get tired?

FIG. 17.1. Would you have defied the majority?

WHAT HE FOUND

Asch's (1955) astonishing finding was that, even though the correct an-swer on each trial was perceptually obvious, participants still often went along with the majority. On critical trials, those on which the majority gave a wrong answer, the lone participants echoed the majority verdict over a third of the time (37% of the time to be exact). Who would have guessed that so much uncoerced compliance would have occurred? Why did participants so often fail to announce what they could plainly see?

Importantly, there were differences among participants in levels of com-pliance. On the one hand, about a quarter of them never agreed with the er-roneous perceptions of the majority. On the other hand, some sided with the majority almost unwaveringly (8% conformed on 10 or more of the 12 critical trials). Most participants fell between the two extremes.

Did the size of the group matter? It did. Participants opposed by only a single group member chose the wrong comparison line only about 4% of the time. With two opposing group members, participants' errors jumped to about 14%. When there were between 3 and 15 opposing group mem-bers' error rates ranged between 31% and 37%. Any variation within this range was not statistically significant. Group influence appeared to asymp-tote (max out) after group size reached about three or four members. That is, no increased compliance was observed thereafter (Fig. 17.2).

Did having an ally—someone who did not side with the majority—make a difference? It did. Asch found: "Disturbing the majority's unanimity had a striking effect" (p. 34). The presence of a supportive partner—an individual who was not aware of the prearranged agreement among the other group members, or a confederate who was instructed to always answer truth-fully—drained the majority of much of its power. Participants with an ally answered incorrectly only about a quarter as often as they did when the rest of the group was unanimous in its opposition. An ally who announced a less incorrect answer than other group members decreased the partici-pant's conformity by about a third, whereas an ally who announced a more incorrect answer decreased the participant's conformity by about two thirds. In the latter case, the participants reported incorrect answers only 9% of the time.

When an ally, after six trials, joined the ranks of the majority, errors on the part of the participant jumped to about what was found in conditions where there had never been an ally (that is, participants yielded to the group on over a third of the remaining trials). In other words, the independence shown by participants disappeared when the ally disappeared. Yet when the ally left the group altogether, his emboldening influence on the participant persisted. The participant's errors increased slightly upon his leaving, but not nearly as much as when he defected to the majority.

Finally, what happened when the difference between the standard and the comparison line chosen by the majority was as great as 7 inches? Asch

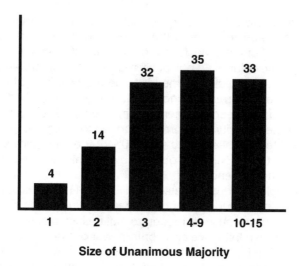

Size of Unanimous Majority

FIG. 17.2. Percentage of trials on which participants went along with unanimous majorities of various sizes, by saying that lines of obviously different length were equal.

found that, even then, a substantial number of participants went along with the group's grossly inaccurate judgements.

SO WHAT?

Asch's (1955) study makes vivid the human tendency to go along with the group. It is unlikely that his participants internalized the majority's position on each trial. The correct matches between standard and comparison lines were too apparent for that to happen. They announced the same judgments as other supposed participants, even though they knew them to be incorrect. They went along, presumably to get along.

Evidently, it doesn't take much to make a powerful majority. Asch (1955) found maximal adherence to the majority as soon its size reached about three or four. Other studies have yielded similar results. For example, Milgram and his colleagues (1969) had 1, 2, 3, 5, 10, or 15 people pause on a crowded New York City street to look up at a sixth floor window. The number of others who followed suit increased as group size increased from 1 to 5, but there were no significant increases with larger groups. Just a small group of apparently distracted passers-by provoked as many as 80% of the others present to mimic their upward gaze. Again, small groups can have great impact. Increasingly larger groups have less and less additional effect (see Gerard and others, 1968).

Also evident in Asch's study was the difference made by the presence of a dissenter. Apparently, a unanimous majority frequently has an irresistible impact on a lone individual. But given just one fellow dissenter, an individual finds the courage and wherewithal to resist social pressure. Other studies bear this out. For example, Nemeth and Chiles (1988) had participants publicly judge the color of an obviously red slide that others were claiming was orange. They correctly claimed it to be red only 30% of the time (in other words, they incorrectly announced orange 70% of the time). However, if they had just seen another lone individual misjudge to be blue a stimulus that the majority had correctly judged to be green, they then correctly claimed to have seen a red slide 80% of the time (they said orange only 20% of the time). Evidently, observing even mistaken defiance can increase one's independence.

Why do people conform? Deutsch and Gerard (1955) distinguished between *informational* influence and *normative* influence. In the first case, others influence us because we recognize that their opinions often reflect reality. We accept their influence and conform out of a desire to be right. The participants in Sherif's (1936) study were not sure how much the light was actually moving (they were in the dark, literally), so they let themselves be swayed by the estimates of others. Presumably they partly accepted the validity of those estimates and adjusted their own estimates accordingly (often settling on a compromise). However, in the case of normative influence, we fall in line because we feel, at some level, pressure to comply. We sense that the group is seeking our compliance. We want to live by its norms and not appear atypical or conspicuous, deviant or strange. The participants in Asch's (1955) study knew which of the comparison lines was equal to the standard lines. They echoed the judgments of the majority not because they lacked information, but because they did not wish to stand out. They wanted to be accepted and liked (see chap. 28 for what can happen when people find themselves chronically rejected). Asch's participants were caught between the desire to be right and the desire to be liked, but the latter desire often proved stronger (see Insko and others, 1985).

Even more basically, people comply with the practices, perceptions, or beliefs of others out of a desire to feel better about themselves. Indeed, it has been suggested that self-esteem primarily reflects how well one feels he or she is fitting in socially (Leary and others, 1995). Fitting in socially, of course, requires meeting approved norms of conduct.

Just as individuals readily submit to group norms, groups readily demand conformity. Deviance threatens the group and its agenda. A group is like a train moving down a track. Deviance derails it. Nonconformity undermines a group's *raison d'etre* and so is seldom welcome. Groups insisting on compliance are found throughout history and in every part of the world. The Catholic Church resorted to torturing and murdering nonbelievers during the infamous Spanish Inquisition. The mafia had a pair of cement shoes for any of its wayward members. The Soviet empire reserved the Gulag for political dissenters. The Chinese government attempted to suppress the hugely popular religious practice of Falun Gong. The infamous

Taliban regime in Afghanistan, now presumably disbanded, once dealt brutally with even trivial violations of their fundamentalist Islamic code: women who did not wear Burkas (or men who did not wear beards) were systematically beaten or worse. Post September 11th, it would take a brave U.S. citizen to publicly claim (rightly or wrongly) that the unjust foreign policies of his government were partly responsible for the terrorist attack.

The more cohesive or tight-knit a group is (the more affinity and loyalty there is among its members), the more it demands conformity. A study by Schachter over 50 years ago (1951) had high cohesive groups and low cohesive groups discuss ways to handle a particular wayward teenager, Johnny Rocco (the very name suggests delinquency!). Three confederates were planted in the group: *deviate, slider,* and *mode.* The first consistently deviated from the majority opinion, the second started out in the same way, but then slid to the side of the majority, whereas the third always sided with the majority. Long story short: the groups, especially the high cohesive group, applied great pressure to the deviate, trying to get him to conform to the group. Group members eventually gave up on him, ceasing to talk with him at all. Needless to say, when jobs in the group were divided up, the deviate got the least desirable ones. No wonder people fear standing apart from their peers.

AFTERTHOUGHTS

Two final thoughts: First, notice how labor-intensive or wasteful Asch's (1955) procedure was. Everyone but one actual participant was part of Asch's conspiracy. Crutchfield (1955) developed a more economical procedure for studying conformity. Participants each sit alone in a booth facing a box with a panel on which there are a number of switches for indicating their responses and lights registering others' responses. Each participant is told that he or she is the last to respond in a preordained sequence. A cover story justifies this set-up. What the participants do not know, however, is that the experimenter manipulates the responses of the other supposed participants. Each real participant therefore responds according to what he or she falsely believes are the responses of the other participants. With this system, there is no need to train and pay a team of warm-blooded research assistants. "Necessity, or perhaps economy, is the mother of invention"! Research using this Crutchfield technique does not find as much conformity as did Asch's research. Evidently, normative pressure is more powerful when it occurs face-to-face, as it did in Asch's study.

The second afterthought has to do with deviance. As history attests, just as groups can influence their members, certain individuals and subgroups can influence their groups or the prevailing social order more generally (Maass & Clark, 1984). Indeed, minorities sometimes sway majorities, and thereby act as potent agents of social change.

Think of Galileo. With the help of a low-power telescope, he spied four moons circling Jupiter and mountains and craters on the moon. This led him to claim, as had Copernicus before him, that the geocentric worldview was mistaken and that the celestial bodies are pocked, not perfect. Though he lived the later part of his life under house arrest, his evidence was not lost on the outside world. Think of Mohandas Gandhi. He led a series of peaceful protests and marches that defied India's salt laws, a symbol of hated British rule in India. Despite encountering brutal police violence, notably at the Dharsana salt factory, Gandhi and his followers courageously persisted, paving the way for Indian independence 17 years later. Think of Rosa Parks. She refused to sit in the back of a city bus in Birmingham, Alabama in 1958. Her bold act was a catalyst for a nationwide civil rights movement, which ultimately led to the abolition of racial segregation. Think of the 9/11 terrorist attacks on the World Trade Center and Pentagon in the United States. These actions were undertaken in an effort to disrupt American financial and military centers and incite a *jihad* or holy war. Only time will tell its ultimate impact. Even in smaller circles—an atheist among believers, a vegetarian among meat-eaters, someone who chooses to "just say no" among pressuring peers—numerical minorities often have a remarkable effect.

One of the most dramatic depictions of minority influence is the vintage film, *12 Angry Men*. A teenager is on trial for murder and a jury must decide the case. In a show-of-hands vote, Henry Fonda is the only holdout against a quick conviction. The film shows his slow but inexorable progress in turning an 11–1 guilty vote into, finally, a 0–12 not guilty vote. Although research finds that the initial positions of jurors are typically strongly predictive of their final verdict, and that group discussion only tends to polarize opinions, this film about minority influence is still a classic.

Deviant individuals or minorities may not always have this kind of dramatic success, but they can still have considerable impact. Research finds that, whereas majorities inspire heuristic judgments ("their sheer number suggests they must be right") and often compliance ("I'd better go along with them"), minorities provoke a more systematic consideration of arguments and, possibly, an internal acceptance of their position (Nemeth, 1986). Majorities tend to have a greater impact on public conformity, whereas minorities tend to have more effect on private conformity (Chaiken & Stangor, 1987).

Research has found that the most persuasive individuals and minorities tend to be those who hold to their dissenting position in an unwavering, self-assured manner (Nemeth & Wachtler, 1974). It also helps if they are not perceived to be arguing in their own interests, dogmatic and inflexible, or psychologically disturbed. In addition, one has a better chance of influencing a group if one first conforms to it. Deviance is better received if it comes on the foundation of having built up ample "interpersonal credits" (Hollander, 1958).

Historically, minority perspectives and deviant behaviors generally have not been readily tolerated. People tend to have little patience or kindness for anyone trying to upset their applecart. Greedy corporations have been known to fire isolated and uncompliant employees who dare to protest against their inhumane working conditions. By the same token, striking labor groups have been known to crack the skulls of fellow workers who refuse to take part in a work action. More than a few deviants have felt the noose tighten around their neck or have otherwise gone the way of public execution. Though people who hold dissenting opinions are often seen as competent and honest, they are usually not liked (Bassili & Provencal, 1988). Deviance is most accepted from high-status persons, most expected from low-status persons, but is rarely tolerated from intermediate-status persons. The latter have neither the credit of the highs, nor do they not have anything to lose like the lows.

Not only does violation of a norm invite public opprobrium, it also can result in self-punishment. Whether as an individual or a group, breaching a social norm is psychologically painful. In a study by Milgram and Sabini (1978), research assistants asked subway riders to give up their seats for them. Making such a request was reported to be extremely unnerving, even though the worst response one typically got was a simple "no." We fear punishment, or reproach ourselves, for breaking social norms. Unless one has a combative nature and thick skin, it is no fun jeopardizing the acceptance of valued others, no fun being socially ostracized (see Williams, 1997).

Yet, in every realm of life there are people who accept being outsiders, often to society's benefit. John Lennon, of Beatle fame, put his nonconformity this way (his words laden with a heavy Liverpuddlian accent): "I'm not gonna change the way I look or the way I feel to conform to anything. I've always been a freak. So I've been a freak all my life and I have to live like that, you know. I'm one of those people." Lennon's nonconformity had him imagining a world where there was "no religion" and "no hell below us, above us only sky."

But if defiance is painful, so too is conformity. One sulks over having to go along with some ridiculous or repugnant norm, and if conformity doesn't cause actual pain, it can produce a harmful numbness. It can kill one's soul, according to British novelist Virginia Woolf: "Once conform, once do what other people do because they do it, and a lethargy steals over the finer nerves and faculties of the soul. She becomes an outer show and inward emptiness; dull, callous, and indifferent."

Clearly, healthy social life requires a deft balance between conformity and autonomy, between compliance and defiance. Chief among the things one must learn in life is when to go along and conform and when to stop in one's tracks and resist the trends and influence of social groups. Solomon Asch (1955) worried about the degree of conformity he found in his research:

> Life in society requires consensus as an indispensable condition. But consensus, to be productive, requires that each individual contribute independently out of his experience and insight. When consensus comes under

the dominance of conformity, the social process is polluted and the individual at the same time surrenders the powers on which his functioning as a feeling and thinking being depends. That we have found the tendency to conform in our society so strong that reasonably intelligent and well-meaning young people are willing to call white black is a matter of concern. It raises questions about our ways of education and about the values that guide our conduct. (p. 34)

Perhaps we, like Asch, should worry too.

REVELATION

Ubiquitous and hard-to-resist norms shape social life. As a result, groups exert tremendous normative influence over their members that only a few brave souls can defy.

— KPF —

CHAPTER REFERENCE

Asch, S. E. (1955, November). Opinions and social pressure. *Scientific American, 19,* 31–35.

OTHER REFERENCES

Bassili, J. N., & Provencal, A. (1988). Perceiving minorities: A factor-analytic approach. *Personality and Social Psychology Bulletin, 14,* 5–15.

Chaiken, S., & Stangor, C. (1987). Attitudes and attitude change. *Annual Review of Psychology, 38,* 575–630.

Crutchfield, R. A. (1955). Conformity and character. *American Psychologist, 10,* 191–198.

Deutsch, M., & Gerard, H. B. (1955). A study of normative and informational social influences upon individual judgment. *Journal of Abnormal and Social Psychology, 51,* 629–636.

Gerard, H. B., Wilhelmy, R. A., & Conolley, E. S. (1968). Conformity and group size. *Journal of Personality and Social Psychology, 8,* 79–82.

Goodall, J. (1971). *Tiwi wives.* Seattle, WA: University of Washington Press.

Gregor, T. (1985). *Anxious pleasures: The sexual lives of the Amazonian people.* Chicago, IL: University of Chicago Press.

Herdt, G. H. (1981). *Guardians of the flutes: Idioms of masculinity.* New York: McGraw-Hill.

Hollander, E. P. (1958). Conformity, status, and idiosyncratic credits. *Psychological Review, 65,* 117–127.

Insko, C. A., Smith, R. H., Alicke, M. D., Wade, J., & Taylor, S. (1985). Conformity and group size: The concern with being right and the concern with being liked. *Personality and Social Psychology Bulletin, 11,* 41–50.

Jacobs, R. C., & Campbell, D. T. (1961). The perpetuation of an arbitrary tradition through several generations of a laboratory microculture. *Journal of Abnormal and Social Psychology, 62,* 649–658.

Langer, E. J., Blank, A., & Chanowitz, B. (1978). The mindlessness of ostensibly thoughtful action: The role of "placebic" information in interpersonal interaction. *Journal of Personality and Social Psychology, 36,* 635–642.

Leary, M., Tambor, E., Terdel, S., & Downs, D. (1995). Self-esteem as an interpersonal monitor: The sociometer hypothesis. *Journal of Personality and Social Psychology, 68,* 518–530.

Maass, A., & Clark, R. D., III. (1984). Hidden impact of minorities: Fifteen years of minority influence research. *Psychological Bulletin, 95,* 428–450.

Milgram, S., Bickman, L., & Berkowitz, L. (1969). Note on the drawing power of crowds of different size. *Journal of Personality and Social Psychology, 13,* 79–82.

Milgram, S., & Sabini, J. (1978). On maintaining urban norms: A field experiment in the subway. In A. Baum, J. E. Singer, & S. Valins (Eds.), *Advances in environmental psychology* (Vol. 1). Hillsdale, NJ: Lawrence Erlbaum Associates.

Nemeth, C. J. (1986). Differential contributions of majority and minority influence. *Psychological Review, 93,* 23–32.

Nemeth, C., & Chiles, C. (1988). Modelling courage: The role of dissent in fostering independence. *European Journal of Social Psychology, 18,* 275–280.

Nemeth, C. J., & Wachtler, J. (1974). Creating the perceptions of consistency and confidence: A necessary condition for minority influence. *Sociometry, 37,* 529–540.

Schachter, S. (1951). Deviation, rejection and communication. *Journal of Abnormal and Social Psychology, 46,* 190–207.

Sherif, M. (1936). *The psychology of social norms.* New York: Harper.

Williams, K. D. (1997). Social ostracism. In R. M. Kowalski (Ed.), *Aversive interpersonal behaviors* (pp. 133–170). New York: Plenum.

MORE TO EXPLORE

Axtell, R. E. (Ed.). (1993). *Do's and taboos around the world.* New York: John Wiley & Sons.

Bartholomew, R. E., & Goode, E. (2000, May/June). Mass delusions and hysterias: Highlights from the past millennium. *Skeptical Inquirer, 24,* 20–28.

Gwaltney, L. (1986). *The dissenters.* New York: Random House.

18 The Unhurried Samaritan: When Context Determines Character

"Where are they who claim kindred with the unfortunate?"
—Caroline Lamb (1785–1828), English novelist

BACKGROUND

The experiments in this volume might be dubbed *empirical parables* (Ross & Nisbett, 1991). Empirical in the sense that their findings derive from controlled observations, and parables because they offer a profound, sometimes even moral, punchline. We now describe an experiment that is based on an actual parable, one that has no doubt inspired many a Sunday sermon:

> "And who is my neighbor?" Jesus replied, "A man was going down from Jericho, and he fell among robbers, who stripped him and beat him, and departed, leaving him half dead. Now by chance a priest was going down the road; and when he saw him he passed by on the other side. So likewise a Levite, when he came to the place and saw him, passed by on the other side. But a Samaritan, as he journeyed, came to where he was; and when he saw him, he had compassion, and went to him and bound his wounds, pouring on oil and wine; then he set him on his own beast and brought him to an inn, and took care of him. And the next day he took out two dennarii and gave them to the innkeeper, saying, "Take care of him; and whatever more you spend, I will repay you when I come back." Which of these three, do you think, proved neighbor to him who fell among the robbers? He said, "The

one who showed mercy on him." And Jesus said to him, "Go and do likewise." (Luke 10: 29–37 RSV, as cited in Darley & Batson, 1973, pp. 100–101)

What comes to mind when you contemplate this parable? Convictions about the importance of helping people in distress? Differences among people in their penchant for doing good deeds? Suspicions that we are attempting to convert you?

To the minds of two prominent social psychologists, John Darley and Daniel Batson (1973), there came the realization that this short biblical narrative features two types of variables known to influence people's behavior: *dispositional variables* (stable, enduring characteristics of the person), and *situational variables* (transient or more permanent aspects of the physical or social environment). Although Jesus seems to have been emphasizing differences in the disposition or character of the unhelpful Levite and priest and the more compassionate Samaritan, features of the situation itself, which might have influenced decisions to help, can also be read into this celebrated scenario. For example, the priest and Levite, religious functionaries preoccupied with temple ceremonies and other liturgical matters, were perhaps more burdened with social obligations and a demanding schedule than was the Samaritan. In the words of Darley and Batson:

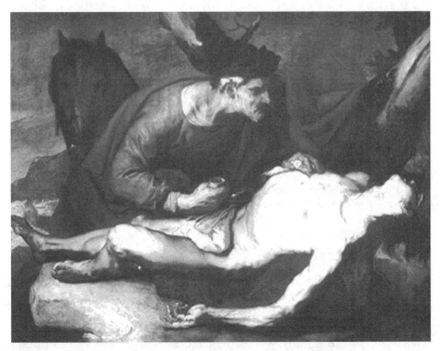

FIG. 18.1.   Would this Good Samaritan have stopped if he'd been in a hurry?

One can imagine the priest and Levite, prominent public figures, hurrying along with little black books full of meetings and appointments, glancing furtively at their sundials. In contrast, the Samaritan would likely have far fewer and less important people counting on him to be at a particular place at a particular time, and therefore might be expected to be in less of a hurry than the prominent priest or Levite. (p. 101)

So, mindful of the Good Samaritan parable, Darley and Batson sought to examine the relative effects of dispositional and situational variables on helping behavior. Darley and Latané (1968) had already conducted celebrated experiments on bystander intervention in emergency situations (see chap. 19). These experiments suggest that at least one feature of the situation, namely the number of people present, greatly influences whether or not one will help someone in trouble. Their concept of *diffusion of responsibility* served as a possible explanation for why it is that the more people there are to witness an emergency, the less likely it is that any one of them will intervene. At the same time, researchers in general were having bad luck finding personality characteristics associated with helping behavior. Such variables as *Machiavellianism* (believing that the end justifies the means), *authoritarianism* (rigid conventionality and submission to authority), *social desirability* (trying to please others and behave in a socially acceptable way), and *social responsibility* (feeling an obligation to help others in need), which were expected to strongly predict helping, in fact hardly predicted it at all. Furthermore, Mischel (1968) had just vigorously challenged the overused trait concept and entrenched notions of cross-situational consistency in behavior, citing, for example, Hartshorne and May's (1928) discovery that moral behavior is not a solid fixture of personality. A child's honesty in one situation was found to be virtually unrelated to his or her honesty in another situation.

Such previous findings and prevailing themes were brought together in a profound way in Darley and Batson's (1973) *Jerusalem to Jericho* study, in which variables that might affect helping behavior were theoretically identified (drawing hints from careful biblical exegesis!) and then ingeniously *operationalized* (defined in terms of how one would experimentally manipulate or measure them). Darley and Batson examined two situational variables: whether or not the norm of social responsibility—the obligation to help people in need—was made salient to participants, and how much of a hurry those participants were in. They also examined one dispositional variable: religiosity—the importance of religion in one's life. Darley and Batson wondered: what are the relative influences of these variables on helping? Was the Samaritan a better "neighbor to him who fell among the robbers" because he was more benevolently motivated, or were the priest and Levite simply worse neighbors to the pitiable (stripped,

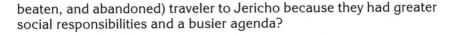

beaten, and abandoned) traveler to Jericho because they had greater social responsibilities and a busier agenda?

WHAT THEY DID

The participants were 67 students at Princeton Theological Seminary (where Batson, himself an ordained minister, had received his doctoral training). The study, said to be concerned with religious education and vocations, had two parts. In the first part, participants completed several questionnaires concerning their thinking about religious issues and, especially, their motives for being religious. Statistical analysis of their responses revealed that the questions measured three somewhat distinct *factors* (underlying dimensions). The first two factors were *religion as means* and *religion as end*. These reflect a distinction made by the eminent personality psychologist, Gordon Allport (1961), between *extrinsic religion* (which is primarily selfish and pragmatic) and *intrinsic religion* (which centers on faith and religious values). The third religiosity factor, promoted by Batson in a challenge to Allport's simple two-factor model, was *religion as quest*, which involves one's search for meaning in life. Darley and Batson hypothesized that people who are religious for intrinsic reasons or as part of a quest for meaning would be inclined to help someone in distress, while people who are religious in order to gain extrinsic rewards would not be.

The second part of the study contained the experimental manipulations. Participants were asked to give a 3–5 minute talk on the jobs they thought seminary graduates would excel at or a correspondingly brief talk on the parable of the Good Samaritan (a printed copy of the parable was provided in case they were unfamiliar with it). An assistant then casually explained:

> Since they're rather tight on space in this building, we're using a free office in the building next door for recording the talks. Let me show you how to get there [draws and explains map on 3 × 5 card]. This is where Professor Steiner's office is. If you go in this door [points at map] … another of Professor Steiner's assistants will get you set up for recording your talk … (Darley & Batson, 1973, p. 103)

This miniature drama ended with the research assistant saying one of three things: "Oh, you're late. They were expecting you a few minutes ago. We'd better get moving. The assistant should be waiting for you so you'd better hurry. It shouldn't take but just a minute" (the *high-hurry* condition) or "… The assistant is ready for you, so please go right over" (the *intermediate-hurry* condition) or "… It'll be a few minutes before they're ready for you, but you might as well head on over. If you have to wait over there it shouldn't be long" (the *low-hurry* condition) (Darley & Batson, 1973, p. 104).

Thus, the study featured a *2 × 3 design*, which means that there were two levels of one independent variable (the topic of the talk they were asked to give—either on the parable of the Good Samaritan or on jobs for seminary grads) and three levels of another (how hurried they were made to feel—a lot, somewhat, or not very). Each participant was randomly assigned to one of the six resulting conditions.

On the way through the alley that separated the two buildings, each participant encountered a person (another research confederate) who was sitting slumped over in a doorway, head down, eyes closed, not moving, and coughing and groaning. If the participant asked what was wrong or offered any help, the seemingly groggy confederate responded:

> Oh, thank you [cough] … No, it's all right. [Pause] I've got this respiratory condition [cough] … The doctor's given me these pills to take, and I just took one … If I just sit here and rest for a few minutes I'll be O.K.… Thanks very much for stopping though [smiles weekly] (Darley & Batson, 1973, p. 104) (Imagine being the thespian confederate in this kind of experiment!)

The confederate was *blind* to (not told about) the participants' religiosity scores, how hurried he was, or what talk he was assigned to give. This prevented him from having a biasing influence on participants' behavior. Incidentally, this part of the study took place over the course of a very chilly December in New Jersey, making the confederate's apparent plight all the more pitiable.

The dependent variable was whether, and how much, the participant would offer assistance. To this end, the confederate in the alley rated the participant's behavior, according to the following scale: 0 if he apparently did not notice the victim; 1 if he noticed but did not offer help; 2 if he did not stop, but indirectly sought help (for example, told someone else that the person needed help); 3 if he stopped and asked if the victim needed help; 4 if he stopped, took the victim inside, and left; and 5 if he took the victim inside and stayed with him.

The participant then met an assistant in the second building and was given time to prepare and privately record his brief speech. Afterward, he completed a questionnaire on personal and social ethics, which contained such questions as "When was the last time you saw a person who seemed to be in need of help?" and "When was the last time you stopped to help someone in need?" These questions served as a check on the participants' perceptions of the situation in the alley.

Participants were then thoroughly debriefed. Darley and Batson claimed that: "All [participants] seemed readily to understand the necessity for the deception, and none indicated any resentment to it" (p. 104). One wonders, however, if a disproportionate number of the participants who failed to help—especially those who unhurriedly went to preach about the Good Samaritan—subsequently felt ill-suited for the ministry, and opted instead for a less pastoral career, perhaps on Wall Street.

WHAT THEY FOUND

Darley and Batson (1973) predicted that the topic of the talk participants readied themselves to give (Good Samaritan vs. vocational opportunities) would not affect their behavior, even though this prediction flies in the face of theories that emphasize the importance of normative influences. In other words, Darley and Batson hypothesized that, regardless of whether or not the norm of social responsibility was made salient (emphasized), participants would help equally. They did predict, however, that how rushed participants were would sway behavior. Participants in more of a hurry would offer less help. Finally, they predicted that participants who were intrinsically religiously motivated or whose faith took the form of a quest would demonstrate more good will than would those who were extrinsically religiously motivated.

As it turned out, 40% of the participants offered some help. Importantly, the hurry manipulation profoundly affected participants' behaviors. Averaging across both talk topics, help was offered by 63% of those in the low-hurry condition, 45% of those in the intermediate-hurry condition, and only 10% of those in the high-hurry condition (Fig. 18.2). At the same time, 53% of those asked to talk about the Good Samaritan parable offered help, while 29% of those asked to speak on the vocational strengths of seminarians offered help, a difference that Darley and Batson concluded was not statistically significant. It should be noted, however, that, using more powerful statistical tests, Greenwald (1975) concluded that this difference was significant. Thus, both of the situational manipulations (the hurry manipulation and the talk manipulation) influenced helping behavior.

In contrast, religiosity—the dispositional variable of choice in this study—was not related to whether participants offered to help. The only exception was religion as quest, which did predict the kind of help that was offered. However, it did so in a manner opposite to what Darley and Batson predicted, luring them into a labyrinth of logic in their discussion.

Darley and Batson's results led them to a provocative conclusion:

A person not in a hurry may stop and offer help to a person in distress. A person in a hurry is likely to keep going. Ironically, he is likely to keep going even if he is hurrying to speak on the parable of the Good Samaritan, thus inadvertently confirming the point of the parable. (Indeed, on several occasions, a seminary student going to give his talk on the parable of the Good Samaritan literally stepped over the victim as he hurried on his way!) (p. 107)

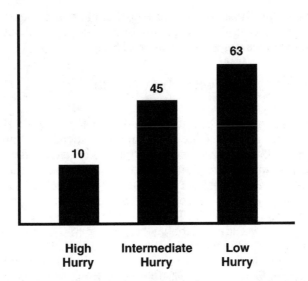

FIG. 18.2.   Percentage of participants who, on the way to give a sermon, offered help to a man slumped in an alley, depending on how much of a hurry they were in.

SO WHAT?

Some of the most remarkable social psychological experiments have been those that have attempted to examine and challenge oft-repeated adages or deeply entrenched assumptions. Darley and Batson's (1973) experiment was a perfect example. It demonstrated how small, subtle aspects of a situation can at times influence consequential behaviors in a way that relevant personality variables do not. Thus, the study contradicted our general proclivity to make internal attributions for others' behaviors (Ross, 1977; see chap. 23). Although we might assume that someone who is currently a bit subdued at a party is typically bashful or that someone who drops money into a Salvation Army pot at a K-Mart entrance is characteristically magnanimous (internal attributions), situational factors may in fact be responsible for such behaviors (perhaps the party music was depressing or a friend did not show up, and maybe the person ringing the charity bell was charmingly good-humored or irresistibly attractive). The causes of behavior are often to be found in the *situation* rather than the *person*, and sometimes it takes a kind of Sherlock Holmesian perspicacity, or the rigor of empirical science, to detect such causes.

In pondering the results of this study, were you surprised (even disturbed) that 60% of the seminarians failed to offer any help at all? Given that all of the participants noticed the victim in the alleyway (as revealed by their answers to the questions at the end of the study), should we say that those who did not help were undeniably coldhearted? A follow-up study by Batson and his colleagues (1978) may help to answer this question. Their study followed procedures that were similar to those in the Darley and Batson (1973) study and likewise found that participants in a hurry were less likely to help (40%) than were those under no time pressure (65%). However, this study further determined that the difference occurred primarily for participants who thought their research participation was essential to the experimenter. When participants were led to believe that the researcher was not counting on their participation, those in a hurry were just about as likely to help (70%) as those not in a hurry (80%). In other words, the hurry and participation variables interacted. When participation was essential, there was a difference of 25% (65%–40%) between the high-hurry and low-hurry conditions. However, when participation was optional, the difference was only 10% (80%–70%)—a difference between differences.

This latter finding suggested that the participants in these studies may have wanted to help both the experimenter and the victim and decided upon a course of action only after a cost–benefit analysis. The nonhelpers in Darley and Batson's study were perhaps, indeed, being Good Samaritans, albeit toward the experimenter. True, being in a hurry may have prevented them from acknowledging the needs of the victim, or even if they had enough time to acknowledge them, they may have concluded that their ethical obligation to the experimenter was paramount.

Perhaps the priest and Levite in Jesus' parable can be similarly pardoned. It is conceivable that they may have made the decision to bypass the man who had fallen among robbers because their business in Jericho imposed an even greater obligation on them. Perhaps Jesus would have made a stronger case (especially to any social psychologists in his audience!) if he had mentioned in his parable that neither the priest nor the Levite (nor the Samaritan) were not on their way to respond to more desperate needs or pressing business.

AFTERTHOUGHTS

In their book, *The Person and the Situation*, Lee Ross and Richard Nisbett (1991) described the many successful attempts of social psychology to show the power of situations to influence behavior, and the general inability of personality variables to do so. Researchers are often able to demonstrate that a particular contextual variable (that laypeople may fail to appreciate) has a substantial impact on behavior, while information about traits or individual differences (that people may believe are decisive) prove to have trivial effects.

Ross and Nisbett also reminded us of the attention that Kurt Lewin—one of the early giants in the field—brought to apparently minor, though materially important, details of a social situation. These *channel factors*, as he called them, are any critical facilitators of, or barriers to, behavior. In Darley and Batson's (1973) study, time pressure was a channel factor. It was a subtly manipulated, but quite powerful, determinant of altruistic behavior. There may be other channel factors affecting Good Samaritan behavior. For example, Huston and others (1981) conducted in-depth interviews with people who had intervened in dangerous crime episodes (bank holdups, armed robberies, and street muggings) or who had passively stood by. Their investigation revealed that those who threw caution to the wind were relatively taller and heavier, had more life-saving, medical, or police training, and were more apt to describe themselves as strong and aggressive. In other words, these Good Samaritans were not more motivated by humanitarian concerns, just physically stronger and better trained.

A final point to make is that the social psychologist (who focuses more on external determinants of behavior) and the personality psychologist (who focuses more on internal determinants of behavior) are typically one and the same person. Many psychologists feel comfortable donning both hats. In fact, one often finds these two disciplines wedded together within psychology departments. (Indeed, the flagship journal of the field is named the *Journal of Personality and Social Psychology*.) Yet if one considers the pure form of each approach, one begins to see what strange bedfellows they are. To the social psychologist, differences among people represent *noise*. Individual differences mask the *signal* (produced by the experimental manipulation) that the social psychologist is hunting for. Randomly assigning research participants to the different conditions in an experiment (so that, in all likelihood, the participants in one condition are no different from the participants in another condition on any given dimension) is the primary way of nullifying such noise. In contrast, to the personality psychologist, the noisy differences among people are of great interest. Alert to people's unique traits, they view situational differences as the source of unwanted noise. Changes in people's behaviors, caused by changes in environments, obscure their underlying dispositions. Fortunately, many psychologists are able to adroitly pursue both approaches simultaneously. Instead of pitting situational and dispositional variables against each other, to see which better explains behavior, they attempt to see how the two add to or, better yet, *interact* with each other, mindful of the famous Lewinian formula, $B = f(P,E)$. Behavior is a function of both the person *and* his or her environment. They are interested, for example, in how a change in the situation will affect behavior, but only for some people, or, conversely, how certain types of people behave in certain ways, but only in some situations. They are also interested in how people tend to seek out or create different situations that in turn affect them (referred to as *niche-building*). Darley and Batson's study is a precious examination of the impact of both the person and the person's situation on a critical human behavior.

REVELATION

Small, subtle, seemingly trivial situational variables often have a greater impact on behavior than do the personality variables that we more readily, but often mistakenly, regard as influential. Something as simple as time pressure can impact something as vital as compassionate behavior.

— KPF —

CHAPTER REFERENCE

Darley, J. M., & Batson, C. D. (1973). "From Jerusalem to Jericho": A study of situational and dispositional variables in helping behavior. *Journal of Personality and Social Psychology, 27,* 100–108.

OTHER REFERENCES

Allport, G. W. (1961). *Pattern and growth in personality.* New York: Holt, Rinehart & Winston.

Batson, C. D., Cochran, P. J., Biederman, M. F., Blosser, J. L., Ryan, M. J., & Vogt, B. (1978). Failure to help when in a hurry: Callousness or conflict? *Personality and Social Psychology Bulletin, 4,* 97–101.

Darley, J. M., & Latané, B. (1968). Bystander intervention in emergencies: Diffusion of responsibility. *Journal of Personality and Social Psychology, 8,* 377–383.

Greenwald, A. G. (1975). Does the Good Samaritan parable increase helping? A comment on Darley and Batson's no-effect conclusion. *Journal of Personality and Social Psychology, 32,* 578–583.

Hartshorne, H., & May, M. A. (1928). *Studies in the nature of character.* Vol. 1. New York: Macmillan.

Huston, T. L., Ruggiero, M., Conner, R., & Geis, G. (1981). Bystander intervention into crime: A study based on naturally-occurring episodes. *Social Psychology Quarterly, 44,* 14–23.

Mischel, W. (1968). *Personality and assessment.* New York: Wiley.

Ross, L. (1977). The intuitive psychologist and his shortcomings: Distortions in the attributional process. In L. Berkowitz (Ed.), *Advances in experimental social psychology* (Vol. 10, pp. 174–221). New York: Academic Press.

Ross, L., & Nisbett, R. E. (1991). *The person and the situation: Perspectives of social psychology.* New York: McGraw-Hill.

MORE TO EXPLORE

Davis, M. H. (1996). *Empathy: A social psychological approach.* Boulder, CO: Westview Press.

Pietromanaco, P., & Nisbett, R. E. (1982). Swimming upstream against the fundamental attribution error: Participants' weak generalizations from the Darley and Batson study. *Social Behavior and Personality, 10,* 1–4.

19 Who, Me?: The Failure of Bystanders to Intervene in Emergencies

"I have always depended on the kindness of strangers."
—Blanche Dubois, in American playwright Tennessee Williams'
(1911–1982) *A Streetcar Named Desire*

BACKGROUND

This chapter's study is grounded in the tragic story of Kitty Genovese. The *New York Times* (March 27, 1964) reported it this way:

> For more than half an hour thirty-eight respectable, law-abiding citizens in Queens watched a killer stalk and stab a woman in three separate attacks in Kew Gardens. Twice the sound of their voices and the sudden glow of their bedroom lights interrupted him and frightened him off. Each time he returned, sought her out and stabbed her again. Not one person telephoned the police during the assault; one witness called after the woman was dead.

During this fatal ordeal, Kitty Genovese screamed numerous pleas, including "Oh, my God! He stabbed me! Please help me!" One onlooker started to call the police, but his wife stopped him: "Don't, thirty people have probably called by now." Another neighbor, after calling a friend in another county for advice, went to the top of his building, across several rooftops, and down into another building, where he asked an elderly woman to call the police. The police later found him in his apartment, guilt-ridden and drunk (Rosenthal, 1964).

FIG. 19.1. When others are present, bystanders often fail to provide assistance.

Although the Kitty Genovese incident is now legendary, it does not stand alone in the annals of heroless situations. Similar occurrences, equally shocking, surface in the news from time to time. Latané and Darley (1970) described how a teenage boy was gutted with a knife as he rode home on the subway. Eleven other riders watched as he bled to death. None of them came to his aid, even after his attackers had fled the subway car. In another example, a young switchboard operator was beaten and raped while alone in her office. Breaking free, she ran naked and bleeding to the street, screaming for help. Forty onlookers watched—but did not intervene—as, in broad daylight, the rapist tried to drag the woman back upstairs. Fortunately, two policemen happened by, did not turn the same blind eye, and dutifully arrested the assailant.

Social commentators, including journalists, professors, and ministers, have a field day probing for the causes of such seemingly callous indifference to the plight of others. Why don't people help in these situations? With so many witnesses, you'd think that at least one would get involved, even if just to pick up the phone and dial 911. Does big-city life turn decent folk into zombie-like bystanders, too jaded to concern themselves with fellow human beings? Do such tragedies reveal an insidious moral decay in our culture?

John Darley and Bibb Latané (1968) put their money on a social psychological explanation. They argued that people witnessing an emergency, especially something as petrifying as a stabbing, are in a state of conflict. Humanitarian norms and the whisperings of conscience prompt them to intervene, but a host of fears, both rational and irrational, hold them back. After all, one could get hurt while helping, experience public embarrassment, or get tangled in police procedures. How might features of the *situation* dictate the way such a conflict is resolved?

Darley and Latané surmised that the presence of other people witnessing the same emergency, rather than spurring one to action, might actually discourage one from helping, for several reasons. First, seeing that no one else is helping may lead one to define the situation as a nonemergency, and so feel no obligation to help. "It's probably just a lover's spat." Collective inaction thereby begets further collective inaction. Second, one may not know how others are responding. This may lead one to infer that others are in fact helping, making one's own involvement unnecessary. Darley and Latané referred to this phenomenon as *pluralistic ignorance* (see also Prentice & Miller, 1999). In fact, many of those observing the assault on Kitty Genovese, upon seeing lights and silhouettes in nearby apartment windows, knew that others were also watching, but had no way of knowing how those others were reacting. Pluralistic ignorance prevailed. Finally, nonintervention may occur due to what Darley and Latané termed a *diffusion of responsibility*. Failure to help occurs because the responsibility for helping is spread among a number of observers, as is any blame for not taking action. An ironic implication is that, had the brutal attack and Kitty Genovese's desperate cries been observed by a single night owl, who believed that he or she alone was witness to this gruesome assault, it might have been prevented from ending so tragically. The pressure to intervene would have focused uniquely on that one witness.

A longish quote from Evans (1980) described a discussion between Darley and Latané (recalled years later by Darley) when the Genovese murder was still a hot news item:

> Latané and I, shocked as anybody else, met over dinner a few days after this terrible incident had occurred and began to analyze this process in social psychological terms ... First, social psychologists ask not how are people different or why are the people who failed to respond monsters, but how all people are the same and how might anybody in that situation be influenced to not respond. Second, we asked: What influences reach the person from the group? We argued for a several-step model in which a person first had to define the situation. Emergencies don't come wearing signs saying "I am an emergency." In defining an event as an emergency, one looks at other people to see their reactions to the situation and interpret the meaning that lies behind their actions. Third, when multiple people are present, the responsibility to intervene does not focus clearly on any one person ... You feel a diffusion of responsibility in that situation and you're less likely to take responsibility.

We argued that these two processes, definition and diffusion, working to-gether, might well account for a good deal of what happened. (pp. 216–217)

This discussion led Darley and Latané to hypothesize that the more by-standers there are to an emergency, the less likely, or more slowly, any one bystander will intervene. They then put this hypothesis to an empirical test.

WHAT THEY DID

Darley and Latané's (1968) experiment required a bit of staging and theat-rics. Just how does one conduct an experiment in which, first, an emer-gency occurs, second, participants are blocked from communicating with others and knowing about their behavior, and, third, it is possible for the ex-perimenter to assess the frequency and speed of participants' reactions to the emergency?

Seventy-two New York University students (males and females) partici-pated in Darley and Latané's study. Upon arriving for the experiment, a par-ticipant found herself in a long corridor with doors opening to a series of small rooms (not a trivial detail). An experimenter took the participant to one of the rooms (leaving the contents of the other rooms to the imagina-tion) and seated her at a table on which a microphone and pair of head-phones lay. The participant filled out an information form and then listened to instructions presented by the experimenter over an intercom.

Participants were told that the study was concerned with the kinds of per-sonal problems that normal college students face in a high-pressure urban environment (remember, these were N.Y.U. students). They were also told that the procedure of the study was designed to avoid any embarrassments that arise from discussing personal problems with strangers. They would each remain anonymous, seated in separate rooms rather than face-to-face. They were further told that, because an outside listener might inhibit the dis-cussion, the experimenter would not be eavesdropping. He would get their reactions afterward, by questionnaire. It was explained that each person would talk in turn, disclosing personal problems, via microphone, to those seated in the other rooms down the hall. Next, each person would, in turn, comment on what the others had said, and finally there would be an open discussion. Importantly, the flow of the conversation would be regulated. That is, each participant's microphone would be on for only 2 minutes, dur-ing his or her turn, while the other microphones would be off, so that only one participant would be heard over the network at a time.

Unknown to participants, however, the 2-minute inputs of others were tape recordings. In other words, participants thought they were listening to the live verbal disclosures of other participants when in fact the "oth-ers" were merely recorded scripts. One of these others—we will call him the victim, for reasons that will make sense in a moment—"spoke" first.

He began by describing a few commonplace problems, like having a hard time getting adjusted to New York City and his studies. He also mentioned, hesitantly and with apparent embarrassment, that he sometimes experienced seizures, especially when studying hard or taking an exam. One by one, the other "participants" also divulged some of their own problems, but with no mention of proneness to epileptic fits. Finally, the real participants, playing their own unwitting part in the elaborate charade, divulged some personal trials and tribulations. When it was again the victim's turn to talk, he made a few relatively calm comments, and then, becoming noticeably louder and more incoherent, continued:

> I-er-um-think I-I need-er-if-if could-er-er-somebody er-er-er-er-er-er-er give me a little help here because-er-I-er-I-er-I-er-h-h-having a-a-a real problem-er-right now and I-er-if somebody could help me out it would-it-would-er-er s-s-sure be-sure good ... because-er-there-er-er-a cause I-er-I-uh-I've got a-a one of the-er-sei-er-er-things coming on and-and-and I could really-er-use some help if somebody would-er-give me a little h-help- uh-er-er-er-er-er c-could somebody-er-er-help-er-uh-uh-uh (choking sounds).... I'm gonna die-er-er-I'm ... gonna die-er-help-er-er-seizure-er-[chokes, then quiet]. (Darley & Latané, 1968, p. 379)

You've got to admit, social psychology has its inspired moments!

The time from the start of this "fit" until a participant left the room and notified the experimenter at the end of the hall was recorded. This constituted the main dependent variable. As soon as a participant reported the emergency, or if she failed to do so after 6 minutes, the experiment was stopped and she was *debriefed* (the true nature of the study was revealed and any ill feelings were sympathetically addressed).

Participants then completed a battery of questionnaires, which measured *Machiavellianism* (cold-hearted ruthlessness), *anomie* (lack of personal values), *authoritarianism* (deference to authority and disdain for the downtrodden), *social desirability* (the tendency to seek approval), and *social responsibility* (social compassion and helpfulness). These additional assessments allowed a comparison between the influences of personality and situational factors on helping behavior. We should point out, however, that the personality variables should have been measured in a separate context. The way things were, nonhelpers especially may have exaggerated their standing on some of these personality dimensions in order to compensate for their embarrassing inaction earlier. This could have obscured any real differences in personality capable of accounting for differences in helping.

Knowing that experiments involve the deliberate manipulation of one or more independent variables, you might be wondering what exactly was manipulated in this study. Well, think back to Darley and Latané's (1968) diffusion-of-responsibility hypothesis: the more bystanders to an emergency, the less likely or more slowly any one bystander will help. This hypothesis led Darley and Latané to manipulate perceived group size. They varied both the assistant's comments before the experiment and the number of voices heard to speak in the first round of the group discussion. Participants were led to believe that the group consisted of two people (just them and the victim), three people (them, the victim, and one other participant), or six people (them, the victim, and four other participants). Keep in mind that the only real people were the participants themselves; the others were merely tape recordings.

The composition of the three-person groups was also manipulated. In one variation, the taped bystander's voice was that of a female, in another that of a male, and in another that of a male who just happened (wink!) to mention that he was a premedical student who occasionally worked in the emergency ward (just the kind of person trained to deal with unexpected seizures). Thus, the major independent variables were group size and group composition, while the major dependent variables were whether and how fast a participant came to the victim's aid by reporting the seizure to the experimenter.

WHAT THEY FOUND

Participants seemed genuinely convinced of, and affected by, the victim's seizure, a matter of *experimental realism* (meaning that the participants felt psychologically drawn into the experiment). Whether or not participants intervened, they clearly believed the sudden fit to be real and serious, saying things like: "My God, he's having a fit!" "It's just my kind of luck, something has to happen to me!" or "Oh God, what should I do?" Unbeknownst to participants, the experimenter could hear these various comments over the intercom. Also, to the experimenter down the hall, participants said things like: "Hey, I think Number 1 is very sick. He's having a fit or something." And when the experimenter checked the situation and reported that: "Everything is under control," they were apparently relieved, although they would still ask: "Is he being taken care of?" or "He's all right, isn't he?" Like the participants in Milgram's (1963) obedience study (see chap. 21), they seemed genuinely upset and concerned.

The number of others that participants believed were present had a profound influence on whether and how promptly they helped. Specifically, 85% of participants who believed they were alone reported the emergency before the victim was cut off (that is, within 2 minutes), whereas only 31% of those who believed that four others were present did so. Moreover, 100% of the participants in the two-person groups, but only 62% of those in the six-person groups, ever reported the emergency (Fig. 19.2). In fact, at any point in time, more participants in two-person than three-person groups, and more participants in three-person than six-person groups, reported the incident. Also, the fewer individuals that participants thought were present, the faster they responded.

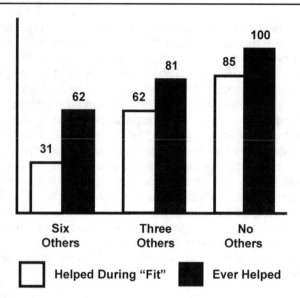

FIG. 19.2.   Percentage of participants who went to help a bogus victim, during his epileptic 'fit' or ever, when they believed that six, two, or no others also heard him.

Interestingly, participants in the three-person groups were equally likely to respond, and responded equally quickly, regardless of whether they believed the other participant (besides the victim) to be male, female, or medically competent. Also, even though males are often given the duty of responding to emergencies, or are regarded as more inclined to assume the role of rescuer in dire situations, male participants in this study were no more likely than females to help, nor did they help more quickly. This may have been, however, because helping in this study involved merely reporting a crisis.

Did some factor of which participants were aware account for the influence of group size on helping? It seems not. Participants indicated which thoughts—from a list presented to them—they had had during the emergency (for example, "I didn't know exactly what was happening" or "I didn't know what to do"). There were no significant differences in their reported thoughts across the three conditions. Although participants in the three-person and six-person groups reported that they were fully aware that others were present to hear the fit, they claimed that this had no effect on their behavior. Research has found, however, that we often do not know the true causes of our behavior (Nisbett & Bellows, 1977; see chap. 1). The nice thing about an experiment is that it allows one to isolate exactly what does cause something. In this case, nothing other than the participants' awareness of the number of others present could explain the group differences in their helping, despite their apparent lack of insight regarding its influence.

Finally, just as was the case in a number of other classic studies documenting the power of the situation (see, for example, chaps. 18 and 21), none of the personality measures was significantly related to the likelihood or speed of participants' responses. In fact, only one variable besides group size correlated with speed of helping: the larger the community a participant grew up in, the less likely he or she was to help. Make of this finding what you will, but the more important result is that it was something *outside* of the person—namely, the number of others present—and not simply something *inside* the person—like a disposition to be socially responsible—that determined how a person would behave in response to the desperate heaving of a fellow student who, by his own account, was "gonna die."

SO WHAT?

According to Darley and Latané (1968), participants in this study experienced an *avoidance–avoidance conflict* (a type of conflict you want to avoid!). They were obviously concerned about the stammering victim, and would likely be ashamed of themselves if they did not take action, but they also did not want to make fools of themselves by jumping to conclusions. For those in the two-person groups ("It's just me and this guy croaking in another room") the conflict was easily resolved: "My help in this situation is crucial." But for those who believed that others were present ("There are four or five of us listening to this guy unfold") the anticipated embarrassment of helping, should no help in fact be needed, increased, thereby leading them to restrain their humanitarian instincts, and heightening their internal conflict. "Should I let the guy continue to suffer, even die, or should I alarm the experimenter and risk embarrassing myself?" It was not that the participants consciously decided to not intervene. Rather they mentally vacillated between two negative alternatives and never actually did anything. Then, after several minutes had passed, it was illogical or simply too late to help.

Darley and Latané's results cast doubt on explanations for bystander unresponsiveness that refer to apathy or indifference. Such explanations assert that crowds of people who stand by and do nothing when others are suffering before their very eyes are somehow different from the rest of us: desensitized by modern culture or just naturally uncaring. Why else would someone watch passively as someone else gets hacked to death? However, dispositional explanations of this sort may be too convenient, allowing us to deny that we, as persons of unimpeachable character or infinite benevolence, would ever be guilty of failing to help in a similar situation. Indeed, none of the personality variables implicated in such pat, self-protective accounts were found in the present study to have anything to do with whether or how quickly participants helped.

The significance of this study is quite apparent if you reconsider the grievous case of Kitty Genovese, or the equally lamentable cases of the subway rider or switchboard operator described earlier. These unfortunates were not only victims of their heartless assailants; they were also victims of the influence that a situation can have on human decision making when pluralistic ignorance, a diffusion of responsibility, or both, characterize an emergency situation. This dynamic is not uncommon and deserves our understanding. Just as we are encouraged to learn CPR and to recycle plastic, should we not also be encouraged to understand and resist the situational pressures that inhibit helping? Bystanders need not be so unresponsive, the crowd so unhelpful.

AFTERTHOUGHTS

Darley and Latané's (1968) study ingeniously captured the critical features of certain types of emergencies, such as the Genovese murder, in which spectators knew that others were watching, could neither communicate with them nor know how they were reacting, and were uncertain as to whether it was up to them to help. Further studies along the same lines followed. In one by Latané and Rodin (1969), participants were busy filling out questionnaires when a young female experimenter left to get more materials from an adjacent room. The unsuspecting participants heard her drag a chair across the floor of the other room, climb onto it, and then emit a piercing scream, after which there was a loud crash that sounded like a bookcase overturning, followed by the ominous thud of a body hitting the floor. Next they heard the woman moaning in pain and crying out "Oh my God! My ankle! I can't move it! I think it's broken!" (All of these sound effects were carefully tape-recorded beforehand and played back from the other room once the woman arrived there.) Think about it: how would *you* have responded as a participant in this study? Would you have rushed to the woman's aid, regardless of the number of observers present? Well, predictably, the woman received help 70% of the time from solitary participants, 40% of the time from either member of two-person groups, and a mere 7% of the time when the other member of the pair was a deliberately unresponsive experimental confederate.

More than 50 follow-up studies, conducted either in the laboratory or in field settings, have confirmed the inverse relationship between group size and helping (see Latané & Nida, 1981). Yet, to be sure, Darley and Latané's study, and numerous replications, do not shed light on all aspects of helping or failing to help. New questions on this topic crop up as quickly as old ones are answered. (That a sense of enlightenment begets further ignorance is not uncommon in science.) One question: how are people socialized to be helpful? Coates and others (1976) found that certain TV shows, like *Sesame Street* and *Mr. Rogers' Neighborhood*, promote helpful behavior in preschoolers by providing likable models that they can imitate. In contrast, ostentatiously rewarding children for helping turns out to be a counterproductive strategy (Fabes and others, 1989; see chap. 8).

Another question: does one's mood influence one's tendency to help? Levin and Isen (1975) demonstrated that adults whose spirits were lifted upon finding a dime planted in the coin return of a public telephone were subsequently more inclined to help a passerby who 'accidentally' dropped a folder of papers. Also, Cunningham (1979) found that people leave larger tips on sunny days than on cloudy or rainy days (the *sunny Samaritan effect*). Furthermore, Harris and others (1975) found that Catholics on the way into confession (presumably burdened by guilt) donated more money to the March of Dimes than did those coming out of confession.

A final question: does gender or race affect helping? A *meta-analysis* (which involves statistically summarizing the results of many individual studies) by Eagly and Crowley (1986) found that men generally help more than women, and are more likely to assist strangers. This is especially true when there are onlookers, when there is potential danger involved in helping, and when the person in need is female. On this latter point, West and others (1975) found that when a motorist was seen to be changing a flat tire along a highway, one in four cars stopped when the motorist was female, but only 1 in 50 stopped when the motorist was male. (Would the same be found today? Probably.) In addition, Brigham and Richardson (1979) found that White convenience store clerks allowed a customer, who "discovered" that he or she did not have enough money to purchase a product, to do so anyway two-thirds of the time if the customer was a White man or woman, or a Black woman, but only one-third of the time if the customer was a Black man.

These and other questions and findings suggest that helping in an emergency, and helpful behavior more generally, is a multifaceted phenomenon, a complex function of many variables. Yet identifying the social conditions that facilitate helping does not establish why people want to help in the first place. Chapter 20 addresses the deeper motivational question of whether helping is ever done for purely unselfish reasons.

REVELATION

The more witnesses there are to an emergency, the less likely it is that any one of them will help. This is because individuals are often not privy to others' reactions, or because they do not feel uniquely responsible for preventing tragic outcomes.

— KPF —

CHAPTER REFERENCE

Darley, J. M., & Latané, B. (1968). Bystander intervention in emergencies: Diffusion of responsibility. *Journal of Personality and Social Psychology, 8,* 377–383.

OTHER REFERENCES

Brigham, J. C., & Richardson, C. B. (1979). Race, sex, and helping in the market place. *Journal of Applied Social Psychology, 9,* 314–322.

Coates, B., Pusser, H. E., & Goodman, I. (1976). The influence of "Sesame Street" and "Mister Rogers' Neighborhood" on children's social behavior in the preschool. *Child Development, 47,* 138–144.

Cunningham, M. R. (1979). Weather, mood, and helping behavior: Quasi-experiments with the sunshine Samaritan. *Journal of Personality and Social Psychology, 37,* 1947–1956.

Eagly, A. H., & Crowley, M. (1986). Gender and helping behavior: A meta-analytic review of the social psychological literature. *Psychological Bulletin, 100,* 283–308.

Evans, R. I. (1980). *The making of social psychology: Discussions with creative contributors.* New York: Gardner Press.

Fabes, R. A., Fultz, J., Eisenberg, N., May-Plumlee, T., & Christopher, F. C. (1989). Effects of rewards on children's prosocial motivation: A socialization study. *Developmental Psychology, 25,* 509–515.

Harris, M. B., Benson, J. M., & Hall, C. L. (1975). The effects of confession on altruism. *Journal of Social Psychology, 96,* 187–192.

Latané, B., & Darley, J. M. (1970). *The unresponsive bystander: Why doesn't he help?* New York: Appleton-Century-Crofts.

Latané, B., & Nida, S. (1981). Ten years of research on group size and helping. *Psychological Bulletin, 89,* 308–324.

Latané, B., & Rodin, J. (1969). A lady in distress: Inhibiting effects of friends and strangers on bystander intervention. *Journal of Experimental Social Psychology, 5,* 189–202.

Levin, P. F., & Isen, A. M. (1975). Further studies on the effect of feeling good on helping. *Sociometry, 38,* 141–147.

Milgram, S. (1963). Behavioral study of obedience. *Journal of Abnormal and Social Psychology, 69,* 137–143.

Nisbett, R. E., & Bellows, N. (1977). Verbal reports about causal influences on social judgments: Private access versus public theories. *Journal of Personality and Social Psychology, 35,* 613–624.

Prentice, D. A., & Miller, D. T. (Eds.). (1999). *Cultural divides: Understanding and overcoming group conflict.* New York: Russell Sage Foundation.

Rosenthal, A. M. (1964). *Thirty-eight witnesses.* New York: McGraw-Hill.

West, S. G., Whitney, G., & Schnedler, R. (1975). Helping a motorist in distress: The effects of sex, race, and neighborhood. *Journal of Personality and Social Psychology, 31,* 691–698.

MORE TO EXPLORE

Latané, B., & Darley, J. M. (1969). Bystander apathy. *American Scientist, 57,* 224–268.

20 Love Thy Neighbor or Thyself?: Empathy as a Source of Altruism

"Act so as to treat humanity ... never as a means only, but always at the same time as an end."

—Immanuel Kant (1724–1804), German philosopher

BACKGROUND

Chapter 19 investigated the phenomenon of bystander nonintervention—the tendency of people in crowds to stand idly by while someone suffers before their very eyes or within earshot. On the face of it, such passive behavior betokens an appalling lack of human sympathy: It seems to prove just how threadbare the fabric of public morality has become. However, social psychological research has established that bystanders stay put for quite another reason: the sheer ambiguity of the situation. Bystanders wonder: Whose responsibility is it to help? Is it really an emergency if no one else is doing anything? Tellingly, when bystanders do define a situation as an emergency, accept it is up to them to intervene, and feel confident they can be of assistance, they quickly channel their concern for victims into concrete action (Latané & Darley, 1968). Hence, the underlying goodwill of people in large gatherings need not be doubted. The problem stems from without. The presence of others fosters perceptions that make the expression of goodwill less likely. True, damsels (and swains) in distress suffer the consequences of being ignored regardless of why they are ignored. Yet it is some consolation that the hearts of passive bystanders are in the right place even if their bodies are not.

In this chapter, we delve deeper into people's motives for helping each other. In particular we consider research that seeks to answer the following question: Are people's motives for performing any act always in the last analysis self-serving?

Ask yourself: Did your friends give you birthday gifts this year out of a genuine desire to make you happy? Were they perhaps trying to endear themselves to you? Or just fulfilling an obligation they would have preferred not to have? Let us grant that your friends really did wish to make you happy on your birthday. Yet, even then, were they perhaps motivated by the anticipated pleasure of seeing you happy? Or by the pride of knowing that they were able to make you happy? How certain can you be, when it comes right down to it, that your friends were interested in fostering your happiness for its own sake? (And by the way: How pure were your motives when you gave them birthday gifts?)

The fundamental issue is whether promoting the welfare of others is ever our ultimate goal—our final selfless aim—or whether it is always and only an instrumental goal—a means to an end that satisfies some selfish desire on our part. Can we ever be disinterested altruists? Or are we forever doomed to be egoists of one sort or another, driven by selfish motives that differ only in their degree of subtlety? A negative answer to this question might offend those who, perhaps because of their faith in God, prefer to view mankind sympathetically. Equally, an affirmative answer might offend those who, perhaps thinking of Darwinian evolution, prefer

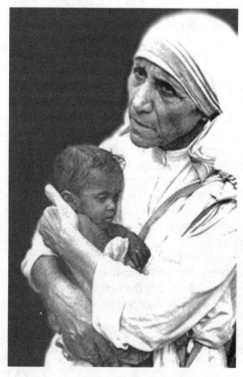

FIG. 20.1. Do we ultimately have a selfish reason for everything we do?

to view mankind cynically. What sort of objective evidence can help us settle the question?

First of all, there is the evidence afforded by everyday observation. It is evident that coming to the aid of others often provides joy and satisfaction, whereas leaving them to suffer often creates distress and guilt. So, we have much to gain, emotionally speaking, from lending a hand, and much to lose by not doing so.

Indeed, research proves that people help in order to repair bad moods. In one study, participants were led to believe that they, or another person, had accidentally harmed an experimental confederate. This manipulation, understandably, left participants rather dismayed. In addition, it also made them more likely to volunteer for a worthy cause later on. However, if participants were given either praise or cash after the initial manipulation, their likelihood of volunteering later dropped to the level of a control group not exposed to that manipulation (Cialdini, Darby, & Vincent, 1973). This study made a convincing case that the desire to make yourself feel better—a thoroughly selfish motive—can lead you to perform good deeds, unless something else makes you feel better first.

The situation might appear to be bleak for proponents of altruism. Everyday observation suggests, and some empirical research shows, that people help for selfish reasons. However, such evidence is not decisive. First, the mere fact that two phenomena are linked is not in itself a guarantee that one causes the other. For example, day and night follow each other with perfect regularity, but neither can be said to cause the other. Second, even if helping others benefits us in some way, it does not follow that we help in order to benefit. Any benefit we receive may conceivably be a by-product of our helping (Nagel, 1979). Granted, psychological rewards can and do motivate us to help. Yet it is a far from settled question whether they always do. Proponents of altruism can cheerfully concede the existence of any number of selfish motives because they do not logically exclude the existence of selfless motives. Hence, the informal evidence for universal egoism in can only ever be circumstantial, never enough to establish it beyond reasonable doubt.

Experimentation in the social psychological laboratory would appear to offer hope of untangling the causal knot. Yet, creating a paradigm capable of yielding evidence in favor of either egoism or altruism presents quite a challenge. What needs to be done?

First, a source of altruistic motivation needs to be identified. What state of mind could be expected to prompt altruistic acts? Thinkers throughout the ages have been fairly unanimous in singling out empathy as the prime candidate, so social psychologists have followed their lead (Batson, 1994). Empathy can be defined as an emotional orientation that comprises feelings of sympathy and compassion for others combined with a tendency to see things from their perspective. The hypothesis that empathy prompts altruistic acts is called—no surprise here—the *empathy-altruism hypothesis.*

Second, a number of potential selfish reasons need to be advanced for why people who feel empathy help. Do such people (whom, for brevity, we from now on call *empathizers*) help to improve their mood, enhance their self-regard, or alleviate their discomfort? Each selfish reason put forward constitutes a rival *egoistic hypothesis* to the empathy-altruism hypothesis.

The last step involves devising experimental tests to decide between the empathy-altruism hypothesis and each of its egoistic rivals. The details differ from case to case, but an attempt is always made to rule out one particular selfish reason for why empathizers might provide help. Of course, given the abundance of such reasons, multiple studies are required to test the empathy-altruism hypothesis fully. Nonetheless, at any point along the way, the empathy-altruism hypothesis could be disconfirmed, and its egoistic rival supported. Hence, if the empathy-altruism hypothesis survives a succession of determined attempts to disconfirm it, and no plausible egoistic alternatives to it remain, then that should be regarded as provisional evidence in its favor. To quote Conan Doyle's Sherlock Holmes, "… when you have eliminated the impossible, then whatever remains, however improbable, must be the truth."

Later, we summarize the many experimental findings that bear on the existence of altruism. For the moment, however, we consider findings that pertain to just one alternative to the empathy-altruism hypothesis. The alternative runs as follows: whenever we feel empathy for others, we help in order to forestall (prevent from occurring in advance) the guilt that would result from not helping.

Advocates of this particular rival hypothesis point out that people typically berate themselves whenever they violate private standards of conduct. They argue that people's reluctance to violate such standards stems from their natural desire to avoid such painful feelings of self-censure. Now, helping other people in distress is a standard of conduct to which most people subscribe. Hence, the argument goes, empathizers help in order to make sure that they avoid painful feelings of guilt in the future. In other words, it is a selfish concern with their own future well-being that motivates them, not any altruistic concern with the well-being of the distressed.

Advocates of the empathy-altruism hypothesis disagree. They propose that empathizers help with the ultimate goal of benefitting the distressed. Any guilt they might forestall in the process is merely an unsought-after bonus. Who is right?

WHAT THEY DID

Danie Batson and his colleagues (1988) had to manufacture an experimental situation in which one outcome would occur if empathic helping derived from a desire to forestall guilt, but another outcome would occur if it did not. Their ingenious strategy was as follows. They realized that the degree of guilt that someone anticipates for not helping is not only a function of the private standards to which they subscribe; it is also a function of the social context in which they find themselves. For example, suppose that, to help your long-suffering mother, you know you ought to wash up after dinner, but you selfishly opt not to, and later feel guilty. Suppose too that your siblings either regularly wash up or rarely wash up. You would probably feel less guilty in the latter case because you would have a credible excuse for not helping: My siblings don't wash up, so why should I? In the psychological laboratory, the social context can also be explicitly adjusted to raise or lower levels of guilt. Such adjustments provide the key to testing whether or not empathy-based helping does or does not stem from the desire to forestall guilt.

The logic goes like this. If forestalling guilt is the ultimate goal of empathizers, then the strength of their resolve to help, and the amount of help they provide, should be reduced by changes in context that provide excuses for not helping. However, if forestalling guilt is not the ultimate goal of empathizers, then neither the strength of their resolve to help, nor the amount of help they provide, should be reduced by such contextual adjustments. One pattern of results would support the egoistic guilt-forestalling hypothesis, the other contradict it.

There is one complication however. Suppose the researchers demonstrated that providing an excuse for not helping had no effect on empathic helping. Would that by itself be enough to refute the egoistic guilt-forestalling hypothesis? No. The absence of a result could be put down to some defect in the study, such as an unconvincing excuse, or an insensitive measure of helping. To meet such objections, the researchers had also to show that they *could* undermine helping with an excuse. In particular, they had to show that providing participants with an excuse when they felt little empathy for a victim would reduce their helpfulness, whereas providing participants with the same excuse when they felt much empathy for a victim would not. Such a result would indicate that empathy made participants immune, so to speak, to the help-undermining effects of excuses. It would indicate that empathizers do not help with the ultimate goal of forestalling guilt, for if they did, the availability of an excuse would have reduced the amount of help they provided.

Batson et al. (1988) conducted three separate studies that relied on this logic. In each study, participants were provided with a different justification for not helping. We focus here on the first of these studies, where participants were led to believe that a minority, as opposed to a majority, of their peers had previously helped in a similar situation. The expectation was that participants would adjust their private standards based upon the reported conduct of their peers.

One hundred and twenty undergraduates from Kansas University took part in the study. Matters were neatly arranged so that the 60 males and 60 females were equally represented in all conditions.

Participants were told that the purpose of the study was to pilot test some new programs for a local university radio station. One of the two programs to which they listened was entitled "News from the Personal Side." It consisted of an interview with a college student named Katie Banks. (The other program, more blandly informational, was included merely to make the cover story look plausible.) As the interview proceeded, it became clear that tragedy had recently befallen Katie. Both of her parents, and one of her sisters, had been killed in an automobile accident. Katie had since struggled to support her two younger siblings because her parents had never taken out life insurance. To make matters even worse, Katie had had to withdraw from college in her final year, because if she did not, her siblings would be put up for adoption.

Before playing the tape, the experimenter instructed participants to listen to each program in one of two ways. They were told either to "imagine how the person who is being interviewed feels about what has happened and how the events have affected her" or to "focus on the technical aspects of the broadcast." These differing instructions constituted the experimental manipulation of empathy. The former instruction encouraged participants to identify with Katie, thereby placing them in the high-empathy condition. The latter instruction encouraged participants not to identify with Katie, thereby placing them in the low-empathy condition.

When the tape had finished, the experimenter "discovered" that the questionnaires he had intended to administer to participants had been made illegible by a photocopying glitch. He explained that he would have to leave briefly in order to obtain replacements. On his way out, he handed participants two letters that the professor in charge of the study had asked him to pass on. The first letter was apparently written by the professor himself. In the letter, the professor explained how, after listening to the tape, he imagined some participants might wish to help Katie. He went on to say that he had asked Katie to write a letter of her own, to indicate how participants could help her if they so desired. The second letter was apparently Katie's. In it, she outlined a number of possible ways in which participants could be of assistance to her, for example, by baby-sitting her younger brother and sister, making transport available, or assisting in fundraising efforts.

Included with these letters was a response form, on which participants could indicate whether or not, and to what extent, they wished to help Katie. Participants had the option of pledging between 0 and 10 hours of assistance. Each response form featured eight spaces, seven of which had already been filled in by previous participants, so that one space remained for real participants to fill in. This was done so that participants would not expect their responses to be seen by other participants, an expectation that might have biased their responses.

The availability of the excuse for not helping was manipulated by adjusting how the number of previous participants had responded to Katie's request for help. In the excuse condition, only two out of these seven participants had volunteered to help, whereas in the no-excuse condition, a full five of them had. An additional control condition was included in which the response form was designed to contain only a single signature. The purpose of this condition was to allow the researchers to test whether empathizers would help more than nonempathizers when no information was available about whether other students' helped.

(Note that, had the experimenter still been present at this stage, difficulties might have arisen. Participants might have been more likely to conclude that the letters were just part of the study, or may have helped Katie simply because they felt that the experimenter was around to monitor them.)

Upon the return of the experimenter, participants were asked to fill out two questionnaires. Most of the items they featured were bogus, but a few served as a check on whether the experimental manipulations had worked as intended. Two items assessed the effectiveness of the empathy manipulation. The first asked participants how much they focused on the technical aspects of the broadcast, the second, how much they focused on the feelings of the person interviewed. Another item assessed the effectiveness of the excuse manipulation. Participants were asked to what extent they believed that other students had an obligation to help Katie. (The researchers reasoned that judgments of peer obligation would closely match judgments of personal obligation, and that both would reflect the availability of the excuse for not helping.) A final item asked participants to rate how much Katie herself stood in need of assistance. After completing these paper-and-pencil measures, participants were debriefed and dismissed.

WHAT THEY FOUND

Preliminary checks indicated that the two manipulations had worked as expected. Participants in the high-empathy condition reported focusing more on Katie's feelings than on the technical aspects of the broadcast, whereas participants in the low-empathy condition reported the opposite. (A gender difference was also noted. Women on the whole were more likely to focus on Katie's feelings than men were.) In addition, participants in the excuse condition thought it less imperative that university students help Katie than participants in the no-excuse condition. At the same time, no differences were found across conditions in how pressing Katie's need was judged to be. Neither level of empathy, nor excuse availability, influenced this perception. This makes interpretation of the study's results more straightforward.

The researchers quantified the help that participants provided in two ways. First, they noted the percentage of participants who volunteered any help; second, they noted the number of hours that participants pledged. For statistical reasons that we need not go into, the percentage measure was deemed the primary index of helping, and the number-of-hours measure the secondary index.

So what did the researchers find? As expected, when empathy for Katie was low, participants with an excuse for not helping volunteered in far fewer numbers than participants with no excuse. This indicates that having an excuse undermined helping when empathy was low, presumably by reducing the guilt that participants anticipated for not helping. However, a different picture emerged among participants who empathized with Katie. Participants who had a good excuse for not helping helped almost as often as participants who did not. In fact, the difference was no greater than would be expected by chance. This means that having or not having an excuse did not influence whether or not these participants volunteered to help Katie (Fig. 20.2).

The secondary measure, the number of hours participants pledged, yielded a roughly similar pattern of results. Far fewer hours were pledged by participants in the low-empathy–excuse condition than by participants in the other three conditions, who did not differ in terms of the average number of hours they pledged.

How should these results be interpreted? The effectiveness of the excuse manipulation when empathy was low, coupled with its ineffectiveness when empathy was high, suggests that, while forestalling guilt is the ultimate goal of nonempathizers, it is not the ultimate goal of empathizers. The guilt-forestalling hypothesis has therefore been disconfirmed, and the empathy-altruism hypothesis has survived one substantial attempt at disconfirmation.

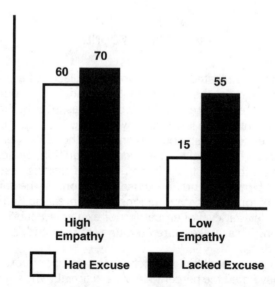

FIG. 20.2. Percentage of participants who helped Katie, when their empathy for her was high or low, and when they had or lacked an excuse for not helping her.

In the study we have described, the excuse for not helping involved leading participants to believe that a minority rather than a majority of undergraduate peers had provided help in a similar situation. In two companion studies, also designed to rule out the guilt-forestalling hypothesis, the researchers provided alternative excuses for not helping. The findings of both of these studies dovetailed those of the present study. Hence, converging evidence was obtained of the falsity of the guilt-forestalling hypothesis as an explanation for why people help when moved by empathy.

SO WHAT?

As mentioned in the introduction, obtaining evidence in favor of the empathy-altruism hypothesis is a cumulative process. The present study and its two follow-ups rule out only a single egoistic alternative to the empathy-altruism hypothesis. Other egoistic alternatives, of equal or greater plausibility, remain. They need to be systematically ruled out in a multipronged program of research.

As it happens, such a program of research is already well underway and may in fact be nearing completion. Numerous studies, analogous in logical structure to the present one, indicate that empathic helping is not motivated by a wide range of egoistic motives, such as reducing distress, enhancing self-image, regulating mood, or taking pride in helping (Batson et al., 1991; Batson, Duncan, Ackerman, Buckley, & Birch, 1981; Dovidio, Piliavin, Gaertner, Schroder, & Clark, 1991). Although the research is not completely consistent (e.g., Schaller & Cialdini, 1988) the balance of evidence suggests that the main egoistic alternatives to the empathy-altruism hypothesis have been credibly ruled out. The odds of the empathy-altruism hypothesis being true have therefore increased. Of course, someone could always come along and identify a new egoistic motive that accounts for empathic helping. For example, it has recently been claimed that feeling empathy leads us to see other people as part of ourselves, so that by selflessly helping them we are in fact selfishly helping ourselves (Cialdini, Brown, Lewis, & Luce, 1997). However, both the reasoning behind this claim, and the data supporting it, have been critiqued (Batson, 1997). Interested readers are encouraged to read further and make up their own minds. Yet, with plausible egoistic motives for emphatic helping dwindling, the contention that human beings are capable of disinterested altruism no longer seems idealistic or naive. Rather, it seems defensible in light of the best evidence that science has to offer.

The results of research on altruism are significant for two reasons. First, they provide a fresh perspective on human motivation. In particular, they imply that psychological hedonism—the theory that all our behavior is governed by the experience, or the anticipated experience, of pleasure and pain—is false. Rather, some motivations may have nothing to do with our own well-being, being focused solely on the well-being of others. (Chapters 6 and 8, saw a refutation of the related, though not identical, theory that behavior is simply governed by rewards and punishments.) As a consequence, the results of research on altruism also tell us something deep about human beings as moral creatures. The cynical view that we are all ultimately selfish—implying that the motives of humanitarians and misanthropists are somehow on an equal footing—need not be endorsed.

AFTERTHOUGHTS

It is interesting to speculate on what sources of altruism might exist in addition to empathy. Batson (1994) considers two possibilities: *collectivism*, the motivation to selflessly benefit a group with which one identifies, and *principlism*, the motivation to uphold some moral principle for its own sake. Collectivism, for example, might inspire a patriot to give up his life for the sake of his country (rather than, say, for personal glory). Or principlism might keep a married man from committing adultery because he believes doing so would be wrong in itself (rather than, say, because he could not live with himself if he did). At the time of writing, no experimental evidence exists for either possibility. However, it may be possible to modify the designs used in the present study to investigate the matter.

The question of whether other sources of altruism exist is important because empathy, for all the accolades bestowed upon it, has two serious drawbacks. We conclude by highlighting them.

First, empathy is largely emotional. As such, it is something that happens to us, not something we freely choose to bring about. Of course, like participants in the present study, we could deliberately try to take the perspective of another person, but this rarely happens in everyday life. Mostly, we are passively seized by tender feelings that prompt us to help others without thought of ourselves. Yet, such feelings are often created by situational factors, many of which are a matter of chance (e.g., whether the victim resembles us, or whether his plight is vividly communicated). This being the case, how much praise do we truly deserve for altruistic acts inspired by empathy? Having pure motives may not make us praiseworthy if those motives are partly the result of factors beyond our control. Altruistic acts inspired by principlism, however, could not be criticized on such grounds. Conforming to a moral principle for its own sake would require a conscious and deliberate act of will. It would not be something that just happens to us; rather, it would be the expression of our deepest character (Kant, 1785/1898). We could therefore justifiably take full credit for any and all altruistic acts we performed when inspired by principlism—unless, of course, it turns out that free will itself is merely a cognitive illusion (Wegner & Wheatley, 1999; see chap. 10).

Another drawback of empathy is that it can inspire actions that violate the moral principle of fairness. Victims who arouse our empathic concern are not always the ones who are objectively most in need of our help (Batson, Klein, Highberger, & Shaw, 1995; Singer, 1995). It may seem legitimate that we put the welfare of friends and family before those of strangers. More ethically worrisome is that the sentimental portrayal of the needs of the few can elicit more empathic help than the impartial description of the needs of the many. Thus, we may give more to a charity for cute mistreated animals than to a charity for emaciated starving children. The virtue of principled altruism is that it transcends parochial concerns. A passionate commitment to universal human rights might prompt one to work towards a fairer distribution of benefits across individuals. However, it may be that abstract principles, at least for most people, have less motivating force than empathy precisely because of their lack of specificity (Eisenberg, 1991). As the dictator Stalin once commented, with ironic insight into the nature of empathy: "The death of one man is a tragedy, the death of a million a statistic."

REVELATION

When moved by empathy, people help not because they are motivated to avoid the guilt that would result from not helping, nor, it seems, for any other selfish reason. Rather, they help with the ultimate goal of benefiting other people.

— APG —

CHAPTER REFERENCE

Batson, C., Dyck, J., Brandt, J. R., Batson, J., Powell, A., McMaster, M. R., & Griffitt, C. (1988). Five studies testing two new egoistic alternatives to the empathy-altruism hypothesis. *Journal of Personality and Social Psychology, 55*, 52–77.

OTHER REFERENCES

Batson, C. D. (1994). Prosocial motivation: Why do we help others? In A.. Tesser (Ed.), *Advanced social psychology* (pp. 333–381). Boston: McGraw-Hill.

Batson, C. D. (1997). Self-other merging and the empathy-altruism hypothesis: Reply to Neuberg et al. *Journal of Personality and Social Psychology, 73*, 517–522.

Batson, C. D., Batson, J. G., Slingsby, J. K., Harrell, K. L., Peekna, H. M., & Todd, R. M. (1991). Empathic joy and the empathy-altruism hypothesis. *Journal of Personality and Social Psychology, 61*, 413–426.

Batson, C. D., Duncan, B. D., Ackerman, P., Buckley, T., & Birch, K. (1981). Is empathic emotion a source of altruistic emotion? *Journal of Personality and Social Psychology, 40,* 290–302.

Batson, C. D., Klein, T. R., Highberger, L., & Shaw, L. (1995). Immorality from empathy-induced altruism: When compassion and justice conflict. *Journal of Personality and Social Psychology, 68,* 1042–1054.

Cialdini, R. B., Darby, B. L., & Vincent, J. E. (1973). Transgression and altruism: A case for hedonism. *Journal of Experimental Social Psychology, 9,* 502–516.

Cialdini, R. B., Brown, S. L., Lewis, B. P., & Luce, C. (1997). Reinterpreting the empathy-altruism relationship: When one into one equals oneness. *Journal of Personality and Social Psychology, 73,* 481–494.

Darley, J. M., & Latané, B. (1968). Bystander intervention in emergencies: Diffusion of responsibility. *Journal of Personality and Social Psychology, 8,* 377–383.

Dovidio, J. F., Piliavin, J. A., Gaertner, S. L., Schroder, D. A., & Clark, R. D. III (1991). The arousal/cost-reward model and the processes of intervention: A review of the evidence. In M. S. Clark (Ed.), *Prosocial behavior* (pp. 86–118). Newbury Park, CA: Sage.

Eisenberg, N. (1991). Meta-analytic contributions to the literature on prosocial behavior. *Personality and Social Psychology Bulletin, 17,* 273–282.

Kant, I. (1898). *Kant's critique of practical reason and other works on the theory of ethics* (4th ed.) (T. K. Abbott, Trans.). New York: Longmans, Green, and Co. (Original work published in 1785)

Latané, B., & Darley, J. M. (1970). *The unresponsive bystander: Why doesn't he help?* Englewood Cliffs, NJ: Prentice-Hall.

Nagel, T. (1979). *The possibility of altruism.* Princeton, NJ: Princeton University Press.

Nisbett, R. E., & Bellows, N. (1977). Verbal reports about causal influences on social judgments: Private access versus public theories. *Journal of Personality and Social Psychology, 35,* 613–624.

Schaller, M., & Cialdini, R. B. (1988). The economics of empathic helping: Support for a mood-management motive. *Journal of Experimental Social Psychology, 24,* 163–181.

Singer, P. (1995). *How are we to live? Ethics in an age of self-interest.* New York: Prometheus Books.

Wegner, D. M., & Wheatley, T. P. (1999). Apparent mental causation: Sources of the experience of will. *American Psychologist, 54,* 480–492.

MORE TO EXPLORE

Kohn, A. (1992). *The brighter side of human nature: Altruism and empathy in everyday life.* New York. Basic Books.

Nagel, T. (1979). *The possibility of altruism.* Princeton, NJ: Princeton University Press.

21 Just Following Orders: A Shocking Demonstration of Obedience to Authority

"Obedience, bane of all genius, virtue, freedom, truth, makes slaves of men, and, of the human frame, a mechanized automaton."
—Percy Bysshe Shelley (1792–1822), English poet

BACKGROUND

Whenever you do something because someone tells you to do it, that is *obedience*. Obedience is often a good thing. It permits society to function smoothly and to accomplish large-scale goals that require hierarchical co-ordination. The ancient Greek philosopher, Socrates, extolled the importance of obedience to the state, even stoically accepting his society's order to drink poisonous hemlock. Yet obedience is not always a good thing. Indeed, Plato questioned the wisdom of obeying unjust laws (mindful of his mentor's sad fate). History since has been replete with poignant examples of obedience-turned-tragedy, leaving the enlightenati of our day wary of all forms of submissiveness to authority.

During the height of the Vietnam War, an American Bravo company swept through a defenseless hamlet, My Lai, slaughtering everyone in sight, because they were suspected of siding with the enemy. One of the invading soldiers admitted in a sobering testimony to pushing men, women, and children into a ravine and shooting them, simply because he was ordered to do so by the officer in charge (Milgram, 1974). That officer, Lieutenant Benjamin Calley, defended his own actions—he too was just following orders. In 1978, over 900 People's Temple devotees of the Reverend Jim Jones obeyed his command to commit mass suicide by drinking cyanide-laced Kool-Aid (although it appeared afterward that some had done so at gunpoint, most had submitted willingly). In 1993, impassioned disciples of David Koresh followed his charge to fire on approaching law enforcement officers and remained barricaded in their Waco, Texas compound for weeks. (Of course, the raiding government troops were likewise being obedient to their superiors.) The standoff ended when the compound was burned to the ground, leaving about 80 Branch Davidian cultists dead, among them 20 children. This is but a fraction of the deplorable historical episodes that inspire the following kind of quote: "When you think of the long and gloomy history of man, you will find that far more, and far more hideous, crimes have been committed in the name of obedience than have ever been committed in the name of rebellion" (Snow, 1961, p. 24).

Social psychologists are well aware of the horrors of history and the world around them. In fact, the *zeitgeist* (spirit of the times) and the *ortgeist* (spirit of a place) very much influence what social psychologists choose to study. When the U.S. government makes some calamitous decision, as it did during the Bay of Pigs fiasco, social psychologists feel compelled to study the pitfalls of group decision making. When a woman is raped on a barroom pool table in full view of unresponsive barflies, social psychologists are driven to study bystander intervention (or lack thereof). When it becomes clear that women earn only two-thirds of what their equally qualified male peers do, social psychologists commit to research on gender stereotypes. Social psychology is perhaps more influenced by current social events than any other field of scientific inquiry.

Social psychologist Stanley Milgram (1963) sought to explain one of the most shameful episodes of human history. As a young assistant professor at Yale University, Milgram had been captivated by the Nuremberg war trials, especially by the trial of Adolf Eichmann, an alleged architect of the Final Solution, Hitler's abhorrent plan to exterminate the Jews of Europe. Eichmann, by all appearances a normal man, repeatedly testified to the Jerusalem court that he had simply been obeying orders, and it was the ordinary demeanor of men like Eichmann that led the social commentator Hannah Arendt to write, in 1965, about the *banality of evil*. Eichmann's plea fascinated Milgram. Had this been an incomprehensively evil man or simply someone who was just following orders? Was Eichmann ruled by unspeakably perverse passions, a deranged ideologue known to fulminate against Jews, or just an ordinary individual who just happened to get caught up in a vortex of indulgent hatred, pride, and vengeance? Just how banal might evil be?

The starting point of what is arguably the most famous (or infamous) of all social psychological experiments was an uncomplicated observation by its designer:

It has been reliably established that from 1933–1945 millions of innocent persons were systematically slaughtered on command. Gas chambers were built, death camps were guarded, daily quotas of corpses were produced with the same efficiency as the manufacture of appliances. These inhumane policies may have originated in the mind of a single person, but they could only be carried out on a massive scale if a very large number of people obeyed orders. (Milgram, 1963, p. 467)

This simple observation produced some obvious questions. What caused those who perpetrated the Final Solution to obey the heinous orders they received? More generally, how inclined are people to obey authority figures, and what factors mitigate or exacerbate such an inclination?

Milgram began as a firm believer in cultural differences. He suspected that the apparent blind obedience on the part of the Nazis during World War II reflected a distinct, and probably rare, German character. In an effort to demonstrate this point, he devised a unique measure of obedience. Specifically, he *operationalized* obedience (that is, he defined obedience in terms of how he would measure it) as the intensity of shock one person, a teacher, would willingly give another person, a learner, at the behest of an authority figure, during what was claimed to be an experiment on the effects of punishment on learning. Having developed this measure of obedience, Milgram speculated that very few of his participants would administer even moderate shocks, let alone intense shocks: "You would get only a very, very small portion of people going out to the end of the shock generator, and they would constitute a pathological fringe" (Meyer, 1970, pp. 3–4). Milgram started out studying adults from the community surrounding Yale University, a reasonably representative sample of the population at large. These participants were to serve as a baseline against which he would later compare German participants expected to possess more authoritarian or Nazi-like characteristics. However, as it turned out, Milgram never got around to studying Germans per se. The results he obtained from Americans were too startling.

WHAT HE DID

Milgram (1963) conducted scores of obedience experiments, altogether involving over 1,000 participants. Many of these studies replicated his fundamental findings, and many served to identify important *moderators* (influences on) and *boundary conditions* (limits of) of those findings. We begin by describing Milgram's basic paradigm and the exact procedure of his first published study on this front.

Milgram paid $4.50 (significant money in the early 60s) to each of 40 men—who ranged from 20 to 50 years old and were from all walks of life— to participate in a study on learning in an elegant laboratory at Yale University. Each participant arrived at the lab at about the same time as did a mild-mannered and amiable 47-year-old accountant, who posed as a second participant. The experimenter—a stern-looking 31-year-old male high school biology teacher, dressed in a gray technician's coat (not Milgram himself)—began by presenting both men with a *cover story* (stated rationale for the study) concerning the presumed relation between punishment and learning:

> We know very little about the effect of punishment on learning, because almost no truly scientific studies have been made of it on human beings. For instance, we don't know how much punishment is best for learning —and we don't know how much difference it makes as to who is giving the punishment, whether an adult learns best from a younger or older person than himself—or many things of the sort. So in this study we are bringing together a number of adults of different occupations and ages. And we're asking some of them to be teachers and some to be learners. We want to find out just what effect different people have on each other as teachers and learners, and also what effect punishment will have on learning in this situation. Therefore, I'm going to ask one of you to be the teacher here tonight and the other to be the learner. (Milgram, 1963, p. 468)

At this point the two participants (the real one and the confederate posing as a participant) drew slips of paper from a hat to determine their respective roles. However, the drawing was rigged so that the real participant was always assigned the teacher role. Then the two participants followed the experimenter to an adjoining room where the hapless learner (the experimenter's accomplice) sat down and had his arm strapped into place.

The experimenter explained that the straps were designed to prevent any undue movement, or any attempt at escape. An electrode, allegedly connected to a shock generator in the adjacent room, was attached to the learner's wrist, and buffered by electrode paste "to avoid blisters and burns." As part of the elaborate subterfuge, the learner asked, with apparent nervousness, if the shocks would be painful, to which the experimenter coolly replied that the shocks, though quite painful, would cause no lasting damage. (In subsequent studies, the learner also mentioned in passing that he had a "heart condition.") Thus, the real participant was made fully aware of the other participant's unenviable predicament.

The experimenter then apprised the participant of his task. He was to read a list of paired words (blue–sky, nice–day, wild–duck ...) over a microphone to the learner in the next room. The learner's task was allegedly to memorize the word pairs. The participant would then read the first word of each pair along with four other words (e.g., blue ... ink, sky, box, lamp) and the learner would indicate which of the four words he believed was originally paired with the first word by pressing one of four switches in front of him. One of four numbers would then light up on an answer box in the next room where the participant sat, indicating the learner's response.

FIG. 21.1.   A replica of Milgram's bogus shock generator.

The answer box was located conveniently above a very authentic-looking shock generator.

The instrument panel of the shock generator included 30 identical lever switches, each with its own industrially engraved voltage designation. The first switch (on the far left) indicated 15 volts, the second 30 volts, the third 45 volts, and so on right up to 450 volts. The first three switches carried the label "Slight Shock." Moving to the right, subsequent triplets of switches carried the labels "Moderate Shock," "Strong Shock," "Very Strong Shock," "Intense Shock," "Extremely Intense Shock," and "Danger: Severe Shock." The final two switches were ominously marked "XXX." Whenever a switch was pressed, a pilot light went on, an electric buzz was heard, a blue light (labeled voltage energizer) flashed, and a dial on a voltage meter swung rightward.

To make matters more convincing still, all participants were given a sample shock themselves before beginning the study. An electrode was applied to their wrists, the third switch was pressed, and a real 45 volt shock was delivered. Their reactions proved to them that the shock was intense. In fact, they often estimated that they had received a higher level of shock. (They might even have calculated that the learner was eligible to receive a maximum shock 10 times that amount!) The participant was told that whenever the learner gave an incorrect answer, he (the participant) was to deliver a shock to him, by throwing one of the switches, and was to "start from 15 volts and increase the shock level one step each time the learner gives a wrong answer" (Milgram, 1963, p. 469).

The participant was instructed to administer shocks in this way until the learner got all of the word pairs correct, even if this required going through the list several times. Unknown to the participant, however, the learner followed a predetermined schedule of responses, answering correctly on only about a quarter of the trials. Moreover, in this particular study, the learner was heard to pound on the wall after (seemingly) receiving a 300-volt shock, but gave no further answers thereafter. The experimenter instructed the typically puzzled and alarmed participant to treat this absence of a response as a wrong answer and to advance to the next level of shock, 315 volts. The learner pounded on the wall one final time after (seemingly) receiving this level of shock, but after that, nothing more was heard from him. Deathly silence reigned.

Participants instinctively turned to the experimenter for advice on whether they should proceed. They often objected to continuing to shock the unresponsive learner. The experimenter responded with a preordained sequence of five statements, made in a polite but firm tone of voice: "Please continue," "Please go on," "The experiment requires that you continue," "It is absolutely essential that you continue," and "You have no other choice, you must go on." To any participant expressing concern about the learner's physical condition, the experimenter would matter-of-factly reply: "Although the shocks may be painful, there is no physical damage, so please go on." If the participant said he wanted to quit the procedure, the experimenter retorted: "Whether the learner likes it or not, you must go on until he has learned all the word pairs correctly. So please go on."

Milgram collected various types of data in this study. Photographs of the participant were sometimes taken through one-way mirrors; notes were kept by the experimenter, and sometimes by additional observers, on any of the participant's eccentric behaviors; and recordings were made of the time that elapsed between when the learner responded and when the participant pressed a shock lever, and of the duration of each lever press. Yet the main dependent variable was the maximum shock a participant would administer before refusing to go on. Milgram's primary objective was to see how far participants would go in their obedience to the experimenter, the authority figure in the situation.

When it was all over, the participant was presented with open-ended questions, projective measures (e.g., inkblots), and attitude scales about his experience as a teacher. The participants were then *debriefed*: the true purpose of the study was explained, after which the learner reintroduced himself and revealed that he was in fact a research accomplice who had in no way suffered harm during the ordeal. The filmed expressions of the unsuspecting teachers when they received this revelation shows *them* now being shocked.

WHAT HE FOUND

What do you think Milgram found? Imagine 100 people that you know with diverse backgrounds and assorted personality traits going through

Milgram's procedure. What percentage of the 100 would likely obey the experimenter and deliver a 15-volt shock to a fellow participant? How many would proceed to 30 volts, 45 volts, 60 volts, and so on? What percentage do you imagine would deliver intense or extremely intense shocks to a fellow human being, even after he demands to be let out, pounds on the wall, and then falls silent? What percentage would go all the way to deliver 450-volt "XXX" shocks? When Milgram posed such questions to his colleagues and Yale University psychology majors, he found that the vast majority predicted that few people would go beyond "Very Strong Shock" levels and that only an insignificant few (0 to 3 percent) would continue obediently to the maximum level of shock. (Forty psychiatrists at a nearby medical school, contemplating a similar follow-up study, predicted that fewer than 1%—only the most twisted and sadistic—would deliver the highest possible shock.) Naturally, when people were asked to predict how *they* would act in such a situation, none imagined themselves delivering any more than the most minimal shocks.

In light of these predictions, Milgram's (1963) actual results were stunning. Not one of the participants stopped prior to delivering the 300-volt shock, the point at which the learner audibly pounded on the wall. Five participants refused to go on at that point. Four more participants refused to go on after delivering 315 volts of shock and hearing the learner once again pound on the wall. Two participants then quit delivering shocks at 330 volts, and one more at each of the next three shock levels (345, 360, and 375 volts) when the learner was no longer pounding or answering. But that was it. The remaining 26 participants proceeded to 390, 405, 420, 435, and 450 volts of shock (Fig. 21.2). In other words, 65% punished the learner (for failing to correctly remember word pairs) with the most potent levels of shock ("Danger: Severe" and "XXX"). These participants often expressed discomfort, fear, reluctance, and indignation, although some remained oddly serene. Milgram commented on their demeanor during the ordeal:

> [When] the experimenter called a halt to the proceedings, many obedient [participants] heaved sighs of relief, mopped their brows, rubbed their fingers over their eyes, or nervously fumbled cigarettes. Some shook their heads, apparently in regret. Some remained calm throughout the experiment, and displayed only minimal signs of tension from beginning to end. (p. 470)

A few further results, from Milgram's subsequent studies (1965), are noteworthy. As mentioned already, once Milgram stumbled upon his unanticipated results, he attempted to isolate factors that would influence obedience within his general paradigm. For example, he surmised that the prestige of the sponsoring institution (namely, Yale University) may have contributed to his dramatic results, so he moved his study to a shabby

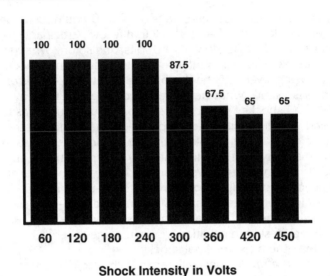

Shock Intensity in Volts

FIG. 21.2.   Percentage of participants who kept on obeying the experimenter's
instruction to shock a "learner," as the level of shock intensity increased.

commercial building in downtown Bridgeport, Connecticut, and found
that more than half the participants there also obeyed to the bitter end.
Milgram also wondered about the effect that the physical or psychological
distance between the participant and either the experimenter or the learner
might have had on his results. Thus, in one study, instead of having the experimenter physically present to give instructions, Milgram had him give instructions either by telephone or tape-recorder. Only 16% of the
participants went all the way in such conditions (and some participants
cheated by giving reduced shocks). In another study, the learner was
placed one and a half feet away from the participant in the same
room—adding visual cues of pain to the audible cues that were present in
the initial study. In that situation, about 40%, rather than 65%, gave extreme shocks. Obedience was even less (but still remarkable) in another
condition where the experimenter ordered the teacher to manually force
the learner's hand onto a shock plate (a plastic shield prevented the teacher
himself from receiving the presumed shock).

   With indefatigable curiosity, Milgram also tested the effects of group
pressure on obedience by having *three* teachers (two of them were actually
research confederates) deliver shocks together (the real participant was by
"chance" the one to actually press the shock levers). When the other two
teachers submissively obeyed the experimenter and showed no sympathy
for the distressed learner, the true participant tended to do the same (72%
delivered extreme shocks). However, when the other two teachers defied

the experimenter (quitting at 150 and 210 volts, respectively), the true participants showed considerably more backbone (only 10% delivered extreme shocks). (See chap. 17 for more on the effects of having a defiant ally.) Interestingly, when participants put through the procedure of the original study were allowed to choose the shock level they would give for each wrong answer, only 1 in 40 ever resorted to 450 volts. Yet when a participant was put in a subsidiary role where he stood by while another participant (actually a confederate) pressed the shock lever, the sobering 65% mentioned earlier jumped to an alarming 93%. Participants in passive roles seldom did anything substantial to stop the shocks. Might this explain why, during World War II, ordinary Germans stood by while the Nazis carried out systematic slaughter?

Finally, to the chagrin of anyone wanting to extol the importance of a person's moral mettle or character in such a situation, Milgram found that personality traits and demographic variables had little effect on his general results. Participants high on the trait of *authoritarianism* (rigid deference to authority and lack of sympathy for the weak and oppressed) did obey slightly more than those low on the same trait. Roman Catholics obeyed slightly more than Protestants or Jews. And those with less education and income obeyed slightly more than those with more education and income. Yet basically, most of what the person brought into Milgram's laboratory (including whether they were male or female) had little to do with what they did in his laboratory, with that very authentic-looking voltage generator sitting in front of them and the imperious experimenter nearby.

SO WHAT?

Milgram's (1963) findings sent shockwaves through academia and the world beyond. They led many to conclude that human nature is easily prodded to brutal and inhumane acts given the presence of a malevolent authority figure. In Milgram's words: "A substantial proportion of people do what they are told to do, irrespective of the content of the act and without limitations of conscience, so long as they perceive that the command comes from a legitimate authority" (1965, pp. 74–75). Milgram's results are an antidote to moral self-complacency, making it harder for us to assume that we could never act like Adolf Eichmann in Nazi Germany, Lt. Calley in My Lai, or one of the suicide victims in Jonestown, Guyana.

Although we would like to think of ourselves as free agents, relatively impervious to situational pressures, this is evidently not the case. Milgram's study reveals how powerful an influence the situation can exert over one's behavior. This is a bitter pill to swallow, and it is a rare person who would admit, as did the novelist Kurt Vonnegut Jr., that "If I'd been born in Germany I suppose I would have been a Nazi, bopping Jews and gypsies and Poles around, leaving boots sticking out of the snow-banks, warming myself with my sweetly virtuous insides" (1966, p. 69). However, such an honest admission is the bleak side of the story. The brighter side has to do with our growing recognition of the potency of such situations and our capacity to prevent or counteract their occurrence.

It should also be noted that, using quite different methods, other researchers have obtained similar results implying similar conclusions. In one study, for example, an unknown doctor telephoned nurses and ordered them to administer twice the maximum safe dosage of an uncommon drug to patients. All but one of 22 nurses would have done so had an alert research assistant not stopped them at the last moment (Hofling and others, 1966). Milgramesque results have also been successfully replicated in other countries (e.g., Kilham & Mann, 1974; Meeus & Raaijmakers, 1995). All this tends to strengthen the conclusion that obedience to authority occurs as readily as it did in 1960s New Haven. Milgrams results were no fluke.

AFTERTHOUGHTS

Milgram's (1963) research leaves us with two important questions. The first has to do with his intriguing results. What produced them? Why did participants obey to such extremes? The second has to do with his questionable methods. Were they excessive? Did Milgram overstep critical ethical boundaries by putting his participants through unnecessary psychological torture?

The first of these questions arises because, although Milgram's research identifies various situational *moderators* (factors that affect the magnitude) of his results, it does little to elucidate the psychological *mediators* (intervening causes) of those results. Why, specifically, did participants feel so compelled to obey the experimenter even though, in many cases, they were so obviously distressed? Milgram's research did not provide many insights at the conceptual or theoretical level. Nonetheless, there has been no shortage of post hoc explanations.

One is that Milgram's participants were, in fact, depraved and merciless. Yet consider how much strain and distress they evidently suffered during the ordeal: succumbing to fits of nervous laughter, sweating profusely, and begging the experimenter to stop. Clearly, his participants did feel concern for the victim, even if that concern was, in truth, more selfish than unselfish (but see chap. 20). It is unlikely that Milgram's participants were sadistic and pitiless. Claiming they were amounts to the *fundamental attribution error*—exaggerating the dispositional determinants of behavior while downplaying the situational determinants of behavior (Ross, 1977; see chap. 23).

Another explanation points to the role of *norms*, societal expectations concerning how one should and should not behave (see chap. 17). The *norm of obedience*, for example, dictates that people should obey those who have legitimate authority. The *norm of social responsibility*, in contrast, demands that people help others in distress. Each of these norms tends to arise or be salient in different situations, as when a police officer orders one to use a crosswalk (obedience) or when one encounters a lost child (social responsibility). In the situation Milgram created, it appears that these two norms competed, so to speak. Opposing psychological forces collided: participants did not want to suffer any disapproval or scorn for refusing to obey, nor did they want to suffer "empathetic distress" over the person they were willfully hurting. The institutional setting and the experimenter's forceful words ("You must continue ... It is absolutely essential that you continue") emphasized the norm of obedience. Less austere surroundings and different words ("Be careful not to hurt the learner ... Be sensitive to his feelings and welfare") would have underscored the expectation to be compassionate and, no doubt, have produced different behaviors. In like manner, the norm of obedience often occludes the norm of social responsibility in everyday circumstances, with regrettable outcomes.

The concepts of *low-balling* and the *foot-in-the-door* have also been offered to explain Milgram's results. One gets low-balled when one commits to a particular course of action (for example, agreeing to buy a cherry-red "classic" from a used car salesman) that proves to be more costly or less attractive than one originally expected (the fail-safe warranty turns out to not be part of the deal; see Cialdini, 2000). The savvy influence peddler gets his foot in the door when he convinces his patsy to make a small commitment that later makes it psychologically difficult to forego a larger commitment (Cialdini & others, 1978; see chaps. 6 and 7). In Milgram's scenario, participants unknowingly committed themselves to a course of action that initially seemed quite benign (the shocks were weak and were intended to improve learning) and meritorious (from a scientific standpoint). How could the participants have known that the learner was going to make so many mistakes and that the shocks would so quickly become so intense? Furthermore, if the teacher obeyed the experimenter at 45 volts, what reason could he give himself for disobeying at 60 volts, and if he obeyed at 390 volts, why disobey at 405 volts? If participants had to increase the shocks in 100-volt increments, would they have been so obedient? Apparently, the gradual step-by-step nature of their obedience to the experimenter's escalating requests kept participants from disobeying. They were on a slippery slope, with no time to think (Gilbert, 1981). Their innocuous acts quickly mutated into unconscionable ones. As sometimes happens in life outside the lab, innocence devolved into evil.

Finally, perhaps Milgram's participants went to such shocking extremes because they were *authorized* to do so. In fact, Milgram (1974) described participants as entering into an *agentic state*—seeing themselves as mere instruments or agents of the experimenter, helpless cogs in the machinery of the situation. Participants were led to focus on details of the task and not on its higher-level implications (Vallacher & Wegner, 1987). When they asked "Who's responsible?" the experimenter stated clearly "I'm responsible," thus absolving them of at least some of the responsibility for their actions.

Perhaps none of these explanations is completely satisfying. However, the blunt truth remains: it was the situation (the experimenter's words, the nature of the task, the trappings of the lab) that in large part made participants do what they did, and the critical features of Milgram's manipulation often have analogies in everyday life.

The second important question: how unethical was Milgram's research? Well, he could have done worse. By way of comparison, about 40 years earlier a researcher by the name of Carney Landis (1924) studied the facial expressions of strong emotions and was quite cavalier in how he went about producing them. For example, to arouse fear, Landis put a participant's hand (sight unseen) into a bucket of water containing three frogs (imagine it is *your* hand and you have no idea what those slimy, warty, leggy things in the water are). To startle his charges, Landis set off firecrackers under their chairs. To produce pain, he sent a strong current of electricity through the water (ouch!). He also exposed his ill-fated participants to pornographic pictures in order to create yet other emotions: shock, disgust, or possibly pleasure. As a finale, Landis commanded each of his participants to use a dull butter knife to decapitate a live rat (perhaps saying "the experiment requires it … you have no choice … please go on"). A participant who refused was still required to watch as Landis did the beheading honors. The point of this detailed description is that such research would today be unequivocally considered unethical and prohibited by ethics committees everywhere.

Milgram's research is obviously less blatantly unscrupulous, but not beyond reproof. In fact, his research has become almost synonymous with issues regarding the fair treatment of human participants, and he probably spent more time and energy than any other social psychologist responding to others' criticisms regarding ethics (see, for example, Baumrind 1964, 1985, and Milgram, 1964, 1977). The primary question is whether Milgram's results, as compelling as they were, justified the psychological cost to participants. Unquestionably, Milgram put his participants through extreme stress. Even he admitted to the aggravation he caused some of them:

> I observed a mature and initially poised businessman enter the laboratory smiling and confident. Within 20 minutes he was reduced to a twitching, stuttering wreck, who was rapidly approaching a point of nervous collapse. He constantly pulled on his earlobe, and twisted his hands. At one point he pushed his fist into his forehead and muttered: "Oh God, let's stop it." And yet he continued to respond to every word of the experimenter, and obeyed to the end. (Milgram, 1963, p. 376)

Milgram's participants were not warned ahead of time about what they were in for (that would have compromised the purpose of the study). Furthermore, he deceived his participants in many ways. Most seriously, he led them to believe that they were perilously harming another human being. Even after a friendly reconciliation with the supposed victim and a thorough debriefing, participants were left forever knowing that they were capable of such perniciousness. Clearly, they had not asked for such painful and dispiriting insights into their own psyches. Even granting the wisdom of the age-old mandate to "Know thyself," most people would rather do so on their own terms and at their own pace.

Milgram countered the profusion of objections with the fact that a follow-up mail survey revealed that defiant and obedient participants alike said that they were glad they had taken part in the study (but note the connection between this finding and the results of the study described in chap. 7). Nearly 85% indicated that they would be willing to participate in further similar experiments. Milgram also managed to find psychiatrists who would attest to the lack of any harmful long-term effects on his participants. These rebuttals aside, however, the ethical furor resulted in permanent changes in how research participants should be treated. It became the majority opinion that strict ethical guidelines should thereafter protect human participants from the wiles of overzealous researchers. Such guidelines have become plenteous: a judicious cost–benefit analysis, use of deception only when justified, avoidance of unnecessary harm, informed consent, and a thorough debriefing. Few today would contend the merits of these guidelines. However, while few today miss research of the Landis (1924) sort, more than a few miss the opportunity Milgram had, and took, to put human participants to such a dramatic test, and with such sensational results.

REVELATION

The power of the situation can incline people to willingly obey authority figures, with the result that they sometimes commit the most abominable and appalling of acts.

— KPF —

CHAPTER REFERENCE

Milgram, S. (1963). The behavioral study of obedience. *Journal of Abnormal and Social Psychology, 67,* 371–378.

OTHER REFERENCES

Arendt, H. (1965). *Eichmann in Jerusalem: A report on the banality of evil* (rev. ed.). New York: Viking Press.

Baumrind, D. (1964). Some thoughts on the ethics of research: After reading Milgram's "Behavioral Study of Obedience." *American Psychologist, 19,* 421–423.

Baumrind, D. (1985). Research using intentional deception: Ethical issues revisited. *American Psychologist, 40,* 165–174.

Cialdini, R. B. (2000). *Influence: Science and practice* (4th ed.). New York: Allyn & Bacon.

Cialdini, R., Cacioppo, J., Bassett, R., & Miller, J. (1978). Low-ball procedure for producing compliance: Commitment then cost. *Journal of Personality and Social Psychology, 36,* 463–476.

Gilbert, S. J. (1981). Another look at the Milgram obedience studies: The role of a graduated series of shocks. *Personality and Social Psychology Bulletin, 7,* 690–695.

Hofling, C. K., Brotzman, E., Dalrymple, S., Graves, N., & Pierce, C. M. (1966). An experimental study in nurse–physician relationships. *The Journal of Nervous and Mental Disease, 143,* 171–180.

Kilham, W., & Mann, L. (1974). Level of destructive obedience as a function of transmitter and executant roles in the Milgram obedience paradigm. *Journal of Personality and Social Psychology, 29,* 696–702.

Landis, C. (1924). Studies of emotional reactions: General behavior and facial expressions. *Comparative Psychology, 4,* 447–509.

Meeus, W. H. J., & Raaijmakers, Q. A. W (1995). Obedience in modern society: The Utrecht Studies. *Journal of Social Issues, 51,* 155–175.

Meyer, P. (1970, February). If Hitler asked you to electrocute a stranger would you? … What if Mr. Milgram asked you? *Esquire,* 72–73.

Milgram, S. (1964). Issues in the study of obedience: A reply to Baumrind. *American Psychologist, 19,* 848–852.

Milgram, S. (1965). Some conditions of obedience and disobedience to authority. *Human Relations, 18,* 57–76.

Milgram, S. (1974). *Obedience to authority: An experimental review.* New York: Harper & Row.

Milgram, S. (1977, October). Subjects' experiences: The neglected factor in the ethics of experimentation. *Hastings Center Report,* 19–23.

Ross, L. (1977). The intuitive psychologist and his shortcomings: Distortion in the attribution process. In L. Berkowitz (Ed.), *Advances in experimental social psychology* (Vol. 10, pp. 174–221). New York: Academic Press.

Snow, C. P. (1961). Either-or. *Progressive,* 24.

Vallacher, R. R., & Wegner, D. M. (1987). What do people think they're doing? Action identification and human behavior. *Psychological Review, 94,* 3–15.

Vonnegut, K., Jr. (1966). *Mother night.* New York: Dell.

MORE TO EXPLORE

Blass, T. (2002, March/April). The man who shocked the world. *Psychology Today,* 68–74.

Blass, T. http://www.stanleymilgrm.com

Layton, D. (1998). *Seductive poison: A Jonestown survivor's story of life and death in the Peoples Temple.* New York: Doubleday.

Miller, A. G., Collins, B. E., & Brief, D. E. (1995). Perspectives on obedience to authority: The legacy of the Milgram experiments. *Journal of Social Issues, 51,* 1–19.

22 Hooded Hoodlums: The Role of Deindividuation in Antisocial Behavior

"To be a member of a crowd is closely akin to alcohol intoxication."
—Aldous Huxley (1894–1963), English novelist

BACKGROUND

Consider the phenomenon of *suicide baiting*. A despondent soul is perched on a building ledge, 10 floors up. A passerby notices and calls attention to his precarious position. Swept up by morbid curiosity, others stop to watch as the desperate individual inches forward and redoubles his resolve to jump. The burgeoning rush hour crowd soon becomes an unruly mob of 500. Police arrive on the scene, hoping to diffuse the situation and rescue the victim above. Nevertheless, a sudden "Let the fool jump!" emanates from the horde and hangs in the growing darkness. Someone shouts a more forceful "Jump!" from another indistinct niche in the volatile mass. Debris is thrown at an arriving ambulance. Jeers and other malicious exhortations follow, and before long a taunting chorus begins: "Jump! ... Jump! ..."

You might wonder: Why do ordinarily conscientious people sometimes behave in such a callous manner? More generally, why do people violate prevalent social norms and hurt, directly or indirectly, those around them? Why do they defy their own moral and ethical standards to engage in unscrupulous behavior? Answers to such pressing questions have implicated a staggering array of possible causes: genetic defects, glitches in moral development, pent up rage, media influences, social disintegration, and so on. A number of social psychologists have suggested that simply being immersed in a large group is enough to cause one to engage in impetuous, wanton behavior. Indeed, Le Bon (1896) described how an individual immersed in a crowd "descends several rungs in the ladder of civilization" (p. 36). Festinger and his colleagues (1952) picked up on this theme and proposed the idea that uninhibited, antisocial behavior is often performed by group members who are temporarily not seen, either by themselves or others, as individuals. Such a state of *deindividuation* involves a mix of possible features: reduced self-awareness, a sense of anonymity, increased autonomic arousal, greater responsiveness to cues in the environment, and a collapse of internal controls against improper behavior.

Zimbardo (1969) sought to demonstrate deindividuation empirically. He led female participants to believe that they were giving electric shocks to another woman (in reality a research confederate, who was never actually shocked). They did so either alone or in groups. When in groups they were told that the experimenter could not tell who was giving the shocks or how hefty the shocks were. Furthermore, participants wore either oversized lab coats that resembled hooded Ku Klux Klan outfits (rendering them anonymous) or normal clothes and an ID badge (making them readily identifiable). Finally, some participants interacted with a pleasant confederate, others with an obnoxious one.

Zimbardo found that being in a group and wearing lab coats increased the duration of the shocks participants gave, consistent with the concept of deindividuation. However, being alone and anonymous had the opposite effect. It reduced the duration of the shocks given to the insolent confederate. Also significant: the identifiable participants shocked the offensive woman more than they did the amiable woman, whereas the anonymous participants gave the same levels of shock to both women. Apparently, being anonymous resulted in more indiscriminate, as well as greater, hostility.

Not all researchers would agree that Zimbardo's research participants experienced deindividuation per se. Some have searched for alternative explanations for why individuals in groups are prone to antisocial behavior. Perhaps *modeling* is a crucial mechanism. Does a sinister type of contagion occur in a group wherein members robotically trigger each other's impulsive behavior? When electric power is unexpectedly lost at a shopping mall, does one immediately start making off with as much costly merchandise as possible because others are observed to be engaging in the same frenzied behavior? Researchers have also wondered about the role of *responsibility*. For example, would intentionally altering a group member's responsibility (by explicitly assigning responsibility to someone else in the group) spur one to even greater extremes of uninhibited

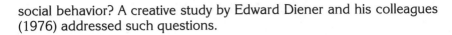

social behavior? A creative study by Edward Diener and his colleagues (1976) addressed such questions.

WHAT THEY DID

The study involved 1,352 children and took place in 27 different homes throughout Seattle on Halloween night. This ambitious study was an example of a *quasi-experiment* in that it featured some of the critical features of a true experiment (such as deliberate manipulation of independent variables) but not others (such as perfect random assignment of participants to conditions or absolute control over nuisance variables). The study thus traded some *internal validity* (the ability to assuredly draw causal inferences) for *ecological validity* (the ability to claim that the results were obtained in a realistic everyday setting, rather than in an artificial laboratory setting).

The 27 homes were all set up similarly: on one end of a low table inside the front door was a large bowl of bite-sized candy bars; at the other end was a bowl of pennies and nickels. Children naturally arrived on trick-or-treat night either alone or in groups. A woman (actually a research accomplice) greeted the children, complimented them on their costumes, and otherwise acted in a friendly manner. Some of the children (both those who came alone and those who came in groups) were deliberately identified. The woman asked each child what his or her name was and where he or she lived, and then repeated the information back to the child. Other children (alone or in groups) were not asked to identify themselves or say where they lived. They remained anonymous. The woman then told the children that they should take just one candy. If a child asked about the bowl filled with coins, she simply repeated her instruction to take only one candy.

In a number of homes, the woman declared that the smallest child (if the children had arrived in a group) would be responsible for any extra candy or money that was taken. There were three variations of this *shifted responsibility* condition: sometimes all the children, including the one made responsible, remained anonymous; sometimes the responsible child was identified while the other children in the group remained anonymous; and sometimes all the children, including the responsible child, were identified. It was predicted that shifting responsibility to the smallest child would make transgressions more likely, because the bigger children could blame him or her if they were found out.

After these various manipulations were in place, the woman casually mentioned that she needed to return to her work in another room. What the children (or child) did not know was that a research assistant was observing them through a peephole in a decorative backdrop, recording how much candy and money they (or he or she) took.

WHAT THEY FOUND

About a third of the children took money, extra candy, or both (each child was scored as simply having transgressed or not). Both anonymity and group presence exerted a significant *main effect*. That is, each alone affected the number of transgressions (in both cases increasing them). A more notable finding, however, was that these factors significantly *interacted* (the effect of one factor depended on the effect of the other). Specifically, 8% of the children stole either money or extra candy when they were alone; 21% stole something when they were anonymous or part of a group; and 57% of the children stole something when they were anonymous and part of a group. Thus, children stole more when they were anonymous, but especially when they were in groups. Another striking finding was that the effects of shifted responsibility and anonymity together were greater than either alone (another interaction). A full 80% of the children swiped money or extra candy when both factors were present (Fig. 22.1).

Diener et al. (1976) also wanted to determine whether the effect of being in a group was attributable to modeling. Does being in a group directly cause one to more freely transgress, or is the effect of the group on an individual's behavior mediated by his or her observing others in the group transgress? Diener et al. (1976) found clear evi-

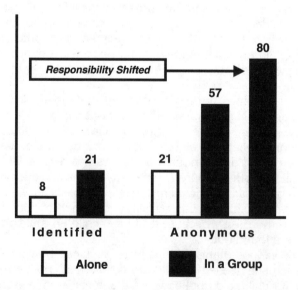

FIG. 22.1.   Percentage of trick-or-treaters who stole, when alone or in a group, when identified or anonymous, and when responsibility was shifted from them or not.

dence for the latter. Transgression rates were notably higher in groups in which the first child took money or extra candy compared to groups in which the first child took only a single piece of candy. However, they also found that first children in groups pilfered more candy or money than children who were alone, suggesting that modeling was not solely responsible for the group transgression rate. Something occurred in the anonymous groups besides modeling—presumably deindividuation—to coax kids into antisocial behavior. Apparently, being anonymous and being in a group influenced the first child's behavior, and then his or her actions created a behavioral norm that was followed by the other children in the group.

SO WHAT?

Diener et al. (1976) were able to show how an interaction of certain variables—namely, group membership, anonymity, and altered responsibility—can lead to a sharp escalation of forbidden behaviors. Roving about in a small pack of other children, and being made relatively anonymous by a witch, mummy, or pirate costume (keep in mind, this was the 1970s, long before *Shrek* and *Scream* costumes), led individual children to grab for extra candy bars and dig freely into a nearby bowl of pennies and nickels. Those children were further emboldened if another child was held responsible for their malfeasance.

Such minor transgressions provide a model for more serious crime. Indeed, deindividuation can pose very real problems. Historical examples of mob behavior (in which deindividuation presumably often occurs) abound. These range from the vigilante lynchings and other acts of violence against Blacks in the United States in the early 1900s; to *Kristallnacht*, a 1938 uprising in which Nazi hoodlums attacked Jews, looted their property, and burned their synagogues; to the riots in Watts, Harlem, and Newark in reaction to White racism in the 1960s. Restless rock concert-goers have been known to stampede stadiums and music halls, leaving dozens injured or dead (although this may be due as much to panic as deindividuation). Sports fans, especially hockey, soccer, and American football enthusiasts, are also notorious for their uproarious and sometimes tragic mob behavior. Even joyous victory celebrations have been known to turn calamitous, as when an NBA team clinches the championship and its home city erupts into a bacchanal of vandalism, looting, arson, and assault. In a similar manner, an outrageous judicial verdict can trigger bedlam. Recall the riotous outbreak that occurred when several Los Angeles policemen were declared innocent after their beatings of a defenseless Black man (Rodney King) had been captured on videotape. To the extent that such events are predictable, preventive measures can be taken, such as beefing up the show of police force. Yet often the sparks that ignite rowdy crowd behavior occur unpredictably. It is always easier to postdict than predict such social upheavals. "Hindsight is 20/20."

An intriguing archival study by Mann (1981) attempted such backward predicting of factors associated with suicide baiting (portrayed at the beginning of the chapter). Mann scoured 15 years of the *New York Times* and *Chicago Tribune* for reports of cases in which crowds were present when an individual publicly threatened and in some cases committed suicide by leaping from a high place. Mann coded the contents of these reports for such variables as location of the incident, position of the victim, date and time of day, duration of the episode, and crowd size, and then compared the baiting episodes to the nonbaiting episodes. He found that a number of factors correlated with baiting. Specifically, baiting occurred more often in large crowds (over 300 people), in which there was a substantial shield of anonymity between individual baiters and the police, and in which baiters were likely to experience increased arousal and diminished self-awareness. Baiting was also found to be more common under the cover of darkness (a majority of the incidents occurred at night), which would, again, make baiters feel more anonymous. The distance between the victim and the crowd also predicted baiting. The mockery

FIG. 22.2. Darkness and disguise suppress individual identity, and often encourage antisocial behavior.

and dares that typify baiting tended not to occur when the victim was too close to the crowd (just a few floors above the street, for example) or when the victim was too far away (many floors above street level or on a bridge). Apparently, baiting requires that the victim be at some optimal distance (though hardly "optimal" from the victim's point of view). Finally, baiting was more prevalent in longer episodes (those that lasted more than 2 hours), which perhaps allowed time for deindividuation to set in and deviant behavior to escalate. It is also plausible that longer episodes fostered a sense of frustration and irritation, even a need for closure ("Come on, jump, I've gotta get home to dinner!"). Evidently, a host of factors combine to cause individuals to join in a baiting chorus. Although it is easy to characterize those involved as cold-hearted and sadistic, and to imagine that "I would never do such a thing," one should not discount the power of the prevailing social situation.

AFTERTHOUGHTS

The research literature on deindividuation is not self-contained or well-defined. The causes, manifestations, and consequences of deindividuation remain to be more rigorously specified. Researchers have been quick to assert that just about any instance of uninhibited behavior reflects deindividuation. For example, stimulus-rich environments—a glitzy casino or Bourbon Street during the Mardi Gras—or even drug-induced alterations in consciousness have been claimed to produce deindividuation. It has also been suggested that *total institutions* (those that control many aspects of one's behavior), such as hospitals, prisons, and military boot camps, alienate people from their personal identities. Such institutions, with their standard uniforms, identification bracelets, codes of conduct, routine schedules, and general lack of freedom, strip people of their individuality.

The deindividuation concept has also been applied to victims as well as aggressors. In chapter 21 we describe how Milgram (1963) found that a teacher was more willing to shock a learner when the two could not see each other. Note how hoods were often placed over criminals when they were publicly hanged in the United States. What purpose did this serve? On a lighter note, Turner and colleagues (1975) found that drivers were more likely to honk at a stalled motorist when a curtain was drawn across the back window compared to when there was no such curtain.

Some researchers have even portrayed deindividuation as a potentially good thing, emphasizing that being absorbed in a group can liberate one from self-strangulating shyness. So-called *encounter groups*, with their intense interpersonal dynamics, have been extolled for having the same type of liberating effect. Even being part of the jubilant anarchy of, say, Times Square on New Year's Eve can give rise to a euphoric sense of freedom or unaccountability. Researchers have even found that when environmental cues make social responsibility salient, deindividuation can lead to more altruistic behavior (Johnson & Downing, 1979; Spivey & Prentice-Dunn, 1990). For the most part, however, researchers have warned of the dark side of deindividuation, claiming that it leads to irrational and harmful behaviors.

Deindividuation is related to the concept of *diffusion of responsibility* (see chap. 19) in that the two can have similar results. In fact, uninhibited behavior occurs for at least two general reasons. An anonymous group member might feel that he or she can get away with certain behaviors (by going undetected), or that he or she will not be held personally responsible for collective behaviors (diffusion of responsibility). Either way, public self-awareness is reduced. The individual feels less conspicuous. He or she is less likely to be singled out, evaluated, criticized, or punished, and so is unconcerned about approval, embarrassment, or retaliation by others. As in the fantasy of being invisible, behavior may be dramatically altered. Technically, however, getting away with things is not deindividuation.

By definition, deindividuation occurs when private self-awareness is reduced. The truly deindividuated person pays little attention to personal values and moral codes. He or she is easily affected by cues in the immediate environment. Seeing others smash through storefront windows and escape with stereos and TVs during a looting spree, the deindividuated person automatically joins in, heedless of personal ethical standards. The perpetrator is temporarily unaware of being an individual. Behavior is released from cognitive control as one becomes immersed in the pulsating crowd.

The distinction between deindividuation and diffusion of responsibility (as well as other distinctions, such as those between group-induced deindividuation and other lapses of self-consciousness) are not inconsequential, and will no doubt continue to be debated and subjected to empirical tests (see, for example, Postmes & Spears, 1998). Such issues do not detract, however, from demonstrations of how a few prosaic conditions, such as being absorbed in a group and feeling aroused and relatively anonymous, can cause the most staid and conscientious of people to go a bit berserk.

REVELATION

Being immersed in a group can lead to heightened arousal, a sense of anonymity, reduced self-awareness, and the automatic modeling of others' behaviors. Such a state of deindividuation can result in unrestrained—often aggressive and destructive—behavior.

— KPF —

CHAPTER REFERENCE

Diener, E., Fraser, S. C., Beaman, A. L., & Kelem, R. T. (1976). Effects of deindividuation variables on stealing among Halloween trick-or-treaters. *Journal of Personality and Social Psychology, 33,* 178–183.

OTHER REFERENCES

Festinger, L., Pepitone, A., & Newcomb, T. (1952). Some consequences of deindividuation in a group. *Journal of Abnormal and Social Psychology, 47,* 382–389.
Johnson, R. D., & Downing, L. L. (1979). Deindividuation and valence of cues: Effects on prosocial and antisocial behavior. *Journal of Personality and Social Psychology, 37,* 1532–1538.
Le Bon, G. (1896). *The crowd: A study of the popular mind.* London: Ernest Benn.
Mann, L. (1981). The baiting crowd in episodes of threatened suicide. *Journal of Personality and Social Psychology, 41,* 703–709.
Milgram, S. (1963). The behavioral study of obedience. *Journal of Abnormal and Social Psychology, 67,* 371–378.
Postmes, T., & Spears, R. (1998). Deinidividuation and antinormative behavior: A meta-analysis. *Psychological Bulletin, 123,* 238–259.
Spivey, C. B., & Prentice-Dunn, S. (1990). Assessing the directionality of deindividuation behavior: Effects of deindividuation, modeling, and private self-consciousness on aggressive and prosocial responses. *Basic and Applied Social Psychology, 11,* 387–403.
Turner, C. W., Layton, J. F., & Simons, L. S. (1975). Naturalistic studies of aggressive behavior: Aggressive stimuli, victim visibility, and horn honking. *Journal of Personality and Social Psychology, 31,* 1098–1107.
Zimbardo, P. G. (1969). The human choice: Individuation, reason, and order versus deindividuation, impulse, and chaos. *Nebraska Symposium on Motivation, 17,* 237–307.

MORE TO EXPLORE

Gergen, K. J., Gergen, M. M., & Barton, W. H. (1973). Deviance in the dark. *Psychology Today, 7,* 129–130.
Mullen, B. (1986). Atrocity as a function of lynch mob composition. *Personality and Social Psychology Bulletin, 12,* 187–198.

23 The Burglar's Situation: Actor-Observer Differences in Explaining Behavior

"People have got to know whether or not their president is a crook. Well, I'm not a crook."
—Richard Nixon (1913–1994), former [crooked] U.S. President

BACKGROUND

Your'e in line at a supermarket, resisting rows of tempting candy bars. Your eyes scan a tabloid headline—*Pet Pig Devours Wedding Cake*—when the woman in front of you suddenly becomes irate. She is trying to get a double-coupon price on an already discounted item (or something like that) and the cashier is explaining that it does not work that way. The woman refuses to budge (as the line behind her grows) and insists on talking to the manager. She starts to ramble incoherently about customer relations and the policies of other supermarkets. You step back a foot or two as her voice falters and then becomes loud again. Will she do something dramatic? Is she mentally ill, or does she simply have a keen sense of justice? Your train of thought continues along these lines. What is it about this woman that is causing her to act this way?

Later the same day you find yourself in what others might view as a similar situation (although you don't see the parallel). You are a student returning a textbook that you discovered you do not need. The book is still in the bag—your hectic schedule has kept you from returning it sooner. A cashier explains that you have missed the 30-day return deadline: "I'll say it one more time: you're too late for a refund. I'm sorry!" But late by only a week,

268

you reason, less if you count Sunday and a holiday on Monday when the bookstore was closed. Rigid, maybe even illegal, policies have you steaming. "Sorry is not enough. I want to talk to a manager and I'm not moving until I do!" Those behind you retreat as your anger swells and finds its targets: "snobby cashier, over-priced textbooks, capitalist society!" The other customers have little sympathy for you, however. They believe that you have been irresponsible, you are being unreasonable, and you are becoming belligerent. Just as your focus was on the woman in front of you at the supermarket, their focus is on you (even if your attention is now on your frustrating situation).

The preceding vignettes make vivid the now well-documented *actor-observer* bias. Jones and Nisbett (1972) were among the first to argue that *actors* (those performing certain behaviors) and *observers* (those witnessing others performing certain behaviors) often offer different *causal attributions* (explanations). Actors tend to attribute the cause of their behavior to the environment, arguably because they have more information about their own intentions and emotions, precipitating events, and external stimuli. Observers, in contrast, tend to attribute the actor's behavior to his or her personality, probably because they are focused more on the actor per se than on the surrounding situation. We often recognize the pressures we ourselves are under, but not the similar pressures felt by others. The one side of this bias has been dubbed the *fundamental attribution error:* as social perceivers, we tend to explain others' actions in terms of personality traits rather than situational factors (Ross, 1977). One of the virtues of social psychology is that it calls attention to this error by revealing the ubiquitous and powerful external influences on human behavior.

A study by Stephen West and his colleagues (1975) was perhaps the most dramatic demonstration of the actor-observer bias. West et al. (1975) were enthralled by the Watergate scandal that dominated news headlines and rocked the nation a few years earlier. In June of 1972, five men were arrested for burgling the Democratic National Committee headquarters at the Watergate apartments in Washington, D.C. The bungled break-in and attempted cover-up came to light during that year's presidential campaign. Congressional impeachment hearings followed, culminating in the resignation of President Nixon in 1974. It was a scandal of grand proportions that begged for explanation. The press attributed the crimes to the paranoid and amoral qualities of the Nixon administration, whereas Nixonites defended the actions by claiming that they were a natural reaction to the nefarious objectives of the radical left. A single event occurred but different insider and outsider explanations followed (see chap. 4 for more on how identical events can produce quite different perceptions).

These disparate accounts of the Watergate imbroglio seemed again to be a case of the actor-observer bias. Some saw the devil in the perpetrators, some in the situation. Intrigued by this, West et al. (1975) sought to elicit Watergate-like behavior from research participants, and then examine their explanations, as well as the explanations of others, for such behaviors. Would the actors tend more toward *situationalism* (claiming that outside forces are at work) and the perceivers more toward *dispositionalism* (believing the cause lies within the person)?

WHAT THEY DID

West et al. (1975) conducted two studies. In the first, an experimenter (known by many to be a local private investigator) invited each of 80 criminology students, a mix of males and females, to his home or a local restaurant to discuss a project he was working on. Every participant approached in this way accepted the mysterious invitation.

A confederate (research accomplice) accompanied the experimenter to the clandestine meeting. In B-movie fashion, the private eye carried a briefcase (handcuffed to his wrist?) containing detailed plans for the burglary of a local advertising agency (a job was going down). The unsuspecting participants were randomly assigned to one of four experimental conditions. In one condition, the Internal Revenue Service was said to be sponsoring the burglary. The reputed ad agency was allegedly harboring a set of bogus accounting records, used to defraud the U.S. government out of millions of tax dollars a year. The agency was really a front for a Miami investment firm. The records were copies of coveted originals; they needed to be microfilmed so that the IRS could obtain a search warrant and subpoena to seize the originals. The participants were told that the IRS would guarantee them immunity from prosecution if they got caught. (If all this sounds farfetched now, it didn't to the aspiring criminologist being briefed by the business-like private eye in a red-leather booth in a dimly lit corner of a smoky local restaurant!)

A second experimental condition was identical, except that participants were warned that there would be no immunity from prosecution if they were apprehended. In a third experimental condition, the cover story described how a second ad agency was secretly offering $8,000 for a copy of a set of designs developed by the first agency. If the burglary succeeded, the participant's under-the-table cut would be $2,000 (a small fortune for a financially strapped college student in the mid-1970s). In a final experimental condition, participants were told that they would break and enter but not actually steal anything, simply to see if the burglary plans of the private eye were feasible. None of the participants protested discussing the proposed crime.

In all of these conditions, a research confederate was introduced as a member of the burglary team. He would serve as an outside lookout. The private eye (really the experimenter) would monitor police calls from an office inside the building. A third member of the team (not present), said to be a lock-and-safe expert with extensive military intelligence training, would also abet the crime. The participant would serve as an inside lookout and do the actual microfilming.

The experimenter and confederate presented the participant with aerial photographs of the building and local area, lists of routes and times of city and state police patrols, and blueprints of the building. All this gave the appearance of a well-planned, professional job. Participants were given a chance to ask questions, most of which were about technical details of the plan. Then a second meeting was arranged. The participant was given time to think things over before committing to the crime or not. The confederate, unaware of the researchers' hypotheses, was on hand to record the participant's decision to join the team or not, and his or her rationale either way.

Anyone with ethical scruples will be glad to know that a break-in never took place. Whether participants agreed or refused to participate in the burglary, and what reasons they gave for their decision, were the main dependent variables. Once this information was obtained, they were carefully debriefed and the deception was explained.

Quite an elaborate ruse! We wish there was hidden-camera footage to show you. Indeed, this first study alone would have been a vivid enough demonstration of compliance. However, a second study was necessary to more fully examine the actor-observer bias. The behaviors and explanations of actors had been recorded. It was now necessary to obtain data on the perceptions of observers.

The 238 participants in the second study (all students in Introductory Psychology classes) were each given a detailed description of one of the four conditions of the first study. Each was asked: "If 100 students were presented with the proposal, how many would you guess would agree to participate?" In response to a second question—"Would you do it?"—each was asked to respond yes, maybe, or no, and to write comments. Half of the participants also responded to the following scenario: "Suppose John, an undergraduate at FSU [the study was conducted at Florida State University], after listening to the proposal previously described, agreed to participate. In two or three sentences, briefly describe why John made this decision." The other half of the participants responded to the same scenario, except that John refused instead of agreed.

The purpose of this second study, then, was to examine observers' explanations of another person's agreeing or refusing to illegally break into a presumed local company and steal information. Comparing these explanations to those given by the participants themselves in the first study represented a direct investigation of the actor-observer bias.

WHAT THEY FOUND

The overall results of the first study are perhaps reassuring to anyone concerned about the ethical standards of college students in the mid-

1970s: the majority of those solicited were unwilling to participate in the burglary. However, agreement rates varied from condition to condition. Four of the 20 participants in the $2,000-reward condition, two in the let's-just-see-if-it-will-work (control) condition, and only one in the government-sponsorship-but-no-immunity condition agreed to assist in the break-in and be the one to copy the desired documents. The differences among these conditions are not statistically significant (the power of the study to detect significant differences is low given the relatively small number of participants). However, 9 of the 20 participants (almost half) in the government-sponsorship-with-immunity-if-caught condition agreed to participate. Because participants were randomly assigned to the four conditions, and because all extraneously variables were carefully controlled, it can be assumed that the greater compliance in the last condition was due to the features of the condition itself. Evidently, the prospect of immunity, or its interaction with government sponsorship, represented a powerful situation that produced alarming rates of compliance.

Did observers believe that they, if put in the same situation, would have joined the crime team? As it turns out, so few thought they would that West et al. (1975) decided to combine yes with maybe answers to allow for a more meaningful analysis. (That participants generally believe that they would not have taken part in the burglary is reminiscent of what others imagine they would or would not do in situations that call upon good character; see chaps. 19 and 21.) Observers were more inclined to think that they would have helped pull off the burglary if there was government sponsorship and immunity than in the other conditions. Interestingly, there were no overall differences between males and females in rates of agreement to participate in the break-in (which is inconsistent with the fact that males are several times more criminal than females in every society ever studied). Yet males merely reading about the situation were almost twice as likely as females to report that they would have gone along with the caper (more consistent with men's greater criminality).

However, compliance is not the main story of this chapter; attributions are. Actors' and observers' attributions for why they (the actor in the situation) or John (the hypothetical FSU student) agreed or refused to take part in the burglary were *coded* (put into one or more categories, allowing statistical comparisons). A 1 indicated a dispositional attribution, a 3 a situational attribution, and a 2 a combination of the two. Which type of attribution was more common among actors? What about among observers? Was there an actor-observer effect?

There was. Actors made more situational attributions than did observers. Put differently, observers made more dispositional attributions than did actors. This effect varied a bit depending upon the condition—government sponsorship with or without immunity, reward, or control—but this does not take away from the striking overall actor-observer difference, which, by the way, occurred for attributions for both agreeing and for refusing to engage in the crime (Fig. 23.1).

SO WHAT?

Under certain circumstances (i.e., with government backing and immunity from prosecution) nearly half the participants—themselves students of criminology—said they would be willing to help pull off a plainly illegal act: breaking into a company's private headquarters to steal confidential documents. Why? Perhaps this was a case of the *foot-in-the-door phenomenon*, illustrated in a study by Freedman and Fraser (1966). In that study, a member of a Committee for Safe Driving approached women in their homes and asked them if they would allow a large, unsightly *Drive Carefully* sign to be staked into their front lawn. Understandably, only 17% agreed to the request. However, women who had first agreed to sign a related petition that would supposedly be sent to State Senators were much more likely, a few weeks later, to agree to host such a sign (55% did). Evidently, getting a foot in the door is an effective technique for inducing compliance. It is possible that, in West et al.'s (1975) first study, agreeing to attend a meeting, in the private eye's home or the shadowy backroom of a nearby restaurant, was tantamount to acquiescing to doing something shady.

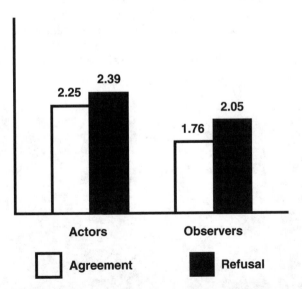

FIG. 23.1.   The degree to which actors and observers attributed actors' agreement or refusal to take part in a burglary to situational rather than to dispositional factors.

The foot-in-the-door concept does not explain the pattern of compliance in the study by West et al. (1975), however. Compliance was exceptionally high in only one of the conditions, that which featured the imprimatur of the IRS and the promise of immunity. Evidently, these features, perhaps along with a foot in the door, set the stage for Watergate-like behavior.

Compliance aside, what about the clear actor-observer bias found in the present study—what explains it? Jones and Davis' (1965) *theory of correspondent inference* holds that we tend to believe that a person's behavior stems from, or corresponds to, his or her dispositional characteristics if the behavior is unflattering (indulgence in criminal escapades tends to be so), out of role (burglary and theft are not formal college requirements), and freely chosen. However, the theory does not state that we should make more correspondent inferences in our judgments of others than of ourselves. Yet many studies, in addition to that conducted by West et al. (1975), have found that we do.

A frequently cited classic, showing the fundamental attribution error alone, is a study by Jones and Harris (1967). Participants were shown essays said to be written by students on a debating team. The essays either supported or opposed Fidel Castro, Cuba's president. Participants who were told that the authors of the essay had *chosen* which type of essay to write—pro-Castro or anti-Castro—judged those authors to be correspondingly pro-Castro or anti-Castro, which makes sense. But what makes less sense is that participants who were told that the authors were *assigned* by their debating coach to a particular side also judged the authors to be correspondingly pro-Castro or anti-Castro. They seemed to ignore the no-choice situation. A study by Gilbert and Jones (1986) found that they did so even when they themselves had assigned the position taken by a speechwriter.

FIG. 23.2.   The Watergate Hotel. What explained the break-in?

A study by Ross and his colleagues (1977), featuring a simulated TV quiz game, showed the more general actor-observer bias. Participants were randomly assigned to be either questioners or contestants. Questioners each created 10 challenging but fair questions. Contestants answered as many as possible (usually getting about 4 out of 10 correct). Interestingly, contestants subsequently judged the questioners to be significantly more knowledgeable than they themselves were, and audience members shared this impression. Again, this makes no sense. The participants were randomly assigned to the two roles; based on the laws of probability, neither questioners nor contestants would have been any more or less erudite.

In another study (Saulnier & Perlman, 1981), when prisoners were asked why they committed their crimes, they emphasized situational factors ("I was out of work, so I robbed the bank" or "the Devil made me do it"). However, their counselors cited characteristics of the inmates' personalities ("He's antisocial" or "she's impulsive"). Furthermore, Nisbett and others (1973) had male college students explain why they liked their current girlfriends and why their best friends liked their girlfriends. They tended to explain their own choice in terms of qualities of the girlfriend (part of the situation) but their friend's choice in terms of his personality. Examples of the actor-observer bias are endless.

Again, what accounts for it? Long story short, it seems to depend on what is salient, on what captures one's attention. For example, in the study done by Ross et al. (1977), the contestants and outside observers alike saw that the questioners knew all the answers to rather tough questions (they seemed to forget that the questioners were drawing on areas of personal expertise). The contestants saw themselves, and observers saw contestants, struggling for answers (perhaps asking Regis Philbin for a life-line), and 6 out of 10 times giving the wrong one. Prior random assignment to the two roles—questioner or contestant—was ignored. Even the contestant, who as an actor would normally be more focused on external factors, was apparently aware of only selective aspects of the situation (the difficulty of the esoteric questions or maybe the condescending smile of the questioner).

The same holds true in any example of the actor-observer bias. When we consider our own behaviors the focus of our attention is more on its context. What events preceded our actions? What are we responding to right now? How is the situation responding back? The effect of the external world on us is subjectively obvious. This is one reason why we generally do not believe that trait labels apply to us (Nisbett et al., 1973). Other people have traits, we have situations, or so we believe. However, when we view others' behaviors, we see them lifted out of context. Lacking information about their life history or current circumstances, we reflexively assume that what they do reflects who they are.

But still, so what? (This is always a legitimate question, especially for consumers of social psychological research.) So we tend to explain our own and others' behaviors differently, chalking the former up to outside influences and the latter to internal forces? So we commit the fundamental attribution error even when we are deliberately attempting to empathize with the person whose behavior we are explaining (as participants in the present study were asked to do with John)?

Well, consider a maxim of social psychology: People do not interact with reality; they interact with their *perception* of reality (see chaps. 1, 2, 3, 4, and 14 for examples of how people mentally construct their social reality). Assuming this maxim to be valid, what happens if we, as individuals or a society, readily view others as the principal cause of, and therefore hold them responsible for, their behavior (even when they have been swamped by external influences)? What happens when we excuse our behavior as being the product of some situation (even when we are, in fact, the primary cause of it)? Might we tend to unfairly explain the plight of rape victims, homeless people, disadvantaged minorities, and other unfortunates in predominantly dispositional terms? Does the actor-observer bias leave us less charitable, or fixated on trying to change individuals instead of the social order? Might the actor-observer bias perpetuate self-righteousness and social coldness?

And yet, the opposite bias might be just as foolhardy: failing to hold people responsible when doing so is justified. Is it true that the observer is always wrong and the actor always right? Might the socially disadvantaged, for example, indeed be partly responsible for their plight? The problem in all of this is that the truth about causality and responsibility is difficult to establish. Nonetheless, if understanding ourselves and others, and rewarding and punishing our own and others' actions, is in any way central to the lives we lead, then comprehending and counteracting attributional biases, of any sort, is vital.

AFTERTHOUGHTS

If you have not read chapter 21, "Just Following Orders: A Shocking Demonstration of Obedience to Authority," please do, because it and this chapter describe what are among the most ethically suspect studies in the history of social psychology. We will not repeat the concerns outlined elsewhere, but recall the results of West et al.'s (1975) first study. A significant number of participants, students of criminology no less, indicated their willingness to engage in criminal activity. Afterward, they were told that the experiment was a setup to see how much they would comply. Think about it: would not this disclosure, however delicately made, lower self-esteem, especially in those who had agreed to participate in the break-in? Would not the knowledge of what one was poised to do create embarrassment or guilt? Watergate had been repeatedly condemned in the press, and here one was, preparing to act much as a disgraced Watergate convict (Cook, 1975). Furthermore, was not this a case of entrapment? Were the participants in this study looking to enter a life of crime, or did individuals they respected and trusted thrust the opportunity upon them?

To be sure, West et al. (1975) went to great lengths to allay ethical concerns. They had a lawyer-psychologist help plan and implement the study. They did not force anyone into anything or have them actually act illegally. They provided a careful debriefing. They noted that participants seemed not to suffer any psychological trauma. Finally, they had the State Attorney's Office review the experiment and declare that its procedures were legally acceptable. Still, concerns remained.

A longer discussion of ethical issues could be offered, but the simple (though difficult) balance is always this: The value of the information gained from the research against concerns for the rights and dignity of the participants. West et al. (1975) believed that their research addressed important questions. What situational factors might induce normally law-abiding citizens to engage in illegal activities that violate the civil rights of others? How can we trust the press, those working in the legal system, or even ourselves to supply valid explanations for given behaviors? You be the judge. Does a contribution to scientific knowledge ever warrant deception and inducement to engage in unethical or immoral actions? Was showing the ubiquity of Watergate-like actor-observer differences worth whatever human cost was involved in West et al.'s (1975) extraordinary experiment?

Ethical considerations aside, whether we are aware of it or not, we are frequently searching for the causes of our own and others' behaviors. The causes we identify may be located inside the person, outside the person, or both. However, it is interesting, and consequential, that we often locate the causes of our behaviors outside and the causes of others' behaviors inside.

How ubiquitous is the actor-observer bias? Interestingly, research has found that it may not occur to the same extent, or even at all, in certain cultures. Miller (1984), for example, explored the everyday social explanations of American and Indian adults and children (the latter were 8, 11, and 15 years old). She found that American adults are more inclined to refer to dispositional factors, and Indian adults to contextual factors, when explaining events. She also found that these cultural differences become more evident in children as they get older, suggesting that the contrasting attributional styles are learned. Individuals in the two cultures come to view the person's relationship with the environment somewhat differently. The individual's influence on the situation is emphasized in the one culture, the impact of the situation on the individual is better recognized in the other culture.

What happens when we are made aware of the actor-observer bias, where it does exist? Perhaps we are made wiser by having a fairer understanding, both of ourselves and of others, regarding the interplay between the person and the situation. Perhaps we then see the woman in front of us at the supermarket (the one losing her cool) and ourselves returning a text-book (also getting a bit steamed) in a new light.

REVELATION

We assume that a person's behaviors reflect fixed traits and underlying attitudes, when we should perhaps pay more attention to factors in the physical and social environment. In the case of our own behavior, we are more apt to recognize situational pressures.

— KPF —

CHAPTER REFERENCE

West, S. G., Gunn, S. P., & Chernicky, P. (1975). Ubiquitous Watergate: An attributional analysis. *Journal of Personality and Social Psychology, 32,* 55–65.

OTHER REFERENCES

Cook, S. W. (1975). A comment on the ethical issues involved in West, Gunn, and Chernicky's "Ubiquitous Watergate: An attributional analysis." *Journal of Personality and Social Psychology, 32,* 66–68.

Freedman, J. L., & Fraser, S. C. (1966). Compliance without pressure: The foot-in-the-door technique. *Journal of Personality and Social Psychology, 4,* 195–202.

Gilbert, D. T., & Jones, E. E. (1986). Perceiver-induced constraint: Interpretations of self-generated reality. *Journal of Personality and Social Psychology, 50,* 269–280.

Jones, E. E., & Davis, K. E. (1965). A theory of correspondent inferences: From acts to dispositions. In L. Berkowitz (Ed.), *Advances in experimental social psychology* (Vol. 2, pp. 219–266). New York: Academic press.

Jones, E. E., & Harris, V. A. (1967). The attribution of attitudes. *Journal of Experimental Social Psychology, 3,* 1–24.

Jones, E. E., & Nisbett, R. E. (1972). The actor and the observer: Divergent perspectives of the causes of behavior. In E. E. Jones, D. E. Kanouse, H. H. Kelley, R. E. Nisbett, S. Valins, & B. Weiner (Eds.), *Attribution: Perceiving the causes of behavior* (pp. 79–94). Morristown, NJ: General Learning Press.

Miller, J. (1984). Culture and the development of everyday social explanations. *Journal of Personality and Social Psychology, 46,* 961–978.

Nisbett, R. E., Caputo, C., Legant, P., & Marecek, J. (1973). Behavior as seen by the actor and as seen by the observer. *Journal of Personality and Social Psychology, 27,* 154–164.

Ross, L. (1977). The intuitive psychologist and his shortcomings: Distortions in the attributional process. In L. Berkowitz (Ed.), *Advances in experimental social psychology* (Vol. 10, pp. 174–221). New York: Academic Press.

Ross, L., Amabile, T. M., & Steinmetz, J. L. (1977). Social roles, social control, and biases in social perception processes. *Journal of Personality and Social Psychology, 35,* 485–494.

Saulnier, K., & Perlman, D. (1981). The actor-observer bias is alive and well in prison. *Personality and Social Psychology Bulletin, 7,* 559–564.

MORE TO EXPLORE

Lee, F., Hallahan, M., & Herzog, T. (1996). Explaining real-life events: How culture and domain shape attributions. *Personality and Social Psychology Bulletin, 22,* 732–741.

Lupfer, M. B., Clark, L. F., & Hutcherson, H. W. (1990). Impact of context on spontaneous trait and situational attributions. *Journal of Personality and Social Psychology, 58,* 239–249.

24 Of Cockroaches and Men: Social Enhancement and Inhibition of Performance

"The chief difference between mankind and the cockroach is that the one continually bitches over his fate while the other stoically plods on, uncomplaining, with never a glance backward nor a sigh for what might have been."
—Jean Shepherd (1921–1999), comic writer and performer

BACKGROUND

The following creepy study is part of a research tradition that began over a century ago, when in 1898 Norman Triplett published "The Dynamogenic Factors of Pacemaking in Competition" in the then nascent *American Journal of Psychology*. There are two things worth remembering about Triplett. First, he loved bicycle racing. He enjoyed taking part in competitions, savored his role as spectator, and was a noted authority on the sport more generally. In fact, it was his rapt inspection of the 1897 records book of the League of American Wheelmen that led him to notice that cyclists who competed against or were paced by others performed better than those who raced against the clock alone. This, Triplett (1898) concluded, is because the "presence of another rider is a stimulus to the racer in arousing the competitive instinct … the means of releasing or freeing nervous energy for him that he cannot of himself release" (p. 516).

The second thing to remember about Triplett is that he was, evidently, a natural-born experimentalist. Venturing beyond casual observation and speculation, he cajoled 40 neighborhood children into winding up fishing reels, each as fast as they could. Sometimes he had them do this alone, sometimes in pairs. (Imagine what the neighbors thought: Something "reely fishy" is going on!) Just as he predicted, winding times were faster when the children wound together. Apparently, the mere presence of other children had resulted in enhanced performance. Triplett's interest in social influences on performance, and his attempt to investigate such influences experimentally, distinguished him as an important forebear of social psychology.

Following Triplett's research, hundreds of studies have looked at the relationship between the presence of others and an individual's performance on a task. Bond and Titus (1983) conducted a *meta-analysis* (quantitative summary) of some 241 of these studies. Various types of performance have been investigated: doing simple arithmetic, making complex calculations, putting on clothes, memorizing nonsense syllables, learning a finger maze, crossing out vowels, shooting pool, and even eating. Studies have focused on the influence of *coactors* (others working simultaneously on the same or even different task) and on the effects of performing in front of an audience. What has become clear from this research is that the presence of other people only sometimes enhances performance (referred to as *social facilitation*); at other times it actually impairs performance (*social inhibition*). For example, although participants cross out the vowels in a newspaper column faster in the presence of others, they are slower to memorize nonsense syllables in the presence of others. For a long time, investigators were perplexed by such inconsistent findings.

Then, in 1965, Robert Zajonc offered an elegant solution to the puzzle. He proposed that the presence of other people serves to heighten arousal (of the physiological, not sexual, sort—unless the other people happen to be naked!). Furthermore, reviving an old behaviorist principle of learning, he suggested that, in a given situation, heightened arousal facilitates *dominant* (simple, well-learned) responses, but inhibits *nondominant* (complex, novel) responses. For example, if you are a fast and proficient typist, others watching you will likely spur you to a nimbler performance, but if you are a slow and clumsy typist, others hanging over your shoulders will likely turn your fingers into stale French fries!

Numerous studies have now demonstrated this particular interaction (the social facilitation of dominant responses and social inhibition of nondominant responses), but one of the classics is Zajonc and Sales (1966). Male students practiced pronouncing 10 different Turkish words (actually seven-letter nonsense words). Two of these were presented for practice once, two twice, two four times, two eight times, and two 16 times, all in a random order. Participants then began the subliminal perception phase of the study. A tachistoscope was used to present the words very briefly, and the participant's task was to guess which word was presented on each trial. Each word was flashed for only 1/10th of a second. Nonetheless participants correctly guessed the words about 90% of the time. Nonwords—31 different configurations of irregular black lines—were also presented, but only for 1/100th of a second in each case—a pace at which the recognition of actual words would be no better than chance. These extra stimuli allowed the researchers to estimate participants' tendency to guess. Altogether the participants saw four blocks of 41 words: 10 pseudo-Turkish words and 31 pseudo-pseudo-Turkish words.

Some participants went through this procedure alone (the use of an automated slide projector and a tape recorder made the presence of the experimenter unnecessary), whereas others went through the procedure in the presence of some unknown students, passively seated a few feet away. These students, actually confederates in the study, had casually mentioned to participants that they were observing the study with the permission of the experimenter. Zajonc and Sales predicted that the presence of an "audience" would facilitate dominant responses, namely, guessing Turkish words that had been more frequently "practiced" (8 or 16 times), and inhibit nondominant responses, namely, guessing Turkish words that had been practiced less frequently (once or twice). This is exactly what they found.

This and other rigorous studies lent credibility to Zajonc's parsimonious explanation for mere presence effects. Yet such studies also ushered in plausible alternative explanations. For example, perhaps the presence of others creates apprehension in participants, spurring them to try harder at a task, but impairs their performance if the task is relatively challenging. Or, perhaps participants are more motivated by the need for approval and spend more time monitoring their behavior in the presence of others, thereby yielding the same pattern of results. Such explanations raise questions about the cause or generalizability of mere presence effects. For example, to what extent are more complex cognitive processes (such as apprehension or self-awareness) responsible for them? Would it be possible to demonstrate such effects with members of another species, ones that presumably have less going on upstairs (in their minds)? Would Zajonc's theory accurately predict mere presence effects in, say, cockroaches? Why not round up a few and find out?

WHAT THEY DID

Zajonc and his colleagues (1969) predicted that, even among cockroaches, simply being in the presence of others (other cockroaches, that is) would facilitate performance on a simple task, and inhibit performance on a complex task. The researchers initially envisioned an uncomplicated 2 × 2 experi-

FIG. 24.1.   The mentally minimal *Blatta Orientalis*.

mental design, in which roaches would run down a straight runway (a relatively easy task) or through a slightly more complex maze (a relatively difficult task), either alone or in tandem (that is, with one other roach). However, they realized that the tandem condition contained a potential confound: If the roaches ran faster with a partner, it might be because the two had *aroused* each other (as suggested by Zajonc) or because they had *directed* each other using mysterious cockroach body language, perhaps with a subtle shake of the legs, or a timely touch of the feelers. Foreseeing this possibility, Zajonc et al. (1969) engineered an additional condition in which roaches performed in front of an audience of other spectator roaches. (By the way, what does one call a group of roaches? A "scuttle"?) While such spectator cockroaches might influence the performing cockroaches by their mere presence, it is unlikely that they would provide any task-relevant behavioral cues.

The participants in this study were 72 adult female cockroaches (*Blatta orientalis*, to be entomologically correct) maintained in dark quarters on a diet of sliced apples. (We had better not say from what university dormitory these roaches were obtained.) The basic apparatus was a clear plexiglass cube, about 20 inches along each edge, outfitted to house either a maze or a straight runway. A 150-watt floodlight, shone into a start box, served as a noxious stimulus (roaches, unlike moths, hate bright lights). A darkened goal box at the other end of the runway or maze beckoned to them. The route in between featured guillotine gates and clear plexiglass runway tubes. Plexiglass audience boxes, positioned along most of the walls of the runway or maze were added in some conditions. These contained small apertures that allowed the transmission of olfactory cues (one whiff would detect any lurking fellow roaches).

Turning on the floodlight and opening a guillotine door spurred the roaches to action. The crucial variable was the time it took the roaches to get through the runway or maze and enter the goal box (another guillotine door was closed just after the roach's last leg crossed the threshold of the goal box).

WHAT THEY FOUND

Zajonc et al. (1969) found strong support for their hypotheses. Roaches that negotiated the maze in tandem took more time than roaches that negotiated it alone, whereas roaches that traveled the simpler runway in tandem took less time than roaches that traveled it alone. The same pattern of results was found when comparing the audience condition to the alone condition: the presence of a roach audience inhibited maze performance but facilitated runway performance (Fig. 24.2). Thus, the coactive and audience roaches had similar effects on performance. This finding (the lack of a significant three-way interaction) was critical, for it eliminated the possibility that the observed effects were due to specific behavioral cues. It is highly unlikely that the audience roaches were communicating—through sound or gesture—hints to the performing cockroaches on the runway but not in the maze. This strongly suggests that it was the mere presence of other roaches that mattered, nothing else.

Worth mentioning briefly is another of Zajonc and company's (1969) experiments, in which roaches traveled either a runway or a maze, in both cases flanked by mirrors, while being exposed either to a smelly egg carton left for a few days in the roach colony or to a fresh egg carton bearing not a trace of *eau de roach*. Again, the runway versus maze manipulation provided a simple versus complex task. The mirrors presumably created the effect of having fellow roaches present. The egg carton—smelly or not— was a manipulation of olfactory (smell-related) cues, again suggesting, in a different way, that other roaches were present or absent. The results of this experiment were not conclusive, but the inclusion of mirrors and the manipulation of odor did highlight an interesting question. What minimal features are sufficient to produce mere presence effects? For example, would cockroaches perform differently in the presence of dead or anaesthetized roaches (assuming that these immobile companions would not unduly alarm them)?

SO WHAT?

"So what?" is an easy question to ask in response to research involving cockroaches. However, bear in mind that this research is backed up by

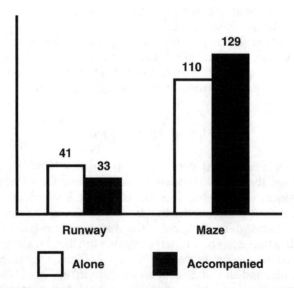

FIG. 24.2.   Number of seconds that it took cockroaches to travel down a runway or to negotiate a maze, when alone or accompanied by other cockroaches.

dozens of other studies on mere presence effects (see, for example, Michaels and others, 1982). Most of these have involved human participants, but comparable effects have been documented in dogs, rats, birds, fish, and even ants (see Chen, 1937, for evidence that ants dig twice as much dirt in the presence of other ants than when alone). Also bear in mind that Zajonc et al. (1969) were not attempting to understand the richness of human social behavior based upon observations of *Blatta orientalis* alone. That is, they were not interested in generalizing directly from cockroach to human. Rather, they sought to show that it is *possible* for mere presence effects to occur in the absence of cognitive mediation. Hence, they conducted an experiment that allowed them to rule out such variables as evaluation apprehension, self-monitoring, or some sort of approval motive as necessary causes of mere presence effects. Unless one is willing to argue that the lowly cockroach is swayed by many of the same passions and vulnerabilities that beset college sophomores, they succeeded in doing just that.

Relevant here is an article by Mook (1980), provocatively titled "In Defense of External Invalidity." Mook astutely pointed out that experimental research serves a variety of objectives, only one of which is to generalize from one population or setting to another population or setting. Instead, one often wants to demonstrate that an effect is simply possible, or that it can be obtained even in the somewhat contrived conditions of the laboratory. Also, one often wants only to test a particular hypothesis generated by a particular theory, without initially caring about generalizability. In other words, the artificiality of the laboratory, or the peculiar characteristics of, say, college sophomores, is often not a problem. In fact, laboratory experiments have the advantage of permitting particular variables to be isolated by paring down the complexity of the situation. In everyday life there is often simply too much going on to figure out exactly what causes what. The laboratory, therefore, provides a means of discovering rare social psychological truths, as the many experimental studies in this book illustrate.

AFTERTHOUGHTS

Science continually unfolds in a dialectical manner. A theory is asserted, then found wanting in some respect, then modified or replaced (see Cialdini, 1995). Sometimes support is even found for competing explanations, in which case it is often concluded that an effect can occur for more than one reason. For example, is it indeed the mere presence of others (sans cognitive mediation) that produces social facilitation and inhibition? Or is some kind of cognitive mediation, such as concern over being judged by others, responsible for such effects? A study by Cottrell and others (1968) found that participants performing a task in front of an audience showed the typical interaction pattern (social facilitation of dominant responses and inhibition of nondominant responses), but not if the others were blindfolded, supporting the claim that mere presence effects are mediated by evaluation apprehension (see also Aiello & Svec, 1993).

Nonetheless, the findings of the cockroach study cast doubt on the necessity of explaining mere presence effects in terms of something so human as evaluation apprehension (though, to our knowledge, nobody has tried the blindfold trick with cockroaches!). (Research by Markus, 1978, also showed that evaluation apprehension need not play a role in mere presence effects.) But what then, if not performance anxiety, might cause roaches to change their pace (sometimes going faster, sometimes slower) in the presence of other roaches? Sanders and Baron (1975) suggested that they get distracted. The distraction caused by coactors or an audience creates a conflict between focusing on the task and focusing on the others present. This conflict then raises arousal, thereby facilitating dominant and inhibiting nondominant responses. Indeed, sudden noises or flashes of light have been found to produce the same pattern of enhancement or impairment. Thus, we might conclude that a small mix of variables mediates social facilitation and inhibition: the mere presence of others, distraction, and, at least with humans, concerns about being evaluated (Geen, 1991; Guerin, 1993; Kent, 1996).

One thing to keep in mind about mere presence effects is that the complexity of a given task falls along a continuum. Arousal, too, falls on a continuum, from very low to very high. The implication is that the higher the arousal, the more dominant the response must be for performance to be facilitated. However, it is possible that arousal can be too high, disturbing performance on even relatively simple or well-practiced tasks. Consider, for example, competitive sporting events. It is well documented that sports teams tend to play better at home where, presumably, they feel more encouraged and possibly aroused than do their beleaguered opponents. And yet, Baumeister and Showers (1986) have empirically determined that when a given contest is particularly crucial and challenging—the final game of a major league baseball playoff, for example—playing at home is statistically a disadvantage. Indeed, one can think of examples—personal or not—of a person's feeling so aroused that even the simplest of tasks are near impossible to accomplish.

More generally, findings of social facilitation and inhibition fit with a more general insight: People greatly affect the person. All sorts of interesting things happen when we fall in among other *homo sapiens*. We begin to like them more as they become more familiar (see chap. 11); their norms dictate our perceptions and behavior (see chap. 17); they cause us to lose our sense of self (see chap. 22); we feel less personally responsible and culpable in their company (see chap. 19); and we look among them for self-flattering connections (see chap. 25). This theme—people affect the person—is all the more fascinating because of the subtle and manifold ways in which it plays itself out.

REVELATION

The mere presence of others enhances performance on simple tasks but impairs performance on complex tasks. This can occur even in the absence of complex mediating cognitions.

— *KPF* —

CHAPTER REFERENCE

Zajonc, R. B., Heingarter, A., & Herman, E. M. (1969). Social enhancement and impairment of performance in the cockroach. *Journal of Personality and Social Psychology, 13,* 83–92.

OTHER REFERENCES

Aiello, J. R., & Svec, C. M. (1993). Computer monitoring of work performance: Extending the social facilitation framework to electronic presence. *Journal of Applied Social Psychology, 23,* 537–548.

Baumeister, R. F., & Showers, C. J. (1986). A review of paradoxical performance effects: Choking under pressure in sports and mental tests. *European Journal of Social Psychology, 16,* 361–383.

Bond, C. F., Jr., & Titus, L. T. (1983). Social facilitation: A meta-analysis of 241 studies. *Psychological Bulletin, 94,* 265–292.

Chen, S. C. (1937). Social modification of the activity of ants in nest-building. *Physiological Zoology, 10,* 420–436.

Cialdini, R. B. (1995). A full-cycle approach to social psychology. In G. C. Bronnigan & M. R. Merrens (Eds.), *The social psychologist: Research adventures* (pp. 52–73). New York: McGraw-Hill.

Cottrell, N. B., Wack, D. L., Sekevak, G. J., & Rittle, R. H. (1968). Social facilitation of dominant responses by the presence of an audience and the mere presence of others. *Journal of Personality and Social Psychology, 9,* 245–250.

Geen, R. G. (1991). Social motivation. *Annual Review of Psychology, 42,* 377–399.

Guerin, B. (1993). *Social facilitation.* Cambridge: Cambridge University Press.

Kent, M. V. (1996). Presence of others. In A. P. Hare, H. H. Blumberg, M. F. Davies, & M. V. Kent (Eds.), *Small groups: An introduction* (pp. 41–57). Westport, CT: Praeger.

Markus, H. (1978). The effect of mere presence on social facilitation: An unobtrusive test. *Journal of Experimental Social Psychology, 14,* 389–397.

Michaels, J. W., Blommel, J. M., Brocato, R. M., Linkous, R. A., & Rowe, J. S. (1982). Social facilitation and inhibition in a natural setting. *Replications in Social Psychology, 12,* 21–24.

Mook, D. G. (1980). In defense of external invalidity. *American Psychologist, 38,* 379–388.

Sanders, G. S., & Baron, R. S. (1975). The motivating effects of distraction on task performance. *Journal of Personality and Social Psychology, 32,* 956–963.

Triplett, N. (1898). The dynamogenic factors in pacemaking and competition. *American Journal of Psychology, 9,* 507–533.

Zajonc, R. B. (1965). Social facilitation. *Science, 149,* 269–274.

Zajonc, R. B., & Sales, S. M. (1966). Social facilitation of dominant and subordinate responses. *Journal of Experimental Social Psychology, 2,* 160–168.

MORE TO EXPLORE

Baumeister, R. F. (1985). The championship choke. *Psychology Today, 19,* 48–52.

25 "We're Number One!": Basking in Others' Glory

> "In victory even the cowardly like to boast, while in adverse times even the brave are discredited."
> —Sallust (86 BC–34 BC), Roman senator and historian

BACKGROUND

It is not uncommon for us to trumpet our accomplishments and virtues, hoping that others will like and respect us more. True, we may on occasion admit to a few personal failures or foibles, particularly among those who know us well (Tice and others, 1995). However, some form of self-enhancement, direct or indirect, is more typical. We seek to persuade ourselves and others that we are uniquely talented, irresistibly charming, and perfectly lovable (Sedikides & Gregg, in press). It is a rare person, perhaps only one suffering from severe depression or bereft of all self-esteem, who is not his or her own best public relations agent. For example, even East Asian folk, who grow up in collectivistic societies where public self-promotion is frowned upon, still show the same fondness for the letters and characters in their own name that Westerners do (Kitayama & Karasawa, 1997), and have an inclination to regard themselves as above-average on traits valued by collectivistic cultures (Sedikides and others, in press).

A familiar example of our tendency to self-enhancement is our attempting to capitalize on someone else's victory or fame, even when we have little if anything to do with it ourselves. Think of how often we use the remotest affiliation to our advantage. We might slip into a conversation the fact that we share the same birthday as, say, a movie celebrity. Or mention with unabashed pride that we hail from the state that has produced the most vice presidents. Or report to everyone's great interest (or so we imagine) that the oldest inland open-air market in the country continues to operate in none other than our hometown. In such cases, we publicize the positive links—however trivial careful thought discovers them to be—emanating from our being.

Another example of self-enhancement by association is when we lay claim to the glory of a sports team's victory. Indeed, the following scene recently caught my eye: The camera pans through an intoxicated L.A. crowd and zeroes in on a guy whose bald head is a painted mosaic of blue and yellow. He's emphatically holding up his index finger and chanting "We're number one! We're number one!" As Robert Cialdini and his colleagues (1976) pointed out, the chant is always: "*We're* number one," never "*They're* number one."

Cialdini et al. (1976) referred to the previous phenomenon as "Basking in Reflected Glory" (or BIRGing for short). To investigate BIRGing, they went to seven different universities (Arizona State, Louisiana State, Notre Dame, Michigan, Pittsburgh, Ohio State, and Southern California) and secretly noted the clothing of introductory psychology students each Monday during football season. Taking note of whether a particular university won or lost their previous Saturday game, they recorded how many students in class wore jackets, sweatshirts, T-shirts, or buttons that displayed either the university's name or insignia, or the football team's nickname or mascot (wearing school colors did not count, nor did university notebooks and book covers). Their results were clear-cut: Students displayed their scholastic affiliation more after their school's football team had won than after it had lost. Moreover, the correlation between the number of students billboarding their school and the margin of victory was a noteworthy .43 (R. B. Cialdini, personal communication). In other words, the more lopsided the score, the more students on the victorious side displayed their school affiliation (and the less those on the losing side exhibited theirs). This was

FIG. 25.1. Utah 'R Us!

just as true for home games (for which it might be argued that cheers from the stands were instrumental in bringing about the victory) as it was for away games (which fewer students would have attended).

What explains such findings? Perhaps students believed, consciously or not, that others would regard them more favorably if they showed off their scholastic affiliation if their team won. The public flattery would boost their self-esteem. We seem to have an intuitive sense, accurate or not, that we are evaluated based not just on who we are, as individuals, but also on who or what we are associated with. We imagine that being seen with prestigious or supercool people will add an inch or two to our own social stature. We also sense that others will like us more when we communicate good news than when we bear bad news, even when we have obviously played no role in matters. We are reluctant to deliver a gloomy message, not because we feel guilty or sorrowful, but because we fear that we, though blameless, will be negatively evaluated as a result. (Mae and others, 1999, found something similar. When a communicator badmouths or praises someone, the described traits get automatically transferred onto the communicator as time passes. The target of the comments is forgotten, and a simple associative link persists.)

Cialdini et al. (1976) were quick to point out, however, that the tendency to wear university-related clothing following football wins may have nothing to do with efforts to exploit an incidental affiliation for egotistical ends. Perhaps doing so simply expresses one's school pride, or is an uncomplicated means of feeling good. In other words, people may BIRG for purely *intra*personal reasons. It is easy to imagine Notre Dame students wearing their *Fightin' Irish* sweatshirts in the privacy of their own dorm rooms, without wanting others to notice them doing so. However, Cialdini et al. (1976) wanted to demonstrate that BIRGing occurs, at least in part, for *inter*personal reasons as well. It is a means of boosting one's self-esteem by winning others' respect and admiration or garnering other social benefits.

WHAT THEY DID

Suspecting that BIRGing is at least partially mediated by interpersonal dynamics, Cialdini et al. (1976) examined students' use of pronouns in their descriptions of the outcomes of football games between their own and rival universities. They predicted that students would tend to use "we" more in references to school victories (as in "we won") and "they" more in references to defeats ("they lost"). They further predicted that this pattern of results would be exaggerated for participants whose self-esteem had recently been attacked.

One hundred seventy-three undergraduates at a large university (boasting a nationally ranked football team) were randomly selected from the university's telephone directory. During a 3-day period midway through the 1974 football season, they were contacted by phone by research assistants who identified themselves as employees of a regional survey center with headquarters in an out-of-state city. The caller said he was conducting a survey of college students' knowledge of campus issues and proceeded to ask six factually oriented questions about campus life (93% of those called agreed to participate in the survey). A typical question: "What percentage of students at your school are married—would you say it's closer to 20% or 35%?" ("I haven't the foggiest idea" was not an option). After participants had answered the six questions, the caller told them either that they had done very well compared to other students (getting *five* out of six questions correct) or that they had done relatively poorly (getting only *one* out of six correct).

These alternative remarks, randomly administered, served to experimentally manipulate participants' state (temporary) self-esteem. Presumably, the participants in the first condition experienced a slight boost in how they felt about themselves, whereas participants in the second condition felt a bit deflated. (The inclusion of a *manipulation check*—some way of demonstrating that the experimental manipulation did, indeed, have an effect—would have enhanced this study. The researchers just presumed that their manipulation worked, a plausible assumption, but a presumption nonetheless.)

The caller then mentioned that there would be a few more questions, the first of which had to do with campus athletics. Half the participants were asked about a football victory:

> In the first game of the season, your school's football team played the University of Houston. Can you tell me the outcome of that game?

The other half were asked about a defeat:

> In the first game of the season, your school's football team played the University of Missouri. Can you tell me the outcome of that game?

If a participant did not know the results of the game, a new participant was called. (It would be interesting to know whether wins were better remembered than losses. Research shows that we tend to selectively forget information that does not flatter the self [Sedikides & Green, 2000] or that otherwise proves uncongenial [Skowronski and others, 1991].) Otherwise his or her verbatim account of the outcome was recorded. The dependent variable was whether participants gave "we" responses (for example, "We won" or "We got beat") or non-"we" responses (for example, "The score was 14–6, Missouri" or "They lost"). Again, Cialdini et al. (1976) predicted that participants would give more "we" responses when describing a victory than when describing a defeat, and that this effect would be greater for participants who had failed the campus issues survey. Those participants, in particular, were expected to emphasize their affiliation with a winning team ("we") and distance themselves from a losing team ("they"), in order to prop up their flagging self-esteem.

WHAT THEY FOUND

Cialdini et al. (1976) found precisely what they had predicted. Usage of "we" was more common in descriptions of team victories than in descriptions of team defeats. Importantly, however, this occurred only among those whose egos had been bruised. For those who presumably experienced a blow to their self-esteem, "we" was used 40% of the time for victories and only 14% of the time for defeats. Notice that, for those whose egos had presumably been bolstered, "we" usage was almost identical for victories and defeats (Fig. 25.2). This pattern of results supports the contention that, when feasible, people flaunt, though perhaps not intentionally, trivial links between themselves and successful others in order to impress others and feel better about themselves.

Notice the difference between Study 1 and Study 2. Study 1 demonstrated a correlation between football team victories and the wearing of the team or sponsoring school's clothing. Study 2 built on Study 1 by experimentally manipulating whether a research participant was contemplating a team win or loss and by testing a theoretical claim about the mediating role of self-esteem in the tendency to BIRG. Ideally, science works in precisely this manner. It builds upon careful observation, rich description, and knowledge of correlated variables by engaging in experimental research that allows for sound causal inferences. It also moves back and forth between the so-called real world and the laboratory (see Cialdini, 1995).

A final study served to verify a further nuance of BIRGing. Benefits should accrue to the BIRGer only if he or she can boast of an association that is not shared by the observer. As an example of this, Cialdini et al. (1976) pointed out that when Californians brag about their state's idyllic climate, they are more likely to do so to people from other states (North Dakota, say) than with fellow Californians. In other words, BIRGing should more readily occur when one's connection with a celebrated something is stronger than the observer's connection. In order to test this assertion, an experimenter called participants up, inquiring, as in the previous study, about campus issues, including the outcome of a recent school football game. He identified himself as an employee of either the university survey center, located on campus, or the regional survey center, located in an out-of-state city. Although the results of this study did not quite reach conventional levels of statistical significance, the trend was clear. Participants were more likely to use "we" to describe school victories and other language ("they") to describe school defeats when they presumed that they were being interviewed by an out-of-state caller than by a campus caller. This marginally statistically significant result reinforces the claim that

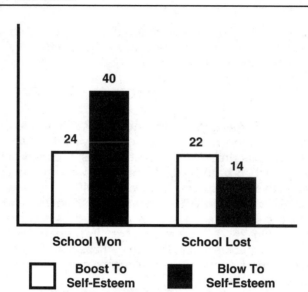

FIG. 25.2. Percentage of participants who used "we" to describe the outcome of their school's football game after they had received a boost or blow to their self-esteem.

BIRGing is not only about wanting to feel good—it is about wanting to feel good by impressing others (especially those who do not share the same source of pride).

Thus, in the last study, the origin of the caller was a notable *moderator* of the BIRGing effect. Y moderates the link between A and B if the strength or direction of that link changes when Y changes. Note how moderation is subtly different from *mediation*. In both cases, a link between A and B depends on some third factor. However, with mediation, the A–B link cannot occur unless that factor is present. With moderation it can, though when the factor is present, the A–B link gets modified. Think of the relationship between your dentist and the pain he or she causes. Whereas the dental drill mediates the link between your dentist and your pain (no drill, no pain), a local anesthetic moderates the link between the two (it reduces the intensity of the pain, hopefully).

These more technical details aside, all three studies by Cialdini et al. (1976) showed that participants were more likely to publicly identify themselves with their university's football team after it had recently been victorious. Evidently, people make known their links to successful groups at least in part because they realize that observers recognize such links and will evaluate them positively as a result. This realization and the desire to enjoy a favorable social image (especially after that image has been tarnished) appear to foster the BIRGing tendency.

SO WHAT?

Cialdini's research illustrates an important truth: One's identity includes both *I* and *we*, personal attributes as well as social contacts and group memberships. One's family, friends, ethnic group, religious affiliations, political party, and professional peers are all part of who one is. As Gordon Allport (1954), one of social psychology's prime movers, put it: "attachment to one's own being is basic to human life ... and along with this beloved self go all of the person's basic memberships ..." (p. 30).

This theme is captured in Tajfel (1979) and Turner's (1985) *social identity theory,* which highlights the role that group identification plays in achieving positive self-esteem (see chap. 28). We feel better about ourselves when our group (which social psychologists call the *ingroup*) has positive distinctiveness, that is, when it appears superior to other groups to which we do not belong or identify with (*outgroups*). Thus, self-esteem is more than just one's personal self-evaluation. It has a collective aspect (see Turner and others', 1987, related *self-categorization theory*).

Merely being associated with someone else's success or failure can have the same effect as personal success or failure. Whomever you root for represents you. If you are an American, and an American wins the Olympic marathon, you are a winner too (as if you yourself have been logging 100 plus miles a week for the past 10 years training for the event). And if you are Brazilian, you are certainly not disappointed that Brazil has just won the World Cup in soccer. We psychologically internalize our team's outcomes. In fact, believe it or not, a sports fan watching a live basketball game in which his team wins is subsequently more likely to predict that he will do well on a task (any task) than if his team loses. In other words, his team's winning boosts his own self-confidence (Hirt and others, 1992).

But keep this in mind: although we try to associate with winners and those who are otherwise successful, we sometimes find ourselves affiliated with losers. When this happens, we have a couple of options. One is to make excuses. For example, we can explain a sports loss on poor officiating (see chap. 4). If excuses do not work, we can distance ourselves from defeated or unpopular individuals or ingroups. That is, we can Cut Off Reflected Failure (CORF).

In an investigation of CORFing, Snyder and his colleagues (1986) had participants work on intellectual problems together in a small group, the "Blue team." Afterward they were given bogus feedback: Some were told that they had essentially failed (scoring below 70% of people in their age group), others that they had succeeded magnificently (scoring above 90% of others in their age group). A control group of participants were not given any feedback. On their way out, participants were told that there was a box of team badges by the door, and that they could take and wear one of the badges if they wished. About 50% of the participants given no feedback took a badge. But get this: Whereas a mere 10% of the participants in the low-scoring group took a badge (the few that did not CORF), a full 70% of the participants in the high-scoring group took a badge (the majority BIRGed). The upshot of research on CORFing is that we tend to distance ourselves from losers. We do not want our reputations tarnished. We do not want to suffer unfavorable associations or, worse, harmful consequences. But if this is true, why do we often champion, or root for, the underdog?

AFTERTHOUGHTS

Cialdini et al. (1976) explored how we compare the performance of ingroups to outgroups, and how our self-esteem and social awareness factor into the comparison. That is precisely what is happening when, as, say, Sacramento Kings fans, we anxiously watch the score in an NBA playoff game against the Los Angeles Lakers volley back and forth. Who is winning? Who is going to win? If "we" win: pride and joy. If "we" lose: heartache and humiliation. *We* is a prominent part of *I*.

However, we also compare our individual performances in life to that of others (Tesser, 1988). Related to the concepts of BIRGing and CORFing is the practice of *social comparison*. Recall how in elementary school you were curious about how well (or poorly) your friend did on a spelling test compared to you, and how as an adult the mere sight of someone else's dazzling new SUV (or dilapidated wreck) causes you to reflect on the relative quality of your own car. An important question: How does social comparison affect how we feel about ourselves? After all, although we might delight in someone else's glory, we might also suffer jealousy over it (Salovey & Rodin, 1984).

Tesser's (1988) *self-evaluation maintenance model* suggests that it all depends on whether the comparison person is close (a friend or relative) or distant (a stranger or foe), and on whether the dimension of evaluation does or does not pertain to our personal identity. An aspiring comedian may be psychologically threatened by a friend's hilarious performance but roll in laughter at the buffoonery of a stranger. We tend to like someone who performs better than us on something of little personal relevance. In more personally significant arenas, however, we prefer them to be slightly inferior to us (if they are too much so then the comparison is not seen as legitimate). As William James (1907), one of psychology's trailblazers, put it:

> I, who for the time have staked my all on being a psychologist, am mortified if others know much more psychology than I. But I am content to wallow in the grossest ignorance of Greek. My deficiencies there give me no sense of personal humiliation at all. Had I "pretensions" to be a linguist, it would have been just the reverse. (p. 310)

BIRGing and CORFing, and more direct social comparison, aside, a larger statement can be made. We all want to be liked and looked up to. We want to be appreciated and empowered in our social worlds, and to avoid heartaches and headaches in our social encounters (Leary and others, 1995). To this end we try to present ourselves in the best possible light. The process of trying to create a desired social image is referred to as *impression management* (Schlenker, 1980). We attempt to influence others' impressions of us by selectively displaying behaviors that convey a favorable image, or that hide an unfavorable one. According to renowned sociologist Irving Goffman (1959), social interactions represent a kind of theatrical performance in which one presents a *line*: carefully chosen words and deeds meant to express a certain self. We each seek to minimize our social blunders and agonizing embarrassments (Goffman refers to this as *face work*), and we have a repertoire of face-saving devices when these occur.

In fact, BIRGing is only one of several impression management techniques (perhaps one of the least obvious and intentional ones). Jones and Pittman (1982) have identified a grab bag of other ploys. One is ingratiation: We give others our attention, conform to their opinions, shower them with flattery, do them favors, and pretend to overlook their foibles, all in order to be liked. We too know "how to win friends and influence people" (Dale Carnegie, 1994). Another ploy is *self-handicapping*: we do or say things that will enable us to either excuse a subsequent failure or take credit for a more unlikely success. For example, we get intoxicated the night before a big exam or mention before a musical audition that we have a sore throat and possibly a fever. (As a long distance runner, I am always amazed at how many of us toeing the start line of a race are not expecting—or so we tell others—to run our best, given the hard workout we ran the day before, blisters we have, problems with shin splints, and so on.) Yet another strategy is *exemplification*. Although we risk appearing sanctimonious, we nevertheless let it be known, through melodramatic self-denial and suffering, how morally exemplary we are ("You go on, I'll finish up here. I'll just quickly clear off the table, wash and dry all the dishes, sweep the floor, make us some coffee, bring out desserts ..."). These are but a few of the schemes we use to manage others' impressions of us.

Interestingly, face-saving devices and impression management techniques can also occur in collusion. When we notice someone picking their nose, we tactfully ask them if they need a tissue. When we trip over our own two feet, they continue talking as if nothing embarrassing has happened. We help one another—especially in a close relationship—maintain a favorable impression and positive self-esteem.

Of course, different people are more or less inclined to monitor their behaviors and employ such strategies (Snyder, 1987). And, indisputably, such strategies require energy and skill. Maintaining one's mask is no easy task. Perhaps this is why we often fall back on the more effortless maneuver of basking in someone else's exultation. I may not be number one, but surely "We're number one"!

REVELATION

People, as well as groups and institutions we are socially connected to, are part of our identity and impact our self-esteem. We personalize their successes and failures, trumpeting the former and distancing ourselves from the latter.

— KPF —

CHAPTER REFERENCE

Cialdini, R. B., Borden, R. J., Thorne, A., Walker, M. R., Freeman, S., & Sloan, L. R. (1976). Basking in reflected glory: Three (football) field studies. *Journal of Personality and Social Psychology, 34,* 366–375.

OTHER REFERENCES

Allport, G. W. (1954). *The nature of prejudice.* Reading, MA: Addison-Wesley.

Carnegie, D. (1994). *How to win friends and influence people.* New York: Pocket Books.

Cialdini, R. B. (1995). A full-cycle approach to social psychology. In G. C. Brannigan & M. R. Merrens (Eds.), *The social psychologists: Research adventures* (pp. 52–73). New York: McGraw-Hill.

Goffman, E. (1959). *The presentation of self in everyday life.* Garden City, NY: Doubleday.

Hirt, E. R., Zillman, D., Erickson, G. A., & Kennedy, C. (1992). Costs and benefits of allegiance: Changes in fans' self-ascribed competencies after team victory versus defeat. *Journal of Personality and Social Psychology, 63,* 724–738.

James, W. (1907). *Pragmatism.* New York: Longmans, Green.

Jones, E. E., & Pittman, T. (1982). Toward a general theory of strategic self-presentation. In J. Suls (Ed.), *Psychological perspectives on the self* (Vol. 1, pp. 231–262). Hillsdale, NJ: Lawrence Erlbaum Associates.

Kitayama, S., & Karasawa, M. (1997). Implicit self-esteem in Japan: Name letters and birthday numbers. *Personality and Social Psychology Bulletin, 23,* 736–742.

Leary, M., Tambor, E., Terdel, S., & Downs, D. (1995). Self-esteem as an interpersonal monitor: The sociometer hypothesis. *Journal of Personality and Social Psychology, 68,* 518–530.

Mae, L., Carlston, D. E., & Skowronski, J. J. (1999). Spontaneous trait transfer to familiar communications: Is a little knowledge a dangerous thing? *Journal of Personality and Social Psychology, 77,* 233–246.

Salovey, P., & Rodin, J. (1984). Some antecedents and consequences of social-comparison jealousy. *Journal of Personality and Social Psychology, 47,* 780–792.

Schlenker, B. R. (1980). *Impression management: The self-concept, social identity, and interpersonal relations.* Monterey, CA: Brooks/Cole.

Sedikides, C., Gaertner, L., & Toguchi, Y. (in press). Pancultural self-enhancement. *Journal of Personality and Social Psychology.*

Sedikides, C., & Green, J. D. (2000). On the self-protective nature of inconsistency/negativity management: Using the person memory paradigm to examine self-referent memory. *Journal of Personality and Social Psychology, 79,* 906–922.

Sedikides, C., & Gregg, A. P. (in press). Portraits of the self. In M. A. Hogg & J. Cooper (Eds.), *Sage handbook of social psychology.* London: Sage Publications.

Skowronski, J. J., Betz, A. L., Thompson, C. P., & Shannon, L. (1991). Social memory in everyday life: Recall of self-events and other-events. *Journal of Personality and Social Psychology, 60,* 831–843.

Snyder, C. R., Lassergard, M., & Ford, C. E. (1986). Distancing after group success and failure: Basking in reflected glory and cutting off reflected failure. *Journal of Personality and Social Psychology, 51,* 382–388.

Snyder, M. (1987). *Public appearances/private realities: The psychology of self-monitoring.* New York: W. H. Freeman.

Tajfel, H. (1979). Individuals and groups in social psychology. *British Journal of Social and Clinical Psychology, 18,* 183–190.

Tesser, A. (1988). Toward a self-evaluation maintenance model of social behavior. In L. Berkowitz (Ed.), *Advances in experimental social psychology* (Vol. 21, pp. 181–227). New York: Academic Press.

Tice, D. M., Butler, J. L., Muraven, M. B., & Stillwell, A. M. (1995). When modesty prevails: Differential favorability of self-presentation to friends and strangers. *Journal of Personality and Social Psychology, 69,* 1120–1138.

Turner, J. C. (1985). Social categorization and the self-concept: A social-cognitive theory of group behavior. In E. J. Lawler (Ed.), *Advances in group processes* (Vol. 2, pp. 77–122). Greenwich, CT: JAI Press.

Turner, J. C., Hogg, M., Oakes, P., Reicher, S., & Wetherell, M. (1987). *Rediscovering the social group: A self-categorization theory.* Oxford, England: Basil Blackwell.

MORE TO EXPLORE

Cialdini, R. B., & De Nicholas, M. E. (1989). Self-presentation by association. *Journal of Personality and Social Psychology, 57,* 626–631.

Kulik, J. A., & Gump, B. B. (1997). Affective reactions to social comparison: The effects of relative performance and related attributes information about another person. *Personality and Social Psychology Bulletin, 23,* 452–468.

Sedikides, C. (1993). Assessment, enhancement, and verification of the self-enhancement process. *Journal of Personality and Social Psychology, 65,* 317–338.

26 Ackmians Are From Mars, Orinthians Are From Venus: Gender Stereotypes as Role Rationalizations

"Sometimes I wonder if men and women really suit each other. Perhaps they should live next door and just visit now and then."
— Katharine Hepburn (1907–2003), U.S. actress

BACKGROUND

Imagine taking part in an experiment on how children play. You are introduced to an 18-month-old infant—"Joey"—and asked to play with him for a few minutes. What would you do? Give him a noisy rattle or plastic hammer to play with? Bounce him on your knee, or playfully toss him a foot or two into the air? But what if you were introduced to "Janie" instead? Would you give her a female doll and accessories to play with? Handle her more gently, and talk to her more softly? Experimental research confirms that this is what people tend to do (Smith & Lloyd, 1978). Consider also the following experiment. Participants watched a videotape of a 9-month-old baby. Some were told that it was a boy, others that it was a girl. When asked why the baby burst into tears over a jack-in-the-box, the participants in the first group often said that it was because *he* was angry, while participants in the second group said that it was because *she* was afraid (Condry & Condry, 1976). What about *your* reactions to boys versus girls? Does something different come to mind when you hear "It's a boy!" versus "It's a girl!'"? Do you associate boys and girls with different traits? Do you think that boys and girls will grow into men and women with different preferences, potentials, and perceptions of the world?

Your answers to such questions might well reflect *gender stereotypes*—distinct sets of characteristics conventionally associated with males and females. A study of gender stereotypes across 30 countries found that, just about everywhere, men are thought to be relatively adventurous, ambitious, dominant, obnoxious, logical, task-oriented, and promiscuous, whereas women are thought to be relatively sentimental, submissive, dependent, people-oriented, and weak (Williams & Best, 1990). In general, people see men as strong and independent, women as nice and nurturing (De Lisi & Soundranayagam, 1990). Does this sound familiar to you?

Do men and women really differ in the way that gender stereotypes suggest they do? Certainly, research has uncovered many interesting differences between men and women—in aggression, depression, odor discrimination, susceptibility to phobia, nonverbal behavior, leadership styles, criminality, suicidal behaviors, preoccupation with sex, and so on. Regarding suicide, for example, more than twice as many women attempt it as men, although twice as many men succeed at it as women, partly because men are more likely to choose surefire lethal methods, like shooting themselves in the head (Berman & Jobes, 1991). Regarding preoccupation with sex, a survey of a random sample of American adults aged 18–59 found that 54% of men and 19% of women report thinking about sex very regularly, 43% of men and 67% of women report thinking about sex occasionally, and 4% of men and 14% of women report thinking about sex only rarely (Michael and others, 1994). Perhaps the most interesting aspect of these results is that, although men generally report thinking about sex more than women do, there are also a significant number of women who report thinking about sex more than men do. (Also interest-

FIG. 26.1. Doctor and nurse. Or is that nurse and doctor? Photo courtesy of www.gaymed.ch

ing, if not incredible, is the fact that there are some people who claim that they almost never think about sex!) Of course, just because research finds some gender differences, it does not follow that all, or even any, gender stereotypes are accurate.

Alice Eagly (1987), one of the first social psychologists to study gender differences, conceded that many gender stereotypes are rooted in real underlying differences between men and women. However, she claimed that these underlying differences are typically small. They become magnified, however, because men and women tend to take on or be assigned to different social roles. Even in progressive societies, men are more likely than women to occupy *agentic* roles, distinguished by self-assertiveness and a willingness to prevail over others. Examples include politician, scientist, business executive, or religious leader. Women, in contrast, are more likely than men to occupy *communal* roles, distinguished by selflessness and concern for others. Examples include homemaker, elementary school teacher, secretary, or nurse. For instance, in my sons' elementary school, 34 of the 36 teachers are female, whereas, predictably, the principal is male.

Thus, although men and women have quite similar personalities deep down, they find themselves in different roles that require them to express different traits. People notice these overtly expressed traits and form stereotypes based on them. In other words, according to Eagly (1987), role-based differences are primarily responsible for gender stereotypes. Put the average woman into an agentic role and you will find that she becomes just as agentic as men in that role. Put the average man into a communal role and you will find that he becomes just as communal as women in that role. Agentic roles bring out masculine traits in both men and women. Communal roles bring out feminine traits in both too. Were men and women more equally dispersed across social roles, the differences between them (and corresponding stereotypes) might still exist, but much less so.

Eagly's social role interpretation of observed gender differences has much to recommend it, given the obviously unequal distribution of men and women in various social roles, many of which can be classified as being one-sidedly agentic or communal in nature. Her theory has also received empirical support (e.g., Eagly & Steffen, 1984). However, some thorny questions remain, including an important one raised by Hoffman and Hurst (1990). Do gender stereotypes arise directly and exclusively from observed sex differences in personality (even if they are partly a product of social roles)? Hoffman and Hurst speculated that they do not. Gender differences, even when amplified by roles, are too small, they claimed, for people to detect them. They quote Nisbett and Ross (1980) on this score: "People's covariation detection capacities are far too crude to allow any ... purely data-based discovery" (pp. 238–239). People simply do not have the perceptual perspicacity to develop such stereotypes on their own.

Hoffman and Hurst (1990) also pointed out that gender stereotypes do not always faithfully map on to scientifically established gender differences. For example, research finds no differences between men and women on such traits as kindness, patience, or ability to make decisions, and yet such differences feature prominently in gender stereotypes. In contrast, men are more restless than women, and women are better than men at decoding body language and facial expressions, and yet these differences feature only peripherally in gender stereotypes.

Another of Hoffman and Hurst's (1990) challenges: If gender stereotypes are purely role-based, why do they exist above and beyond more specific stereotypes of, say, homemakers, stockbrokers, brain surgeons, or daycare helpers? Why do people have notions of what men or women are like in general? What purpose might such stereotypes serve?

Hoffman and Hurst (1990) argued that merely categorizing people into social roles is sufficient to produce stereotypes; perceiving actual gender differences is not necessary. Yet if that is the case, then what accounts for the connection between roles and stereotypes? According to Hoffman and Hurst, the two are connected because gender stereotypes serve to *rationalize* the roles of men and women in society. That is, gender stereotypes are explanatory conveniences that allow people to justify the social status quo:

> "Women care for children, and understandably so—they are by nature kinder, gentler, and more sensitive than men. Men run the businesses and fight the wars, and that is obviously because they are naturally more logical, independent, and competitive than women." In essence, we propose that gender stereotypes be regarded not primarily as summary abstractions of males' and females' personalities based directly on observed differences in those personalities, but at least partly explanatory fictions that rationalize and make sense of the sexual division of labor. (Hoffman & Hurst, 1990, p. 199)

To say that people's assumptions about gender differences are explanatory fictions is a bold assertion. A hard-nosed social psychologist would demand: "Show me the data!"

WHAT THEY DID

Hoffman and Hurst (1990) sought to show that gender stereotypes can arise as a direct result of two groups taking on different social roles, even when the members of those groups share similar traits. To this end, they had participants (a mix of 80 males and females) imagine two fictional social groups—*Ackmians* and *Orinthians*—living on a faraway planet. These groups were said to reside in the countryside near large cities. Participants were told that the adult members of the two groups were either *child raisers* (caring for and teaching the young) or *city workers* (involved in business, industry, technology, and higher education).

Participants were presented with brief individual descriptions, and head and shoulders "photos," of each of 15 Ackmians and 15 Orinthians (randomly ordered). Each photo and description was printed on one page of a booklet and presented for 15 seconds. The description included the individual's name, group membership, social role, and three personality traits. The three personality traits included one relatively agentic (masculine) quality, one communal (feminine) quality, and one neutral quality (as determined by the ratings of independent judges). Example: "Dolack, an Ackmian who raises children, is outspoken, compassionate, and reliable." Another example: "Damorin, an Orinthian who works in the city, is resourceful, individualistic, and soft-spoken." Each Ackmian and Orinthian was described by a unique set of traits. Importantly, given that every target was described by all three of the trait types, neither the group to which the aliens belonged, nor the social role they occupied, made any difference to how agentic or communal they really were overall.

For half the participants, 12 out of 15 of the Ackmians were described as city workers (the remaining three being described as child raisers) and 12 out of 15 Orinthians were described as child raisers (the remaining three being described as city workers). Participants in an alternate experimental condition were presented with the opposite combination: most Ackmians were described as child raisers and most Orinthians as city workers. Thus, Hoffman and Hurst experimentally manipulated the degree of overlap between social group (Ackmian or Orinthian) and role (child raiser or city dweller). They predicted that this group-role overlap would cause participants to form role-based personality stereotypes of the two alien races, though the targets' personalities did not differ by group or role. In addition, they also predicted that these stereotypes would influence participants' perceptions of group members even when the members' social roles were specified.

Another experimental manipulation was important. For half of the participants, the distinction between Ackmians and Orinthians was claimed to be *biological*. The two groups were said to be distinct species, with their respective members unable to interbreed, and physically resembling each other more than members of the other group. For the remaining participants, the distinction between the Ackmians and Orinthians was claimed to be *nonbiological*. The two groups were said to represent different subcultures, with their respective members able to interbreed, and in appearance distinguished only by the color of their clothing. Hoffman and Hurst predicted that stereotypes would more likely arise when the groups were described as biologically, as opposed to culturally, distinct. (Note: Agentic and communal social roles were not themselves described as biologically or culturally distinct.) The researchers reasoned that *priming* (making mentally available) the idea of biological inevitability would encourage stereotyping, whereas priming the idea of cultural relativity would discourage it. Portraying a social distinction as genetically preset is a notorious way of rationalizing it. For example, to justify opting out of childcare responsibilities, men might conclude that women are just innately better at nurturing children.

After reading the descriptions of the Ackmians and Orinthians, the participants were asked to indicate the percentage of each group that were child raisers and the percentage that were city dwellers (with the two percentages equaling 100 for each group). This procedure was followed by yet another experimental manipulation. Half of the participants were asked to explain why the Ackmians and Orinthians might tend to occupy their respective roles; the remaining participants were not asked to give an explanation. Hoffman and Hurst predicted that having to explain the overlap between group category and social role would prompt gender stereotyping. The researchers reasoned that having to come up with an explanation would kick-start the process of stereotypical rationalization. Research shows that focused thinking about a topic, or the overt expression of opinions, is enough to make attitudes more extreme (Abelson, 1995).

Next came the actual measures of stereotyping. Participants were asked to rate the personalities of Ackmians in general and Orinthians in general on each of six agentic traits (ambitious, assertive, competitive, independent, out-spoken, and self-confident) and six communal traits (affectionate, emotional, gentle, helpful, kind, and understanding). They then rated Ackmian child raisers, Ackmian city workers, Orinthian child raisers, and Orinthian city workers on each of the same 12 traits. All ratings were made on a scale from 0 (not at all) to 9 (extremely).

WHAT THEY FOUND

Participants were evidently aware of the relation between the alien groups and social roles. They reported that most of the Ackmians were city workers (in one condition) or that most were child raisers (in the other). They were also aware that some members of each group occupied atypical roles. For example, none reported that 100% of the Ackmians were city workers.

Hoffman and Hurst (1990) subtracted each participant's ratings of Ackmians and Orinthians on communal traits from their ratings of them on agentic traits, to arrive at an index of stereotyping. Differences from zero in the positive direction represented a masculine stereotype; differences from zero in the negative direction represented a feminine stereotype. Using this index, it was found that Ackmians or Orinthians in general were viewed as being relatively agentic if most of them worked in the city, or relatively communal if most of them were child raisers, even though no group personality differences existed to warrant such biased impressions. Also, greater stereotyping occurred in the biological condition than in the nonbiological condition, and in the explanation condition than in the no-explanation condition (Fig. 26.2).

Another important result was that stereotyping of the Ackmians or the Orinthians occurred even when the role of child raiser or city dweller was

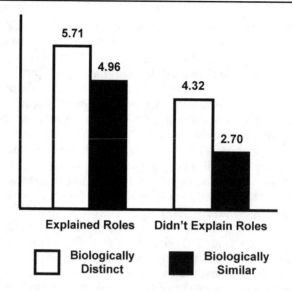

Explained Roles   **Didn't Explain Roles**

☐ **Biologically**   ■ **Biologically**
   Distinct   **Similar**

FIG. 26.2. Stereotyping of two "alien" races, when they had been described as biologically distinct, when participants tried to explain their social roles, both, or neither.

specified. Again, greater stereotyping occurred in the biological than nonbiological conditions, and in the explanation than no-explanation conditions. Of course, the roles themselves also determined the direction of the stereotyping. The child raiser role was, as expected, associated with communal traits and the city worker role with agentic traits. These associations were the equivalent of gender-based stereotypes. If participants had not associated particular attributes with certain social roles, then such attributes could not have become associated with the categories of individuals (Ackmians and Orinthians) who to a greater or lesser extent occupied those roles.

Thus, Hoffman and Hurst found, as predicted, that participants would develop personality stereotypes of Ackmians and Orinthians based upon these supposed aliens' typical roles even when no personality differences existed. They also demonstrated that these stereotypes impacted perceptions even when social roles were specified. Participants came to believe that the Ackmians and Orinthians had quite different personalities—again, even though objectively no personality differences existed—and that their differences existed independent of role constraints.

Hoffman and Hurst also obtained support for their claim that stereotypes are, at least in part, rationalizations for social role divisions. Almost three quarters of participants giving explanations attributed the correlation between group and role to personality differences. For example, one wrote:

"Orinthians are on average the kind and sensitive … species. The Ackmians are more self-confident and forceful, therefore better suited for working in the city." Simply because the majority of the members of a group occupied a certain role, it was automatically inferred that they must possess the personality traits required for that role. Similar assumptions or rationalizations are heard every day: "Most nurses are women, because women are naturally more empathetic and caring than men."

Worth mentioning is a follow-up experiment by Hoffman and Hurst—reported in the same article. During interviews following the first experiment, participants were asked to guess its true purpose. A small percent mentioned that they thought it had something to do with gender. Although statistical analyses that excluded data from these participants yielded the same results, Hoffman and Hurst were concerned that participants were implicitly equating the two alien groups (Ackmians and Orinthians) with the two human sexes (males and females). They reasoned that participants' stereotypes of the supposed aliens might have been based, not on their typical social roles, but on already held stereotypes of men and women here on earth! They therefore conducted a second experiment, in which the roles of child raisers and city dwellers were replaced with the roles of businesspersons (extroverted, ambitious types) and academics (introverted, intellectual types). They argued that, whereas the former pair of roles may have brought to mind gender stereotypes, the second pair was not likely to do so. The results of this second experiment mirrored those of the first experiment, bolstering Hoffman and Hurst's confidence in the validity and robustness of their findings.

SO WHAT?

Hoffman and Hurst (1990) showed that stereotypes can form even when no objective differences exist to warrant their formation. All that is needed is the perception that different groups of people occupy different social roles. This prompts the formation of group stereotypes to rationalize why the members occupy those roles. In other words, the generalizations that we make about people in particular groups can serve as after-the-fact justifications for their roles in the social world. Famed social psychologist Gordon Allport (1958) expressed the same view: "the rationalizing and justifying function of a stereotype exceeds its function as a reflector of group attributes" (p. 192). Much of Allport's attention was on racial stereotypes. Indeed, he suggested that the American stereotype of Blacks as lazy and mentally dull served to rationalize slavery.

Whether stereotypes are based on actual perceptions of group differences, a need to rationalize the social order, or both, they tend to be self-perpetuating (see chaps. 4 and 14 for more on how people's beliefs and expectations can create their own reality). For example, exceptions to a stereotype are often explained away as special cases that do not require one to amend the stereotype itself, a process known as *subtyping* (Rothbart & John, 1985). Thus, post

September 11th, meeting a mild-mannered Arab nonbeliever may not convince a media-saturated American that Arabs in general are not Islamic fanatics.

It's not only that stereotypes are easily formed and perpetuated, it's also that they are potentially harmful. Stereotypes, by definition, ignore the unique qualities of the individual, even if they allow us to deploy our cognitive resources economically (Macrae and others, 1994). Stereotypes may also channel people into certain occupations and other social roles, thereby limiting their options. Thus, women may be steered away from potentially fulfilling careers as physicists, men from potentially fulfilling careers as florists. There is even evidence that people will endorse stereotypes that do not benefit themselves, and rationalize their own inferior status, as, for example, when a Catholic woman sees herself, and all women, as unworthy of ordination to the priesthood (Jost & Banaji, 1994). As rationalizations, stereotypes maintain the current structure of society, even when that structure is not fair or otherwise best. In this sense, stereotypes can be likened to *ego defense mechanisms* (mental strategies to ward off anxiety) that tie up psychic energy and prevent growth (Freud, 1946). Bottom line: stereotypes—including gender stereotypes—have a dark underside.

Also important about gender stereotypes is that they can overlap with other stereotypes, thereby targeting even more specific groups of people. For example, in research by Niemann and others (1994), participants listed the first 10 adjectives that came to mind when thinking about each of eight groups: African American men, African American women, Anglo American men, Anglo American women, Asian American men, Asian American women, Mexican American men, and Mexican American women. They discovered a number of gender stereotypes that were unaffected by ethnicity. For example, women from all groups were described as pleasant and friendly. They also found ethnic stereotypes that were unaffected by gender. For example, African Americans, whether male or female, were described as athletic, and Asian Americans, whether male or female, as intelligent. However, they also found distinct gender stereotypes within specific ethnic groups. For example, Anglo American and Mexican American women, but not men, were described as attractive. Asian American and Mexican American men, but not women, were described as hard working. Hoffman and Hurst's findings continue to raise the question: Are these various specific stereotypes the result of actual perceptions, or are they a form of rationalization?

AFTERTHOUGHTS

The fact that human beings come in two biological flavors, men and women, is a fascinating one, and makes for much excitement. Indeed, most people would probably prefer two sexes to just one. Of course, one might pine for even greater complexity—three or four sexes, say—but God has not decreed, or nature has not selected, such numbers (think how that might complicate the reproductive process!). Our species consists of but two sexes, and no doubt people throughout history have wondered about differences between them.

Social psychologists would like to have a full and precise account of the ways in which men and women are, or are not, different, whatever the social or political fallout. Plenty of research, including *meta-analytic* research (which involves statistically summarizing the results of many related individual experiments), now exists on this topic (see, for example, Buss, 1989; Eagly & Crowley, 1986; Eagly & Johnson, 1990; Eisenberg & Lennon, 1983; Gabriel & Gardner, 1999; Konrad & others, 2000; Oliver & Hyde, 1993; Pratto & others, 1997; Tannen, 1990). Though informative, such research does not entirely put to rest the hotly debated issue of gender differences.

It is obvious that men and women are different anatomically, even if it is unclear what tomorrow holds in terms of breakthroughs in genetic engineering or reconstructive surgery. Claims about psychological differences are more controversial, however. Is it true that men, when they get lost while driving, generally refuse to stop and ask for directions, or that women are not psychologically equipped for military combat? Is it the case that men and women engage in different types of moral reasoning, with men being more concerned about *justice* (people getting what they deserve), and women being more concerned about *care* (preserving harmonious relationships; Gilligan, 1982)?

Moreover, consider some of John Gray's (1992) assertions in his bestseller. Men and women are claimed to seemingly hail from different planets—Mars and Venus, respectively. Their values, coping strategies, sources of motivation, communication styles, emotional and sexual needs, means of "keeping score" in a relationship, and so on, all differ. regarding intimacy, men are said to be like *rubber bands*: "when a man loves a woman, periodically he needs to pull away before he can get closer" (p. 92). And women are said to be like *waves*: "A woman's self-esteem rises and falls ... when she hits bottom it is time for emotional housecleaning" (p. 113). However, is such an obsession with gender differences warranted? Does Gray gloss over the fact that men and women overlap considerably on most dimensions? Take something as uncontroversial as height. Clearly, men are, on average, taller than women. Nonetheless, many women are still taller than men. In light of this, should all women be treated as small and all men as big? Similarly, do I, as a male, not need time for "emotional housekeeping" and my wife, as a woman, not need to emotionally "pull away" occasionally?

Furthermore, is it true that men and women want different things from relationships? A popular book by clinical psychologist and marriage counselor Harley (1998) lists men and women's separate marital can't-do-withouts:

The man's five most basic needs in marriage tend to be (1) sexual fulfillment, (2) recreational companionship, (3) an attractive spouse, (4) domestic support, and (5) admiration. The woman's five most basic needs in marriage tend to be: (1) affection, (2) conversation, (3) honesty and openness, (4) financial support, and (5) family commitment. (pp. 12–13)

Learning that women do not need an attractive spouse is certainly comforting to this author (KPF)! But one has to wonder, with such a list, where does truth end and storytelling begin?

Finally, why are there separate gender roles for men and women in the first place, if not because men and women have quite different personalities? Why the sexual division of labor in virtually every society? Hoffman and Hurst (1990) suggested that it is an evolutionary accident caused by biological differences, something as elementary as women's ability, and men's inability, to bear and nurse infant children. Accordingly, it has always made sense, at least until quite recently, for women to remain at home and care for children. And as long as they were involved in childcare, it made sense for them to do the household chores as well. That left the hunting, fighting, and trading to the men. (Who does one find in a hunting cabin, in a combat zone, or on the floor of the Stock Exchange—primarily men or women?) The latter roles are relatively dangerous, but better to lose a substantial number of men (in which case reproduction easily goes on) than to lose a substantial number of women (in which case the whole reproductive enterprise may skid to a halt).

Yet not everyone would agree that it is something so quotidian as the ability to nurse offspring that explains the remarkable differences in social roles and divisions of labor we find in the world today. Some would argue that such differences arise because of real personality differences, ones that go back to the beginning of time. They believe that men gravitate to agentic roles and women to communal roles because of their intrinsically different natures. At the same time, however, we see cultural differences and historical shifts in gender roles, calling into question the validity of related gender stereotypes. How accurate are gender stereotypes, and what is their origin? The debate rages on.

REVELATION

Gender stereotypes do not only arise from perceptions of actual gender differences. They also arise as ways of rationalizing the different social roles that men and women occupy.

— KPF —

CHAPTER REFERENCE

Hoffman, C., & Hurst, N. (1990). Gender stereotypes: Perception or rationalization? *Journal of Personality and Social Psychology, 58,* 197–208.

OTHER REFERENCES

Abelson, R. P. (1995). Attitude extremity. In R. E. Petty & J. A. Krosnick (Eds.), *Attitude strength: Antecedents and consequences* (pp. 25–42). Hillsdale, NJ: Lawrence Erlbaum Associates.

Allport, G. W. (1958). *The nature of prejudice*. New York: Doubleday.

Berman, K. F., & Jobes, D. A. (1991). *Adolescent suicide: Assessment and intervention*. Washington, DC: American Psychological Association.

Buss, D. M. (1989). Sex difference in human mating preferences: Evolutionary hypotheses tested in 37 cultures. *Behavioral and Brain Sciences, 12,* 1–49.

Condry, J., & Condry, S. (1976). Sex differences: A study of the eye of the beholder. *Child Development, 47,* 812–819.

De Lisi, R., & Soundranayagam, L. (1990). The conceptual structure of sex role stereotypes in college students. *Sex Roles, 23,* 593–611.

Eagly, A. H. (1987). *Sex differences in social behavior: A social-role interpretation*. Hillsdale, NJ: Lawrence Erlbaum Associates.

Eagly, A. H., & Crowley, M. (1986). Gender and helping behavior: A meta-analytic review of the social psychological literature. *Psychological Bulletin, 100,* 283–308.

Eagly, A. H., & Johnson, B. T. (1990). Gender and leadership style: A meta-analysis. *Psychological Bulletin, 108,* 233–256.

Eagly, A. H., & Steffen, V. J. (1984). Gender stereotypes stem from the distribution of women and men into social roles. *Journal of Personality and Social Psychology, 46,* 735–754.

Eisenberg, N., & Lennon, R. (1983). Sex differences in empathy and related capacities. *Psychological Bulletin, 94,* 100–131.

Freud, A. (1946). *The ego and the mechanisms of defense*. New York: International Universities Press.

Gabriel, S., & Gardner, W. L. (1999). Are there "his" and "hers" types of interdependence? The implications of gender differences in collective versus relational interdependence for affect, behavior, and cognition. *Journal of Personality and Social Psychology, 77,* 642–655.

Gilligan, C. (1982). *In a different voice*. Cambridge, MA: Harvard University Press.

Gray, J. (1992). *Men are from Mars, Women are from Venus: A practical guide for improving communication and getting what you want in your relationships*. New York: HarperCollins.

Harley, W. F. (1998). *His needs, her needs*. Grand Rapids, MI: Fleming H. Revell.

Jost, J. T., & Banaji, M. R. (1994). The role of stereotyping in system-justification and the production of false consciousness. *British Journal of Psychology, 33,* 1–27.

Konrad, A. M., Ritchie, J. E., Jr., Lieb, P., & Corrigall, E. (2000). Sex differences and similarities in job attribute preferences: A meta-analysis. *Psychological Bulletin, 126,* 593–641.

Macrae, C. N., Milne, A. B., & Bodenhausen, G. V. (1994). Stereotypes as energy-saving devices: A peek inside the cognitive toolbox. *Journal of Personality and Social Psychology, 63,* 37–47.

Michael, R. T., Gagnon, J. H., Laumann, E. O., & Kolata, G. (1994). *Sex in America: A definitive survey*. Boston: Little, Brown.

Niemann, Y. F., Jennings, L., Rozelle, R. M., Baxter, J. C., & Sullivan, E. (1994). Use of free responses and cluster analysis to determine stereotypes of eight groups. *Personality and Social Psychology Bulletin, 20,* 379–390.

Nisbett, R., & Ross, L. (1980). *Human inference: Strategies and shortcomings of social judgment.* Englewood Cliffs, NJ: Prentice-Hall.

Oliver, M. B., & Hyde, J. S. (1993). Gender differences in sexuality: A meta-analysis. *Psychological Bulletin, 114,* 29–51.

Pratto, F., Stallworth, L. M., Sidanius, J., & Siers, B. (1997). The gender gap: Differences in political attitudes and social dominance orientation. *British Journal of Social Psychology, 36,* 49–68.

Rothbart, M., & John, O. P. (1985). Social categorization and behavioral episodes: A cognitive analysis of the effects of intergroup conflict. *Journal of Social Issues, 41,* 81–104.

Smith, C., & Lloyd, B. (1978). Maternal behavior and perceived sex of infant: Revisited. *Child Development, 49,* 1263–1265.

Tannen, D. (1990). *You just don't understand: Women and men in conversation.* New York: Marrow.

Williams, J. E., & Best, D. L. (1990). *Measuring sex stereotypes: A multinational study.* Newbury Park, CA: Sage.

MORE TO EXPLORE

Eagly, A. H. (1995). The science and politics of comparing women and men. *American Psychologist, 50,* 145–158.

Hyde, J. S., & Plant, E. A. (1995). Magnitude of psychological gender differences. *American Psychologist, 50,* 159–161.

Pease, B., & Pease, A. (2001). *Why men don't listen and women can't read maps.* New York: Doubleday.

27 When Two Become One: Expanding the Self to Include the Other

"How do I love thee? Let me count the ways."
 —Elizabeth Barrett Browning (1806–1861), English poet

BACKGROUND

The best-known love story of modern times may be Erich Segal's (1970) *Love Story*. In this 20-million-copy best-seller, Oliver Barrett IV is a Harvard ice-hockey jock born into family money. The great-grandson of the man after whom a colossal dormitory and several other campus buildings are named, Oliver is ambivalent about his family's in-your-face Harvardism. Moreover, he positively loathes being programmed into the Barrett tradition: "It's all crap" as he unambiguously puts it. Jenny Cavilleri, on the other hand, is a sarcastic Radcliff music major with gorgeous legs (by Oliver's account). Her mother's death in a car crash left her to be raised by her roughhewn, big-hearted, pastry-chef father (whom she lovingly calls "Phil") and welcoming neighbors in Cranston, Rhode Island.

Oliver and Jenny meet in the Radcliff library. From the word go, she calls him "preppie"; he calls her "snotty Radcliff bitch." A few dates later, however, opposites have attracted, and Oliver utters those immortal words: "I think … I'm in love with you." Despite initially telling him he's "full of shit," the couple soon marry, though without the blessing of Oliver's father, "Old Stonyface" ("Marry her now, and I will not give you the time of day").

At their do-it-yourself wedding, Oliver and Jenny stare blissfully into each other's eyes, while she recites a sonnet from Elizabeth Barrett Browning:

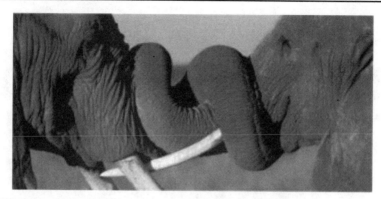

FIG. 27.1. Close others become intertwined with the self.

When our two souls stand up erect and strong,
Face to face, silent, drawing nigh and nigher,
Until the lengthening wings break into fire ...
... a place to stand and love in for a day,
With darkness and the death hour rounding it.

In turn, he reads aloud a piece of Walt Whitman's *Song of the Open Road:*

... I give you my hand!
I give you my love more precious than money,
I give you myself before preaching or law;
Will you give me yourself?
Will you come travel with me?
Shall we stick by each other as long as we live?

Afterward, they reflect on their new status as husband and wife: "Jenny, we're legally married!" he exclaims. "Yeah, now I can be a bitch," she quips. With Oliver still estranged from his imperious father, and cut off from the family fortune, the couple move into a cheap apartment and eke out a living. Despite their poverty, they are immeasurably happy. Though conflicts arise ("God damn you, Jenny, why don't you get the hell out of my life!"), their love always prevails. Jenny works to support Oliver through Harvard Law School. He finally graduates third in his class and makes the *Law Review.* "I owe you a helluva lot," he acknowledges. "Not true," she replies, "You owe me everything." Further along in the story, just as Oliver is apologizing for his generally insensitive behavior, Jenny utters her most memorable line: "Love means never having to say you're sorry."

We will not reveal more of this celebrated story, including its heartrending ending and final consolation. Suffice it to say that *Love Story* leaves one shaken, yet grateful, for what love is, or can be.

But have you ever asked yourself: What is love? What is the source of the poignant, often unaccountable, attraction between particular people? How are we to understand the dynamics of a close, personal relationship? What are the causes of satisfaction or conflict in relationships? Why do some flourish and endure, others deteriorate and end? More generally, how do *personal relationships* (with family members, friends, and romantic partners) differ from *social relations* (with neighbors, coworkers, and strangers)? Historically, social psychology has mostly concerned itself with the latter, although a vibrant relationship science has emerged in recent decades.

Though we will attempt to address a few of the previous questions in this chapter, our focus is mostly on the simple question: What is a close relationship? In the research literature, *behavioral* definitions stipulate that close relationships involve mutual interdependence and influence. Thus, relatives, friends, and lovers typically spend considerable time together, share a diversity of activities, and reciprocate guidance and protection. Yet what is the *cognitive* significance of being in a close relationship?

Taking hints from William James (1890/1948) and Kurt Lewin (1948) (known as the fathers of American psychology and social psychology, respectively), Arthur and Elaine Aron (1986) suggested that people relate to close others much as they relate to themselves. To put it metaphorically, they tend to include close others in the self, seeing and treating them as largely equivalent to their own person. This inclusion is said to occur in the case of resources, perspectives, and characteristics.

To begin with, in a close relationship one tends to allocate resources to one's partner as if one were allocating them to oneself. One views benefits to a partner, or joint benefits, as accruing to the self. One wants to help or give to the other because the other is cognitively part of the self. Furthermore, in a close relationship, one views the other's behavior much as one does one's own behavior. For example, one recognizes how much the other's behavior is influenced by the prevailing situation. This means that in close, loving relationships there is less of an *actor–observer effect* (in which one attributes what one does to situational factors, but what others do to dispositional factors; Nisbett and others, 1973; see chap. 23). The contention that our perspective of the other is different depending on whether the other is an intimate or a stranger is supported by a number of empirical findings. For example, whereas research participants remembered their own performance on a laboratory task better than they did the performance of a stranger, they remembered the performance of a friend or romantic partner nearly as well as their own (Brenner, 1973). Finally, in close relationships, others' characteristics are easily confused with one's own. Thus, it is more difficult, and requires more time, to say that a particular trait describes oneself when a close other lacks it, and to say that a particular trait does not describe oneself when a close other possesses it. For example, suppose that either Jack or Jill (but not both) were shy. Jack and Jill would then need to think harder and longer about whether they were personally shy than if both happened to be shy or not shy.

Although there are undoubtedly other ways in which *other* might be cognitively incorporated into *self,* Aron, Aron, Tudor, and Nelson (1991) sought to test the foregoing three claims—pertaining to resources, perspectives, and characteristics—in three corresponding experiments. We describe the methods and results of their first experiment in the next two sections, and then more briefly describe their second and third experiments in the *So What?* section. In the *Afterthoughts* section, we draw a distinction between relationships involving strangers and those involving lovers, before returning to the topic of love per se.

WHAT THEY DID

In their first experiment, Aron et al. (1991) adopted a procedure previously used by Liebrand (1984) to compare how participants would allocate money to themselves or to another, when that other was a stranger, friendly acquaintance, or best friend.

Twenty-four college students were presented, on a computer screen, with a series of choices having to do with allocating money to themselves and another person. For example, one choice was between (a) the self gaining $14.50 and the other losing $3.90, and (b) the self gaining $16.00 and the other losing $7.50. Each choice was preceded by an instruction to imagine that the other was a stranger, friendly acquaintance, or best friend, who would or would not know the participant's allocation choice. Participants made 24 choices for each of the six possible combinations of instructions. For example, one set of 24 trials had them choose between allocation options while assuming that the other was a best friend who would know their choices.

Following the logic of the inclusion-of-other-in-the-self approach, Aron et al. (1991) predicted that the difference between self-allocations and other-allocations would be least when other was their best friend, intermediate when the other was a friendly acquaintance, and greatest when the other was a stranger. They further predicted that this pattern would be unaffected by whether participants assumed the other would or would not know about their choices. That is, they predicted that allocations would be based on including or not including other in the self, and not on self-presentational concerns or hopes of obtaining something in exchange for a favorable allocation. Thus, they did not expect the manipulation of relationship closeness (friend–acquaintance–stranger) and the manipulation of others' knowledge of the allocation (knowing–not knowing) to interact (i.e., for the effects of one to depend on the effects of the other).

The task in the forgoing procedure may seem a bit abstract or artificial. However, previous research had shown that hypothetical allocations are significantly correlated with real ones (Liebrand, 1984). This gave Aron et al. (1991) some confidence that their methodology had *experimental real-*

ism (it absorbed and involved participants). Nonetheless, this did not deter the researchers from conducting a follow-up experiment in which participants were led to believe they would be allocating hard cash to real people, in some cases disclosing details of the allocation by letter. In this follow-up experiment, the friendly acquaintance condition was excluded, and more emphasis was put on the manipulation of whether the other would or would not know about a participant's allocation. This experiment also included checks on whether participants understood the manipulation instructions. (For obvious reasons, such checks are called *manipulation checks*. They are used in research to ensure that what is intended to be manipulated in an experiment is indeed manipulated.)

Again, it was predicted that the difference between the amount of money participants allocated to themselves and to other people would be smaller when the other person was a best friend than when he or she was a stranger. Aron et al. (1991) conducted yet another experiment that featured a friend, stranger, and *disliked* acquaintance, but we will not go into it here.

WHAT THEY FOUND

Aron et al. (1991) analyzed their data in several ways, but always found the same pattern of results. Using allocations to self minus allocations to other as a dependent variable, they found the pattern of allocations they had predicted: the least difference for self and best friend, intermediate difference for self and friendly acquaintance, and greatest difference for self and stranger. In fact, participants actually allocated more money to their best friend than to themselves, an altruistic gesture consistent with feeling greater empathy for close others (see chap. 20). Importantly, they did not find any differences in allocation choices based on whether or not the imagined other would or would not know about their choices. Thus, self-presentation was effectively ruled out as a cause of the findings obtained (Fig. 27.2).

In the follow-up experiment involving real money and people, a similar pattern of results emerged. In particular, the self–other difference in allocation was smaller for best friends than for strangers. Best friends, unlike strangers, were allocated almost as much money as the self. Again, these results did not hinge on whether the friend or stranger was subsequently told about the allocations. (The experiment involving a *disliked* other also dovetailed with the results of the main and first follow-up experiments.) Aron et al. (1991) thus concluded that, "we treat close others as if their resources were, to some extent, our own" (p. 246).

SO WHAT?

The results of this first experiment provide important insight into the cognitive consequences of being in a close relationship: Rewards to one's close family member or friend, or romantic or marital partner, are experienced

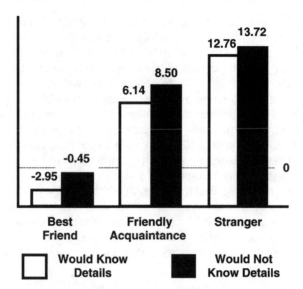

FIG. 27.2. Extra dollars that participants allocated to themselves over three types of other person, when told each type would or would not know the details of the allocation.

much as rewards to the self are. Aron et al.'s (1991) second and third experiments yielded complementary insights.

The second experiment featured a procedure first used by Lord (1980). Participants were presented with a series of concrete nouns each projected on a screen for 10 seconds. The participants were instructed to form as vivid and interesting mental images as possible of either themselves or a target person interacting with whatever each noun denoted (a mule, for example). The target person was either their mother or Cher (the singer and movie actress who had just performed in several successful movies and had that year won an Academy Award). Participants were given 20 seconds to write down a description of their image before a new noun was presented. Once all the nouns had been presented, participants were given a surprise memory test. Specifically, they were asked to write down as many of the nouns as they could recall (in whatever order).

In previous research (Lord, 1980) participants had been instructed to form (again in response to concrete nouns) mental images of themselves, their father, or Walter Cronkite. Perhaps contrary to what you might expect, participants best recalled those nouns earlier linked to Walter Cronkite and worst recalled those earlier linked to themselves. Recall for nouns earlier linked to their fathers fell in between. Such results are explained in terms of perspective: Socially distant others are viewed as part of the outer world (*figures* in one's *phenomenological* field) whereas one's intimately familiar self is viewed as part of the inner world (the *ground* of one's phenomeno-logical field). Evidently, it is easier to form vivid images (and subsequently recall those images, and the nouns they bring to mind) of objective others than of the self. At any rate, Aron et al. (1991) found precisely the same pat-tern of results for the self-mother-Cher manipulation. Participants remem-bered more nouns referring to things that were imagined to be interacting with Cher than they did nouns referring to things imagined to be interacting with their mother or themselves. The slight difference in recall for the mother and self nouns was no greater than would be expected by chance alone.

The same pattern of results was found in a follow-up experiment that in-volved, instead of Cher, a not-too-close female friend or relative of the par-ticipant's mother. Participants in this follow-up experiment were asked to rate how close they felt to their mothers. As predicted, their ratings of close-ness were substantially correlated with the extent to which their memory for mother nouns was similar to their memory for self nouns, showing that in-clusion-of-self-in-the-other is not an all-or-none phenomenon, but a mat-ter of degree.

These various, and admittedly complex, findings all suggest that partici-pants treated someone with whom they have a close relationship much as they would themselves.

A final experiment by Aron et al. (1991) highlighted two independent ef-fects—a *descriptiveness effect* and a *distinctiveness effect* (Mueller and others, 1986). The first refers to participants being quicker to say that a trait applies to them the more descriptive of them it is. The second refers to par-ticipants being slower to say that a trait applies to them the more unique to them it is. Aron et al. (1991) reasoned that, because in a close relationship the mental representation of one's partner is blended with that of one's self, there will be more confusion and slower reaction times in cases where the self and other do not share the same trait.

In order to test their hypothesis, Aron et al. (1991) had participants rate a series of trait adjectives for how well they described themselves, their spouse, and the comedian Bill Cosby. Participants then engaged in a distraction task (serving to clear their minds of the previous ratings), followed by a series of timed trials where they classified those words into the categories "Me" or "Not Me." Aron et al. (1991) examined reaction times for four sets of traits: those rated as (a) true of participants and their spouses but not of Bill Cosby; (b) not true of participants and their spouses but true of Bill Cosby; (c) true of participants, not true of their spouses, and true of Bill Cosby; and (d) not true of participants, true of their spouses, and not true of Bill Cosby. Aron et al. (1991) predicted that participants, who they believed would mentally incor-porate their spouse into their self, would experience more confusion (result-ing in slower reaction times) for traits on which they differed from their spouse. Being dissimilar to Bill Cosby (a distant other), however, was not ex-pected to slow reaction times.

The foregoing procedure and prediction were admittedly quite complicated, but the results were straightforward enough. Participants were slower to respond to traits on which they and their spouse differed than to traits on which they and their spouses were the same or they and Bill Cosby differed. Furthermore, in a follow-up experiment that required participants to indicate how close they were to their spouses (similar to the second experiment), it was found that perceived closeness was substantially correlated with slower reaction times for traits on which self and spouse differed. This correlation between closeness and self-other confusions was exactly what Aron et al. (1991) had predicted, and recalls the results of the previous experiment.

The findings of all these various experiments gel nicely. They support the contention that people in close relationships process information as if their partners are to some extent included in their selves. Never before had such an experimental examination of the cognitive significance of being in a close relationship been conducted.

To return to the "Love Story" with which we opened this chapter, how might such results illuminate the love affair between Oliver and Jenny? They do so by revealing that such an affair involves the breakdown of cognitive boundaries. The distinction between self and other, in both Jenny and Oliver's minds, was presumably blurred as the two fell in love. Each became an extension of the other's self. Neither partner was particularly concerned about receiving a greater allocation of resources than the other: Any benefit to a partner was most likely viewed as a benefit to the self. Moreover, typical differences between actors and observers, in terms of perceptions and attributions, may have all but disappeared in Jenny and Oliver's case. Rather than looking at each other, the two were each looking out from within the other, just as they would look out from within their own selves. Furthermore, they probably came to characterize themselves and their partners similarly—each other's traits becoming blended into closely overlapping schemas. This would have resulted in a failure to appreciate actual trait differences. Differences in traits between two people so close may even have proven to be a source of *cognitive dissonance* (a state of mental tension or uneasiness; see chaps. 6 and 7). Indeed, Aron et al. (1991) suggested that dissimilarity between one's own and a close other's attitudes may cause dissonance in the same way that holding opposite attitudes within oneself can cause dissonance. Thus, dissonance may at times be a function of the closeness of a relationship—the degree to which other is included in the self. It may even have been such dissonance—resulting from any of Jenny and Oliver's personality differences—that motivated the characteristic sarcasm of their relationship.

Taken together, the set of experiments conducted by Aron et al. (1991) reveals love to be an inclusionary process. One mentally includes a close or loved other into oneself. In this sense, a friend or lover is a second self.

AFTERTHOUGHTS

Most of the research described in this book addresses how relative strangers think about and influence one another. This focus characterizes social psychology more generally, although the situation is changing as more and more researchers investigate such meaty topics as attraction, love, communication, resource allocation, jealousy, conflict, conflict resolution, satisfaction, and commitment in close, personal relationships.

One classic theory of human relationships is *social exchange theory* (Kelley & Thibaut, 1978; Thibaut & Kelley, 1959). It applies an economic analysis to interpersonal interactions. Relationships are said to afford various *rewards* (love, status, money, goods, services, and information) and *costs* (time, energy, money, stress, loss of identity, and loss of freedom), and the underlying assumption of the theory is that people seek out and maintain relationships in which the rewards exceed the costs. Thus, a person is likely to compare their current relationship to past relationships ("Hey, I'm not used to being treated this badly in a relationship!" or "I've never felt so loved in all my life!"). He or she is also likely to compare their current relationship to possible future relationships that might prove more rewarding ("Sure I'm engaged, but there's no reason I can't get friendly with that guy who keeps checking me out!").

Social exchange theory helps to explain the so-called *matching principle* (Berscheid and others, 1971)—the tendency for people to choose partners who are fairly similar in physical attractiveness (not to mention age, height, intelligence, educational plans, social background, religion, attitudes, and values). One possible reason for relationship matching is that people know their own *market value* (what their looks, personality, and social standing can buy in the marketplace of people and relationships). Someone who's drop-dead gorgeous does not hook up with someone who looks like a potato (unless that potato has compensating qualities, like wealth). (This might explain why Brittany Spears never returned my calls.) Social exchange theory also helps to explain the *principle of least interest* (Waller, 1938)—the partner who is least interested in a relationship wields the most power. Such a person is in a position to call the shots and make demands in a relationship ("Stop drinking and get a job, or else!") because he or she is more liable to leave, perceiving more rewarding relationship opportunities elsewhere. In general, social exchange theory claims that people focus on the outcomes—the profits and losses—of a relationship. They seek relationship bargains. A relationship is a commodity bought at a price, a stock to invest in, to belabor the economic metaphors.

Yet do economic metaphors fully explain relationship dynamics? Might social relations (among relative strangers) operate differently than personal relationships (among family members, friends, and lovers)? Clark and Mills (1979), in drawing a distinction between *exchange* and *communal* relationships, claimed that they do operate differently.

In an exchange relationship, it is appropriate to give a benefit in return for one of equal value. "The neighbors lent us their garden tools, so we should have them over for dinner." In a communal relationship, however, it is appropriate to give a benefit in response to the need for it. "Our in-laws have fallen on hard times, therefore we should have them over for dinner more often and help watch their kids until their situation improves." Emphatically *not* tit for tat. In exchange relationships, each partner seeks *equity*—what each person gets from the relationship should correspond to what he or she gives to the relationship. Thus, one person's giving a lot when the other gives only a little is not a problem so long as the first person gets proportionately more out of the relationship.

What are the empirical implications of this exchange–communal distinction? Clark and Mills (1979) demonstrated that, whereas tit-for-tat behaviors are welcome and increase attraction in exchange relationships, such behaviors decrease attraction in communal relationships. Clark and others (1989) also demonstrated that members of exchange relationships, concerned about equity, monitor their own and their partner's inputs into a joint task, whereas members of communal relationships do not. Conversely, Clark and others (1986) found that people in communal relationships are more inclined to keep track of others' needs. Finally, Clark and Taraban (1991) found that, whereas people in communal relationships tend to talk about emotional topics, people in exchange relationships tend to talk about unemotional ones (and problems can arise when these norms—see chap. 17—are violated). The research by Aron et al. (1991), focused on in this chapter, is important because it is among the few experiments in social psychology that have featured the cognitive consequences of being in a communal relationship.

It is important to recognize that, although love has been contemplated by poets and philosophers (and practically everyone else) for thousands of years, it has only been studied scientifically (let alone experimentally) for a few decades. What has been learned about love and close relationships in this relatively short time? A great deal, although we can only mention the smallest fraction of it here. One interesting line of research has focused on the *components* of love. According to Robert Sternberg (1986), love is shaped like a triangle, with each of its three sides representing an important component of love: *passion* (an intense longing for union with the other), *intimacy* (the degree of breadth and depth of friendly communication with the other), and *commitment* (the determination to stick with the other). More or less emphasis can be placed on any one of these components (each side of the triangle can be a variable length), so that there are innumerable possible love triangles (not to be confused with three-way relationships!). Indeed, the various components can combine to produce different types of love. A relationship that includes only intimacy: *liking*. One that includes only passion: *infatuation*. Only commitment: *empty love*. Intimacy and passion, but no commitment: *romantic love*. Intimacy and commitment, but no passion: *companionate love*. Passion and commitment, but no intimacy: *fatuous love*. Finally, a love that involves a good measure of all three components: *consummate love*. If you are in love with someone, you may want to read more about these types and reflect on your type. In the fictional case of Oliver and Jenny, there is evidence of all three components of love. Might their story be so appealing because it so eloquently describes a case of consummate love?

Another theoretical approach to love that has prompted much research and received a fair amount of empirical support is that of John Alan Lee (1973) and, later, Clyde and Susan Hendrick (1986). After surveying adults in Canada, the United States, and Great Britain (keep in mind the possible cultural bias here), Lee identified six distinct styles of loving: *eros* (romantic love), *mania* (possessive love), *storge* (best friends love), *pragma* (pragmatic love), *agape* (altruistic love), and *ludus* (game-playing love). Each individual's love style is said to be some combination of these idealized styles. Indeed, measures of these styles yield a somewhat unique profile for each respondent. Hendrick and Hendrick (1986) viewed the styles more as attitudes that can change over time than as fixed traits. Also, different relationship partners and other situational constraints can bring out different love styles in a person. Hendrick and Hendrick's (1986) *Love Attitudes Scale* can help determine your own love style.

One can see in Oliver and Jenny the expression of all six love styles, and some differences between the two lovers. If Oliver and Jenny do exhibit different love styles, perhaps they do so in a way that fits with research findings of gender differences in this regard (Hendrick & Hendrick, 1995) or with prevailing gender stereotypes (see chap. 26). Perhaps too, their approach to love reflects the prevailing culture (America in the late 1960s).

Social psychology continues to provide many other insights into love and personal relationships. There are now entire journals and many books devoted to relationship science. But then too, there is much to discover about love and relationships from life itself.

REVELATION

To love another person means, among other things, to include that person in one's self. This involves perceiving, characterizing, and, critically, allocating resources to that person in much the same way one does one's self.

— KPF —

CHAPTER REFERENCE

Aron, A., Aron, E. N., Tudor, M., & Nelson, G. (1991). Close relationships as including other in the self. *Journal of Personality and Social Psychology, 60,* 241–253.

OTHER REFERENCES

Aron, A., & Aron, E. N. (1986). *Love as the expansion of self: Understanding attraction and satisfaction.* New York: Hemisphere.

Berscheid, E., Dion, K., Walster (Hatfield), E., & Walster, G. W. (1971). Physical attractiveness and dating choice: A test of the matchmaking hypothesis. *Journal of Experimental Social Psychology, 7,* 173–189.

Brenner, M. (1973). The next-in-line effect. *Journal of Verbal Learning and Verbal Behavior, 12,* 320–323.

Clark, M. S., & Mills, J. (1979). Interpersonal attraction in exchange and communal relationships. *Journal of Personality and Social Psychology, 37,* 12–24.

Clark, M. S., Mills, J., & Corcoran, D. M. (1989). Keeping track of needs and inputs of friends and strangers. *Personality and Social Psychology Bulletin, 15,* 533–542.

Clark, M. S., Mills, J., & Powell, M. C. (1986). Keeping track of needs in communal and exchange relationships. *Journal of Personality and Social Psychology, 51,* 333–338.

Clark, M. S., & Taraban, C. (1991). Reactions to and willingness to express emotion in communal and exchange relationships. *Journal of Experimental Social Psychology, 27,* 324–336.

Hendrick, C., & Hendrick, S. S. (1986). A theory and method of love. *Journal of Personality and Social Psychology, 50,* 392–402.

James, W. (1948). *Psychology.* Cleveland, OH: Fine Editions Press. (Original work published 1890)

Kelley, H. H., & Thibaut, J. W. (1978). *Interpersonal relations: A theory of interdependence.* New York: Wiley.

Lee, J. A. (1973). *The colors of love.* New York: Bantam.

Lewin, K. (1948). The background of conflict in marriage. In G. Lewin (Ed.), *Resolving social conflicts: Selected papers on group dynamics* (pp. 84–102). New York: Harper.

Liebrand, W. B. G. (1984). The effect of social motives, communication and group size on behavior in an N-person, multi-stage mixed-motive game. *European Journal of Social Psychology, 14,* 239–264.

Lord, C. G. (1980). Schemas and images as memory aids: Two models of processing social information. *Journal of Personality and Social Psychology, 38,* 257–269.

Mueller, J. H., Thompson, W. B., & Dugan, K. (1986). Trait distinctiveness and accessibility in the self-schema. *Personality and Social Psychology Bulletin, 12,* 81–89.

Nisbett, R. E., Caputo, C., Legant, P., & Marecek, J. (1973). Behavior as seen by the actor and as seen by the observer. *Journal of Personality and Social Psychology, 27,* 154–164.

Segal, E. (1970). *Love story.* New York: HarperCollins.

Sternberg, R. J. (1986). A triangular theory of love. *Psychological Review, 93,* 119–135.

Thibaut, J. W., & Kelley, H. H. (1959). *The social psychology of groups.* New York: Wiley.

Waller, W. (1938). *The family: A dynamic interpretation.* New York: Dryden Press.

MORE TO EXPLORE

Aron, A., Aron, E. N., & Smollan, D. (1992). Inclusion of other in the self scale and the structure of interpersonal closeness. *Journal of Personality and Social Psychology, 63,* 596–612.

Clark, M. S., & Mills, J. (1993). The difference between communal and exchange relationships: What is and is not. *Personality and Social Psychology Bulletin, 19,* 684–691.

Reis, H. T., & Rusbult, C. E. (2002). *Close relationships.* Philadelphia: Taylor and Francis.

28 The Wrath of the Rejected: Being Shut Out Makes One Lash Out

"No man is an island, entire of itself; every man is a piece of the continent, a part of the main."
—John Donne (1572–1631), English metaphysical poet

BACKGROUND

One sunny morning in April 2000, two students, Eric Harris and Dylan Klebold, arrived at their high school a little later than usual. Their goal that fateful day was to murder as many of their classmates and teachers as possible. Dressed in black trenchcoats, and carrying two duffel bags stuffed with firearms and explosives, they gleefully embarked on a killing spree. Within 15 minutes, they had slaughtered 13 people, and wounded a further 21. Had all their explosives detonated as intended, the death toll would have been several times greater. Half an hour later, cornered by police, and knee-deep in human carnage, Harris and Klebold turned their guns on themselves.

Whenever something very bad, unexpected, or out-of-the-ordinary happens, people want to know why (Pyszczynski & Greenberg, 1981). The massacre at Columbine high school is a case in point. In the days and weeks following the tragedy, the question on everybody's lips was: Why? Why did two students try to wipe out an entire school? What made them believe that such ghastly acts were worth committing? What fanned the flames of their hatred, and led them to express it in such an indiscriminate way?

FIG. 28.1. What made them do it?

All sorts of explanations were offered. Perhaps Harris and Klebold were natural-born killers acting on their instincts for destruction. Perhaps they were corrupted by sinister influences in their environment: the North American gun lobby, the glamor of movie violence, the pessimism of Goth subculture. Or perhaps it was all their parents' fault. They had not shown their sons enough love, brought them up to respect others, or cared enough to notice what monsters they were turning into.

As with many unique events, there may be no simple explanation for the Columbine killings. Several factors likely conspired to prompt Harris and Klebold to act as they did. Singling out any one as the cause does not solve the mystery, even if it does bring a sense of closure to the afflicted. All that can be done is to critically survey the set of possible causes, and hope to piece together a provisional understanding of what turns small-town teenagers into big-time killers.

What sorts of insights do social psychologists have to contribute? They usually start from the assumption that the power of the situation is underestimated (see especially chaps. 19, 21, and 23). They wonder: What social influences, perhaps not immediately apparent, might have driven Harris and Klebold over the edge?

A few of the usual suspects can be dismissed at once. For example, there was no pressure on Harris and Klebold either to conform to social norms (chap. 17) or to obey authority figures (chap. 21); Nobody had been around to set a bad example or to issue a hostile order. In fact, what the duo did was an act of brazen self-assertion. They flagrantly disregarded all the dictates and conventions of civil society. If any social influence did acted on them, it must have operated distally (far removed in space and time) rather than proximally (in the immediate context) and must have gradually rather than suddenly tainted their outlook. Extracts from Harris's diary indicate that he had been contemplating a massacre for a year.

What sorts of distal social influences could have made Harris and Klebold run amok? One possibility is *social exclusion*. The boys had lived for some time on the fringes of their teenage community. They had been denied access to the dominant cliques that would have accorded them the popularity and status teenagers typically crave. Their diaries indicate how alienated they felt, and how much they resented their peers for rejecting them. Klebold, for example, wrote: "I swear—like I'm an outcast, and everyone is conspiring against me." The official police report noted that: "Harris and Klebold both wrote of not fitting in, not being accepted ... They plotted against all those persons who they found offensive—jocks, girls that said no, other outcasts, or anybody they thought did not accept them."

In keeping with this possibility, several lines of research do document an association between social exclusion and antisocial behavior. For example, most violent crimes are committed by young men who lack strong interpersonal ties (Garbarino, 1999). In addition, children who are rejected by their peers are more likely on average to intimidate and attack other children (Newcomb, Burowski, & Pattee, 1993).

Such correlations are consistent with the thesis that social exclusion prompts antisocial behavior. However, they are equally consistent with the mirror-image thesis, namely, that antisocial behavior prompts social exclusion. Violent people tend to make disagreeable company. A person who, without good reason, insults or assaults the other members of his social group, is liable to be shunned, at least in a well-organized, civil society.

It is not clear, therefore, whether social exclusion triggers antisocial behavior or vice versa. On the one hand, being excluded certainly thwarts one of the strongest drives in human nature—the need to belong (Baumeister & Leary, 1995). One might therefore expect that the failure to form harmonious relationships with others would cause mental disturbance, possibly spilling over into antisocial behavior. On the other hand, if the need to belong is so pressing, might not socially excluded individuals try even harder to be liked than their socially included fellows? Would they not be expected to redouble their efforts to be friendly, cooperative, and generous?

As matters stand, then, the case for social exclusion being a cause of antisocial behavior is not yet compelling. To make it compelling, the best approach is to run an experiment. This allows social exclusion to be isolated from everything else with which it tends to be naturally confounded (e.g., a nasty disposition) and permits its unique impact on antisocial behavior to be assessed. Twenge, Baumeister, Tice, and Stucke (2001) adopted precisely this approach.

WHAT THEY DID

Twenge et al. (2001) reported a total of five studies in their paper. We begin by focusing on just one of them, and later comment briefly the remaining four.

Thirty undergraduates, 17 males and 13 females, served as participants. The study kicked off with a manipulation of social exclusion. It involved giving some participants the proverbial cold shoulder. The study was run in same-gender groups of four to six. Participants engaged in an exercise ostensibly designed to acquaint them with one another. During this exercise, they memorized each other's names, and took turns sharing thoughts and feelings. Fifteen minutes later, they were transferred to private cubicles. There, they were asked to write down on a sheet of paper which two participants that they would most like to collaborate with on an upcoming task. The experimenter then took the sheet away, promising to return shortly with information about the composition of the new groups. During the experimenter's temporary absence, participants passed the time writing an essay in which they expressed their opinions about abortion. (The purpose of this essay will be made clear in a moment.) When the experimenter returned, she told them either one of two things. In the *acceptance* condition, she told them: "I have good news for you—everyone chose you as someone they'd like to work with." In the *rejection* condition, she told them: "I hate to tell you this, but no one chose you as someone they wanted to work with."

Twenge et al. (2001) were interested in finding our how participants felt after being rejected or accepted. They hypothesized that rejection would create feelings of sadness or anxiety; after all, the fear of social exclusion is a prominent correlate of mental distress (Baumeister & Leary, 1995). To check how participants felt, the researchers had them fill out a self-report measure of mood. It assessed both their positive and negative feelings.

While participants were busy reporting their mood, the experimenter took their essay on abortion, and allegedly gave it to another participant for the purposes of evaluation. This participant was described as being the same gender as the real participants but as not being a member of the original group.

Soon after participants had finished filling out the mood measure, they received feedback from the participant on the quality of their essay. This feedback was severely critical. The summary comment on the feedback sheet blatantly announced: "One of the worst essays I have ever read!" Various aspects of the essay (e.g., organization, style) were given correspondingly miserable ratings.

Participants now began a computer game. They were led to believe that they would be competing against the very participant who had so tactlessly bruised their egos. The game was allegedly a test of who could press a computer key more rapidly in response to a prompt. On each trial, the person who was slower was supposed to receive an unpleasant blast of white noise through a pair of headphones. The entire game, however, was made up. The computer merely delivered the occasional blast of noise to participants to maintain the cover story. The important feature of the set-up was that participants had some control over the unpleasantness of the blast. In particular, they could set the intensity of the blast prior to each trial (its level ranged from 0 to 10) and vary its duration during each trial by holding down the mouse button for a longer or shorter period. Participants' level of aggression was indexed by the intensity and duration of the blast that they administered on the first trial (which their fellow participant conveniently went slower on). Previous research had shown this to be the most sensitive measure of aggression.

After the study participants were carefully debriefed. Twenge et al. (2001) were mindful of the fact that the manipulations they had employed were somewhat stressful (telling participants that they had written a hopeless essay, or that no one wanted to work with them, or both). Consequently, the experimenter did not permit participants to leave until they fully understood that they had not really been rejected, nor their essays really evaluated. The experimenter reassured participants in the rejection condition that other participants had chosen to work with them, as was almost invariably the case. The experimenter also apologized for any discomfort participants might have experienced as a result of being deceived.

We leave it to the reader to decide whether the scientific value of the study justified its methods. Note, however, that temporarily being left out or harshly evaluated are not uncommon events in most people's lives, and most of us get over them quickly. Chapters 21 and 23 provide a fuller discussion of the ethics of experimenting on human participants.

WHAT THEY FOUND

The key question was whether the experience of social exclusion would augment participants' aggression toward a person who had (apparently) harshly criticized them. It did. Participants who had previously been rejected were substantially more aggressive toward the participant than those who had previously been accepted. They chose to deliver more intense blasts of noise for a longer period of time. Feeling themselves to have been cut off from other people made them retaliate with greater venom (Fig. 28.2).

The results of some other studies reported by Twenge et al. (2001) reinforced this finding. In these studies, social exclusion was manipulated in a more abstract way: Participants were told, on the basis of a bogus personality profile, that one of two contrasting futures lay in store for them. In the exclusion-feedback condition, they were told that they would likely spend their later years in solitude. Although they might currently be enjoying satisfying social relationships, over time these relationships would weaken and disintegrate. In the inclusion-feedback condition, they were told that they would likely spend their later years in the convivial company of many other people. Their network of social affiliations would remain reassuringly intact.

Aggression was also measured in a different way. Participants were told that the person who had earlier denounced their essay was applying to become a research assistant in the Department of Psychology. The experimenter claimed that the Department was interested in knowing what those who had taken part in the study thought of the person. Participants responded to a questionnaire that featured such items as "If I were in charge of hiring research assistants, I would hire this applicant." In this and further studies, participants were consistently found to be more hostile following social exclusion. The value of using various manipulations and measures is that research findings are less likely to be an artifact of any one research methodology. This builds confidence that the effects observed are real and related to what the researchers are conceptually interested in.

Some studies also featured a third condition, in which participants were told that they would be accident-prone later in life, even if they currently showed no sign of being that way (misfortune-feedback). The purpose of including this condition was to allow the researchers to separate out the effects of anticipating social exclusion from the effects of anticipating an unpleasant but nonsocial eventuality. As predicted, only the receipt of exclusion feedback made participants act more aggressively.

Yet why does social exclusion make people act more aggressively? One possibility is that it puts people in a bad mood, and that their bad mood then induces them to go on the offensive. To their surprise, however, Twenge et al. (2001) did not find that being sidelined by peers (the present study) or expecting to end up alone (the other studies) made participants feel any worse. The effects of social exclusion on aggression did not seem to depend on the positivity or negativity of their feelings. Hence, although social exclusion prompted aggressive behavior, it did not seem to do so by making people feel bad.

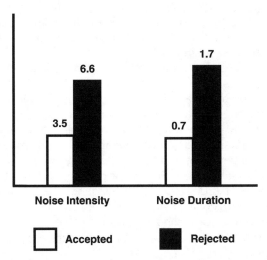

FIG. 28.2.   The intensity and duration of a blast of noise that the participants gave to someone who criticized them, after they had been accepted or rejected by peers.

SO WHAT?

Prior to the research conducted by Twenge et al. (2001), it was not clear whether social exclusion could in principle amplify aggression. Now we know that it can. That makes it more probable that social exclusion is one variable in the equation of why troubled people like Harris and Klebold embark on their campaigns of terror.

That equation can take on complex forms. For instance, the situational impact of social exclusion, and the dispositional impact of a problem personality, can combine to reinforce each other. Take the case of Ted Kaczynski, the notorious Unabomber. Over a 20-year period, this former mathematics professor mailed deadly explosives to (mostly) computer specialists, in protest against what he regarded as the evils of modern technology. As a child, Kaczynski had been painfully shy and socially awkward. His difficulties were only compounded by his intelligence, which led him to skip grades in school (where the older boys bullied him) and to enter Harvard at the tender age of 16 (where he became more isolated still). Finding himself unable to relate to others, Kaczynski entered into a pattern of ever-increasing reclusiveness, culminating in a decision to live alone in the Montana wilderness. At each step of the way, his avoidance of other people would have only further impaired his ability to relate to them. Denied the consolation of friendship, he was eventually led to view technological society as hopelessly corrupt, and to kill those in favor of it as a way of publicly airing his discontent. The point we wish to bring out here is that Kaczynski's preexisting propensity for introversion led him to make life-choices that placed him in situations liable to exacerbate his feelings of social exclusion. It is not implausible that, over time, such acute feelings could have nurtured his aggression, eventually transforming him from a diffident whizz-kid into a heartless assassin.

Laboratory research has shown that social exclusion fosters a variety of antisocial tendencies (Tice, Twenge, & Schmeichel, 2001). For example, undergraduates led to believe that they would end up alone in adulthood are more likely to cheat on a test (by exceeding a time limit), to behave antagonistically (in a tit-for-tat game), and to refrain from helping others by not donating money. Ironically, being cut adrift from the mainland of social life tends to make people less fit to live there.

Still one wonders: What is going on inside the mind of the rejected? Recall that Twenge et al. (2001) found little evidence that positive or negative emotion were responsible for aggression. If anything, socially excluded participants reported not feeling much of anything, a sort of emotional numbness. Some other mental process must therefore provide the missing internal link.

One possibility is that, after being socially excluded, people attempt to suppress their growing sense of isolation. Their attempt is largely successful, and they manage to cultivate a more-or-less neutral emotional state.

However, the effort they exert doing so induces a state of ego-depletion in which reserves of willpower become temporarily scarce (Baumeister, Bratslavsky, Muraven, & Tice, 1998; see chap. 10). As a consequence, the socially excluded are prone to act on urges that they might otherwise resist. Several studies support this line of reasoning (Baumeister et al., in press). For example, when offered the choice between a high-fat candy bar and a healthy food snack, socially excluded participants chose the former option—the impulsive and imprudent one—more often than other participants did.

Perhaps individuals who are chronically cut off from others are mentally worn down much of the time, with the result that they lose interest in long-term constructive goals, and opt instead for more harmful short-term alternatives. Or perhaps, unaccustomed to fulfilling the duties and obligations of social life, their ability to restrain their antisocial inclinations diminishes (Baumeister & Exline, 1999). Either way, the socially excluded can be prone to lash out at enemies they perceive to be around them.

To an outsider the targets of their aggression often appear arbitrary. Take Harris and Klebold again. The media made much of the fact that, prior to their shooting spree, they had drawn up a hit-list of hated schoolmates. However, only one of their eventual victims was actually on that list. As witnesses testified, the killing was haphazard and capricious. This fact squares with another finding by Twenge et al. (2001): Socially excluded participants behaved more aggressively, not only toward a person who had given them offense, but also toward a person whom they had never met before. Their vengeance appears to have an equal-opportunity quality, directed not only at the guilty but also at the innocent.

One of the tragedies of social exclusion is that it thwarts not only the need to belong, but also other fundamental needs. According to *self-determination theory* (Deci & Ryan, 2000) people have intrinsic drives for relatedness, competence, and autonomy that must be satisfied if their minds are to keep running smoothly. Obviously, being socially excluded makes it difficult to relate to others (i.e., satisfy one's need to belong). But it also makes it difficult to show competence in dealing with others (e.g., organizing a successful social event) or autonomy in asserting oneself creatively (e.g., pursuing a rewarding career by forging professional links). Perhaps the terrible deeds that alienated people sometimes carry out represent a drastic way of satisfying their frustrated needs: to become infamous in the eyes of others (relatedness), accomplish something important (competence), or take control of their destiny (autonomy).

Given that social exclusion produces such damaging effects, what can be done about it? A final study by Twenge et al. (2001) suggested one possible answer. It found that, although socially excluded people behaved more aggressively towards both someone who offended them earlier and a stranger, they did not behave more aggressively toward someone who had earlier praised them (commended their essay). It follows that a kind word may negate the antisocial tendencies that social exclusion breeds. Perhaps if Klebold and Harris had received a genuine compliment now and again from their classmates they would never have been driven to murder them.

Of course, the most direct way of undoing the damage caused by social exclusion is to bring the shy, lonely, and alienated back into the embrace of society. Unfortunately, such people tend to be regarded as undesirable interaction partners by those with greater social skills. This is because they are objectively less rewarding to spend time with and because associating with them carries with it a social stigma. What is necessary, therefore, are policies to ensure that social cohesion is maintained within various social institutions, and in society at large. Small-scale programs to get lonely schoolchildren more involved can work exceedingly well (Bagley & Pritchard, 1998). However, finding ways to reverse the increasingly individualistic trend in Western societies is a much taller order. Yet, if we value our collective well-being, we should do something about it: a lack of social integration goes hand in hand with a host of other social pathologies (Twenge, 2000).

AFTERTHOUGHTS

As mentioned in the introduction, social exclusion is merely one factor among many that disposes people to commit violent acts. In itself, social exclusion is not sufficient for violence. Most solitary individuals are inoffensive and law-abiding. Neither is social exclusion necessary for violence. Most violence is committed, not by loners, but by organized collectives of individuals who have long-standing political grievances. Indeed, the causes of antisocial behavior are manifold, and differ from situation to situation. We close this chapter by discussing a factor that has, nonetheless, been widely invoked as an explanation for antisocial behavior (and for a variety of personal and societal ills): self-esteem.

Should you care to browse through the many books located in the Self Help section of your local bookshop, you will repeatedly encounter the view, asserted or assumed, that human misery is predominantly a product of low self-esteem. If only we could all learn to see ourselves in glowing terms, the argument runs, a golden new age would be ushered in. People would become spiritually fulfilled and financially prosperous; groups and individuals would resolve their long-standing enmities and live forever in peace and harmony. If you suspect that this Panglossian ideology is overstated, you are right. The benefits of self-esteem are modest, and are mostly of a personal nature. People with high self-esteem feel happier, are surer of who they are and what they like, and persist longer in the face of adversity (Sedikides & Gregg, in press).

The notion that high self-esteem has substantial interpersonal benefits is reflected in the off-quoted proposition that unless one first loves oneself one cannot love other people. One merit of this proposition (widely regarded as a truism by non-psychologists) is that it can be tested. Simply divide people into those with high and low self-esteem and then examine their relative propensities to engage in antisocial behavior. If the received wisdom is correct, then people with high self-esteem ought to be more peaceful and well-behaved, whereas those with low self-esteem ought to be more belligerent and ill-mannered.

In two laboratory studies (Bushman & Baumeister, 2002), participants went through a procedure similar to that of the present study. All began by writing an essay expressing their views on abortion; the essay was then favorably or unfavorably evaluated by another participant; and an opportunity to punish the participant was provided (he or she could be blasted with an aversive noise). It turned out that self-esteem was irrelevant to how aggressively participants behaved. Those whose self-esteem was low were no more likely to retaliate against the participant than those whose self-esteem was high.

These studies did turn up one positive finding, however. Participants who were high in narcissism—the tendency to entertain an unduly inflated, grandiose view of oneself—were more likely to retaliate than those who were low in it. This suggests that it is not so much an inferiority complex that predisposes people to aggression but rather a superiority complex. When narcissists encounter a threat to their cherished view of self, they react more harshly against it than a humbler person would.

Data from everyday life corroborates the results of these experiments. Perpetrators of serious violence everywhere—murderers, wife-beaters, gang members, dictators—all tend to be rather fond of themselves (Baumeister, Smart, & Boden, 1996). They are not the sort of people who are uncertain of themselves or who fret over their own unworthiness. When someone disses them, they have the self-assurance to strike back. If their self-esteem were low, this is not how they would react. Instead, they would go on the defensive, internalizing the pain and attempting to escape.

Research suggests, however, that people with high self-esteem are something of a mixed bag of individuals. For example, one study categorized participants both on the basis of their self-esteem being high or low and on the basis of it being stable or unstable (i.e., staying the same over time or fluctuating). Results showed that participants whose self-esteem was both high and stable showed the least hostility, whereas those whose self-esteem was both high and unstable showed the greatest (Kernis, Grannemann, & Barclay, 1989). It seems that some people with high self-esteem are quietly self-confident, and relatively impervious to social irritations, whereas others are vainly puffed up, and acutely sensitive to criticism.

How does the psychology of these two groups differ? One suggestion is that some people's sense of self-worth is more contingent than that of others. That is, it depends on certain conditions being met—on gaining popularity, achieving coveted goals, or fulfilling prescribed duties. In contrast, people whose self-worth is noncontingent see themselves positively regardless. They are not unduly perturbed when someone criticizes them, or when they mess up. They accept themselves, warts and all. Studies confirm that having noncontingent self-esteem is associated with equanimity in the face of threats to one's self-esteem (Kernis, in press).

Looking back on the Columbine killings, we can probably characterize Harris and Klebold as individuals who had high self-esteem overall. They did not respond to their marginalization with despair and self-pity; rather, they responded with brutality and disdain. Their self-esteem, however, appears to have been unstable, highly contingent upon the respect and admiration of their peers. Unable to accept the fact that their peers would never hold them in as much esteem as they held themselves, they exacted a terrible revenge. Those who glibly advocate raising self-esteem levels as a panacea for social problems should take note.

REVELATION

Social exclusion causes aggression. People ostracized by others are more likely to hurt those who offend them, and even those who do not.

— APG —

CHAPTER REFERENCE

Twenge, J. M., Baumeister, R. F., Tice, D. M., & Stucke, T. S. (2001). If you can't join them, beat them: The effects of social exclusions on aggressive behavior. *Journal of Personality and Social Psychology, 81,* 1058–1069.

OTHER REFERENCES

Bagley C., & Pritchard C. (1998). The reduction of problem behaviours and school exclusion in at-risk youth: An experimental study of school social work with cost-benefit analyses. *Child and Family Social Work, 3,* 219–226.

Baumeister, R. F., Bratslavsky, E., Muraven, M., & Tice, D. M. (1998). Ego depletion: Is the active self a limited resource? *Journal of Personality and Social Psychology, 74,* 1252–1265.

Baumeister, R. F., & Exline, J. J. (1999). Virtue, personality, and social relations: self-control as a moral muscle. *Journal of Personality, 67,* 1165–1194.

Baumeister, R. F., & Leary, M. R. (1995). The need to belong: Desire for interpersonal attachments as a fundamental human motivation. *Psychological Bulletin, 117,* 497–529.

Baumeister, R. F., Smart, L., & Boden, J. M. (1996). Relation of threatened egotism to violence and aggression: The dark side of high self-esteem. *Psychological Review, 103,* 5–33.

Baumeister, R. F, Twenge, J. M., & Ciarooco, N. (in press). The inner world of rejection: Effects of social exclusion on emotion, cognition, and self-regulation. In J. P. Forgas &

K. D. Williams (Eds.), *The social self: Cognitive, interpersonal, and intergroup perspectives*. Philadelphia: Psychology Press.

Bushman, B. J., & Baumeister, R. F. (2002). Does self-love or self-hate lead to violence? *Journal of Research in Personality, 36*, 543–545.

Deci, E. L., & Ryan, R. M. (2000). The "what" and "why" of goal pursuits: Human needs and the self-determination of behavior. *Psychological Inquiry, 11*, 227–268.

Garbarino, J. (1999). *Lost boys: Why our sons turn violent and how we can save them*. San Francisco: Jossey-Bass.

Kernis, M. H. (in press). Towards a conceptualization of optimal self-esteem. *Psychological Inquiry.*

Kernis, M. H., Grannemann, B. D., & Barclay, L. C. (1989). Stability and level of self-esteem as predictors of anger arousal and hostility. *Journal of Personality and Social Psychology, 56*, 1013–1022.

Newcomb, A. F., Burowski, W. M., & Pattee, L. (1993). Children's peer relations: A meta-analytic review of popular, rejected, neglected, controversial, and average sociometric status. *Psychological Bulletin, 113*, 99–128.

Pyszczynski, T. A., & Greenberg, J. (1981). Role of disconfirmed expectancies in the instigation of attributional processing. *Journal of Personality and Social Psychology, 40*, 31–38.

Sedikides, C., & Gregg, A. P. (in press). Portraits of the self. In M. A. Hogg & J. Cooper (Eds.), *Sage handbook of social psychology*. London: Sage Publications.

Tice, D. M., Twenge, J. M., & Schmeichel, B. J. (2001). Social exclusion and prosocial and antisocial behavior. In J. P. Forgas & K. D. Williams (Eds.), *The social self: Cognitive, interpersonal, and intergroup perspectives* (pp. 175–187). Philadelphia: Psychology Press.

Twenge, J. M. (2000). The age of anxiety? The birth cohort change in anxiety and neuroticism, 1952–1993. *Journal of Personality and Social Psychology, 79*, 1007–1021.

MORE TO EXPLORE

Aronson, E. (2001). *Nobody left to hate: Teaching compassion after Columbine*. New York: Owl Books.

Baumeister, R. F., & Beck, A. T. (1999). *Evil: Inside human violence and cruelty*. New York: W. H. Freeman and Company.

Revelations

- The fact that we are aware of our own beliefs, feelings, and desires does not automatically make us experts on where they come from. Introspection is therefore an unreliable guide to how the mind works, reflecting cultural truisms rather than providing infallible insights.

- Our intuitive theories about how things are subtly shape our memories for what has been. Thus, we unknowingly reconstruct the past in terms of the present rather than simply remembering the past in its original form.

- Although we are fairly adept at predicting how events will make us feel, we overestimate how long those feelings, especially when unpleasant, will last. One reason for this is that we possess a psychological immune system that, over time and without our knowledge, softens the impact of life's trials and tribulations.

- Our group loyalties and preconceptions cause us to perceive events and other stimuli in a biased manner. One consequence of this is that partisans on both sides of an issue tend to overestimate bias in media reports.

- People avoid risks when they stand to gain, but take risks when they stand to lose. Consequently, how a choice is framed, in terms of loss or gain, can influence how people choose, over and above the objective consequences of choosing one way or the other.

- If you wish to change somebody's opinion, subtly induce them to act at odds with it while letting them think they did so of their own free will. This tactic works because people readily rationalize objectionable actions for which they feel responsible by adjusting their attitudes to match them.

- When people voluntarily undergo an unpleasant experience to achieve something, they come to value that something more, not less. This helps explain why people become committed members of groups even when membership entails considerable initial sacrifice and offers scant subsequent reward.

Receiving a reward for doing something makes people want to do it more. However, when the reward is withdrawn, people want to do it even less than they did before receiving the reward.

 People deceive themselves by acting so as to create signs that everything is well even when they cannot make everything well. They then deny that they have acted in this way because admitting as much would imply that those signs are bogus.

 Attempts to bring about a desired mental state tend to backfire if people are distracted or preoccupied. Under such circumstances, they would be well advised to abandon the attempt, or, even better, to try not to bring about that the mental state, as this will ironically tend to bring it about.

 How we feel about a person (or any other stimulus) is influenced by a host of factors, but most basically, it is governed by mere exposure. We tend to like people more the more often we encounter them.

 Social psychologists use technical tools, not subjective interpretation, to tell more about people than they are willing or able to say about themselves. Using such tools, they can detect underlying prejudice in people who explicitly deny it, and predict subtle forms of discrimination.

 Although the hidden persuaders are the stuff of fiction, stimuli presented outside of awareness can nonetheless have surprisingly profound effects on thoughts, feelings, and behavior. In particular, merely calling to mind thoughts about social groups can improve or worsen intellectual performance.

 Although our expectations of people are based on their behavior, it is likewise true that their behavior is the result of our expectations. Simply believing that someone is attractive will lead to their actually being attractive.

 We make sense of ambiguous novel situations by using superficially similar past experiences as a guide, often making unwarranted inferences as a result. For example, belief in personal telepathic ability can be mistakenly engendered by a recent experience of close rapport (good vibes) with others.

 Although commonsense suggests that we suspend belief or disbelief until after we have understood a message, research shows that, initially, belief accompanies understanding, and that doubt follows later only if mental resources and motivation are sufficient.

 Ubiquitous and hard-to-resist norms shape social life. As a result, groups exert tremendous normative influence over their members that only a few brave souls can defy.

 Small, subtle, seemingly trivial situational variables often have a greater impact on behavior than do the personality variables that we more readily, but often mistakenly, regard as influential. Something as simple

as time pressure can impact something as vital as compassionate behavior.

- The more witnesses there are to an emergency, the less likely it is that any one of them will help. This is because individuals are often not privy to others' reactions, or because they do not feel uniquely respon-sible for preventing tragic outcomes.

- When moved by empathy, people help not because they are moti-vated to avoid the guilt that would result from not helping, nor, it seems, for any other selfish reason. Rather, they help with the ultimate goal of benefitting other people.

- The power of the situation can incline people to willingly obey author-ity figures, with the result that they sometimes commit the most abominable and appalling of acts.

- Being immersed in a group can lead to heightened arousal, a sense of anonymity, reduced self-awareness, and the automatic modeling of others' behaviors. Such a state of deindividuation can result in un-restrained—often aggressive and destructive—behavior.

- We assume that a person's behaviors reflect fixed traits and underlying attitudes, when we should perhaps pay more attention to factors in the physical and social environment. In the case of our own behavior, we are more apt to recognize situational pressures.

- The mere presence of others enhances performance on simple tasks but impairs performance on complex tasks. This can occur even in the absence of complex mediating cognitions.

- People, as well as groups and institutions we are socially connected to, are part of our identity and impact our self-esteem. We personalize their successes and failures, trumpeting the former and distancing ourselves from the latter.

- Gender stereotypes do not only arise from perceptions of actual gen-der differences. They also arise as ways of rationalizing the different social roles that men and women occupy.

- To love another person means, among other things, to include that person in one's self. This involves perceiving, characterizing, and, crit-ically, allocating resources to that person in much the same way one does one's self.

- Social exclusion causes aggression. People ostracized by others are mor likely to hurt those who offend them, and even those who do not.

Author Index

Subject Index

Note: *f* indicates figure